MONICA

A Life of Monica Dickens

ANNE WELLMAN

First Printing September 2018

ISBN-13: 978-1548704582

ISBN-10: 154870458X

Acknowledgments

My thanks to Dr Howard Bailes, St Paul's Girls' School archivist and to Nicholas Baldwin, Great Ormond Street Hospital for Children archivist. I am grateful also to Shirley and Morris Karnovsky in Massachusetts for access to their correspondence with Monica Dickens, to Sally Casper in Massachusetts for sharing her memories, and to Falmouth Public Library and Falmouth Museums on the Green in Massachusetts for their particular assistance.

BBC copyright content reproduced courtesy of the British Broadcasting Corporation. All rights reserved.

Table of Contents

Chepstow Villas...1

One Pair of Hands..21

War 59

A Cottage in the Country............................98

Roy..133

Navy Wife..142

Cape Cod...153

The Miseries of the World.........................170

Emma Chisit..202

Henry and Fanny..205

The Literary Life...213

The Listeners...231

Taking Stock..260

The Dickens Connection............................280

Roy..290

Return...294

Chepstow Villas..321

Last Word...323

Bibliography and sources 332

Introduction

'All I have ever done is to report the experiences of my life.'

So said Charles Dickens' great-granddaughter Monica Dickens, author of twenty-five novels and many classics for children, and one of the most popular writers of her day. Born into the upper classes, as a bored and unhappy debutante in the 1930s she took the incredible step of going into domestic service and then writing a book about it. *One Pair of Hands*, published in 1939, sold in the millions and has never been out of print. Her subsequent works, calling on her rich experience as a wartime nurse, Spitfire factory worker, GI bride and more, sold in similar numbers but are now largely forgotten.

Often dismissed as a 'light' writer, and her widespread appeal deflecting serious recognition, Monica Dickens was nevertheless highly praised by some of the most respected authors of the twentieth century, and indeed beyond. Far from writing lightly, in her middle period she addressed issues such as child abuse, suicide, and inner-city deprivation. Her novels, always threaded with humour, were immensely understanding of human frailties, but at the same time urged resilience and responsibility for one's fellow man. These were qualities that Monica herself possessed in plenty. After becoming a volunteer for the Samaritans in England, this deeply compassionate woman went on to found the first branch of the organisation in America and hence to save countless lives. Her name is engraved on a marker near the soaring bridges over the Cape Cod Canal, where she campaigned for the erection of higher barriers to stop desperate people jumping to their deaths.

In her early sixties Monica produced an account of the experiences in her life which had influenced her writing, her 1978 memoir *An Open Book*. 'This is not the whole story of a life,' begins the first chapter, and in truth much was omitted or by her own admission confused with the semi-autobiographical works she had written as a young woman. *An Open Book* is a valuable starting-point but this first biography seeks to fill the gaps and to tell the story of her later years, with the help of contemporary accounts, family histories, interviews with close friends, articles and private correspondence, and not least Monica's major works and their critical reception.

All her writing life Monica was compared to Charles Dickens, not always favourably. And yet the similarities between them are there: eccentric characters, humorous observation of the English scene, social conscience, an optimistic and moral view of life – but above all, talent for the written word.

Chepstow Villas

MONICA ENID DICKENS was born on a London spring morning in 1915, the second year of the First World War. Her mother was Fanny, second daughter of German sugar baron Charles Herman Runge, who in the suspicious atmosphere of war had dropped the German pronunciation of his surname in favour of making it rhyme with the more British-sounding 'sponge'. Monica's father was barrister Henry Charles Dickens, known to all simply as Hal. Henry's grandfather was Charles Dickens himself.

The birth took place in a brass bed in the front room of 52 Chepstow Villas, a square, double-fronted Georgian-style house in Notting Hill which faced a respectable road at the front but was bordered by the more disreputable Portobello Road to the side. Outside, straw had been spread in the road to muffle the sound of horses' hooves. Fanny, at nearly forty, must have been relieved that it was all over, after the earlier births of a healthy son and first daughter but also the anguish of a miscarriage and twin babies who died. As it was, blue-eyed, fair-haired Monica only just made it into the world: many years later Fanny told her daughter that men were not interested 'that way' in their wives after the wives reached forty.

For two well-deserved weeks Fanny, as was the custom at the time, recovered in bed with Monica tucked up beside her, attended by the same nurse who was always engaged for the first month after a birth in the family. In due course the new baby was relegated to the nursery and to the care of the children's nanny Ethel May Gathergood, a Norfolk girl who had just arrived at the age of nineteen and was to remain with the Dickenses for the rest of her working life. As in other upper-middle-class families at the start of the twentieth century, the children saw less of their parents than they did their nanny. It was Nanny Gathergood who changed the nappies, washed the children's clothes, combed the tangles out of their hair, told them off, got them ready for school and listened patiently to endless tales as she sat with the mending. She was a reassuring and much-loved presence in Monica's existence. Only years later did it occur to Monica that they had selfishly assumed

1

Nanny was happy to devote thirty years of her life solely to their family (after the Dickens children were grown Nanny Gathergood took care of her brother's offspring too). But after retiring to take care of her elderly mother Nanny wrote to the adult Monica to say that she never regretted her wonderful life; Fanny had been kindness itself, and she had many happy memories. In Monica's memoir *An Open Book* she wrote that Ethel May Gathergood did indeed gather good, out of her kind and selfless heart, and heaped it upon their family.

Already in the nursery on baby Monica's arrival was her older sister Doris, a toddler of one and a half nicknamed Doady after David in *David Copperfield*. Monica's brother Gerald, nicknamed Bunny, was a divine being a full nine years senior and away at school.

While much of the little girls' time was spent in the nursery or being taken for walks by Nanny, they nevertheless had the benefit of Fanny and Henry's fairly advanced ideas about child-rearing. In later life Monica was to describe her parents as middle-class, conventional on the surface but unconventional underneath and extremely liberal for the era. Thin, dark-haired Fanny was with her children more than most mothers of their class. She would invent treats, spend all day with them when the family was on holiday abroad, read to them and play paper games or turn the dining-room table upside down to make a boat. Nanny was the children's bedrock; Fanny was 'pleasure and stimulation'.

Henry, too, was more available to them than most fathers. He had enjoyed a comfortable and lively upbringing as one of a large family produced by his barrister father Sir Henry Fielding Dickens, Charles Dickens' eighth child, and his formidable but devoted French mother Marie. Henry's father was the only child of Dickens to go to university. (Writing about Dickens in his memoir, Sir Henry remembered that when as a young man he told Dickens that he had won one of the principal mathematical scholarships of his year at Trinity College, Cambridge, his father, a graduate only of the boot-blacking factory, at first responded with just a disappointing 'Capital, capital!', then shortly afterwards broke down completely as he gripped his son by the hand with tears in his eyes. Dickens had a habit of 'strange reticence', an intense dislike of letting himself go in private life or using over-effusive language – except when he was deeply moved.)

Sir Henry, the most successful of Dickens' sons, went on to become a King's Counsel and quite a performer. At Christmas gatherings in the billiard room at the family home, 8 Mulberry

Walk in Chelsea, he would imitate his father giving one of his famous recitations, leaning on the same velvet-covered stand used by Dickens during his tours and sporting the great man's favourite geranium. Some of these recitals were also given in public in support of various charities, or privately to friends, one of whom remembered Sir Henry's word-perfect rendering of *The Death of Steerforth* declaimed 'with unforgettable verve and fire'. Although too young to accompany

Dickens on his reading tours, Sir Henry – who had inherited Charles Dickens' folded eyelids – had presumably listened to him many times and gave what was considered to be an amazingly like performance, though somewhat marred by loosening false teeth as he aged.

At these private readings his wife Lady Dickens would sit busily knitting at Sir Henry's side. As Monica grew older she took her place in the circle of children listening to *A Christmas Carol* on Christmas Eve, during which Dickens' own tones were thought to be heard in her grandfather's terrified shout of 'I know him!' followed by a hush and a creaking whisper: 'Marley's – ghost!' She would listen, too, to Sir Henry's rendition of *Mrs Gamp*, a character study for his reading tours that Charles Dickens had worked up from *Martin Chuzzlewit.* Much of this was to pass her by in her earliest years – in fact as an adult she once referred to the readings as a 'bloody bore' – but for the whole of her life she would remember two particular images which she greeted with joy when eventually she read *Chuzzlewit* herself: Mrs Gamp, with her face for all occasions, looking out of her window among the first-floor flower pots with her 'mourning countenance', and Mrs Gamp in the sickroom in her cabbage nightcap and watchman's coat, sliding her nose backwards and forwards along the brass fender while she waited for the kettle to boil. Just the mention of the words 'Mrs Gamp', or even the word 'midwife', was always enough for these two images to spring immediately to mind.

The several offspring of the canny, humorous Sir Henry and the bossy Marie were noisy and opinionated. Monica's father Henry inherited at least some of Sir Henry's dramatic inclinations: he loved to read aloud, both Dickens to his children and a great variety of books to his wife Fanny, a habit he continued all their married life. As Monica lay in bed during her childhood illnesses she would listen to Henry reading *Great Expectations*, only realising later in life how much she had missed as she dozed. Henry was an affectionate father and more interested in his small children than many men of his era. In the evenings on his return from the Bar he used to fling open the front door with a crash which shook the whole house, then whistle and shout 'Where's my baby?' Tiny Monica would go downstairs one step at a time to meet him, in later years sliding down the smooth and knobless banister to land halfway across the hall. When they grew older Doady and Monica had to go into their father's dressing room for Catechism or French lessons while he was shaving, which Monica hated. The girls angrily banged their heels against the rungs of a chair or picked at the leather top of an old table as Henry put them through their paces. He gave them twopence if they were good or, more often, gave them the twopence anyway.

When at home, her father used to sit for hours, reading or making lists of symphonies he had listened to on the wireless, the places he had been to, or the books he had read to Fanny, or with a special machine cutting out jigsaws from posters pasted onto plywood. Sometimes Monica went to sit underneath the table to watch the soft sawdust piling up on the dining room carpet.

§

By 1917 the Germans were making extensive use of the rigid Zeppelin airships to conduct their bombing raids over London and elsewhere, and Monica's earliest memory, at about two, was of a maid screaming that the Zepps were coming and throwing her apron over her head. When policemen blew warning whistles in the streets on moonlit nights when the Zeppelins might come, Doady and Monica would be placed to sleep under a mattress folded backwards to make a cave, to guard them against the British anti-aircraft shell splinters that posed more of a threat than the Zeppelins themselves. On Armistice Day Monica remembered being made to run through the streets with Doady, waving flags and shouting, 'Hooray Hooray! It's peace today!', which hideously embarrassed both of them as they had no idea what it was all about.

Monica, 3 & Doady, 5

When Fanny taught five-year-old Doady to read, Monica sat under the table imbibing the lessons unconsciously and had learned to read by three and a half. As she got older she discovered that she could win at paper games and party competitions but if she did not win, there was no fun in playing. She began to be known to august great-aunts as 'that clever little Monica' (pronounced 'Moaneeca' by those of European extraction), but as they patted her head they wished that she would not frown so much. She had grown into a stolid, obstinate, somewhat grumpy child, accepted as such by her parents who sensibly made no attempt to jolly her out of it. When Nanny told her off for bad behaviour, saying she was making herself conspicuous, Monica's response was a vehement 'Good!' When Henry shouted for his baby on his return in the evenings from the Law Courts, Monica would now sulk and play hard to get: 'No come see my baby. Go down write papers.' Henry and Fanny responded by allowing her to be herself. If Monica was scowling and sullen, they simply acknowledged it by saying 'She's scowling and sullen,' and let her be. She loathed being dressed up for parties, even when Nanny tried to bait the hook with a frilly dress of the sort that Doady adored. It was always a struggle to get Monica ready although once at the party she plunged into the fray and thoroughly enjoyed herself.

The daily routine of childhood was punctuated by dreaded weekly visits to Henry's mother Marie Dickens at Mulberry Walk. Even Doady the clothes-lover groaned along with Monica when, the night before, Nanny put out the tussore silk dresses and white socks, cleaned their patent leather shoes with milk and brought out the strips of rag to curl their hair. The next day Monica would make a fuss as Nanny dressed her, hoping to get hit with the bristles of the hairbrush so that it looked like incipient disease and she might not have to go. Their combative French grandmother Marie Dickens was rather fearsome, shouting at the servants and insulting them in French. Monica's mother Fanny had been afraid of Marie when she and Henry were first engaged, and continued to be so as a young wife.

The Dickenses had initially tolerated the young Henry's holiday romance with the slender, skating Fanny Runge when he met her at St Moritz – less so at the prospect of an actual connection with the Runges, who had more money than the Dickenses but were 'in trade'. The Runges, for their part, were suspicious of the impecunious young barrister who had been brought up as a Roman Catholic, and would not allow their daughter to marry until the prospective bridegroom could afford two servants. There was no romantic proposal: Henry never did get down on bended knee to Fanny, just began talking and writing in terms of what they would do when they got married. They were at last allowed to do so after a four-year engagement (and no doubt promised, as required by the Catholic Church of a 'mixed' marriage, to bring up any children in the faith). The young couple were then required to go to supper at Mulberry Walk every Sunday night, where little was heard from Sir Henry but a great deal more from Marie as she bossed Fanny about. Although Fanny suffered, they came home with kind gifts of food they could not refuse as they were so poor. In the end she learned to love her mother-in-law and to be bossy to Marie in return, which worked far better than trembling. Doady and Monica were never afraid of their grandmother and enjoyed her pride in them, though embarrassed by her matriarchal passion and energetic attempts to get them to perform comic rhymed sketches in French. Amateur dramatics at Sir Henry's were a constant.

At age four Monica was bridesmaid at a big Dickens wedding when her aunt, Henry's youngest sister Elaine, married a Major at Brompton Oratory, where the Dickenses went to Mass. A full Cardinal officiated at the ceremony. Sir Henry gave away the bride, who was swathed in satin and tulle, and Monica was one of eight bridesmaids in flounced white silk dresses, a full five of whom were great-granddaughters of Charles Dickens. Present at the ceremony were viscounts, admirals, countesses, barons and generals (although Monica was only ever to describe her background as 'bourgeois' and 'not rich, but comfortable').

Monica when grown up lamented in public that, as a child, having a famous ancestor meant nothing. She and Doady were photographed putting flowers on Dickens' gravestone in the floor of Westminster Abbey, and the adults talked of him all the time, but to the little girls it did not seem important. With a child's egotism the young Monica assumed that other people were only there for *her,* and in any case Sir Henry was a remote, imposing figure, always formally seated in an armchair – not someone you could put questions to, she remarked as an adult. He was not fond of small children and did not spend much time with them, Monica recalled, so she had no memory of him talking to any great extent about Dickens, at least to her. Once grown up it was hard for her to accept that her own grandfather knew Dickens so well, and that she had never thought to raise the subject; perhaps a little ashamed of the fact (or possibly genuinely forgetting), she was to claim at various points in her life that he died when she was only five, or six, or nine, or twelve, implying that she had been too young to have a proper conversation with him. She did say that she remembered Sir Henry describing Dickens' parties and theatrical evenings, and casually reminiscing about his father. In truth, at her grandfather's death Monica had reached the relatively mature age of eighteen and it had still apparently never occurred to her to talk to him about Dickens, despite Sir Henry continuing in full possession of his faculties and practising law into his eighties.

§

In due course Monica joined Doady at the private Norland Place School, where the teachers were young ladies. Monica remembered Norland as a wonderful place which did not just teach the children their letters, but also taught them how to learn. Her reports described her as a 'capable little girl' who produced excellent work 'at times'; her English was only 'good'.

The school had a way of fostering expectations of being liked and being successful, and was ruled by loving kindness and trust, Monica was to recall later; when she moved up to her next school she found she had a better grounding than many from much larger schools with lesser ideals. There was nothing at Norland for the naturally mutinous Monica to rebel against, although her school reports indicated that she could be a nuisance, and needed to exercise more self-control and consideration for others and to do better in conforming to school rules. One friend at the school, Sylvia Levinson, remembered Monica in those early days as a natural leader, very clever, and a brilliant story-teller who excelled at sport and was full of fun. Her talent for mimicry gave her a slightly caustic edge, even at that young age, so that according to Sylvia she was 'really quite *spiky*'.

Nanny Gathergood would walk the girls to school in the morning and take them home at the end of the day. Monica insisted that Nanny take the same streets every time because already she was feeling the first stirrings of a 'passion for glimpsed lives'. She wanted to follow the doings of the inhabitants she saw in the windows of the terraced basements as they passed by: a couple arguing, a maid adjusting her cap in the mirror. It was a dawning writer's awareness of the fascination of other people, and Nanny had to drag her crossly away as she lingered at railings to see what was going on, tightening her grip on Monica's hand and saying, 'Don't *stare*, don't look.' Monica was instinctively more interested in the servants in the basements than their employers in the upper storeys, she declared, not because she was sorry for them, but because she felt they were having a better time. It was the beginning, too, of her lifelong attempt to understand why the lives of others looked so attractive from the outside, while from the inside it was the passers-by who held the allure. At times Monica lived in a dream world because she wanted to be those other people; she had already embarked upon her permanent habit of staring at others and, when she could, listening to their conversations.

As Monica grew she became more aware of the area she lived in. Chepstow Villas, with its nannies and scrubbed front steps and pollarded plane trees, was perfectly respectable when the house had first been bought by the Dickenses, but not so Portobello down the hill. At night, men buttoning up their trousers emerged from an alley at the side of the Lord Nelson pub and then came carousing up towards Chepstow Villas, singing drunkenly and frightening Monica if she happened to be sleeping in her brother Bunny's room at the front of the house when he was away. The Portobello Road market – in Monica's childhood just on Saturdays, and still a proper flea market of odd shoes and chipped china – started two streets down from Chepstow Villas and wandered northwards slowly getting worse, although Monica remembered it as fun and cheerful, never depressing. Her mother would do her shopping there, which was considered very progressive as most women of her class had groceries delivered at the back door from Whiteleys or Barkers.

At the far end, where it degenerated into fly-ridden fruit and vegetable stalls, Doady and Monica became briefly involved with a gang of local boys. Their misdemeanours were fairly innocent: stealing sweets, kicking chocolate vending machines, cadging pennies from drunks. Their mother Fanny allowed the girls to play in the streets and to bring the boys home to play in the backyard, and from here the mildly criminal gang of boys and girls discovered a way of getting all the way to the Lord Nelson along the tops of walls and over rooftops without setting foot to the ground. Monica and Doady would signal to the boys from their mother's bedroom, where the window faced onto the Portobello Road at the side of the house. Monica knew one of the urchins as Harry Asker, only finding out years later that his name was actually Harry Housego.

52 Chepstow Villas

Despite the Georgian style, number 52 itself was Victorian, detached and solid, a flight of steps leading to an imposing porticoed door. Monica described it as 'not grand', comfortable to live in, but inconvenient and difficult to clean. The kitchen and its stone sink (plus scullery, pantry and wine cellar) were in the basement, and there were tubes in the rooms to whistle the servants up from the nether regions. All four old-fashioned lavatories in the house had Delft china bowls and wooden seats. The rooms were heated by gas fires, where the children crouched in the winter holding out their underwear to warm before putting it on.

The plastered front of the house in its small paved garden was well maintained, the steps regularly cleaned with hearthstone. But at the back the house was down-at-heel, with bare bricks and window sills left unpainted. Here in the backyard on a Sunday afternoon family and friends played 'stump cricket', a mixture of cricket and squash invented by Henry which involved the ball ricocheting off the walls of the surrounding houses and notional runs being scored according to which wall the ball hit. After the game, beer would be fetched for the men in jugs from a nearby pub, appropriately named The Cricketers.

As a small child Monica maintained a list of the people she was in love with, which she kept under her pillow. These were not people she actually knew, which would have held no magic. The inventory included the Prince of Wales, a soldier in a play she had seen with his arm in a sling, one of the Lost Boys in *Peter Pan* and a couple of members of the Surrey County cricket team. Her father, who took Monica to cricket matches at The Oval as though she were a boy, could have introduced her to the cricketers, but that was not the point.

§

During the spring and summer school holidays the family would spend time at Chilworthy, the country house of Fanny's parents in Somerset. In London the senior Runges lived in a large flat in Berkeley Square, where Monica and Doady had to endure formal Sunday teas of soggy cucumber sandwiches and *Sachertorte* with their German grandparents. The holidays in Somerset were something else. The Runges were as tribal and sociable as the Dickenses and there were always twenty or thirty people packed into the comfortable old manor house, not counting the servants. (A photo of the indoor and outdoor staff at Chilworthy House in 1912 shows eight male servants standing behind ten female seated on the lawn in their capacious white aprons and caps.)

Herman, Fanny's father, was originally from Bremen. He started a prosperous sugar business in Cuba which later became part of the British firm of Tate and Lyle, and with his German wife Emma he then settled in Britain and set about becoming more English than the English. In the country he strode around dressed as an English squire in tweeds and breeches, sometimes brandishing a riding whip, although Monica never saw him ride, and sometimes a gun; his pronounced German accent remained. The anglicisation of his name during the First World War had followed local suspicions that he was an enemy agent and had built the tennis court at Chilworthy as a gun emplacement. His only son, British-born Julius, also worked at Tate and Lyle and became business manager for the wartime Sugar Commission. The House of Commons had to be reassured in 1917 that 'No reason exists to doubt his absolute loyalty to the country of his birth.'

Courteous and open-handed to all his guests, Herman nevertheless seemed rather distant and alarming to the swarms of grandchildren who descended on Chilworthy in the holidays. They hardly ever spoke to him. Their German grandmother Emma was also distant, but not so daunting. She was an invalid dressed in dark colours and mostly confined to bed or sitting supported with pillows in a chair. At the age of forty she had been diagnosed with a weak heart and thereafter had remained captive in bedroom or drawing room, gazing out at the beautiful lawns and parkland. She never descended to the dining room or sat by the fire in the large central hall, where family and guests knocked back the whisky and sherry and consumed huge teas only a few hours before dinner. On warm days she would sit outside in a hooded wicker chair, occasionally being taken to join the tea parties in the summer house, feasts of peaches and raspberries and yellow Jersey cream brought from the nearby farm.

The grandchildren would speak to her usually only once a day, each in turn visiting her at bedtime in her warm and fragrant bedroom (not shared with Grandpa), where she nestled in bed eating a soft-boiled egg mixed with chopped toast and sherry out of a delicate porcelain cup. Each child would be given a square of chocolate in silver paper and an occasional alcoholic taste of egg. Nothing much was said, but Monica felt that Granny liked her and looked forward to their visits. None of the children ever wanted to miss their turn, even after Granny became iller and there was no more chocolate.

The other adults at Chilworthy, Fanny and Henry and Fanny's siblings with their spouses, were a shadowy and unreal presence in comparison to the intensity of existence amongst the cousins. Once a week the children took turns having lunch with the grown-ups in the elegant dining room, where two parlourmaids waited by the sideboard as Henry or another of the fathers carved great haunches of beef or several roast chickens at a time. For lunch in the dining room, announced by a gong, Monica had to change out of the boy's shirts and shorts and snake-buckle belt that she habitually wore to tear around in with the other children. She was suddenly shy at being surrounded by grown-ups but found compensation in the gooseberry fool or salty blackcurrant ice-cream produced by the kitchen maid endlessly churning in the stone-flagged scullery.

At other times the children's meals were in the nursery, attended by Nanny Gathergood and the other nannies and sundry servants from the house. The cousins' bedrooms were at the top of one wing of the house, small white-painted rooms from which the older children escaped to visit each other via the rooftops after they had supposedly gone to bed. The maids' rooms, less comfortable, were at the top of another wing. The housekeeper and Granny's maid had their rooms on yet another level. Downstairs, behind the swinging green baize door, lay the tiled kitchen, sculleries, pantries and larders. The children were allowed into the kitchen but never into the servants' hall or sitting room or the housekeeper's room, which were sacrosanct, no matter how friendly the servants. There was even a code of etiquette for the nannies, who were somewhere between family and servants. They did not always dare to ring for the servants themselves, and equally the housekeeper and Granny's maid had to be issued an invitation to visit the nursery for tea or morning cocoa. Outside staff consisted of the chauffeur, a groom for the few horses, numerous gardeners to care for the cricket lawn, the park and the dredged-out pond for swimming, and a man who operated the generator in a pulsating shed.

The grown-ups at Chilworthy knew as little about the children's world as the children knew about theirs.

There were fiercely bonded friendships, loosening in the distances of different schools in term time and re-forming with someone else next holidays. There were gang wars, pogroms against the nurses, love affairs, hero worship, torture sessions, hauntings, obsessive cults, and displays of long distance urination by the boys.

(Monica Dickens, *An Open Book*, 1978)

§

Chilworthy was to make solid appearances in Monica's first two books and more faintly in some of the others. Her home in Chepstow Villas also frequently manifested itself in her writing, including the last book she ever wrote.

Monica only became aware in later life that few people experience the love and security she had enjoyed in childhood, both at Chilworthy and in London with the deeply loving Fanny and Henry (whom she called by their first names from a very early age). She had the solidity of the Dickens and Runge clans behind her and the 'strengthening reassurance' of parents who liked and approved of her and often told her so. Fanny was not the motherly type, too spare and bony for cuddling, but she would pat an upset child on the back and hum until they felt better. Fanny was never in one place for long, unlike Henry with his lists and jigsaws, habitually ensconced somewhere with a lap available for any passing child. Monica and her siblings were not with their parents all the time but Fanny and Henry were always there, always accepting of their children's individual ways. As she grew older Monica naturally found them old-fashioned and embarrassing, although their unchangeability was a facet of the security they provided. She understood as an adult that a secure childhood lasted a lifetime, and felt guilty that she had been so lucky when many were not. Even Nanny's tellings-off for bad behaviour were an indication that she had importance and a place in the world.

Her relationship with Doady was almost as though Doady were the younger sister and she the elder; it seemed to Monica that it was she who should be lecturing Doady on how to grow up, not the other way round. Doady cried from emotion (and not from fury, like Monica) and was more easily wounded. She constantly

13

forgot her glasses so that she was unable to see at concerts and pantomimes, and was forever needing to relieve herself at awkward moments. As she grew older and imbibed more of the Catholic faith, Doady was tormented by her conscience and troubled by sin. (Monica's attitude to religion was more robust. Seeking to ring the changes at Confession, she once brought up some infantile shop-lifting from Woolworths in the hope of shocking the priest, but to Monica's disappointment he only rejoined that at such an early age it was not a sin.)

The girls' older brother Bunny, meanwhile, was on a pinnacle and hardly known to them. At first away at school, and then later a cadet at the Royal Naval College on the Isle of Wight which he entered in 1919 when Monica was four, he would come home for the holidays in his cadet's uniform and do forbidden things like drinking wine and putting his feet up on the sofa. Monica would try and get his attention, watching his moods for an opportunity to make him laugh by pulling faces or repeating what the grown-ups had said.

It was not Monica but Doady who showed signs of nascent literary ability. Monica was not the kind of child who constantly wrote stories and plays; as an adolescent she never spent hours in a tree house mooning over poetry. She did no writing at all; in fact her mother Fanny thought her more likely to become a painter. It was Doady who wrote the dramas for the cousins to act at Chilworthy, constantly editing the script to suit the talents and inclinations of her actors. These were performed in the children's playhouse with the parents made to watch. Others might play the hero or villain, but Monica would only play comic charwomen.

Fanny, too, wrote dramas, romances, and poetry all her life and in Monica's view was as creative as the Dickenses. Family occasions were invariably marked by clever doggerel from Fanny, as when her father Herman Runge surprisingly won a medal for skating: '...you tightened every nerve, to get the proper perfect curve'.

As the number of children in the extended family grew, Fanny wrote the lyrics for some first-rate musicals which were performed in real theatres, supposedly for charity but in Monica's later view more because Fanny and her ambitious sisters-in-law wanted to produce plays. The adult Monica came to understand that her mother was very clever and completely frustrated because she had never been allowed to have a job. Had she been born in a different generation, Monica realised, she might well have been a journalist.

In Fanny's play *Rainbowland*, produced in 1924, Monica played Pinkie the white rabbit and appeared in a photograph scowling, with her face turned away from the camera.

§

In November 1921 Monica's Runge grandmother died at the age of seventy-three. The funeral service was held at Christ Church near Kensington Gardens in central London. The death of her remote grandfather Herman Runge followed in 1925 and in 1926 the old manor house where Monica had spent so many happy holidays was put up for sale. Harrods department store disposed of the estate, which comprised 400 acres with views of the Somerset coast and a Tudor house (although in fact it was just a nineteenth-century replica, later described by Somerset County Council as a 'very successful pastiche'). Monica and Doady continued to see their many cousins but with the passing of this 'privileged paradise', as Monica termed it in her memoir, gone too was the intensity of feeling between them all – both loves and hates – that had permeated those youthful springs and summers. The smell of the first raspberries, so redolent of Chilworthy, was always to sadden Monica.

Holidays with the Runges had been in Somerset; holidays with the Dickens side of the family mostly took place in the same seaside hotel in Belgium. These were big, noisy clan affairs where the Dickenses and their friends and children and nannies more or less took over the whole establishment. The Dickens party filled the little tram cars that ran past the sandy golf course, employed their own children as caddies instead of the locals, and held sway over the annual tennis tournament. On Saturday nights the family likewise dominated the line of people holding lighted Japanese lanterns as they marched down to the beach behind the town band. To Monica, her family's unruly singing as they paraded was not unlike the sound of the drinkers staggering up the Portobello Road at home.

These group holidays had been going on for years before Monica's birth and on one occasion in 1906 included the venerable 'Auntie' – Georgina Hogarth, sister of Charles Dickens' wife

15

Catherine. Georgina remained with Dickens as his housekeeper even after his separation from Catherine, and was remembered in Dickens' will as 'the best and truest friend I ever had'. She lived to the age of ninety, dying when Monica was nearly two.

§

When Chilworthy was to be sold after the death of her parents Fanny, knowing what a loss awaited the children, decided to buy a cottage in Oxfordshire where a young American friend would live and keep ponies for the family. This was the start of eleven-year-old Monica's lifelong love affair with the horse. She was already passionately horsy and desperately wanted a pair of brown riding boots she used to see in the window of a second-hand shop down in Portobello (on finally going in she had found they were actually men's, and far too big). Once, seeing a picture of a soldier saying farewell to his wounded horse Monica had rushed home, locked herself in the bathroom and dissolved into floods of tears. Doady and Bunny banged on the door and told her to open up. 'Come out, Monica, you silly...It's all right. It's the man who's dying, *not* the horse,' they lied.

The girls began to spend their weekends in the white cottage in the village of Britwell Salome at the foot of the Chiltern Hills. On Friday afternoons the family's chauffeur would collect them from school with their friends in the blue Wolseley car, which already contained Nanny Gathergood, and then return to pick them up on Sundays for the reverse journey back up to London. The cottage was small and primitive with no indoor plumbing; water for the tin baths taken in front of the kitchen fire came from a creaking rainwater pump in the scullery. The kitchen itself was always festooned with saddles and other riding tack which usually had to be moved from chairs before anyone could sit down. In winter there were coal fires in the bedrooms and everyone went to bed in their jumpers and socks, Monica giggling with her friends in the light of the fire reflected on the ceiling; in summer, they dismantled the iron beds and set them up on the lawns outside to sleep under the stars.

A photograph of Monica aged about twelve shows her sitting straight-backed on her horse in jodhpurs and jersey, gazing sternly ahead from beneath the fringe of the short springy bob she had sported throughout childhood. All weekend she rode her first pony, Chips, at Britwell Salome, on Sunday afternoons only very reluctantly hanging up the baggy jodhpurs in her small white bedroom. The drive back to London was spent in dumb misery and, having refused to wash the smell of horse from her hands, Monica would sit crying into her food at the supper table. ('She's watering the soup with her tears,' Fanny and Henry would observe sympathetically.) Chilworthy had been a world of fantasy and minor freedoms set within an adult sphere but at Britwell it was purely a children's universe, created by the children themselves. 'There was total freedom,' remembered Sylvia Levinson, Monica's friend at Norland Place School. 'We could ride, sing, act plays, do as we liked all day long.' Nanny was there to do the cooking and family friend Biddy, in her twenties, was nominally in charge but only got serious where the horses' welfare was concerned. To Monica riding was true pleasure, and what felt like complete liberty. The unaccompanied children would swim their horses in a river or race a whistling train, the driver grinning and the passengers waving. Those horsy days at the cottage were the best of her childhood, Monica was to write later, an adult-free world of adventure which she was never to forget.

§

Monica won a scholarship for a free place at St Paul's Girls' School in London and the two headmistresses at Norland Place hugged her in their chintzy office and wept for joy. But arriving at St Paul's in September 1928 at the age of thirteen, Monica found a very different world from kindly Norland: large, competitive and mercilessly ambitious. Many there did not come from her privileged background, and to Monica it was a jungle compared to the 'milk-and-marie-biscuits' atmosphere of her prep school. Many of the girls were rough and sometimes even sadistic. Monica's more aggressive side, gently held in check at Norland, perforce emerged to enable her to survive; a rebellious streak began to show itself as she launched her school career protesting the exclusion of the Roman Catholic and Jewish girls from the Church of England Assembly, where she thought the hymns were better.

But the mix of backgrounds also made it an exciting place. For the first time, Monica met girls whose parents were more interested in their daughters' education than in their social contacts. No one was stupid, which Monica found a joy: she was surrounded by intelligent people, pupils and teachers alike.

Her method of finding friends in youth was to select a few 'loyal dodos' over whom she could have the upper hand, as well as some who were more attractive and sophisticated and to some of whom Monica was the dodo. She felt that some girls in this second category perceived her as all right to be seen out with, but 'just far enough behind' not to pose a threat. Despite this somewhat clinical method of choosing her comrades she was to describe the friendships she made at St Paul's as 'fierce and enduring'. Her sister Doady, thin, anaemic, and conscience-stricken, was already at the school when Monica started and had found her own way after leaving behind the protection and tolerance of Norland. When she arrived at St Paul's nobody had taken any notice of her so Doady decided to act mad in order to get attention, and began to behave 'very weirdly indeed'. Other girls would come up to Monica to ask if her sister was ill. At one point Doady spread the rumour that their mother Fanny was even madder and had been chained up in a padded cell.

Monica was later to describe her reports at the academically pressured St Paul's as 'not good', although she also stated that she had won scholarships and gained honours in exams. At various times she claimed that she both was and was not pushed to achieve there, but in any case she had an instinctive inclination to aim for the top. Henry and Fanny always encouraged their children to succeed: it was a dominant theme in their family life, a distinct impression imparted of 'you can do it', which the adult Monica acknowledged as tremendously helpful – although success had to be on her own terms. In this atmosphere she became driven, and looking back described herself as a 'rough and ruthless child' with a desperate need for love and admiration which meant she aspired to be the best at everything, whether riding horses or passing exams. At St Paul's she fought her way to being the captain of the second eleven at cricket because, she observed as an adult, if she could not be captain then she did not want to play. She was also Hockey Secretary and later Hockey Vice-Captain.

As her adolescent years progressed Monica became increasingly unhappy, feeling lonely, unloved and unloveable, despite the great affection she received at home. She was not a natural scholar, and according to her mother, disliked being at school because she hated hordes of women. At the age of seventeen came rebellion. Sick and tired of the academic force-feeding, Monica wrote in her memoir that she threw the ugly black felt bucket of a hat and the gym tunic – a hideous item with a box-pleated bodice intended to flatten the chest – into the Thames off Hammersmith Bridge. On returning to the school, she lied that her mother could not afford to buy another uniform (an excuse she had already employed on an earlier occasion after giving the hated hat to the dog). She was expelled.

It was a good story, one that Monica was to wheel out many times throughout her life, once including the not insignificant detail, if true, that she had actually divested herself of the gym tunic on the bridge and arrived home wrapped in a blanket and accompanied by a policeman. However, despite the oft-told tale, school records at St Paul's do not concur. At that point mandated school uniform items for older girls like Monica comprised just the hated hat and a pair of gloves, to be worn with their own clothes; only much younger girls wore the gym tunic, and even then it was not obligatory. Expulsion was extremely rare and the Governors were usually informed of any such cases, but there is no mention of Monica's disgrace in the Minutes of the Governors' Meetings. The records show that Monica took Matriculation and the Leaving Certificate, with Honours, in 1931, and the period of her attendance at the school was the normal length: as would be expected, she was documented as leaving in July 1933 when she was eighteen.

There was clearly some incident with the uniform but the tale may have grown with the telling. Returning to St Paul's as a guest speaker in much later life, Monica talked to the girls about getting expelled but added the words 'or, in those genteel days, I was asked to be removed'. It is likely that at the school's request she departed just a little earlier than she would have done, without any formal expulsion and resultant stain on the record.

On another occasion Monica amplified that she was also expelled for not wearing the uniform, not trying hard enough, going shopping in Kensington High Street (presumably when she should have been at school) and being 'sullen and impertinent and lacking in team spirit'. She may have been staying on at school beyond her natural inclinations in any case: she once claimed that because Henry could afford St Paul's fees Fanny had given the scholarship away to the daughter of a local family, and Monica had then been obliged to remain at the school for two years longer than she wanted to in order to keep the scholarship going for the girl in question. However, this account does not appear in *An Open Book*.

The High Mistress for most of Monica's career at the school was the redoubtable Ethel Strudwick, a statuesque lady who climbed mountains in her spare time. Politician Shirley Williams, a near contemporary at St Paul's, recalled Miss Strudwick as a person of authority who measured the success of her rebukes by whether a girl was reduced to tears, which she took as evidence of shame and regret for misbehaviour. It is hard to imagine Monica being reduced to tears (equally so Shirley Williams, who certainly was not) but she did find Miss Strudwick 'austere and terrifying'. When Monica was asked to go, Miss Strudwick told Fanny that as her daughter was not suited for University, or indeed any sort of life that included the use of the brain, she might try for a civic post such as sanitary inspector.

Before this ignominious end to her school career the adolescent Monica had become subject to 'pashes' for older girls. At this all-female institution the only man was the music master, composer Gustav Holst, who wrote *The Planets* whilst working at the school. In this manless hothouse of academic achievement Monica fell in love with a series of thrilling older girls. She learned to get the full benefit out of the ups and downs of her unrequited amours: the hanging around for a glimpse of the loved one, the blindness to their true nature, the scheming and the dashing of hopes. These lessons in love were to stand her in good stead when in the fullness of time the love object was male: Monica found the heights of joy and depths of despair exactly the same.

All her life Monica was grateful that she went to St Paul's. She maintained that she had had no idea she would become a writer (a teacher once told her that she 'ought to be able to write better than that'), but she recalled that the teaching of English and Literature at the school was superb and inspiring. She recognised later that the school had also taught her to be tough and independent and to fight for what she wanted – as she was about to do.

One Pair of Hands

Fanny and Henry's reaction to Monica's 'expulsion' remains unrecorded, and the seventeen-year-old Monica was sent to a Paris finishing school to be taught deportment and the social graces. Part of the time she stayed with a French family in the well-to-do Passy area of the city, where she learned little French because everyone in the house was anxious to learn English. She also boarded at the school, where, according to her memoir, the girls had to urinate out of the windows at night because they were locked in their rooms. Monica later claimed to have been kicked out of the French finishing school as well.

On her return from being 'finished', Monica decided she wanted to go on the stage, and begged Henry and Fanny to be allowed to have drama training. Her long-suffering parents signed her up at the Central School of Speech Training and Dramatic Art, at that point housed in the Albert Hall in kidney-shaped classrooms ranged around the circular walls. Here Monica, in black tights, mimed a range of emotions and dragging along an unwilling dog, and floundered her way through the maid's part in a poor play. The principal of the school, the terrifying Elsie Fogerty, told Fanny that Monica had bow legs. (What did she expect after eight years of riding horses? Monica asked.) Told that these defective legs would have to be broken and reset, Fanny made some vague but dignified reply, and shortly afterwards, fortunately, Monica was thrown out of the school for lack of talent. If she could not be the best at something, she either dropped out or got kicked out, she remarked in later life. After making such a fuss to get in she was too scared to tell her parents immediately.

In her semi-autobiographical work Monica's failure at drama school is described humorously, but the agony of having to perform in public without talent is excruciatingly conveyed in her later novel *Mariana*, when a drama school teacher orders the heroine Mary to mime Shakespeare's impish character Puck:

Why couldn't she give it to someone else who knew how to do whimsical things with their arms and legs? All Mary could think of was to poke her outspread fingers at the air in the traditional pantomime manner, and mince about on tiptoe, pausing occasionally to strike a sort of 'hark' attitude. She felt herself going crimson, suffused with waves of heat as from an open oven door, and finished her act as soon as she dared.

(Monica Dickens, *Mariana*, 1940)

§

As Monica sought to find her way in the world, events of note had been occurring in the Dickens family. In December 1933 the eighty-four-year-old Sir Henry Fielding Dickens, Monica's barrister grandfather and son of Charles, was knocked down by a motorcycle near his home at Mulberry Walk. Sir Henry had been standing on an island in the middle of the road on Chelsea Embankment, looking the wrong way from the flow of traffic, and then suddenly started to run across in front of an oncoming motorcyclist. His right leg was fractured in two places and there were wounds to his scalp and temple. Taken to St Luke's Hospital in Chelsea, Sir Henry's first words on recovering consciousness were to his wife Marie: 'My poor dear, what a shock for you.' He shortly died, after having retired only a little over a year previously. An inquiry was opened; the motorcyclist stated that the collision had been unavoidable, despite sounding his horn and shouting a warning. Monica's father Henry testified that Sir Henry's health and eyesight had been very good but that his hearing was defective. The coroner called for witnesses to come forward but when the inquiry resumed none had appeared, and a verdict of accidental death was recorded. Following the funeral – at which Henry's brother Pip knocked an intrusive reporter backwards over a gravestone and broke his camera – a memorial service was held in January 1934 at London's famous Temple Church. Henry and Fanny and Doady were there but, for unknown reasons, not Monica, now eighteen. A host of legal and other luminaries were present, including the Mayor of London and the usual clutch of titles.

Monica's feelings on the loss of her remote grandfather are not mentioned in *An Open Book,* which she intended only as a selective memoir of experiences which had shaped her writing. In any case, there had been happier events to occupy her. In 1933, the year of Sir Henry's sudden death, her sister Doady became engaged to Denys Danby, a handsome vet all the rage in Mayfair and the grandson of the Earl of Aylesford. The two were married in August 1934 at the Catholic church of St James in Marylebone, with Monica one of ten bridesmaids in white tulle and georgette dresses, their hair wreathed in wild white roses.

Yet another engagement followed, that of Monica's adored brother Bunny. His marriage to Joyce Miller took place in May 1935 at the Catholic church of St Anne's in Caversham. Monica and the other bridesmaids were resplendent in chiffon and matching caps and capes.

Monica now remained the only one of the Dickens children left at home, her future still a blank.

§

In June 1935, at the age of twenty, Monica was presented at Court. She was decidedly unenthusiastic, later claiming that she was forced into it and hated every minute. Fanny's sister had taken a house in Belgravia for her own daughter's Coming Out season, and had convinced the suggestible Fanny that becoming a debutante was imperative to Monica's chances of making a good marriage. Monica later came to the conclusion that her removal from St Paul's was also instrumental in Fanny's decision to launch her as a deb, presumably meaning that Fanny hoped her troublesome daughter would find a suitable man and settle down. Monica was duly togged out in a sleeveless gown of blush-pink satin, its neckline trimmed with a garland of velvet roses and leaves atop what she considered an overlarge bosom; the costume was completed with elbow-length gloves, a double satin train from the shoulders and the traditional three feathers at the back of the head reflecting the heraldic badge of the Prince of Wales, who was presiding at the ceremony.

In the family's chauffeur-driven blue Wolseley she and Fanny queued for hours to get into Buckingham Palace amongst even posher Rolls Royces and Daimlers, some with coronets on the door to betoken aristocracy. When they finally arrived at the palace Fanny had to make for the ladies' room, which turned out to be just chamber pots in curtained cubicles. In Monica's opinion the money that had been spent teaching her to curtsey was not worth the single minute she then spent in the throne room, too scared to look at the bored Prince of Wales standing in for George V. A photograph taken in the backyard of number 52 shows an unsmiling but handsome Monica in her pink gown, holding a bouquet of matching tinted rosebuds. She was officially 'Out', a marriageable debutante launched on a path of teas at the Ritz and balls at which lipsticked girls sat about giggling as they waited to be asked to dance by the chinless youths they hoped to ensnare.

Unfortunately, Monica was not at her best. At this stage overweight (which had made her subject to teasing), shy, and very gauche, she had no small talk and tended to fall over her feet. At her first debutante ball nobody asked her to dance, so she disappeared to read *Vanity Fair* in the Ladies and never went to another. (When she later came across Charlotte Bingham's *Coronet Among the Weeds* in the early 1960s, Monica was much amused to read about a similar wallflower hiding in the bathroom who supposedly got right through *War and Peace*.) On other social occasions she tagged along with a friend whose partner could produce a male friend for Monica, most of them dreadful in her eyes. Short men were known as 'bent knees' because tall girls like Monica had to wear flat shoes and bend their knees when they danced. Rather than leave a restaurant with a short man walking beside her, Monica would make an excuse, head to the Ladies and then meet him outside. Whenever she did manage to get a boyfriend one of her more attractive girlfriends stole him.

She could be confident and sure of her looks sometimes in a new dress and hairdo, but would immediately feel a mess if a better-groomed girl walked into the room. Brooding over her appearance, depressed by what she considered its defects, she was capable of being plunged into gloom at a party if one side of her hair was not right. With the young men Monica met as a debutante and her friends' brothers at Oxford and Cambridge she stayed in frozen manor houses to attend balls in the Shires, despite disliking house parties, dancing, and often even the men themselves. She had to accept the invitations or feel a failure for staying in London over the weekend. Everyone always seemed to have paired off before Monica arrived, and she would spend her time worrying about whether to risk infection by squeezing her pimples or just to let them break through the heavy make-up she wore as camouflage. Along with many other girls she let virtually any man kiss her rather than return home untouched, or without having her clothing fumbled with, and used to breathe heavily to demonstrate the arousal she supposed she ought to be experiencing. There was little talk about sex in that era, either in public or in private, and she was not quite sure what everyone else was doing.

At the end of August 1935 Monica and her father sailed off aboard *RMS Laconia* to see the wonders of New York, a trip the two took alone together as they had occasionally done in Europe. Americans were fascinated by the pretty blonde great-granddaughter of Charles Dickens and Monica, despite her problems, was caught up in a social whirl and greatly enjoyed herself, although still shy and diffident. One of their engagements in the city was lunch at the Ritz-Carlton with Samuel Stockton White, an old friend of Henry's from his Cambridge days, and his much younger wife Vera, with whom Monica became friendly. They went to stay with the Stockton Whites at their home in Philadelphia, where over-excited newspaper reporters for some reason mistook Henry for Kipling. Monica's interest in these intriguing new acquaintances, however, was but slight. At that stage she was more interested in herself and her own doings than in other people, she subsequently admitted:

> *I lived in a shell, walled in by security, habit and tradition, moving round in my own narrow circuit and* that *revolved round the fascinating subject of myself.*

(Monica Dickens, *Housewife* magazine, March 1954)

At this period she was ignorant 'of life itself', Monica recalled. She knew the date of the Battle of the Boyne, and (after her spell being finished in France) the French for 'Go away, you nasty old man', but she had simply no understanding or curiosity about the people she encountered.

Monica and Henry stayed in the States for over a month, finally sailing home via Boston and Ireland in early October. It was sobering to return to London where nobody sent her orchids and rang her in the morning as she was starting her breakfast in bed with iced orange juice, to thank her for letting them take her out, or 'invited you to stay for a weekend or for ever on the strength of five minutes' chat at a cocktail party'. The anti-climax made Monica feel flat and dissatisfied with her life; the aimlessness was worse than ever. She drifted, bored and discontented, going nowhere, anti-social and impossible at home. She thought all her friends more sophisticated and better-looking, and they were certainly thinner. Her weight had swollen to eleven stone, and she had thighs 'like trees' and a heavy bosom not helped by the hammock-like bras of the 1930s. She could not even see her feet. Feeling 'extremely fat...and far from attractive', Monica went to nightclubs and dinners with any man who asked her, believing that someone her size could not afford to be fussy and that she ought to be out every night of the week like everyone else (afterwards creeping late into number 52, taking off her shoes and avoiding the creaking floorboards to save waking her parents). When there was no one to take her out she secretly went to cinemas all over London to watch the same Hollywood musicals over and over again.

With her best friend from St Paul's, Ann Stoker, she would also hang around the Fleet at Portsmouth and Southsea. (A photograph of the two, both inexplicably in boiler suits, shows a hefty young Monica not displayed to best advantage next to the more petite Ann.) They had to avoid her brother Bunny if he was in port and likewise her Uncle Gerald, brother of Henry, who was captain of the battleship *Repulse*. With another friend she used to drive up to Oxford and Cambridge, a wind-up gramophone in the back of her Sunbeam Special sports car playing *Jeepers Creepers*, and go to balls and parties in students' rooms and be very jolly. One night, somewhat the worse for wear, Monica somehow got her long-nosed Sunbeam tightly jammed in the driveway at number 52 and was unable to back it out after sobering up. It remained there for months, or so the story went.

At a Magdalen College sherry party one day she was wearing a ribbed jersey dress, unflattering to her size, and heard two men on the other side of the room sniggering the Mae West line 'Come up and see me some time', which she knew meant not that she was sexy, but that she was fat. Desperate, Monica turned to her mother for help. Fanny took her to a newly fashionable endocrinologist, who diagnosed thyroid deficiency and prescribed pills.

Wondrously, on a couple of thyroid pills a day, the bust, thighs and thick waist all disappeared. It changed her from a 'droopybosomed piece into a stark skeleton with no bosom at all', Monica recalled. It was a miracle. She weighed herself several times a day and, consumed with the thought of losing more weight, began to eat less and less and finally not to want food at all. Although her energy had evaporated along with the weight she walked all over London in an effort to lose even more. When she had eaten only a salad all day she liked herself; if she had given in and eaten a meal she hated herself. Sometimes, overcome with hunger in the middle of the night, she used to creep downstairs to cram in cakes and white bread and fried onions and then, aghast, take a dose of castor oil to get rid of it all. Finally, the family doctor found out what was happening and threatened Monica with force-feeding in hospital. She came to her senses and cautiously began to eat; energy and normality returned and for the rest of her life Monica was to remain slender.

With the depression gone she no longer crossed the street to avoid people. But as she walked in the park with her dog Ugly, seeing other women with boyfriends and husbands and children, Monica was still without love or direction. Doady was happily married and so was her brother Bunny; friends and cousins were also getting engaged and marrying. Monica had been to too many weddings, aimless, envying the bride but not quite wanting the groom in question, conscious merely that she lacked something the bride now had: a point to life, or perhaps status. As people in the park passed by without noticing her, Monica promised herself that one day they would know who she was – what for, she could not say. But she had great ambition. Monica later recognised that beneath the shyness and self-consciousness of a very young woman there lurked a confidence that was simply looking for a chance to surface.

§

A number of Monica's activities must have felt a little more worthwhile, such as her fund-raising work for the Great Ormond Street Hospital for children (just as Charles Dickens himself had done the previous century). In early 1936 she was also a guest at a celebratory dinner of the Dickens Fellowship, the worldwide association of Dickens fans – some of whom occasionally dress up as Dickens characters. Monica was to remain involved with the Fellowship all her life, although without the dressing up as far as

27

is known. At the 1936 dinner her fellow guests included Fanny and Henry, her grandfather Sir Henry's widow Lady Dickens, an Ambassador, an Archbishop, and the Lord Mayor of London.

A full Dickens clan holiday of family and friends took place in August 1936, this time to Jamaica. On this occasion Fanny was along too, as were Doady and her husband Denys and a brother of Henry's with his own brood, Monica's cousins; the whole party, as ever, sailed First Class. They were warmly welcomed in Jamaica, where Monica's barrister grandfather Sir Henry Dickens had previously fought a very famous case on behalf of a number of insurance companies following an earthquake there in 1907. The insurance coverage had contained a clause ruling out payment in the event of fire caused by earthquake, and Sir Henry's task was therefore to prove that the fires were indeed caused by the shock and did not occur independently – in other words acting against the interests of the Jamaicans, whose capital city Kingston had been all but destroyed. Sir Henry lost the case and the insurance companies were forced to make good all the damage caused by the fires, thereby enabling Kingston to be rebuilt and Sir Henry to be remembered quite fondly. Kingston's *Daily Gleaner*, welcoming the 'Two Sons of Late Sir Henry Dickens and Their Children and Distinguished Party', printed a photograph of the family with Monica and Doady looking pretty in calf-length white suits and heavy lipstick. On their departure Monica's father spoke to the press about his enjoyment of their beautiful island and the excellent service received by his party; he declared Jamaicans most charming and obliging, adding kindly that 'the general standard of intelligence of the ordinary people is creditable'.

On their return came devastating news. Monica's brother Bunny had contracted malaria in the Canary Islands and in October, at the age of just thirty, had died at sea. His widow Joyce was left expecting their first child.

Bunny had been a god to Monica, a far-off being whose attention she had always desperately sought after when younger. Fanny and Henry used to argue about whether, as their brilliant first child long before the advent of Doady and Monica, he had been spoiled. But he was too endearing to deserve that description, Monica believed. Without being self-centred or insistent he simply expected things to go right for him, because he was funny and delightful. People loved him. Summer holidays in Belgium were more thrilling to the young Monica when Bunny was there, even if only for a few days: she carried his golf clubs and picked up his tennis balls and fetched beers for him from the hotel bar. She was less thrilled when, many years later, Bunny fell in love with a friend of hers during a family holiday in Sweden in 1933 when Monica was eighteen. This was her old schoolfriend, the petite and attractive Ann Stoker, granddaughter of *Dracula* author Bram Stoker (perhaps the two had been drawn together by the coincidence of famous forebears.) Love suddenly blossomed between Ann and Bunny and, failing to see what was happening, Monica happily tagged along with the two of them under the impression that her friend had come on the holiday to be with *her*. Ann finally had to tell Monica she was not wanted, a hurt which left 'an indelible wound'. Bunny and Ann proceeded to get engaged, leaving Monica feeling savagely jealous of each of them: her beloved brother and her best friend, both of whom were meant to be hers. The engagement later fell apart but too late: the friendship with Ann was over, Monica wrote later – although in fact she continued to see Ann and was bridesmaid at her wedding to a Navy Lieutenant. Relations with Bunny, too, slowly returned to normal. He used to loan Monica his glamorous open MG sports car to drive while he was away at sea, and she had enjoyed racing other cars through the revolutionary new traffic lights on the equally new Great West Road. When he eventually instructed her to deliver it to his new fiancé Joyce, Monica was suddenly pierced by the old hurt of Bunny's affair with her friend, but by then it was really more about the car, and any remaining jealousy had evaporated by the time of Bunny's marriage.

Now this god was gone. In the navy Bunny had risen from midshipman to become a lieutenant and a torpedo officer, and served on a number of cruisers and destroyers. He was buried in Gibraltar and a Requiem Mass was held at Brompton Oratory in London, celebrated by the same Father John who had officiated at Bunny and Doady's weddings. Monica and her parents were there. Fanny and Henry seemed shrunken by grief, Monica remembered. Bunny's pregnant wife Joyce, staying with the family at number 52, crept unobtrusively about almost as though she had ceased to be alive herself. The baby, Christopher, was born in 1937.

In December Henry and Monica made a trip to Gibraltar together, probably to visit Bunny's grave.

§

Some time around these painful events Monica decided to get a job. Although she probably received an allowance from her father, she wanted to earn money. The problem was what to do. Drama school had been a fiasco. She had learned a little dressmaking at a Polytechnic but was unenthusiastic at the notion of working in a dress shop. She had picked up some knowledge of cooking, both in Paris and, as the in vogue thing to do, at a few classes with other debs at the Petit Cordon Bleu school in Sloane Street. There she had been taught some fancy sauces and the French way of poaching eggs. After another course at an everyday cookery school she had emerged able to make simpler and more useful dishes as well, like rissoles. Monica decided to become a cook, even though unable to practise at home because the family cook objected to trespasses into what she viewed as 'her' kitchen, but Monica reasoned that what she did not know she could learn as she went along.

Her first idea was to do dinner parties, thinking that after her Cordon Bleu training she could be the superior type of cook who catered special dinners when people's own cooks were not quite up to it. She needed an agency to find her some employment and decided on Universal Aunts, a business originally set up to provide aunt-like figures to meet lone ex-pat children arriving from India, and shepherd them across London to get their train for boarding school via a stop for tea. But they also supplied domestic staff and as Monica's mother had never used them, the agency would not know the Dickenses. In great excitement, and without telling anyone, Monica set off for the Universal Aunts office disguised in a servant-looking raincoat and inoffensive hat.

An accurate account of Monica's next couple of years is difficult to pin down. The astoundingly successful book that Monica subsequently wrote about her short career as an amateur cook, *One Pair of Hands*, was generally taken to be a verbatim account, and still is. In fact, of course, names were changed, characters invented or embroidered, events or aspects of one job transposed to another and the sequence of jobs altered (if she had not revised reality in this way, she might well have been subject to some serious libel suits). The real story may not even be recounted in Monica's memoir, written four decades after the event. In this the account of her two years as cook and housemaid was, by her own admission, confused between what actually happened and what she wrote about it in *One Pair of Hands*. It is also likely to be something of an unreliable memoir, given that Monica included long chunks of comic dialogue which she can hardly have accurately recalled after so much time had elapsed. However, *An Open Book* is probably an honest attempt at a record, and the account which now follows tries to reconstruct the reality using not only that record but additional sources such as interviews, articles, and elements of the original synopsis written for her publisher.

Arriving at Universal Aunts, Monica told the woman behind the desk about her lessons at the Cordon Bleu school and was given the telephone number of someone in North London who wanted a competent cook for a large dinner party. On making the call and pretending to be a competent cook Monica was accepted as such, to her great surprise, and she spent the intervening period alternating between fright and excitement. She decided not to tell Henry and Fanny anything about it but to wait until it was all over and then astound them with her 'tale of disaster or triumph'.

It was, of course, a disaster, according to Monica. She had no idea how long the various courses would take to prepare and cook, and nothing was ready on time for the hired-in serving staff to take to the dining room. Everything went wrong – the fish was dry, the cheese sauce separated, she tore the pheasants apart with her bare hands because she was unable to carve and she hurt her finger on a tin of lobster. She broke glasses and a tureen lid and burned a wooden spoon. The waiting staff were angry because things were not ready when they needed them. Her employer was fuming and at the end of the evening paid Monica off with probably less than her due, indicating that her services were no longer required.

It did not matter. Monica thought she had found her role in life, not so much because she had enjoyed the cooking but because she suddenly felt she belonged somewhere.

The staff at the dinner party had been annoyed by Monica's incompetence but afterwards they all sat around the kitchen table, bonded together in the common cause of servants against mistress, and enjoying the choicest bits of pheasant reserved by Monica and the wine discreetly kept back by the temporary butler. As they discussed their employer and her guests with below-stairs relish,

Monica was accepted as one of them. At restaurants and dinner parties she had always suspected that the waiters and servants were having a better time of it than the guests, and now she knew. They were, and she felt more at home in her employer's kitchen than she ever had in any dining room upstairs trying to make small talk to each neighbour in turn and slowly dying of boredom.

I've always wanted to be down at the bottom, you know. I'd rather be doing the thing than having it done for me – I'd rather be the waiter than the dinner guest.

(Monica Dickens, *Saturday Review*, July 1966)

Unusually perhaps for her era and class, Monica had established friendly, egalitarian relationships with the servants at home. In addition to Nanny Gathergood, serving their family of four (five when Bunny had been home on leave) there was a cook, a parlourmaid, a woman who came in to sew, and the golden-haired young chauffeur who resignedly polished out the scratches inflicted by Henry on the Wolseley at weekends. Most important of all at number 52 was Minnie, the beloved char, a roly-poly countrywoman who had started off as one of Henry and Fanny's two servants when they first married in 1904. The Dickens as a family were unstuffy with their servants and Monica followed suit. Henry used to yell at Mary the maid when he lost his glasses and Mary would yell back that she had not touched the rotten things; then Henry might find them in his pocket and back down, smiling. Mary would tell Monica that a titled lady visiting Fanny was 'some old bag with a handle'. There was a happy and casual atmosphere in the house – apart from the time they were all intimidated by a part manservant, part butler called Dowson; Monica, mortally afraid, described him as appearing in sinister fashion in the drawing room like a terrorist eyeing his hostages and forever giving an insulting tone to her name as he announced the telephone for 'Miss Monica.' For the most part, though, the long-standing servants in the house were more like old friends to the young Monica, and treated as such.

But for all of her twenty-one years Monica had been the served, not the server. Although she may have thought of Ellen the cook, Minnie the char, Mary the irreverent maid and Majer the chauffeur as friends, she had never really been more than a visitor in their world. Now she found herself of their company, and liked it.

At the same time, naturally, social distinctions did not suddenly dissolve for Monica, and never would. For the Dickenses and their various relatives, being 'common' was almost as great a crime as being stupid, and the aunts even used the label against the young Monica for wearing too much make-up. Monica necessarily imbibed the views of the class from which she came, and references to being common were to surface in her books and letters until quite late in life. Nevertheless, Monica claimed to find those below stairs to be more likeable people living life in a real way, and, taken with her impatience and disillusion with the emptiness of existence as a deb, a job working below stairs may well have beckoned with a siren call. She returned to the agency for more work.

Henry and Fanny did not object because they were very enterprising and had a good sense of humour, according to Monica, and were glad to see her with a job. This was confirmed by Fanny in a later interview when she declared that she and Henry did not mind their daughter doing domestic work in the least, although outsiders were shocked. 'We were just a little ahead of our generation,' said Fanny. She admitted that she did not think it would last long (and that she felt rather sorry for the recipients of Monica's efforts). However, some of the older members of the family thought it was 'pretty disgraceful' and felt awkward when Monica came to dinner, not wanting their five or six servants to know what Monica was doing. But after a while the telephones stopped ringing between the aunts. Monty, as she was called with the usual family habit of bestowing nicknames, was simply being eccentric again.

Monica by this time could have done without the nickname. When she was running around in boy's shorts and mad about horses it had not mattered, but now, as an adult finally entering the real world, it was beginning to grate.

§

Conditions for servants in the 1930s were not all that different from the Victorian era: the hours were long, time off was limited and pay was low. Uniforms were mandatory and employers had to be formally addressed as 'ma'am' and 'sir'. The work was hard, with few labour-saving devices yet available and most houses not constructed with servants in mind – kitchens were often in basements, with food needing to be carried up steep flights of stairs to the dining room, and heating consisted of dirty coal fires and kitchen ranges that required constant intensive cleaning. Washing was still done by hand. In the more modern houses servants were often forbidden to use their employers' indoor bathrooms, and servants who lived in were usually confined to washing in handbasins in their bedrooms.

On the benefit side, many employers genuinely concerned themselves over the welfare of their servants and might be more like parents, especially to the younger skivvies. For live-in servants accommodation and food were free, so that despite the low wages money could be saved. However, by the 1930s fewer domestic workers were residential although their lives were still closely monitored by their employers, even to the point of being restricted as to what they were allowed to do during their free time. Servants were also encouraged to put the needs of their employers first, for example to work late if required. As in previous eras they might be subject to sexual predation from their employers, or from tradesmen calling at the back door. There was little redress in such cases as domestics relied on their employers for their 'character', meaning a good reference to secure another post should they hand in their notice. Insubordination, such as disobeying 'proper orders', could lead to instant and perfectly legal dismissal. The employer had to provide either one month's notice or a month's wages, but they were not legally obliged to provide a reference. Without one, servants were unable to get another job.

This was the world that well-educated, privileged Monica was about to take the most unusual step of entering. The question naturally arises as to why she did so, and whether her claim that it was because she felt more at home in the company of servants can be taken at face value. It has been suggested that in embarking on a reversal of roles from master to servant, Monica Dickens may have been influenced by the politically-based social realism and documentary nature of works such as George Orwell's *Down and Out in Paris and London* and Walter Greenwood's *Love on the Dole*, both published in 1933. She was not the first to carry out such a role reversal, the results usually being written up in 'slumming journalism', often for purposes of sensationalism. However, while it is true that in *One Pair of Hands* Monica mentioned her 'Bolshie instincts', and that she certainly had some interesting comments to make (in a now excised final chapter) about the need to break down the class system, there is nevertheless no hard evidence to suggest that she ventured out with a political agenda – even if she may have ended up with one. There is also nothing to suggest that she had any intention of writing up her experiences. Her motives in diving below stairs may well have been more complex, of course, than she herself either perceived or understood.

§

Monica realised that she needed to get more hands-on experience and decided to go out as a 'cook-general', a species which did housework as well as cooking. According to Universal Aunts there was a particular demand for cook-generals, because fewer women were willing to be servants but just as many people needed them. Monica felt that it was better to be working somewhere on her own in this way because from her first exploit she knew that as a cook she could fool her employers, but not other servants.

In *An Open Book* Monica wrote that she re-invented herself at the agency as someone who had fallen on hard times and was having to go out to work to support her widowed mother. Elsewhere she admitted that she put on a slight cockney accent and lied to Universal Aunts that she had worked at a couple of places before and could supply references, which she got Doady or friends with aristocratic addresses to forge. Armed with all this duplicity and with the current servant shortage Monica was easily able to secure a series of jobs, declaring later that she never failed to get a job she tried for (if only because often she was the sole applicant).

To start with she opted to live out rather than in, as a counterbalance to the seediness of spending her days in a basement. This meant that she continued to enjoy the ease of life at 52 Chepstow Villas, being waited upon by its cook and maid and Dowson the repellent butler, while going out early every morning to perform menial work for others. 'It was the first time I'd ever done any work. I'd never even made tea.'

In her memoir Monica's first job as cook-general, part-time, was for a boring old couple who hardly spoke to each other and almost never to Monica. Then came a stint with a glamorous divorcée in a studio flat with whom Monica used a false name and a special voice to accompany it. Here she picked up how to make things like omelettes and quiches and soufflés – never learned at the Cordon

Bleu school because she had not progressed far enough – while bluffing that her many previous and (invented) titled employers had preferred good plain cooking. She also banged and broke her way through the housework, taking an aeon to do each task because she was discovering how to do it for the first time. The divorcée was stringing along several men friends and when she came upon one of them putting his arm around the very young and blonde 'Miss Dixon', she found some spurious reason to give Monica the sack. Assaulting maids below stairs had not gone out with the Victorians, Monica was to find.

Back to Universal Aunts, where her basically true if prejudiced account of her dismissal was accepted, and several more jobs proffered. Her second placement as cook-general was with the gay interior designer Derek Patmore (Monica's signal for gay in her 1970s account being that Patmore was willowy and lived with his mother. Patmore was to write a number of well-regarded design manuals and other works, and reviews of his later books would sometimes appear in the same newspaper columns as reviews of his former cook's). Her new employers lived in a tall terraced house near Harrods, and here she found herself much more hard-worked than at the divorcée's and required to turn out fancy cuisine as well. The mother had an unpleasant, rat-toothed little dog which Monica was expected to take for walks in addition to all her other duties as cook, parlourmaid and cleaner. At least she had quite an amusing time in the kitchen – some of her friends found out where she was and took to dropping in when the coast was clear and insisting she go out with them to parties and night clubs on her free evenings. Despite her exhaustion Monica would stay out until three or four in the morning, even if she was not enjoying herself, and then have to get up a grim two hours later to bring early morning tea to her employers in their fusty bedrooms. She drove there in her little Sunbeam which she left around the corner to avoid revealing that the cook-general had her own car, unusual in those days. It would have been easier to catch a bus, but she usually left work so late at night that the car was necessary to get home.

Derek Patmore's house was being done up and one compensation for Monica's drudgery was the company of the workmen, who fancied themselves as comedians and played elaborate jokes like placing a fish's eye on a block of margarine to give her a turn, and cried 'There she goes!' as she fell off a stepladder or burned the toast. Her other social pleasure was the delivery men ringing at the back door, all of whom added a great deal of fun to life and came to her assistance when they saw she was just an amateur. (Monica had never seen a refrigerator before and to start with she used it as a handy extra cupboard, keeping the door open to save trouble, until the friendly grocer explained what it was and why everything in it was melting.) In fact it all became quite sociable below stairs and Monica actually took to giving parties for both the tradesmen and her friends when her employers were out. In the end, though, the hard work and the constant changing of her outfit to be the parlourmaid and then the cook and then the parlourmaid again, and then the black-frocked waitress at dinner, all got too much. She became very bolshie, in her own words, and there were several disputes before a final showdown with the designer's mother about fatty gravy and broken vases. Monica then walked out without giving notice, but everything was left tidy with dinner in the oven and last week's wages under the flour shaker to make up for it. She left a poem there too, which in *One Pair of Hands* became a 'very rude limerick indeed'.

Monica did not go back to Universal Aunts because she had heard the designer's mother on the phone to the agency complaining about her. She went to another agency and took a number of temporary jobs as cook, cocktail and banquet waitress or daily woman, whatever she could find that meant she would not stay too long. She needed a breathing space. Sometimes Monica saw people she knew socially at these affairs and had to keep her eyes on the floor, although she found that they never looked at waitresses as anyone they could possibly know, and no one ever recognised her.

Two more of her friends got married and Doady had her first baby, leaving Monica once again longing for a real role in life. Back with Universal Aunts to inquire about a proper position, she was directed to a well-known actress whom in her memoir she chose, or was advised, to call 'Elektra' (in earlier interviews, in fact, she had already indiscreetly revealed the woman to be Equity co-founder Margaret Rawlings). 'Elektra' was beautiful, husky-voiced, and humorous. They liked each other when Monica went for interview, and she got the job. Here again a mother was installed, although this time it was a mousy little woman desperate not to give any trouble to her daughter. It was congenial and fun working for 'Elektra', who would stand up and declaim Shakespeare or Sheridan in the middle of a dinner party as Monica's waiting soufflé slowly sank on the sideboard. A famous and respectable writer occasionally stayed the night, Monica later recalled, and one morning 'Elektra' informed Monica that she was going to have to let the gentleman go. Monica in her role as servant knew it was not her place to express surprise but asked why. 'He's a prig in bed,' was the reply. (This was quite possibly the playwright and *Times* drama critic Charles Morgan, who wrote his first play for Margaret Rawlings; the two were rumoured to have had an affair. In an interview with the *Daily Express* before her book came out, Monica gave the recipe for the red mullet meunière she had made for Charles Morgan when he came to Margaret's for lunch.)

After a few months Monica was bored and ready to try somewhere else. There had been a few rows and after a stand-up battle in the kitchen, as she later described it, she was again out of a job. Meeting an amused Margaret Rawlings years afterwards in a restaurant, neither could remember if Monica had walked out or been sacked, but both felt it had been the right decision.

The jobs continued and in the approximately two years Monica was a cook-general she had about twenty posts (sometimes taking her half-sheepdog, half-foxhound dog Ugly along with her). Work was relieved by occasional rests and at least one family holiday to Alsace, where she conscientiously explored French restaurants and kitchens to add to her skills. She worked for couples and singles, and country places where she shelled peas on the doorstep. She worked for dull people, entertaining people, people who ate too much or too little, and people who behaved as if they had battalions of serfs to command. She worked for employers who wanted 'terribly plebeian things like blancmange'. She learned to make and serve cocktails – White Ladies and Sidecars – in between opening the door to guests (always in a quickly changed apron) and cooking all the food. Some of the jobs were fairly hard to take but Monica felt that she could stand anything as long as she knew it was not for ever. She became very friendly with someone in the employment agency and when a job got too much she simply rang up and asked what else there was.

There was no point talking about her work at home. If she complained, the family just asked why she did not give it up, but Monica felt it was all she had. When later established as a writer she said in a public talk she had been badly paid and overworked as a cook but had not minded because she was having a better time than she had ever had in her life and was discovering so much about her fellow humans. Employers made no pretences in front of their servants, she recalled. You really saw them as they were, with all their meanness and pettiness and selfish indulgences exposed, and no holds barred with family quarrelling. Nothing was ever hidden from the maids because maids did not exist as human beings, just as her social acquaintances never looked at servants as if they were people. She was a complete nonentity.

This does not exactly sound like an enjoyable existence, and indeed in the future Monica was to admit that she had been unhappy quite a lot of the time and that it was not as much fun as *One Pair of Hands* made out. But despite exaggerations and glossing it seems generally true that she enjoyed herself as a domestic far more than she had as a debutante. 'It was an escape route for me,' she said, admitting also that it absolved her, for a while, from taking any responsibility for her life.

Towards the end of this period Monica was working for a young couple who were expecting a baby but, at the age of only twenty-two, she was feeling worn out and in a rut. At home she had reverted to the bad-tempered Monica of days gone by. Then all at once her brain seemed to wake up. Whether it was the effect of the continuous thyroid medication or a late-dawning maturity she did not know, she reflected forty years later, but in the same way that it had suddenly occurred to her a few years previously to get a job, it now occurred to her that she should use her brain. Since its overworking at St Paul's it had gone to sleep, but now it twitched like a waking monster, as she put it. She decided to write a cookery book from her vast knowledge of what can go wrong, experienced first-hand in other people's kitchens. To make it stand out from other cookbooks, such as that written by her great-grandfather Charles Dickens' wife Catherine who under a pseudonym had produced *What Shall We Have For Dinner?*, she decided it should be written in verse.

Her collaborator in this rather unlikely project was her mother Fanny, the family's great scribbler of comic doggerel. Fanny's contributions were not kept but Monica could remember some of her own embarrassing attempts:

Here's a thing you'll not forget,
Never beat an omel<u>ette</u>.

(Monica Dickens, *An Open Book*, 1978)

The work progressed and in some way reached the press, or at least the Australian press. In November 1938 a London stringer for a small Queensland daily, the *Townsville Daily Bulletin*, wrote a short item on a cookery book being written by 'blue-eyed, golden-haired Monica Dickens', the great-granddaughter of the famous writer. The book was presented as the real intention behind Monica's spell below stairs. Monica Dickens had taken jobs as a cook, ran the article, in order to find out for herself the conditions under which meals were produced in small households. Only in this way could the cookery book be of real use 'to the young married woman starting off housekeeping on a limited income'. No mention was made of its flowery format.

Then out of the blue there came a possible opportunity for publication. In December 1937 Monica was invited to dinner at a friend's followed by a fund-raising and recruitment dance at Paddington Baths in aid of the ARP (Air Raid Precautions), an organisation recently set up to protect civilians from air raids. She did not initially want to go, knowing that after a day's work she would probably be too tired – but changed her mind when she heard that among the guests would be someone from a publishing firm whom she might possibly be able to interest in the rhyming cookbook idea. The someone turned out to be young Charles Pick, then a London salesman for the publisher Michael Joseph.

At the dinner Charles hurriedly changed the subject on hearing about the book; in those days cookbooks did not really sell, as the middle classes were still unused to doing their own cooking and were not interested in the kitchen. But at the dance – as he gazed in horror at her roughened hands, according to the anecdote Monica would later tell – Charles asked what she did. He was fascinated as Monica revealed her switch from debutante to char and embellished her servant experiences with a few choice stories to keep him entertained. During an interval he took the opportunity to squeeze his dinner host for more information, and learning that Monica was the great-granddaughter of Charles Dickens he suddenly became very interested indeed, so much so that his

40

future wife Beryl went home alone in annoyance. With the intrinsic enthusiasm which was to encourage many other writers in the future, he suggested that Monica write about her life as a cook-general: if she could write as well as she told her stories, Charles told her, he believed she could produce a best-seller, especially with the current interest in books showing real lives. (One contemporary work then popular dealt with the working life of a waiter, and another with the quirky passengers picked up by a taxi driver.) He suggested she come in and talk to Michael Joseph in Bloomsbury Street.

In Charles' memory, interestingly, Monica at this point revealed that her private ambition was to be a writer, an account at odds with the way Monica herself narrated her path to authorship – as a matter of sheer fortuitousness. In *An Open Book*, describing her reaction when Charles suggests she should write a book on her experiences as a cook, Monica states merely that she 'felt vague', as though she had never previously given real writing any thought. Much later she told him she would never have been an author without his encouragement, although in his opinion her compulsion to write was such that it was bound to emerge.

Monica was astute enough to see that Charles Pick had been impressed by her name: clearly, a likely selling point for whatever she might be able to produce.

§

Michael Joseph, himself a writer, started as a literary agent and began his own publishing house in 1935 as an associate company of Victor Gollancz, with Gollancz providing office space in Henrietta Street. The first Michael Joseph books were published in 1936 but the big break did not arrive until Monica's book and, in the same year, *How Green Was My Valley* by Richard Llewellyn. Michael was utterly to change Monica's life. For Charles Pick, who had started with Gollancz at the age of sixteen and then moved to Michael Joseph, Monica was to be his first 'find' and the start of a lifelong passion for discovering new authors and helping them develop. After reporting his find Charles admitted to his boss that as yet he had not actually read anything written by Monica; Michael Joseph reportedly snapped in reply that one did not have to read anything by a great-granddaughter of Charles Dickens, especially when it was an account of such extraordinary activities.

41

When Monica nervously turned up at the publisher's on her next free afternoon Michael Joseph met her at the top of the stairs, charming, amused and gratifyingly interested in Monica, who had been almost too scared to come. As he talked encouragingly she began to feel that this new world of writing could really be hers. She was captivated by the persuasive Michael and felt jealous of a picture on the wall of writer Daphne du Maurier (who had just published *Rebecca*), signed 'To Michael, with love'. He offered her a contract on the spot – leading Monica to suppose this was what happened to all young authors even if they had not yet written a word – and wrote out a cheque. She told him she was 'practically illiterate' but she knew enough to spot an opportunity, and naturally signed on the dotted line.

She turned back at the door to ask, 'Suppose I can't write?' The agreeable and, as it seemed to Monica, fatherly Michael Joseph (although he was not yet forty) assured her that in that case she could simply tell them the story and they could write it for her. Monica, of course, was unable to resist the challenge – understanding in retrospect that this was probably Michael Joseph's intention – and immediately decided to write it herself. She gave notice to the nice young couple she was still working for, who naturally were upset, but she helped them find another cook through Universal Aunts. Telling only Henry and Fanny, who were pleased that she would not after all be dissipating her youth in the kitchens of strangers, Monica prepared to put pen to paper. The first step was to spend some of her saved-up meagre wages on clothes 'to be an author in'.

But arriving home one winter day with her shopping she found Fanny, forever a repository for other people's woes, consoling a despondent middle-aged man who had been sent over by Universal Aunts. He was in dire straits: his wife had TB, and in those pre-antibiotic days the only cure was fresh air and rest, so she had moved into a little hut in their Sussex garden leaving the desperate Major with a houseful of children and no help. He begged Monica to come, and she tried to tell him that she no longer did that kind of work. In fact, even without the book she did not want to go just from the description. But the kind and compassionate Fanny put in her own plea, persuading Monica that she could do the 'you know' (the book, still a secret) in the evenings. The Major, looking like a mournful dog, hastened to assure her that they never entertained and that all her evenings would be free.

Monica knew she had to go.

This final experience as a cook-general made it into *One Pair of Hands*, in all its detail, and after publication the Major wrote to Monica in anguish. He had not known how cold she was in the big, ramshackle old house where the fireplaces in the bedrooms were boarded up to stop the wind coming down the chimneys and where snow drifted in through broken window panes. Monica did her best with the heart-rending situation she found on arriving in Sussex. The Major's wife, twenty years younger than her husband, lay deathly cold in her hut in the garden and worried about the family; he could not really afford his five young children, sired late in life, or his wife's medical bills. Three of the children were out at school during the day but the two youngest were in Monica's care, and she battled with their chilblains and hacking coughs and the nappy-washing in cold water when the water could not be heated. She did what she could and loved them all dearly, and would probably have stayed had not the family finally moved to South Africa. Monica returned to London to write her book at last.

§

But how to do it, Monica asked herself.

She bought some exercise books and pencils, not even realising that a typewriter might be in order. Then she sat in a corner of the sofa in the drawing room where Fanny was wont to sit with her cocktails and mending basket. With people constantly coming in to polish the furniture or have tea or play the piano, she wrote *One Pair of Hands* in three weeks. She did not know writing was difficult; she thought you just sat down and did it. While she was writing the book she sometimes looked for inspiration by sitting in Charles Dickens' chair (which, with his desk, had ended up in a corner of their drawing room with one of Henry's old ties across the arms to stop visitors sitting on the worn-out cane seat).

It felt important to be writing a book. Now, walking Ugly in the park, Monica fantasised that everyone looking at her understood that she was deliberately alone in order to think, and would be envious if they knew she was a writer. Her long disused brain was excited by the novelty, causing her some sleepless nights when she would get up to be sick in the bathroom at the thought of being an author. The sympathetic and equally excited Fanny lent assistance. On occasion she and Fanny sat up till three o'clock in the morning and then had to feed each other sleeping pills. At the same time, however, neither one of them seriously expected anything to come of the growing manuscript. Fanny recalled that as a child her daughter never put pen to paper except for school homework, and not always then, and she perhaps doubted that Monica had any writing ability.

Michael Joseph had offered some counsel about how to write, which Monica saw not so much as editorial as a tip from one author to another. He gave her what all her life she considered a superb piece of advice, which she subsequently made sure to pass on to other writers. Imagine that something extraordinary has happened, he told her, and then write it down as though bursting into a room full of people, crying, '*Listen* to what just happened to me.' The reader is the listener. He and Monica were to become 'loving friends', in Monica's words. When she took him home she introduced him to Fanny as 'my publisher', and he gently teased her about not being allowed to have boyfriends. He was happily married, Monica knew, and was playing a game with her, so she flirted gently back, caught up in the fun and excitement of suddenly being an author. Michael eventually hung her picture up next to Daphne du Maurier's and guided and encouraged her through many more books, always doing her the favour, she said, of laughing at her when she became too serious.

Henry was very proud of Monica and the book contract, just as he had been proud of girlish achievements such as becoming captain of the second eleven at cricket (so that she could choose herself to bowl, Monica recalled). Taking her to another annual dinner of the Dickens Fellowship in February 1939, he fondly announced his daughter's upcoming literary achievement to the soon-to-be Fellowship president Compton Mackenzie, famed author of *Sinister Street*. In her memoir Monica, an admirer of the pointy-bearded Mackenzie, who shared her 'Monty' nickname, professed to be horribly embarrassed; Mackenzie's recollection of the event, on the other hand, was that Henry said his daughter had pestered him into asking the celebrated author for advice. Whatever the true story, Mackenzie kindly agreed to look the draft over (admitting he had been 'completely charmed' by the fair-haired young Monica). She duly turned up at Mackenzie's cottage on Hampstead Heath with the typescript in her hands. Mackenzie hoped against hope that he would be able to give an encouraging verdict. But he need not have been anxious, he wrote subsequently: 'I recognised on the first page that the great-granddaughter of Charles Dickens was a genuine novelist'.

However, Mackenzie recognised too that the law of libel would not allow the book to stand as it was. Extensive cuts of Monica's 'delicious book' were required, and he deeply regretted the need for culling. He tidied up the draft generally and taught Monica a valuable lesson in how to convey cockney dialect, as he himself had done in his novel *Carnival*. Not, as Monica had attempted, by means of numerous apostrophes for the dropped aitches and glottal stops, but by appropriate rhythm and use of phrase to help the reader create the accent in their mind. He also taught her how to write dialogue in a way which avoided the 'he said, she said' trap. Because Mackenzie took so much trouble with her as a beginner, Monica on becoming a seasoned author made an effort to help young writers herself, seeing it as Mackenzie's legacy.

Compton turned into a friend and mentor (as Monica's own grandfather Sir Henry Fielding Dickens had been to Compton himself when the author was briefly a law student). She became very fond of him, and he offered, unasked, to write a foreword to *One Pair of Hands*. In this he mentioned the friendship that had existed between Charles Dickens and his own grandparents and described the book as a remarkable work for a young woman in her twenties, and a brave start to Monica's literary career: he felt 'agreeably optimistic about her future'. He added that Monica's book was not quite as good as *Pickwick Papers*, although it had some of her great-grandfather's exuberant vitality and he believed Dickens would have delighted in the 'warm humanity' and unfailing sense of humour of his descendant. (Monica took the reference to *Pickwick Papers* as a fair comment, or at least did so decades afterwards.)

Mackenzie continued in his foreword that the record of Monica's adventure was a faithful one, so far as the law of libel allowed – elucidating that to prevent any possibility that her ex-employers might recognise themselves Monica had been obliged to become as much novelist as historian. As he knew all too well the difficulties of reconciling exact portraiture with reluctance to hurt people's feelings, he wrote that he was astonished at the skill with which Monica had conveyed the essential truth of her experience and at the same time avoided any photographic accuracy.

§

Before appearing in shops the book was serialised in March 1939 in the popular and now defunct *Sunday Chronicle*. The editor, a literary Scot named James Drawbell, enjoyed taking a risk with new talent and wanted only the best for his paper: over the years he was to feature some of the most outstanding writers and thinkers of the period and Monica was in good company: John Buchan, J. B. Priestley, Rose Macaulay, Compton Mackenzie, Sinclair Lewis, H. G. Wells, Bertrand Russell – even Albert Einstein.

At one of the daily staff meetings at the paper the Features Editor had drawn Drawbell's attention to a disreputable pile of tattered manuscript he had been carrying about for several days (presumably passed to him by Michael Joseph). Informed that it was by Dickens' great-granddaughter, and that the work described her experiences as a domestic servant, Drawbell exploded that they should already be running it. Wading through the grubby mass of paper that evening – pencilled here, inked in there, in places typewritten – he knew that his luck was in. He could see that the writing was youthful and undisciplined, but also real and vivid and individual; Monica had a love of words, a keen observation, and a sense of humour, Drawbell later recollected, and her understanding of character and raciness of expression would cut through the untidiest manuscript.

He immediately bought the book for serialisation and was introduced to Monica. He found her 'a very young twenty-three', with honey-coloured hair and bright blue eyes. (Monica's mother always thought her young for her age, behind other girls in most things.) Monica began to be seen around the office, helping with photographs and cutting or rewriting her story to shape it for the paper, and soon seeming like one of the staff.

She was bubbling with anticipation about her book, but two days before the serialisation was due to appear she came to see him, clearly troubled. She had already described to him her family's reverence for their illustrious forebear, and the editor had guessed that some condemnation might fall on Monica's 'lovely head' in daring to follow in the footsteps of the great man. He suggested drink and dinner to celebrate her future, but as a tear began to well in Monica's eye Drawbell shepherded her quickly out of the office. They drove off in his car, and when she began to cry in earnest he drew to a halt at the side of the road.

There had been trouble in the wider family about her temerity in writing a book, Monica confessed, and she wanted to know if it was too late to stop publication. Drawbell responded that retreat was not an option, adding that in any case he would not have allowed it. Monica could not see how good her book was, he informed her firmly, and neither could her family because they were all too close to it. Nothing was going to stop her being a writer, and the book must go ahead.

An advance advertisement in the paper showed blonde and slender Monica, in a spaghetti-strapped evening gown, draped languorously next to large type announcing her as the literary sensation of the century. 'Brilliant, beautiful Monica' had written a book comparable to Dickens' *Pickwick Papers*, the ad inevitably trumpeted, despite the reservations in Compton Mackenzie's foreword. The eventual series, *From Court to Kitchen*, was launched with much fanfare in a striking two-page spread, illustrated with the photo of debutante Monica in her pink satin Court dress juxtaposed with a more recent publicity shot of a considerably thinner Monica in an apron scouring the kitchen floor at number 52. (The family cook failed to see the point of the photograph as she had only just washed the floor herself, Monica recalled.)

Other shots showed her in maid mode and drinking champagne at the Café de Paris. Monica had relished the whole thing as a glorious lark. She also remembered enjoying her first meetings with energetic newspapermen, with their cups of tea and sodden biscuits on the edge of littered desks and casual phone calls to California.

She appeared on BBC radio to talk about her decision to turn her back on her own milieu and work as a servant (meeting with a few sniffs from reviewers about taking jobs away from the needy.) More puff pieces in the press heralded the book's eventual publication in May, including a layout in the *Daily Mirror's* Sunday picture paper featuring photographs of a heavily lipsticked Monica gambolling with her dog at home, and as a uniformed maid holding a tray. *Why I Was Sacked 5 Times!* shrieked the headline.

§

Monica's original synopsis for Michael Joseph more or less reflects the way the book ultimately appeared, with the exception of a proposed section on French cuisine culled from the tour of Alsace she had taken with her family during the period she was working as a cook. Michael probably quite rightly excised it as not in keeping with the general tenor of the book. Her synopsis also proposed melding into the text her personal conclusions about the current so-called 'servant problem' (meaning shortage), based on her painfully acquired first-hand knowledge. Some elements of this idea did survive, woven into the text as she had suggested, but as laid out in the original synopsis it was something of a rant: that while domestics could be irritating and resistant to being imposed upon, nevertheless employers were often to blame for the maids' attitude because of their blatant miserliness in providing inferior food and poor accommodation.

Other, nicer employers deserved better service than they got, Monica maintained, because the older type of servant was near extinction and the newer generation was inefficient and had little interest in performing competently. She argued for greater focus on domestic science in schools, and indeed for treating it more as a real science. With the servant shortage it was now so easy getting a job that there was no incentive to do it well.

Monica professed herself unable to remember doing well at writing at school, but now it seemed that she was a natural. The upshot of Michael's advice to write as though telling an exciting story to friends resulted, in *One Pair of Hands*, in exactly that: a confessional, chatty narrative which draws the reader straight in. It is intensely readable and hugely funny.

The characters Monica paints are stock types, the more sympathetic ones tending to be those of either her own level in society or the honestly working class; middle-class pretensions are firmly ridiculed. The dialogue is perfect, completely nailing the relevant class of whoever is speaking. Monica's flair for capturing character in a single sentence stands revealed:

Godfrey was a large panting man with protuberant eyes and teeth, and a distinct tendency to pinch servants' behinds.

(Monica Dickens, *One Pair of Hands*, 1939)

The necessary fictionalisation meant that real names were not used, of course: Monica's erstwhile employer the interior decorator Derek Patmore, for example, appeared in the book as the invented, nastyish dress designer Martin. Despite such departures from reality Monica nevertheless always firmly labelled the book non-fiction, and at least as regards Patmore she may have held fairly closely to the truth: in the original synopsis for *One Pair of Hands* she made it clear that she loathed Patmore and his mother and their grubby ways, and that she had been witness to some very odd things. Something along these lines certainly emerged in the Martin chapter. Others of Monica's actual employers never featured in *One Pair of Hands* at all, even in disguise. One such was the well-known actress Margaret Rawlings (she of the priggish lover), who despite being included in the synopsis did not make it into print – no doubt on the advice of a nervous Michael Joseph. Also not there were some of Monica's unsuccessful interviews, at least from the evidence of her synopsis: a single man who expected more from Monica than just cooking, a family with an appalling child, and a woman who did not think Monica looked honest enough to be trusted with the housekeeping money.

The title of the book was taken from the despairing cry of servant to mistress: 'I've only got one pair of 'ands, Madam.' The Monica in the book, as in all three of her semi-autobiographical works, plays the role of bumbling novice lurching comically from one situation to another. The people and events she describes may be fictionalised but are very much based on her real experiences as a domestic, and additionally on the more distant past of her childhood. A description of one post as cook in a country house called 'Chilford', for instance, was clearly less an account of an actual place she worked in than an opportunity to recreate long-lost Chilworthy: here again is the green baize swing-door separating the upper and lower regions, a semi-invalid mistress in a hooded basket-chair, a master who ambles about in a tweed jacket, a swarm of children at war with their nurses and a housekeeper with her own sitting-room. It was also an opportunity to introduce a blackmailing butler, Dawkes – perhaps with her family's own unpleasant butler Dowson in mind.

The 'I' of the book is not necessarily the real-life Monica any more than her novelised employers, fellow servants and various misadventures are real, but in and around the comic action there is a story that has the ring of truth – Monica's actual experience as a hitherto privileged young woman trying to find her way in the alien world of domestic service. At first the fictional Monica is more or less play-acting. There is her sudden realisation at an early job interview that the prospective employer can either accept or contemptuously reject her (which induces in her a strong desire to giggle); the purchase of a frilly uniform at an Oxford Street store on her mother's expense account, becoming so entranced with herself in the short-skirted outfit that she keeps it on all evening; and being brought breakfast by one of the family servants before going out to wait on others in her turn. When she starts actually working as a cook she enjoys having a little kitchen all of her own to mess about in, and the cooking itself gives her enormous pleasure. She is amazed how quickly the hours pass when busy working, and thinks back to how she used to have to find things to do to occupy her time.

Housework is a little less enjoyable than the cooking – when cleaning a bathroom, the Monica in the book averts her eyes from 'one piece of furniture' in case she is expected to clean it. As the real Monica certainly was expected to clean it, one wonders what her employers thought about its exclusion, or whether in reality she just got on with it. She learns for the first time how to clean out a grate and light a coal fire and how to polish parquet flooring with a duster wrapped around a broom; she finds ways to cut down on labour, such as always using the same few pieces of silver to avoid having to polish the rest; and realises that it's more efficient to do the washing-up as she goes along. The sociable backdoor traffic is enjoyable and adds a fillip to life, although she finds it difficult to respond in kind to the teasing of workmen.

Then, gradually, the difficulties and hardships of her new career become more apparent. When she acts as both cook and serving maid she must learn to hide her dirty hands underneath the (too hot) dishes as she passes them round at the table – as well as repeatedly having to change her apron to fit each role. She discovers what a chaotic effect a bell has on a maid's nerves: employers ring for her at the precise moment a delivery man rings at the door, which for Monica is a continuous conflict and one of the most annoying aspects of domestic service. There is the constant struggle to master temperamental boilers for a supply of hot water, and the overwhelming tiredness that suddenly hits at the washing-up stage after the excitement of producing an elaborate dinner. She gets into a muddle with invoices and finds life a perpetual battle of wits with her employers, they keeping a sharp eye out for dirt and skimping, 'and me trying to disguise my slovenliness by subterfuge'. Above all else there is the dullness and drudgery of the domestic round – and the cumulative exhaustion.

Monica also discovers exactly what it is to be a menial in terms of behaviour: *One Pair of Hands* provides intriguing insights both into the world of domestic servitude in the 1930s and into the English class system of the era. A servant must be deferential, not talking unless the employer starts the conversation and leaving the room if the employer has finished what she wants to say. A maid is an ideal person to talk to for those who want to go on about themselves and not be answered back, she learns. Employers and their friends talk French (execrably) in front of Monica if they do not want her to understand what is being said, and of course Monica never lets on that she understands because of the fun of it.

But in those days a servant was also a source of entertainment in herself. Employers deliberately drew her out in order to get amusement

...out of the screamingly funny idea that she may have some sort of a human life of her own...Once you get used to the idea of being suddenly hauled out from the oblivion of servitude into the spotlight of attention, and expected to provide entertainment until they just as suddenly tire of you...it's quite an easy game to play. You have to humour them by saying amusing and slightly outrageous things so that they can retail them to their friends, or 'dine out' on quotations from your conversation.

(Monica Dickens, *One Pair of Hands*, 1939)

Other aspects of domestic work take their toll. She gradually moves from conscientiously completing the washing-up at the end of the day, however tired, to leaving it in a dirty pile for the next morning – and begins to perceive the dispiriting effect of domestic service. To her alarm she identifies in herself the servant's 'rather cold-blooded tendency' to view the trials and tribulations of her employers with a certain detachment, almost as if they were actors in a play. (These concerns ring particularly true. The real Monica wrote in her synopsis for Michael Joseph that she had ended up adopting the servant mentality and had found it to be degrading and demoralising. Monica further admitted in an interview after the book came out that she had found herself peeking at keyholes and had worried about her morals.)

With her growing exhaustion leading to mistakes in her work and a feeling of 'sulky apathy', the fictional Monica finally decides that being a servant is no sort of existence and throws in the towel.

She has had enough of 'Life in the Raw' and the squalor of kitchen existence. At the end of *One Pair of Hands* Monica, seemingly as herself, writes that she is still too close to the experience to view her period working as a cook-general as anything but 'a most depressing chapter of my life', although she can see that in the fullness of time she might look back with more nostalgia. She recognises that during the aberrant period of her career as a domestic her family have had to bear both moody silences and fits of rage from her, and yet were remarkably good-natured about it. Feeling guilty, she determines to be nothing but a little ray of sunshine in the future. The first week after leaving her last job is spent either sleeping or having hot baths until she feels more human and has lost the smell of the kitchen, and then she spends all the money that has accumulated from her wages 'on the adornment of my person'. The family heave sighs of relief at the termination of her lunacy.

The book ends on something of a low note. After missing out on a social life for so long the fictional Monica breaks out in a frenzied search for fun – but knows that she is using the clamour of deliberate gaiety to stifle a cold internal voice warning of an imminent return to the boredom whence she started.

The epilogue chapter in the original *One Pair of Hands,* now no longer included, was written in the third person as a comic account of Monica delivering a lecture on the future of the domestic servant to an audience of middle-class women at an ideal home exhibition. As 'Miss Dickens' fluffs her way through her notes the women variously doze off, read letters, long for a cup of tea, or stand up to object to what she is saying.

Monica struggles on, trying to get her message across about the need for reform in domestic employment. The inclusion of this chapter, although as much a piece of comedy as the rest of *One Pair of Hands*, had some serious points to make. Domestic service should be professionalised, she argued, with proper training, conditions of service, and fixed wages. Monica's account of her trials as a cook and char was written to amuse, but at the same time her story brought out the poor conditions and overwork that servants in the 1930s were expected to put up with. The unpleasant treatment meted out by her employers and their condescending attitude to those whom they considered their inferiors had infuriated Monica, and she wanted the world to know and to do something about it.

She may not have been too hopeful. Her proposals during the fictional lecture meet with little response.

'...*what did all that talk amount to*?' asks one woman of another as the audience departs.

'*Don't ask me, dear. I was asleep.*'

§

Monica had wanted to be well-known for something and all of a sudden she was. It was hugely exciting, and equally so for her mother Fanny, herself a frustrated and talented writer. The reaction from the rest of the family was mixed, as might be guessed from the horror expressed before publication. Some of the Dickens aunts continued to be scandalised that another member of the family had dared take up the pen: Dickens as a name was sacrosanct, and present-day Dickenses were expected to be successful, but not pushy. It was a form of blasphemy for a descendant even to try to write. 'Dickens was God,' Monica was to comment. 'It was like someone coming along after Christ and saying they were Christ too.' Her grandmother, Henry's mother Lady Dickens, threatened to cancel her account at Harrods if they continued to display the book, while even a wealthy Runge aunt put her copy under lock and key lest one of her several maids read it and became corrupted by Monica's insidious propaganda.

Monica always readily conceded that who she was did help her to get started, and that being Dickens' great-granddaughter had never been anything other than 'tremendously helpful'; in fact, she doubted whether her first book would ever have been published at all had she not borne the name of Dickens. Michael Joseph, too, was of course aware of the power of the name: on hearing from Charles Pick about Monica's exploits he had thought there might be a book in it, but, on learning that she was the great-granddaughter of Charles Dickens, he was certain. At the same time, however, Monica was aware that bearing the name of Dickens was a double-edged sword and that she was condemned from the start. She knew that readers would either expect too much and be let down, or suspect her of trading on the name and write her off without reading the book at all. She was right. Certain well-known writers were 'very rude' to her because they thought she was a young upstart, she later disclosed (without revealing any names). Even the general public could be hard on her. One letter from a reader abused her roundly for desecrating the name of Dickens with a split infinitive on page 124, line 16.

The book was an immediate best-seller, despite Monica's ultimate recognition of its naivety and prejudices and her lifelong conviction that she had inherited none of the talent of her famous ancestor, whose writing in her eyes was 'extraordinary, freakish stuff' ranking with Shakespeare and Tolstoy. In her memoir she declared that *One Pair of Hands* probably got by on a 'certain spontaneity and youthful enthusiasm'; it was badly written and she blushed for it, she commented elsewhere, yet there was life in it because of the way she just sat down and 'splurged the whole thing out'.

Critics in the main were enthusiastic: the *Times* review took it as a hugely amusing story of 'extraordinary pluck, endurance and adventurousness', but also as a social document laying bare the nonsense of households trying to live beyond their means. The *Manchester Guardian* believed the work would do more for understanding of the servant problem than any number of essays if only because it presented, with equal verve, the problem with employers. Others extolled Monica's eye for character and the humour and gusto of the writing, although there were a few references to the seeming 'carelessness' of her style. One or two general readers made the apt point that while most servants were stuck with their lot, Monica Dickens was able to walk away. Without exception, of course, reviews made a point of mentioning Monica's relation to Charles Dickens, no doubt to the aunts' great disgruntlement, and indeed to Monica's own: the name of Charles Dickens was to become a thorn in her side. Inevitably, too, there were comparisons – some positive, others less so.

Interest in the US mirrored that in Great Britain, with an initial announcement in the *New York Times* in May 1939 that the President of Harper and Bros. publishers had just returned from England with Monica's book for publication in America. Miss Dickens had 'the same interest in the lower half of the people that Dickens was so well known for', the publisher rather bizarrely reported. The same paper gave a glowing review to the book in

October, describing Monica as a natural and her exploration of the servant problem completely unlaboured. The book had 'gay adventurousness' and 'keen-eyed and blithe-hearted experience'. On this first occasion there was not the universal comparison with Dickens which future American reviews of Monica's work would unfailingly draw.

Elsewhere in the English-speaking world an equal degree of interest was shown in this first output of a Dickens descendant bearing the same name. In the more egalitarian Antipodes, critics found the book entertaining and well written but some pointed to the less defensible aspects of Monica's charade. The Melbourne *Herald* wrote sharply that Monica had none of the social consciousness of her great-grandfather – she never forgot to let readers know that she was the 'great lady who has voluntarily gone in for a bit of slumming'. Her portraits of her fellow domestics were consciously or unconsciously superior, the *Herald* continued, and judging from her plea in the final chapter for servants to be treated as human beings, it appeared that in England such a status was 'not yet fully recognised'. The Melbourne *Australasian* observed that Monica aping the accent and lower educational standards of the working class (as when she pretended to her employers not to know the meaning of the word Adonis) was somewhat questionable behaviour. Only a real slave knows the meaning of slavery, said the *New Zealand Herald* pertinently, quoting the passage from the book where an exhausted Monica is put to bed by her mother with a cup of hot milk, and further drawing attention to the fact that she was able to hand in her notice when she felt like it and not face destitution as a consequence. Other critics saw her as much more of a sympathiser with the domestic classes and recognised the real power in her writing – perhaps the result of inherited talent, they suggested – and *The Press* correctly foresaw that Monica would produce an unusual novel some time before 1950.

Monica, at the age of just twenty-four, was a celebrity and best-selling author. *One Pair of Hands* sold 6,622 copies in its original edition and thereafter sales never stopped, reaching an average of twenty to thirty thousand a year for many decades. Nearly ten years later the book was still popular enough to be serialised on *Woman's Hour* on the BBC. It continued to sell well for the rest of the twentieth century, and beyond, and to receive dramatisation on BBC Radio 4 as late as 2001.

Owing to the war the sale of foreign rights was not an option but after 1945 the book was touted abroad by Monica's literary agents Pearn, Pollinger and Higham. In Paris the firm's contact was the famous agent Jenny Bradley, friend and supporter of James Joyce. There were no takers until 1950, when the rights were finally bought by Éditions Julliard and published in 1951 as *La Meilleure des Bonnes* (The Best of Maids). Sales must have been healthy as another edition of 10,000 French copies followed in 1955 – this time headlined as 'The Most Indiscreet Novel of the Year'.

§

Monica's life was transformed almost overnight: invited to publishers' parties, to write book reviews and articles on careers for women, and do a cookery series for the *Daily Express* (recipes including a rather strange risotto out of a leftover joint). At Harrods that May she gave a Harrods Authors' Talk on *The Kensington Housewife*, and in June she was amongst a series of 'famous Authoresses' gracing a Foyles Book Club tea for a discussion on whether romance was still alive (tea and sherry included in the price).

In August 1939 a short story by Monica featured in the popular pocket magazine *Lilliput*, an eclectic monthly featuring short stories and discreetly posed photographs of female nudes. The narrator of *Love Below Stairs* is a cook called Monica who is looking for love, and engages first in the hopeless pursuit of a red-haired Irish chauffeur and then in a backdoor flirtation with an enticing greengrocer. When she is too busy for boyfriends, she is reduced to making up outrageous stories about her love life to amuse her employers as she serves them at table. Finding the very idea of romance among the 'pond-life of the basement' hugely funny, the family press her for more and more comic revelations. The cook finally comes out with an (unspecified) anecdote so sordid that she is thrown out of the house and her boxes hurled after her onto the pavement. Clearly, the attitude that Monica had met with from some employers – amusement that a servant might have some sort of human life of her own – was still rankling.

It now seemed to Monica that writing might be her true calling. In the 1939 Register, a census of the civilian population taken just after the outbreak of World War II, Monica firmly declared her profession as 'Writer'. Knowing that a second work would be carefully watched by critics ready to pounce with accusations that the first had been a flash in the pan, Monica determined on a complete departure – a first novel. She bought a second-hand typewriter and tried to work, but number 52 was suddenly swelled by the return of sister Doady in need of help with her growing family. She and the children took over Monica's front bedroom, while Monica moved into her brother's little room next door which had been rigged up like a ship's cabin when he was a naval cadet at Osborne. The house became noisy and crowded.

On 3 September 1939 war was declared on Germany. Monica cancelled a planned trip to the States. Rents dropped when people began to flee London in fear of bombing, and with the help of her new income she was able to take a small flat in Mayfair to finish her book at speed before the expected conscription of women began.

As her brain continued to recover from its long disuse and she discovered the joy of creativity, Monica's old dissatisfaction and restlessness slowly fell away,

...as the pleasure in creating something, however trivial, began to take hold of me and as new interests crowded round, [my] first tentative steps into the world of books and authors and publishers, I began to feel properly alive for the first time in years.

(Monica Dickens, *Making the Most of Life*, Women's Journal, 1944)

War

In January 1940 came the death of Monica's formidable French grandmother Lady Dickens, wife of Charles Dickens' eighth child Henry Fielding – she who had frightened Monica's mother Fanny so much in the early years of marriage to their son Henry. Marie Dickens, known to her family and intimates as 'Mumsey', had lovingly cared for Dickens' estranged wife Catherine in her last illness and had been with her to the end; she had likewise ensured that Catherine's sister (and Dickens' housekeeper) Georgina Hogarth – the family's beloved 'Auntie' – was able to spend her last years living comfortably with other members of the Dickens clan. She collected and preserved Dickens memorabilia such as his desk and chair, which, before finding their way to number 52 to be looked after by Monica's family, had been objects of reverence in the billiard room at 8 Mulberry Walk. Marie had also amassed a collection of translations of his work into other languages. Obituaries and tributes on her death revealed more of Lady Dickens' life: born Marie Thérèse Roche, she was the granddaughter of the musician Ignaz Moscheles, a friend and pupil of Beethoven's who had arranged financial help for the composer as he lay dying and destitute. The accompaniment for her wedding to Henry Fielding Dickens in 1876 had been a wedding march written by the French composer Charles Gounod for his 'petite amie Marie'.

Another link with the literary past was gone. Monica herself had never been afraid of Lady Dickens, and in her memoir wrote sadly that her grandmother's death was the end of the old lady's intense grief for her youngest son Cedric, killed at the Battle of the Somme in 1916. Together with her parents and Doady and other family members, and many devoted old friends, Monica attended the Requiem Mass at Farm Street Church in Berkeley Square on 15 January.

Meanwhile she continued her hard (and fast) work on her second book, the novel *Mariana*, based in part on her childhood and growing up. Other, more minor items appeared in the interim, including a 1939 story about a woman's escape from a Nazi death camp, just after the existence of the camps had been revealed to the public in a Government White Paper. Book reviewing, a cookery column and cookery correspondence were still ongoing irons in the fire. Monica at this stage was already well launched on her life's path of speedily produced books interspersed with a gossipy journalism which kept her in the public eye. An ad for a June 1939 article in the *Sunday Chronicle*, for instance, promised a story on Monica's undercover job as an ice-cream seller at the seaside.

However, she was also trying her hand at war work, although this early in the war little was happening. There was a brief stint cooking in a canteen for women drivers in London's Auxiliary Ambulance Service, operated by volunteers in a mustard yellow uniform and tin hats, but Monica found it consisted of too much sitting around knitting while the women discussed their love affairs. Cooking toad-in-the-hole at this or another canteen had brought her into contact with the oily-overalled 'Bobs and Nobbys and Toms' who were actually longing for an air raid.

Monica's intention was to get involved in war work when there was some real action. Meanwhile she was mainly living with Henry and Fanny in the country, to which they had temporarily retreated from London, but she would come up to Mayfair to write in peace in the flat. Interviewed there in March 1940 by an American journalist as the snow fell outside the windows, she talked about coping with London's nightly blackout and having recently suffered another car crashing into hers in the gloom – she wanted to take the woman to court and get some money out of her. Monica was described as tall, blonde and willowy, fond of riding, tennis, swimming and dancing. One of her current pet dislikes about the war, she told the interviewer, was 'unattractive women with big legs blustering around in uniforms'. She also made a point, perhaps not unconnected with the blustering women, of mentioning her dislike of the old school system and people who found jobs through contacts rather than ability.

Mariana, titled after the melancholy poem of the same name by Tennyson, came out later in the year with Michael Joseph but was published in the US as *The Moon Was Low* (a quote from the same poem). It was dedicated to Henry and Fanny. The world suddenly woke up to what a talented author was now on stage, not merely witty and observant but truly gifted. Reviewers considered *Mariana* a remarkably mature first novel and that Monica had shown herself to be a writer of 'admirable gifts and equipment'. In France it proved enduringly popular, going through several editions, and was well received in America, particularly for its evocation of English countryside and culture. The *New York Times* was distinctly impressed: '...a gusto in character creation and an ability to limn a physical portrait in an effective stroke or two that speak, in no uncertain terms, of inherited tendency'.

A book to read for its vitality, simplicity and humanness, commented the *Mercury* in Tasmania. Similar plaudits came from several other Antipodean papers, with all of them discerning inherited gifts; 'wittily-turned sentences and an exuberant vitality', praised the *New Zealand Herald*.

At home the *Times Literary Supplement* enjoyed Monica's 'refreshing acidity' and the *Daily Mail* declared her a genius. *The Scotsman* admired her sure hand and humorous understanding of human nature. More condescendingly, *New Statesman and Nation* remarked only that '*Mariana* will be fun for those who like to look through other people's snap-albums and listen to the usual commentary'. But *Mariana* has withstood the test of time. A new edition after six decades was greeted enthusiastically by the *Spectator* as 'fresh and funny...written with such verve and humour', and by *The Lady* as so enjoyable that it was impossible to understand how it had disappeared from view for so long. Time has placed *Mariana* exactly where it belongs, amongst the classics of women's fiction.

The novel tells the story of young Mary Shannon and her growth to adulthood in the 1920s and '30s, the early years in particular drawing heavily on Monica's own experience. Here again in all its glory is the old country house at Chilworthy, this time reincarnated as 'Charbury', reached by the same exciting journey down to Somerset via the main line from Paddington and then a branch line to the sleepy local station. Here again is the pack of cousins at war with the nannies, and the grandmother, like Emma Runge, an invalid in a basket chair. The young Mary loves horses, and runs around in boy's clothes. The children put on a play, acted out for the grown-ups in their playhouse as Monica and her cousins had done in those long ago days. The young ones take it in turns to have lunch in the dining room, and pay visits to the grandmother's room at bedtime to be given a chocolate. And, just as Monica herself experienced, Mary revisits her grandparents' former home in Somerset as an adult only to find it shockingly small and the lengthy drive she remembered as a child now ridiculously short.

Mary eventually goes to a girls' school in London called St Martin's, wearing a velour hat of 'unbelievable hardness and ugliness'. Here she is lost and lonely until she makes a friend, who, exactly like Monica's sister Doady, deliberately plays mad to get attention. Here are the crushes on older girls that Monica herself suffered, and a moment of rebellion against a teacher when Mary blurts out that it is none of the teacher's business what she does outside school and that she is only paid to boss her inside. Describing Mary in this moment as overtaken by a 'blinding madness', Monica may well have been depicting her own feelings during her rebellion against the ugly uniform at St Paul's. Like Monica, the grown-up Mary is hopeless at drama school and is kicked out; she too stays with a French family in Paris. Love affairs and meaningless jobs follow as Mary searches for her place in life and the right man to share it with.

Mariana is also notable for a lengthy description of a day out with the hounds and an exhilarating run after the fox across furrowed fields. Monica hunted, and clearly enjoyed it, although it is indicative that the fox during this description goes to ground and cannot be dug out. It was the thrill of the chase that Monica enjoyed, not the kill, and she was to renounce hunting while still a young woman.

But *Mariana* is not straight autobiography. Mary Shannon is not Monica, and although the heroine moves through various of Monica's own experiences there are obvious points of departure. Mary is petite and dark-haired, for one, and does not produce a best-selling book at the age of twenty-three. However, there are clear similarities, probably including a first love. Fictional Mary loves her dark-haired cousin Denys, for whom she nurses first a youthful and then a more mature passion; Monica admitted very late in life that when young she had been in love with a handsome cousin. A number of Monica's male cousins would have been about the right age for romantic yearnings. These included the darkly attractive Charles Orr-Ewing, who was likely part of the pack at Chilworthy and who in due course became the distinguished Conservative politician Baron Orr-Ewing. Monica as a child was close to his sister Phoebe, who was definitely one of the cousins holidaying at Chilworthy and, like Denys' sister in *Mariana*, was later presented at court.

Mariana remains a delight to read, gripping and funny and affecting, if somewhat rushed towards the end, and a vehicle for Monica's real skill as a writer to emerge for the first time. Although not a comic novel, humour is nevertheless present, as it was to be in all her novels, often blended with pathos. It is also a historical record of a young girl's upbringing between the wars, before teenagers were invented, or at least a girl of a certain type – the book is again permeated with Monica's sense of social class, if forgivably so for the era she was writing in. The *Times Literary Supplement* detected that Mary's experiences had been portrayed by someone to whom the joys of youth and the agonies of adolescence were still close enough to be living and vivid, and praised Monica for her feat in giving power and personality to an ordinary girl stumbling in and out of unsatisfactory love affairs.

In one way it is indeed mainly a romantic novel about the search for love, but in another it is about finding and retaining true identity:

> *When you were born, you were given a trust of individuality that you were bound to preserve. It was precious. The things that happened in your life, however closely connected with other people, developed and strengthened that individuality. You became a person.*

(Monica Dickens, *Mariana*, 1940)

Tennyson's poem *Mariana* concerns a woman waiting hopelessly for her lover, just as Mary waits throughout a long night to hear if her beloved new husband has gone down with his ship in the early days of the war. The ending is poignant and perfectly realised.

§

With the proceeds from *Mariana* Monica bought a new typewriter as well as the first refrigerator ever installed in number 52, a tiny thing with the ice trays soon beaten out of shape by Henry trying to extract the ice.

As the book was nearing completion, Monica had begun to think again about what she could do for the war effort. For a while she collected scrap iron with a pony and cart borrowed from a stable in the Portobello Road, picking up bedsteads and old pipes to be converted into guns. But the draft for women was now clearly in sight and as Monica later commented, it was obvious that if you did not choose your own war work you would be drafted into something awful like peeling potatoes in a bleak kitchen on Salisbury Plain. In fact she had already decided: she wanted to train as a nurse.

There is always the possibility that Monica was deliberately looking for something else to write about, although according to her memoir she believed as a probationer that she had abandoned writing and would be a nurse for ever (despite the recently acquired new typewriter). She declared that she was 'saturated' with Hemingway's *A Farewell to Arms*, in which beautiful English nurse Catherine falls in love with her soldier patient. In Monica's subsequent book about being a nurse, called, of course, *One Pair of Feet*, she refers to Hemingway's novel and mentions that she was also influenced by seeing Madeleine Carroll as a selfless nurse in the 1940 film *Vigil in the Night* (in fact, the part was played by blonde lookalike Carole Lombard). She wrote, too, that nursing had long attracted her, even in peacetime.

She began by enrolling as a Voluntary Aid Detachment nurse in the Red Cross, a voluntary role without the full training and qualifications of a professional nurse. Volunteers to the VAD service usually came from the upper and middle classes but tended to be given the unskilled work around the wards and were often looked down upon by the proper nurses, which no doubt came as a shock to some of the upper-crust VADs. It seems a surprising choice given Monica's stated interest in real nursing, but she clearly enjoyed wearing the romantic VAD uniform with its flowing white veil, and Catherine in *A Farewell to Arms* was a VAD. It is also likely that volunteering may have been more the done thing, for a young woman of Monica's class, than actually to become a member of the nursing profession.

Part of the VAD training was getting experience on a hospital ward and here Monica was only allowed to make the bread and butter and sweep the floor. And there was not enough to do: London hospitals had not yet felt the worst of the war casualties. The Assistant Matron one day found her cowering in the kitchen, too scared to go onto the ward without being invited to by the real nurses; the woman suggested that Monica see the Matron about receiving proper training. This she did and was accepted as a probationer. The hospital was the King Edward VII in Windsor, which in 1939 had been made part of the Emergency Medical Service for treating war-injured patients evacuated from London hospitals.

With Windsor some distance from London commuting was out of the question, so Monica was given a place in the nurses' residence (a building which was to find fame in 1963 as a location used in the film *Carry On Cabby*). She found a stables nearby on the edge of Windsor Great Park for her horse Tonia and dog Ugly so that she could take them out when she had the time and energy, which did not prove to be very often. Monica had worked hard as a cook-general but it was nothing to what she experienced as a probationer at King Edward's. She was afraid some of the time, hungry most of the time, and tired all of the time, she wrote in her memoir. But, just as she had recognised a spiritual home on first descending into her employers' kitchens as a cook, so she recognised as her own the isolated world of the hospital. It was also Monica's first experience of the close friendships born of being in a like situation and driven by the same purpose, and of the intense, fleeting closeness of caring for people in the moment of their greatest need.

In the 1940s a nurse was half nun, half slave, and a probationer was about as low in the pecking order as it was possible to be, despite the fact that more of them were now needed because of the war and they were probably becoming more valued. The uniforms consisted of long blue pleated dresses and the caps were finicky and impractical, arriving from the laundry in a stiff semi-circle which had to be sewn into shape and affixed to the head with iron grips. Monica was unable to master the sewing technique and usually offered a bribe of cigarettes or sweets to anyone who could. The uniform's high studded collars shrank in the wash and pinched the neck with a red line, which for Monica was extra painful on the loose skin remaining after losing her thyroid weight. Shoes and stockings were black, belts were starched, and the long sleeves of the dress had detachable stiff cuffs which became the bane of her existence. On the ward the cuffs were taken off and stowed away and the sleeves rolled up for work – except when there was a formal briefing or a doctor to be addressed, in which case on went the cuffs again; off the wards, for instance in the corridors or in the nurses' dining room, the cuffs had always to be on. Monica once made the mistake of saying hello to a doctor friend on the ward, and Sister was horrified not only that Monica knew a doctor socially, but that she had addressed him cuffless. On another occasion she was running without her cuffs to the kitchens to fetch ice for a patient's uncontrollable nosebleed and was ordered back to the ward to get them by a prowling Assistant Matron.

The wartime food for the nurses was atrocious. At seven in the evening before they went on duty the night staff would have to eat what was left over from the day staff's breakfast – cold scrambled substitute eggs and soggy toast – and in the morning when they came off duty after a long night on the wards they used to get what the day staff had endured for supper the day before. On one occasion this was baked sheep's hearts and macaroni, which Monica was made to go and eat before returning to the ward to finish laying out a body. Henry wrote a letter about this incident to the *Daily Telegraph*, which printed it, but of course nothing changed.

Conditions for the patients, before the creation of the National Health Service, were hardly more palatable – because of wartime food shortages, for example, if patients wanted eggs they had to be brought in by relatives. Hospitals then were mainly run on funds from charities or from local authority rates, or, in small towns, from public subscription. Frills were few, and treatment limited. Bed rest was the major remedy for heart attacks, ulcers and tuberculosis, and patients often stayed for weeks. There were no curtains or screens between the beds and the humiliated patients were all constipated; money spent on the enemas necessary to address the constipation could just as easily have been spent on more wheeled screens, in Monica's opinion. It was also the era before antibiotics and people still died of simple infections. This meant that the standard of the nursing care was crucial and Monica was impressed by the dedication and skill of a number of the senior nurses, and by their determination to pass on what they knew even to the lowly probationers. Others were not so kind. There was still a tremendous amount of sadism amongst the older Sisters, Monica observed years later; some of them were 'really vile' to the younger nurses.

Inevitably, Monica's first experience with death came as a nurse. Initially terrified, she instantly realised on seeing her first dead body that the person was no longer there. Later in life she could never understand the American obsession with the actual body, the need to view 'this thing' lying there with its glasses on and all made up:

> ...*because it is not a person, the person isn't there, the person may be looking down and watching you but they're certainly not inside the body.*

(Monica Dickens, interview with Leigh Crutchley, BBC, 1964)

After several months Monica was sent to the private wards, where patients were not always that ill but were rich enough to pay for it, and treated the nurses like servants. One of her nicer patients was the literary agent Curtis Brown, who brought books in for her and to whom she had presumably revealed her identity. (It is likely that as a rule she did not reveal herself as the famed author of *One Pair of Hands*, even as she continued her journalism and her broadcasts for the BBC. In April 1941, for example, as she was handing round the bedpans, Monica was also on the radio with film star Leslie Howard on the programme *Answering You*, responding to questions from America, and in December that same year she gave a talk on *Christmas and Dickens*.)

Work on the private wards was slightly easier and Monica began to feel less exhausted. The decreased tempo gave her time to think

and to feel the stirrings of writer's guilt. In nursing she had seen so much that was comic or tragic or fascinating that she simply had to start writing again, so on one of her days off she lugged her new typewriter back from London and began to record her experiences. In the nurses' home she still had the single room given to her after contracting chicken pox from a patient with shingles, and here she tapped surreptitiously away every evening instead of working for her Preliminary exams. When she had to go on nights she wrote in bed in the mornings when she was supposed to be sleeping, stuffing the papers under the blankets and the typewriter under the bed when Sister came round checking the night staff were asleep and waking them up in the process. She no longer felt as excited as she had when writing *One Pair of Hands*; being a writer was no longer the heady business of her first book but simply a part of life.

Then a patient innocently showed the Matron a magazine story written by Monica the previous year, and Matron was livid that one of the nurses was, in her words, making a public spectacle of herself; she did not believe nurses should be articulate or set themselves above the common herd. Brought up before Matron to explain herself, Monica let drop that she would shortly be publishing a book about being a nurse, and handed in her notice.

§

One Pair of Feet, dedicated to Doady and her husband Denys, came out in 1942. Mainly humorous but with the occasional darker note, *One Pair of Feet* is Monica's account of training to be a nurse in the 1940s; it does not concern itself with the big issues of the day, such as the world war raging beyond the hospital gates (although Monica and the other nurses do voice objections to caring for two German airmen injured when their plane is shot down near the town). It is equally a gripping account of health care before the widespread use of antibiotics or the advent of the NHS.

The book closely mirrors Monica's real experience but again, of course, she altered names and embroidered events for comic effect, albeit perhaps sailing a little close to the wind on occasion. The Matron at her real hospital in Windsor was in her forties with 'greying sausage curls'; the fictional Matron in the book is a youngish 'plucked boiling fowl' with a ridged perm. *One Pair of Feet* is set in the Queen Adelaide Hospital in the fictional town of Redwood, described as not far out of London, as was Windsor. Monica skipped that she started her nursing life as a VAD and in the book she dismisses VADs as never getting beyond the charring stage, which she knew from experience.

Monica's supposed course as a probationer is charted at the invented Queen Adelaide as a series of comic episodes taking her from first tentative steps as an idealistic trainee to final exhaustion and disillusion. This seems very like real life, only with humour, and *One Pair of Feet* is immensely readable. Monica is again the error-prone novice, getting in the way and giving the patients the wrong supper trays as she encounters her fellow probationers, the frigid Matron, the know-all nurses above her in the hierarchy who cannot be bothered to instruct her, the comical or touching patients, and not least a number of selfless and dedicated members of the nursing profession who devote themselves heart and soul to saving lives. All of these characters are invented or composites, not real people, but like the details of nursing, closely based on Monica's actual experience.

She conveys the claustrophobic all-female world of nurses who for the most part are only interested in their own immediate concerns and indifferent to news of the war, and who constantly threaten to leave a profession which Monica cannot understand why they entered in the first place. She undergoes a period of night duty, breakfasting at the end of her night's shift on rabbit stew and ginger pudding, and sneaking out during the day instead of sleeping. She works in Theatre, where she is terrified of the surgeons and once or twice renders them unsterile by accidentally touching them, thus necessitating a furious repeat of the scrubbing-up process. She acts as general dogsbody on the private wards where there is no real nursing to be done and she runs around to the constant clamour of patients' bells ringing; she tries, and fails, to quieten the yelling babies on Maternity. Off duty she fills up on sausage, chips and beans at a local greasy spoon, or drags herself home for a spell of normality.

The fictional Monica has quite a lot to say about the hospital food, doubtless inspired by appalling reality. Meals for the nurses at the Queen Adelaide consist of vast amounts of carbohydrate – mostly bread and nursery puddings – and little in the way of meat or fresh vegetables. At first she is repelled by the diet but then, made ravenously hungry by the demands of the long days galloping up and down the wards, finds herself packing it away with the best of them. Her new life is ruled by the need to 'get done', the requirement to get through a certain amount of work without enough time to do it in. She is furious if a patient throws her off her stride by upsetting a glass of water or asking for an extra slice of bread and butter, and develops a knack of going at such a speed that it becomes impossible to slow down. At night her feet are on fire and she has to try sleeping with them on a pillow and even raising the foot of her bed with books.

The Ward Sisters rule with a rod of iron, insisting on an inflexible routine of scouring and polishing even in the midst of death and disaster. The rigid and pointless hospital etiquette dictates that a probationer like Monica can only speak to a doctor through the medium of a senior nurse; junior nurses cannot consort with seniors and she has to allow nurses senior to her, if only by a few weeks, to go through the door first and to help themselves to the salt at meal times before she does. She describes the agony of the constant, absurd cuff-changing and throws in the real incident of the cuffs and the nosebleed.

Monica's real response to the iron grip of the hospital machine is clearly stated. Surprisingly, she recognises the futility of resistance and makes no protest. The hospital system was too big and too ingrained to try, she wrote, never mind the absurdity of treating grown women responsible enough to deal with life and death like children, turning off the lights in the nurses' home at ten-thirty every night and subjecting their bedrooms to inspection. She submits to being scolded – on one occasion by Matron herself for being overfamiliar with the seniors and too opinionated – and cries in the sluice. Despite her often truculent attitude to life thus far, Monica confesses in *One Pair of Feet* that she does not have the nerve to answer back to bullying senior nurses. She can remember a time when she might have been more rebellious and less 'blindly acquiescent', but believes that working to routine and never to initiative has dulled her brain. This intellectual enfeeblement is not noticeable in the hospital itself, where conversation is uninspiring and humour is mainly of the toilet variety, but is certainly obvious outside, where she feels boring and inadequate. She now understands why people beyond the hospital gates tend to view nurses as a 'race of screaming bores'.

Even so, Monica in the book is angered by the requirement to attend lectures during off-duty hours, especially when these occur on a full day off and prevent her from going home for a decent meal and a long sleep in her own bed. At first she simply gives the lectures a miss and goes home as usual, but is soon brought up before Matron. Still just bolshie enough, she continues to evade the lectures with a repertoire of excuses about dentists and long-lost relations and even a mythical fiancé, and wishes heartily that nurses had a Union. She also admits to a 'wedge of Red' being inserted into her politics after experiencing the hell of being at the beck and call of private patients.

But regardless of the irritations and inequalities of hospital life, and her own professed ineptitude, Monica in *One Pair of Feet* declares that she loves nursing. It is clear that she finds the work interesting, and the bonding with both staff and patients worthwhile. She is nevertheless reluctant to sign on for real after her first few months' trial, and, without elaborating, justifies missing her lectures because she does not believe she will be there to take her exam. She makes a bet with a fellow nurse that she will not stay a year. Again, no reason is given, although at a guess the rigid discipline and lack of opportunity to use her own initiative might well have been a problem for Monica, and perhaps in addition a communal life in the unalloyed company of other females (which she had disliked as a schoolgirl), most of them from vastly different backgrounds.

In the end the fictional Monica becomes more and more tired. She has no energy to go out at night. She tries to work for her pending exam but constantly falls asleep over her books or in lectures and loses all hope of passing, and has in any case begun to think she might be better employed in an aircraft factory. She admits to herself this might be as much about being fed up with nursing as about wanting to kill Germans for the war effort. At the same time she recognises that, when stripped of all its petty tyrannies and discomforts, hospital life has the power to hold her, and its bonds would be hard to break without regret.

Then, as really occurred, Matron hears of a story that Monica has written for a magazine and forbids her ever to do such a thing again. That settles it and Monica hands in her notice, telling Matron she wants to go and make a tank.

§

Monica in *One Pair of Feet* returned to an account written in the first person, her tone gossipy, that of a friend confiding her good moments and occasional disasters on the wards and admitting to the odd fag behind Sister's back. The book found an appreciative audience, perhaps not least because despite her frankness about the hospital system, Monica nevertheless managed to convey her belief in the essential nobility of the profession and the selflessness of the many doctors and nurses she had met who were dedicated to saving lives. But she made clear distinctions between the type of nurse who treated patients with care and concern, and those who treated them (and subordinate nurses) like imbeciles. It was also very funny, and scalpel-sharp: like *One Pair of Hands*, the work was an opportunity to vent about the kind of people that obviously drove Monica up the wall. Here is the woman patient who does not complain or make a fuss outright but gets her own way by revealing Monica's mistakes in front of Sister, and is repellently self-centred:

> She was the sort of person who says: 'Of course, I'm frightfully interested in people. I find them fascinating' – which usually means that the speaker's interest is confined almost wholly to the fascination of herself. 'Of course,' Mrs Drucker once said to me, 'I have a horror of war.' Everyone else loved it, of course.

(Monica Dickens, *One Pair of Feet*, 1942)

Or the egotistical fiancé of a friend at the hospital:

> ...everything that was said he capped with a story which centred round the word 'I'. He aborted any discussion by being unable to keep it impersonal, and the only heed he paid to anyone else's opinion was occasionally to wait without listening until they had finished talking and he could go on undisturbed.

(Monica Dickens, *One Pair of Feet*, 1942)

Monica again demonstrates her happy facility for encapsulating a whole character in a single sentence: a patient's husband is a 'humble old man with faded blue eyes and the walk of a man who has spent his life with horses'; a senior nurse is a 'nut-coloured raw-boned woman, who prowled round the hospital on silent feet, with a venomous fang for a tongue'. However, the humour is often directed at stock types, sometimes with the casual racism of the era: senior nurses are either dragons or eccentric spinsters, working-class patients are ungrammatical, a Jewish woman keens 'like the lost tribes of Israel'. Such humour was mitigated, as a review by the *Times Literary Supplement* pointed out, by the author's instinctive sympathy for those disadvantaged by illness or poverty. And, like *One Pair of Hands*, class consciousness is again an integral element: choosing to forget the intense snobbishness of her own social class, Monica digs into the petty snobberies and class discrimination then rife in the nursing profession (and elsewhere), mercilessly reproducing the accents of the would-be refined and castigating the apparent desire of many nurses to set themselves above others as 'odious'.

The book sold well, although not accompanied by the same fanfare as *One Pair of Hands*, and was serialised on the BBC's *Woman's Hour* in 1946-7. The subtle novelist Elizabeth Bowen was impressed, finding it 'brilliantly funny' and Monica shrewd, with a quick eye and an excellent heart. 'Her character sketches of sisters, nurses, public-ward patients, the grandees of the town are little masterpieces.' The *Daily Express* critic James Agate picked up on Monica's talent for characterisation, highlighting her ability to pack into one sentence what most took a page to express. The left-leaning political and literary review *Time and Tide* considered the book to have 'high documentary value', showing how much change was needed in hospital organisation and atmosphere – but found its entertainment value higher still. Another critic predicted some turbulence in the real hospital so frankly described and referred to the independence of mind which had caused so much trouble for Monica during her youth. Still another made the inevitable comparisons between Monica's style and that of her ancestor, observing that she was able to convey a personality or the humour of a situation with the same effective economy as Dickens and that she was just as focused on certain social aspects. James Agate, too, believed Monica a 'chip off the old block'.

In the US, however, there was less willingness this time to see anything of Dickens in Monica – and in one review, raised eyebrows at the conditions described ('here in America similar conditions have not existed for fifty years, if ever') and some surprise at the conspicuous absence of love affairs between the doctors and nurses.

After the war was over Monica's agents tried without success to interest French publishers, but although Julliard asked for an option on the work when it accepted *One Pair of Hands,* this was apparently not taken up. However, it was published in Germany as *Schwester Dickens* (Nurse Dickens) and in Italy with the original title in translation, illustrated with a pair of shapely legs in very unnurse-like high heels.

Press reviews may have been appreciative but nursing journals were outraged, mainly because Monica had dared to be funny about their profession. Miss Dickens was seemingly not acquainted with the 'wholesomely-humoured' women who nursed with 'balanced minds and intelligence', sniffed one. The *Nursing Times*, clearly not understanding that the book was fictionalised and intended to be humorous, castigated Monica for choosing her training hospital on the basis that the bath water was reputedly always hot, and had lied to avoid being sent off the ward to put on a clean apron. The *American Journal of Nursing*, with the same total lack of humour, was aghast that Monica had evidently written her own references and concerned that her apparent antics might have harmed the patients. 'We have known so many fine and admirable English nurses,' the review commented uncomprehendingly, 'that it is hard to believe that those in the hospital...were almost without exception unattractive personally, dull mentally, and inferior socially.'

A senior nurse wrote to the Editor of the *Nursing Times* pointing out that the book was either fiction, in which case it was all lies, or if it was non-fiction the hospital in question should immediately be struck off the list of approved training centres. The book was of course a mix of both: names and scenes were altered but many real incidents, such as the cuffs and the nosebleed, were included. Other real incidents were excluded because Michael Joseph was concerned about libel. On one occasion, for instance, Monica when on night duty had been helping with a patient having an emergency operation on a clot in a femoral artery. The surgeon was unable to find his assistant, a young resident, and Monica was sent to fetch him. She knew where he was – drinking in the sitting room of the very Sister who had told her off for directly addressing a doctor. During the operation the drunk resident, holding up the artery with a tape to cut off the blood while the blood vessel was being worked on, passed out. He fell across the patient's body and as the tape slipped from his hand a fountain of blood shot up and hit the ceiling. Fortunately, the patient recovered. Monica was naturally not allowed to include this particular event in the book, but in the main *One Pair of Feet* was a realistic account of a probationer's existence in the 1940s.

Monica's real hospital, the King Edward VII in Windsor, was, not surprisingly, horrified by it. Thereafter, new probationers were gathered together at the start of their training and asked if they had read Charles Dickens, and then in a leading way if they had read any Monica Dickens. One or two of the dimmer nurses admitted that they had, and the storm duly broke. The book was dismissed as lies and the nurses forbidden to read it; one nurse told Monica that the hospital thought it was being laughed at. In later life Monica defended the book as neither lies nor subversive but the truth, with a few changes to avoid libel or hurting people.

In 1943 a government-funded film loosely based on the book, *The Lamp Still Burns*, came out with the intention of attracting new recruits to nursing. Monica had apparently sold the rights completely and was not credited for the screenplay, although a press report in 1942 suggested some collaboration. The same report stated that the film would be based on fact, but in the event a romantic plotline distanced the film from Monica's original work except as regards her implicit plea for better conditions and better treatment of nurses in British hospitals. The story follows a woman architect who changes careers to train as a nurse and, like Monica, finds that her independence of mind gets her into trouble when she fails to wear her cuffs properly or questions hospital regulations such as not speaking directly to a doctor. Nurses at that point were not allowed to marry, and in the end the heroine turns down a marriage proposal in order to help improve the deplorable conditions endured by nurses and patients alike. Her lover, played by a smouldering Stewart Granger, vows to wait.

The film was produced by the popular actor Leslie Howard, star of *Gone With the Wind*, who died before the film was completed when the Luftwaffe shot down the civilian aircraft in which he was flying (giving rise to a number of still unresolved conspiracy theories). Profits from the film's premiere went to the London Hospital, which Howard had enlisted as technical adviser on the film, and after his death the actor Laurence Olivier unveiled a plaque there to the actor.

Made with the assistance and collaboration of the Ministry of Health, the film opens with an announcement that it is a tribute to all who nurse. Criticised later as flag-waving, clichéd and dated, its frank portrayal of conditions for nurses also seems strangely at odds with its ostensible goal of attracting new recruits to the profession. Apart from a scene in which an operation is carried out during an air raid, the war hardly features. Problems in British hospitals are firmly linked not to the war but to endemic flaws in the system, such as the dependence on charitable donations and nurses being unable to combine career with marriage. As a propaganda piece the film therefore seems way off beam and in fact closer to the spirit of Monica's critical stance on the realities of being a nurse. The intention of the film may well have been to attract women into the profession primarily by a portrayal of nursing as romantic, noble, and self-sacrificing (hence the silly plot), but at the same time to be frank about the need for reform. Its actual effect on potential recruits – and on reform of the nursing profession – is not known.

Despite criticisms from the nursing profession generally, Monica's scathing depictions of hospital life reportedly enjoyed the support of at least some nursing leaders in the influential London teaching hospitals and likewise of the Ministry of Health, both of which were certainly involved in making the critical *The Lamp Still Burns*. It is possible that as well as a propaganda piece the film was intentionally a call to reform on the part of these bodies. The Ministry of Health had just contributed to the revolutionary Beveridge Report, which laid the foundations for the National Health Service, and one of the Ministry's revised conditions for service in its 1945 nursing recruitment campaign was acceptance of married nurses. If the Ministry was indeed bent on reform of Britain's health system through the medium of film, perhaps part of its visionary message was the appearance in *The Lamp Still Burns* of a young Joyce Grenfell as an efficient woman doctor.

Some years later Monica was invited to co-script another nursing recruitment feature film, this time commissioned by the Crown Film Unit for the Ministry of Information. There was a chronic shortage of qualified nurses in post-war Britain, fuelled in part by the increased demand from the newly established NHS. For *Life in Her Hands*, which appeared in 1951, Monica and her co-writer Anthony Steven wrote a strong script which more clearly presented a positive image of nursing for the film – although the hierarchical divides are just as evident. Nevertheless, the film depicts nursing as an attractive career choice. Despite all her criticisms, Monica is unlikely to have supported this message without feeling the genuine admiration for the profession she so obviously evinced in *One Pair of Feet*.

§

Monica's book has been called the single most influential portrayal of the nursing profession in the 1940s and '50s, albeit through the prism of humour. She highlighted the slave-like servitude of nurses and pointed to the hopeless inadequacy of a trained nurse's pay, though conceding that in the early stages of becoming a nurse the profession trained and maintained the probationers while giving them a wage packet. She may not have created a timeless character like her great-grandfather's Sairey Gamp, the drunken nurse who attends a birth or a death with equal relish and who instructs her clients to leave the bottle on the chimney piece where she can get at it, but her frank portrayal of the state of contemporary nursing had a similar impact. (Gamp had remained the archetypal nurse until the advent of reformer Florence Nightingale, who remarked that her well-to-do parents' reaction to her announcement of nursing as her chosen profession was as if she had wanted to be a kitchen-maid – perhaps the same horrified response evinced by some of the Dickens family when Monica made known her intention to be exactly that.)

Monica's own view of her third success was that she had been lucky, as she thought she had been with her writing from the outset, particularly in regard to the name which had helped her to get started. But in addition, she recognised that up until that point nobody had ever written a comic work set in a hospital: 'Nobody had ever laughed at nursing.' It also attempted to tell the truth about what nursing was like, which she believed no nurse had ever done before either. In later life she was to consider *One Pair of Feet* a better book than *One Pair of Hands*.

Just after the war, the National Book League (now Book Trust) asked readers to submit lists of ten outstanding and significant books published during the years of conflict which, in their opinion, would be of general interest to POWs and service personnel on their return home. *One Pair of Feet* by Monica Dickens was amongst the winners.

Decades later, the writer and journalist Libby Purves was to reflect on the psychological influence of *One Pair of Hands* and *One Pair of Feet,* Monica's two books about female servitude. When read in one's teens, she observed, some books could reinforce patterns of thought for the rest of one's life. For Purves (while recognising that nursing was a profession), Monica had permanently defined the dead-end female job: what the exhaustion of servitude felt like, how impossible it was to think of going out for the evening because the only thing on your mind during a night shift was a plate of sausage and bacon at the nearest transport café. But equally, Monica had made clear that even the lowliest employee has the right to laugh at her employers, whether overbearing Ward Sisters or effete bachelors, and her serious concerns about domestic service and nursing had been expressed lightly. When Purves herself was stuck in dead-end jobs during her teen and student years, Monica's spirit had remained with her. Her genius was to convey how it is to be 'tired, down-trodden and not particularly competent, and still to find life – observed from underneath – a riot'.

§

From spring 1941 women in Britain aged 18-60 had to register for war work, and by December conscription of women aged 20-30 was already in force. Monica needed to keep contributing to the war effort and, after leaving King Edward's, she began training as a fitter at the Park Royal Government Training Centre in the London suburb of Perivale. Here she learned about the specific gravity of metals and, achingly slowly, how to file male and female squares so that one fitted exactly into the other. The publicity picture (above) of a heavily made-up Monica in boiler suit and cap, metal file in hand – presumably propaganda to encourage others into similar work – appeared as far afield as Australia.

Monica provided an account of the half-hearted training at Perivale in one of her later novels, caustically describing the girls' larking about, their speedy disillusionment with the course and inability to find a real job once they had the essentially meaningless qualification. The heroine of the novel abandons the course (which may well have been exactly what Monica did) and finds proper war work. Monica herself ended up with a job in the inspection department at London's Sunbeam Talbot factory, helping to repair Rolls-Royce Spitfire engines damaged in crashes or which had failed during testing.

The engines were broken down and washed in the dismantling section, and were then brought in pieces for the crews to inspect. Each worker knew their own bit and worked on it engine after engine, some remaining on valves or oil pipes for the entire war. Monica worked mainly on the supercharger, the air compressor that increases the pressure of the air supplied to the internal combustion engine. She became quite fond of it, but also learned all the other sections to ward off boredom. She enjoyed the chatting and joking around the inspection bench, and the efforts of the foremen to control their motley wartime teams of housewives, violinists and part-time prostitutes, as she later described them in *An Open Book*. But at the same time she was shocked, and disillusioned, by the fact that her fellow workers were more interested in their pay packets than in the aircraft they were working on in order to win the war. Some of the other women on the bench with men away fighting were equally shocked.

Doing an extra bit for victory, Monica in 1942 wrote for the BBC's *Britain to America*, a series of broadcasts to the US and Canada billed as a typical British variety programme of comedy sketches and song, with pieces by celebrities and talks by ordinary people involved in the war effort. This was part of a combined attempt to cement Anglo-American relations now that the US was firmly in the conflict. A talk she had first broadcast earlier in the year, *My Work in a Factory*, was possibly used in the series. Monica declared that she loved being one of a hundred girls in white overalls working at a bench:

> *Gear wheels galore, writhing pipes, valves – look, there's half a carburettor, and there's a supercharger. And here's me perching by it, handling it with almost affectionate familiarity – me, who, a few months ago, thought a supercharger was a kind of horse. We've each been taught our particular job thoroughly, but if we get into difficulties there's Bill, the foreman of our section, running about all day with his hair on end and his sharp cockney face contorted with mock fury, pursued by female cries like the mewing of seagulls.*

(Monica Dickens, *My Work in a Factory*, BBC, 1942)

What did her workmates crouching over their engine parts make of this celebrity in their midst, broadcasting to the world about their lives (if they knew who she was), or her fellow fitters at the government training centre make of her boiler-suited glamour shot in 1941? Was Monica able to establish genuine relationships with the other women, or were they wary of her fame and cut-glass accent, and suspicious that she might be looking for copy and amusing types for her next book? She did indeed begin to write about her adventures in this latest of social milieus. In an article at the time she wrote frankly of the tedium of factory work, living for weeks in a state of suspended animation with one eye on the crawling clock and one eye out for the even slower end to the war which would enable her to get on with her own life again. However, as the thrust of her article was to exhort readers to make the most of the opportunities afforded by wartime, Monica of course added that she used to stop short and remind herself of all the things she was getting which she would not otherwise have known: friendship, meeting an entirely new set of people and getting to know them, the experience of punching a clock and queuing up on Friday evenings for a pay packet with GO TO IT stamped on the outside. She now knew the difference between a foreman, a charge hand and a section leader and had penetrated some of the mysteries of Trade Unionism, she wrote, and was savouring the atmosphere of free and easy Christian names, backchat, and the good honest hunger that made her only too ready for tea at the peculiar hour of half-past two. She had obtained a glimmering of how an internal combustion engine worked and could now undo a tight nut, change a fuse and do a few elementary plumbing repairs. Some women had even discovered an unsuspected bent for engineering, she noted (admitting she was not of their number).

In tandem with her factory job and producing the odd broadcast or piece of journalism, Monica in early 1942 was still trying to finish *One Pair of Feet*, although she was usually too tired to work in the evenings and waited until her parents went down to the country at weekends. She had moved back in with Henry and Fanny at Chepstow Villas, sending her horse to live with Doady in the country and leaving her dog Ugly with the man at the stables on the edge of Windsor Great Park near her old hospital. Ugly was happy there, and to Monica it seemed kinder to leave him near a park than to haul him back to the dangers of the Blitz in London.

Not surprisingly the new experience of factory work eventually found its way into Monica's fourth book, this time a novel published in 1943: *The Fancy*, mainly about a diffident, rabbit-breeding young foreman in charge of a bench of women and girls at an aircraft factory. Monica was continuing to produce at speed, squeezing her real-life experiences for her fiction. The work includes a fair amount of technical detail on engine parts and functions, and perhaps rather too much on breeding rabbits, but the book has an easy, conversational style and the by now expected array of comic types delivered in a single trenchant phrase. More of a domestic than a war novel, the story centres around the lives and loves of foreman Edward and the girls (after whom, according to the vagaries of their characters, he names his rabbits). The unhappily married Edward has growing feelings for a timid young girl on the bench, but he plays it straight and it is his unpleasant wife Connie who breaks up the marriage, thus allowing Edward his chance at happiness with someone else.

As the story unfolds the reader is drawn into the hard daily life of a factory and its mainly female workers in time of war. In a mirror of Monica's magazine article on the dreariness of the long hours, a typical tedious day at the workbench is feelingly related by one of the main characters:

> *She had gone through all the usual phases: cold and depressed at first and inclined to wish that whoever it was had never invented the internal combustion engine, softening towards him after tea and a margarine roll at half-past nine had brought her fingers alive at last, bearing up until at about eleven-thirty it became evident that lunch time would never come, quite lively after the hour's break, but falling away after an early tea into the state that made her shake her watch unbelievingly at half-past four and at intervals afterwards, until at half-past five she struck an interesting patch of work and looked up suddenly to see that it was five to six and she would have to fly for the toilet if she wanted to be out when the bell rang.*

(Monica Dickens, *The Fancy*, 1943)

Monica's evident sympathy for women in this novel, so hard-worked both at the factory and at home, might suggest a possibly emerging feminism as a new element in her instinctive social crusading. The same character indignantly describes woman's double load: getting the children dressed and their husband's breakfast in the mornings, then trailing round to the day nursery to drop off the children and on to the factory for a hard day's work and probably a missed lunch because of needing to shop. In the evening everything in reverse, followed by cooking the supper, putting the children to bed and doing the housework. And even this heated account leaves out the fact that the nursery may be two miles in the opposite direction to the factory, as Monica brings out elsewhere. Additionally, many of the men in the book are pointedly self-centred and helpless in the kitchen and expect slavish attendance from their wives, who bear the brunt of managing all the wartime privations.

However, far from being in the feminist vanguard Monica was of her time, and a more conventional message prevails. Unattractive female characters, like Edward's wife, are slovenly housekeepers, while a sympathetic character positively enjoys doing her spring cleaning. The happiest marriage in the novel is one where the wife wholeheartedly embraces her domestic role. Similarly, sex outside of marriage for one woman leads to abandonment, debt and blackmail. It is doubtful that Monica was rethinking the female role, even if instinctively on the side of the downtrodden.

A propaganda film that came out that same year, *Millions Like Us*, had the aim of convincing young women that working in an aircraft factory was a noble and necessary contribution to winning the war: in stark contrast to these selfless characters, Monica's factory workers are only too human, moaning about the job and the foreman, and desperate for a skive away from their benches. For these workers any kind of community feeling or sense of pulling together for the good of the nation, as rosily depicted in *Millions Like Us*, is anathema. The picture painted by Monica no doubt mirrors what she herself had experienced and is likely to be a far more accurate representation of women's attitudes to conscripted factory work.

The book had the 'quality of good art', enthused the *Scotsman*, while the *Times Literary Supplement* noted the light, authentic touch, the rapid movement in the book from one little factory or domestic drama to another to build up a picture of wartime women at work, and the truthfulness and humour of its portrayal of largely female manners. The *Observer* liked its humour and infectious energy, whilst writer Elizabeth Bowen declared *The Fancy* a humane and entertaining story which she had read in a single sitting. For Bowen it was essentially about a cross-section of different lives, the mixing of Londoners of many different ages and classes and of other innocents who have come to London for war work. Monica was one of the most engaging of comic authors, Bowen wrote, but one who never sacrificed either fact or genuine feeling to comedy.

The poet John Betjeman, later Poet Laureate, dug a little deeper in his *Daily Herald* review. He wrote that naturally he was tempted to draw a comparison between Monica and her great-grandfather: in his view Monica shared with Charles Dickens a keen delight in ordinary people, and they both crammed their novels with interesting characters. However, Betjeman believed that Dickens had had a high moral purpose in most of his books and he doubted that Dickens would have approved of the happy ending (involving divorce) that Monica gave to *The Fancy*. He felt that Monica was primarily an observer rather than a moral writer. Nevertheless, *The Fancy* was the best novel Betjeman had read that week and he claimed to have missed his station on the train through absorption in the 'richly packed' book.

Abroad, for the *Sydney Morning Herald* the book was written with more enthusiasm than skill, although 'always sincere, often surprisingly sympathetic, and, occasionally, very amusing'. The *New York Herald Tribune* described the novel (called *Edward's Fancy* in the US) as 'a robust story of the British common people'; the *New York Times* enjoyed the book but wished that Monica had paused now and again to give her characters a chance to grow on the reader. As a prime example their review pointed out the Dickensian qualities of Monica's peripheral character Mrs Urry, who in Monica's succinct description has a face 'like the uneatable kernel of an old walnut', and who with her equally decrepit husband has bedded down in the Underground for the duration and goes out cleaning to keep herself in gin.

Mrs Urry was not the only memorable figure. Perhaps the best commentary about *The Fancy*, and about Monica's writing as a whole, came from the intellectual novelist and critic Rebecca West during a broadcast to France as part of the BBC series *Chronique des Lettres et des Arts en Angleterre* in October 1945. Rebecca described Monica Dickens as a young and pretty woman who presented an interesting example of the power of heredity. She saw in Monica's books several of Dickens' most pronounced characteristics which she believed Monica would not have been able to imitate intentionally, and some of which she felt were not even very desirable – but those that *were* desirable were gifts from the gods. Monica resembled her ancestor in 'unevenness and vitality', she wrote too much and too quickly, putting in too many characters and too much incident; she was not sufficiently attentive to form. 'Her haste is often abominable, but it is life itself which is caught up in the pages of her books.'

The line about life itself being caught up in Monica's books – without its opening clause, of course – was to become a frequent quote in relation to Monica's work.

Rebecca West dismissed Monica's earlier efforts as negligible (citing *One Pair of Hands* in particular) but she considered *The Fancy* a very fine work. The characters had real flesh and blood and were as real as any in Dickens, she observed. The second part of her talk was devoted to reading aloud, in French, a particular section of the book which had 'authentic quality': a passage about Edward's objectionable wife unexpectedly returning to the marital home, after more or less leaving her husband, only to find factory girl Wendy and her mother installed there because they have nowhere to live. This scene Rebecca West described as a masterpiece of oblique communication between two completely dissimilar women, one of whom wants Edward and one of whom does not.

Despite this eulogising of Monica *The Fancy* was not, however, fancied by the French. It was finally accepted by Fontaine in 1945 but the deal was unaccountably cancelled a year later. Monica's agents Pearn, Pollinger and Higham expressed their astonishment, but in France *The Fancy* was only to see the light of day in its original English.

There is a Monica figure amongst the other women in Edward's charge – Sheila, a pretty young blonde who wears a lot of make-up and has fled her middle-class existence to work in the factory. When a working-class friend from the factory visits her flat and sees the photograph of Sheila's home and well-heeled family, and jars of preserves made by her mother, Sheila is ashamed and wishes that she too had been brought up in working-class Paddington Green. She has a love affair with a young reporter whose hair grows 'so absolutely the right way', and whose voice (no doubt meaning accent) is 'absolutely right' – calling to mind *Mariana* and Mary Shannon's 'incredibly *right*-looking' husband.

Monica, too, was looking for someone exactly *right*. She was now a very attractive twenty-eight and still single. There is little information about her love-life in the early works, apart from her heroine Mary's childhood passion for a cousin in *Mariana* (based on Monica's own experience). Nothing of significance is revealed in either of the semi-autobiographical *One Pair of Hands* and *One Pair of Feet*, apart from asking how to recognise love for the first time if there is nothing to compare it with except a furtive romance with a stable boy at the age of fourteen (in her memoir a caption on one of her childhood photographs mentions being in love with the kennel boy). Perhaps in connection with this early amour, Monica in her old age was to describe the moment as a girl when suddenly her early passions for the handsome cousin and the Prince of Wales and the thrilling older girls at school were revealed as mere childishness:

The pure loves of childhood can be as sweet and painful as the complicated turmoil of grown-up emotions and desires for which they are the prologue. The turning point was a farmyard in Oxfordshire when a boy with whom I had been childishly jumping off a haystack grabbed me in the loose hay and kissed me violently.

The world stood still. The sky reeled above my open, astonished eyes. No loves were ever quite the same again.

(Monica Dickens, *First Loves*, When We Were Young: Memories of Childhood, 1987)

§

Monica was at the factory for about a year, eventually getting ground down by the monotony and starting to feel as she had with nursing that, despite working on such a vital task, her job had little to do with winning the war. In the end, riding her bike each morning through the bleak North Kensington streets to Sunbeam Talbot, battling the hills and the wind, Monica felt unable to stand the job a single day longer. The factory was always freezing on a Monday morning after the heating had been turned off all weekend, and in the evenings after bicycling home through the fog an appalling oily reek rose up from her clothes as she tried to thaw out in front of the fire. Nothing got rid of it, no matter how many hot baths she steeped herself in. The coming of spring only increased her restlessness, as did a sweaty, oily summer with her forehead turning black from wiping it with the back of her dirty hand. Long before *The Fancy* came out, Monica had made a momentous decision: to leave factory work and go back to nursing. On an unexpected visit to a patient at her former hospital, the King Edward VII in Windsor, she had been bitten again by the nursing bug.

The visit was a result of an accident that occurred while staying with sister Doady and her four children in the country, where Doady had moved to whilst husband Denys was in the forces. Monica found a little cart, and hitched up her seemingly docile horse Tonia – which she mistakenly thought was harness-broken – to take the children and their Nanny Brown out for a drive. There was some kind of upset on the road and Monica awoke to find herself sitting on the grass verge, cradling Nanny's bloody head in her lap, and no sign of the children or Tonia. Neither she nor Nanny Brown had any memory of the cause of the accident. Luckily the little ones had been picked up by a passing driver, who had called for an ambulance, and Tonia was found that night still attached to bits of broken cart.

Monica suffered minor facial injuries but Nanny Brown, in turning to shield the baby from the horse, had suffered a hoof in the head and fractured her skull. Monica, feeling very guilty, went to see her at the King Edward wearing dark glasses (and not just because of her bruises and bloodshot eye – she was not unaware of the hospital's reaction to *One Pair of Feet*). Entering King Edward's she was immediately pierced with a pang at the familiar smell of carbolic and ether, and sick with envy of the porters and their trolleys, the hurrying doctors and the nurses who looked at visitors like Monica as nuisances in their busy day.

For Monica the visit was 'wildly nostalgic' and she again experienced the draw of belonging somewhere – even at the price of losing her independence and being once more shut up in a nurses' home. She wanted to go back to being a nurse, in fact felt she had never really ceased to be one. Knowing nurses were in very short supply because by now, in 1942, so many had gone into the Services, she began to apply to the big London hospitals.

None of them would take her. The upper echelons had been insulted by Monica's jokes about cuffs and protocol and probationers being lower than the bed wheels. 'Every matron in England was crackling with indignation,' her mother Fanny commented. In hospital after hospital, an encouraging interview would end with her name being recognised and Monica being shown the door. She resorted to using a false name but was routed out by her identity card and insurance papers, thus proving to at least one hospital that she was dishonest as well as subversive.

Monica could not switch war work without securing another job first, and she toiled on at Sunbeam Talbot. Hope slowly receded until she began to feel that a lifetime at the factory stretched before her. Listening to Churchill on the nine o'clock news kept her going through long patches of boredom and resignation to a wartime status quo in which the jam ration was more on people's minds than the progress of the struggle. Like everyone else she suffered the privations and shortages of wartime, stood in interminable queues, and did what she could to obey the dictates of fashion, surprisingly still much in evidence.

Back at number 52 Henry was an air raid warden, and had built an underground shelter in the backyard where in happier times family and friends had played stump cricket on Sundays. In the shelter were two bunk beds divided by a narrow space. Here Monica slept with her parents when there was a raid, rising at dawn when she heard the All Clear to steal a couple of hours in her own bed before pulling on her overalls and bicycling to the factory. In the evenings, if the warning siren had gone, Henry had his dinner brought out to the shelter by one of the servants – apparently left in the house during the raid – despite the squadrons of bombers humming over Kensington and the anti-aircraft guns firing at them from the Park. When it was Fanny's birthday he wore a dinner jacket.

One evening in September the garden next door was hit by an oil bomb, a device containing an oil mixture and a high-explosive bursting charge – the closest call the family was to suffer. Henry had returned to the house in search of the port decanter and a bowl of walnuts and only just made it back to the shelter with decanter in hand: 'Thank God the port's all right.'

Either this or a different bomb which came 'warbling past my ear' added to Monica's growing sense that life must be seized with both hands. Her possibly final conscious thought as the bomb sailed by, she wrote in an article, was not to see her past life flashing before her eyes but to feel regret that now she would be unable to do all the things she planned. Life must be lived in the moment, she impressed upon her readers, and the utmost got out of it. She believed the secret of happiness for a woman was to create something, and her own creative task was to write.

§

Finally, amidst the gloomy hopelessness and grinding tedium at the factory, a letter came from a hospital inviting Monica for interview. The Sister Tutor there wrote that unlike others in her profession she had enjoyed *One Pair of Feet*, and that if Monica had trained at her hospital her experience would have been very different. Monica's application was accepted, and she quickly handed in her cards at Sunbeam Talbot. Because she had never passed her State exams, the period at King Edward's carried no weight and she was obliged to start again as a lowly probationer, which she did some time in probably 1943.

At the new hospital she was obliged to wear the old blue uniform from King Edward's until the arrival of her new black-and-white striped one, and naturally she stood out and felt self-conscious. Not only that, but Monica soon realised that the other nurses were deliberately avoiding her, both when working in the hospital and at meal times. A lone friendly colleague revealed that the management had warned them to stay away from her, and Monica then understood that the only reason she had been taken on was that they were desperately short of staff. The embargo eventually evaporated, but for Monica this disturbing period of isolation was enough for her to understand why people thought of suicide.

One advantage of that initial situation at least was that she had been given her own room in the nurse's hostel, which was a converted set of flats and bedsitters in tall buildings down an alley off Queen Square in Bloomsbury. The single occupancy was not because Sister Tutor wished her to have somewhere quiet to turn out another great work of literature, Monica discovered, but in order to keep her from infecting the others. In the end there were complaints about what looked like preferential treatment and Monica was made to share with another nurse, who objected to her typing in bed. After that Monica hauled her typewriter back to the hospital each night, placed it on an emergency operating table in the basement and sat on the anaesthetist's stool trying to get on with *The Fancy*. Hitler now became a personal annoyance because if there was an air raid, emergency operations had to be performed in the basement and Monica had to move.

As the Sister Tutor had indicated, Monica found herself in a very different kind of establishment. The London Homoeopathic Hospital (its original spelling) in Queen Square was founded in 1849 by Dr Frederick Quin, one of the first doctors to practise homeopathy in Britain, and coincidentally a personal friend of Charles Dickens – who was one of his patients – and godfather to one of Dickens' children. At the outbreak of the war the hospital became an independent unit in the Emergency Medical Service for the treatment of casualties, and was itself severely damaged by the Luftwaffe. The gallantry of the staff during air raids, and particularly during actual bombing of the hospital, was to be recognised by the awarding of four George Medals and an MBE.

After the war the hospital, now the Royal London Homeopathic, was subsumed into the NHS as part of the widespread post-war nationalisation of the health system. In its early years it had been at the centre of the nineteenth-century dispute over the efficacy and status of homeopathic medicine, a dispute which continues: as recently as 2007 an eminent surgeon dismissed homeopathy as no better than witchcraft and urged the hospital's NHS Trust to consider other uses for the Royal London's buildings. In the 1940s Monica, however, was intrigued by the homeopathic treatments, which operate on the principle that like cures like and that an infinitesimally tiny amount of a substance which causes similar symptoms to an ailment has the ability to cure it. During the war the London Homoeopathic had changed to more generalised work and some of the staff practised homeopathy and some did not, leading to sometimes dangerous confusion about treatment. There was no time to instruct all the nursing staff in the proper administering of the homeopathic medicines, with the result that on occasion Monica and the other nurses did not give them at all, or gave them wrongly, and she must have found it difficult to form proper conclusions. Nevertheless, Monica was impressed by amazing results from the natural herbal and plant ointments in the skin clinic, and the resolution of gastric complaints via a combination of diet and homeopathic treatment. She was heartened to see the body curing itself when it could. But, even after an eventual two and a half years at the hospital she felt she had learned little about the practice of homeopathy, and there is a sense in *An Open Book* that she reserved judgment on its efficacy.

She was able to observe the efficacy of placebos, however. The hospital employed the startling practice of trying harmless lactose pills on patients first to discover if they were hypochondriacs, and Monica had direct experience that this could work.

General nursing training was very good at the London Homoeopathic, if tough, and with the shortage of staff in civilian hospitals a great deal was expected from the nurses, right down to the lowly probationers who might suddenly find themselves given frightening responsibility. Monica had learned to work hard at King Edward's but now she learned commitment, and that nursing was more than 'technique and muscle and endless endurance'. Discipline in the hospital was hard too, and intrusive, albeit rooted in protectiveness: the Matron watched out of the window of her office to see which nurses were late arriving or went out without wearing their gloves, and what kind of men were waiting for them by the corner lamp post. Strangely enough for one of her temperament, Monica at this stage did not particularly mind this close supervision; there was a certain sense of security within such a system and it saved her from having to think for herself, which she could now see was probably a blessing when things got difficult. On one occasion she told a superior that she thought a patient was dying, and was informed she was not there to think but to do as she was told.

Along with some other nurses Monica was eventually moved into residential quarters in the evacuated Hospital for Nervous Diseases, a building which joined the back of the London Homoeopathic. Access to their rooms was through the door of their own hospital and therefore still under Matron's watchful eye. But before long Monica and other young nurses discovered an alternative route, via the glass roof of the mortuary, to go and meet their men friends under a different lamp post. Matron was pleased that more nurses seemed to be staying in at night and studying.

Working at the London Homoeopathic for a longer period, Monica enjoyed even more intense friendships there than she had at King Edward's. Some of her nursing friends lived too far away from London to get home much and so she invited them to join her at number 52 for some decent food and a hot bath, sharing the tub to conserve hot water. Eating sausages from a wooden sponge tray across the bath, they spun tales of the hospital to a tolerant Fanny keeping them company – everybody else had long ago lost patience with Monica's stories. They had all been bored stiff listening to her fixated tales of being a cook, Monica reflected later, and stories from a nurse confined in a hospital day and night were if anything duller. People learned not to ask her about her work at dinner parties because she tended to tell them (if she had managed to keep awake).

As well as continuing her own writing Monica was still producing book reviews for the *Sunday Chronicle,* including on Mary Lavin's latest in 1944, a thriller from Nigel Balchin in 1945 and a book of theatre critic James Agate's in which her reference to Agate's 'ungullible critical faculty' greatly pleased him. She even weighed in on a life of Beethoven. Her editor at the paper was still the paternalistic Jimmy Drawbell, who had serialised her first book in 1939 and who continued to encourage her efforts. In an advert for the paper in 1945, *Why I Write for The Sunday Chronicle*, Monica wrote that she did so because she was grateful for the encouragement the paper had given an unknown author but also that she found it 'streets ahead of the rest of its class for intelligence, entertainment and broad-minded thought'. She was proud to have a permanent connection as a book reviewer with such a fine paper, she declared. (In fact the *Sunday Chronicle* was very much a middle-market newspaper which eventually merged with the *News of the World*.)

Other articles appeared, including a sort of propaganda piece in 1945 for the Government's new Home Help Scheme in which she related various domestic hard-luck stories in a bid to attract volunteers to work for the service. She was sure, she wrote, that none of the volunteers would try to be superior or critical about the homes where they helped out, because now everyone lived in shabby surroundings and was short of food and fuel. She also continued a steady stream of broadcasts for the BBC, often on a Dickens theme, including in 1942 an imaginary conversation with her great-grandfather which George Orwell broadcast to an Indian audience when working for the BBC's Eastern Service. There was a Christmas talk for the Pacific Service the following year to mark the centenary of *A Christmas Carol,* another on *A Dickens Christmas* in 1944 (broadcast to the French under the billing *Noel à la Dickens*, though still in English), and for the overseas series *What War Means to Me* some laboured humour about the lack of servants and constant queuing: '...my mother stands in line for hours to get a bit of Dover sole and it turns out to be Icelandic cod'. Being on night duty when asked to record this last offering, Monica told the BBC that she was happy to come any morning required but the earlier the better – presumably to get back to the hospital in time to snatch some sleep. She asked that anything pejorative she might say about nursing be attributed to her first hospital and anything good to her present one, in order to avoid the necessity of submitting the script to the Homoeopathic. She was on the wrong side of the hospital authorities just then, she explained without going into detail, and did not want to say anything that would cause trouble.

More interestingly, Monica in early 1944 gave a talk for the Pacific Service on the problems of a civilian hospital in wartime. BBC editors requested changes to her initial script, considering her to have painted a depressing picture which might lead their overseas listeners to think that Britons were 'nearly starving and frozen stiff'. The changes were duly made but the resultant talk still gave a rather bleak impression. Hospital life in this the fifth year of the war was an unending struggle to give peacetime service under wartime conditions, said Monica. She described how many hospitals had been taken over for the Forces, leaving fewer facilities for civilians, and how even these were obliged to keep whole wards empty and ready for emergency casualties. This meant fewer beds for more patients, she observed, and although the population remained astonishingly well after several years of war it was clear that people's resistance to infection was naturally lower than in normal conditions. She gave as an example the (perhaps invented) story of Charlie, a backstreet shoemaker who was weakened by all-night firewatching and by patriotically working in his shop without warmth in order to save on fuel, and who eventually collapsed with influenza and was taken into hospital. He died. The hospitals were full of people like Charlie, she said, people who became seriously ill through overwork, irregular meals and keeping going with too many cigarettes and cups of coffee or tea. Once in hospital, the special diets required to build them up were hugely difficult because of rationing, despite the priority and extras given to hospitals. She talked too of the lowered contributions to her 'voluntary' hospital (meaning that funding was from endowments and subscriptions), how money was no longer so available for donating after the rises in income tax and the cost of living, and the pressure on people to buy War Savings. Linen, drugs, disinfectants, instruments, all were expensive and having to be eked out on the wards. Staff shortages meant that the overworked doctors were either very old or very young, while the young women that were now being drafted into hospitals as nurses did not have the passion for the job and were insubordinate – just as she had been in her day, Monica admitted. She even professed to regret the threatened loss of starched aprons and cuffs in order to save on laundry.

It was a grimly realistic snapshot of wartime privations endured by both populace and hospitals alike, albeit written in Monica's usual humorous vein: Sister was marking the bottles of disinfectant the way drinkers in the London nightclubs were marking their gin, the unruly young women called up to nursing were only interested in getting off duty in time for their dates with handsome Canadians. But Monica ended on a decidedly upbeat note, no doubt mindful of the BBC's request for positivity for their overseas audience – and, in spite of everything, probably herself an ardent believer in the staunch capacity of British hospitals to survive and overcome. Somehow the Sister in charge of housekeeping managed to provide special food for the patients, she maintained, *and* feed the ravenous nurses. Morale remained high and unlikely to be sapped. Hospitals had kept going throughout the Blitz, she reminded her listeners, even when casualties were piling up in the corridors, the nurses did not take off their uniforms for days and blue-chinned doctors operated twelve hours at a stretch. Whatever Hitler had up his sleeve, Monica declared, they were not giving up: whatever he tried, the hospitals would be ready for him.

§

Trying to combine nursing, writing and broadcasting was hard work and Monica found it more and more difficult to focus on the books she needed to read, and to write the reviews themselves for the *Chronicle*. She was forever behind with her copy, flying down Gray's Inn Road on her bike to the *Chronicle* office and hoping no one she knew there would see her in her nurse's uniform. After *The Fancy* came out she embarked on yet another book, this time a novel set, naturally, in a hospital like the London Homoeopathic. With exams looming she had trouble getting started, but eventually settled into it.

When Monica finally underwent her Preliminary Examination for State Registration, three Matrons from other hospitals arrived to conduct the oral and to observe the nurses carrying out practical demonstrations. Monica heard from her own hospital's Sister Tutor that over lunch the visiting Matrons had been sounding off about *One Pair of Feet*, commenting that the author must have been a hopeless nurse. Sister Tutor had been tempted to retort that the Matron had just passed Monica Dickens for her Prelim, with praise.

Conditions inevitably deteriorated as the war went on. Hospital food got worse and worse, everyone's weekly two-ounce butter and sugar rations seemingly getting smaller. In June 1944 came the first V-1 flying bombs, nicknamed Doodlebugs, which were essentially bombs with wings like a cruise missile. Monica described their horrific operation:

No one who lived through that time will ever forget the ponderous 'De dum, de dum', as the evil thing, obscenely cruciform, lumbered overhead, while you dived for cover, fell on your face, or just stood and hunched your shoulders. When the engine cut out, it fell. Silence. A whistling. The explosion. The enormous relief: They didn't get me, followed by guilt at being relieved that they got somebody else.

(Monica Dickens, *An Open Book*, 1978)

During the worst of the Doodlebugs, and just after the appearance in London of the first V-2 rocket in September that same year – the world's first guided ballistic missile launched in retribution for Allied bombings of German cities – some of Monica's hospital was evacuated to a large pseudo-country house on Coombe Hill near Kingston. There was a limited fleet of nurses and no Matron; Monica, now past her second year and heading towards Finals, was given more responsibility and was the senior nurse on night shift. She enjoyed being able to make her own decisions and patients and staff alike felt more relaxed at night without supervision.

The evacuated hospital had one resident woman doctor, and surgeons came down once or twice a week to operate in a converted study. Clean sheets were draped over the walls for the operations but it can hardly have been a very sterile environment. One of the surgeons was leading the way in the now common practice of making patients get up out of bed as soon as possible after a major operation, and one evening as she went onto night shift Monica was given orders to get a patient out of bed when he woke from the anaesthetic. He was a likeable family man with whom Monica had chatted as she prepared him for surgery. She now found him clearly in pain and unwilling to be moved, and was caught in a dilemma which had often troubled her: whether to follow her own instinct or do as the doctor ordered. No one was awake to consult with and she did not want to worry the probationer on duty with her by discussing it.

At five in the morning Monica made the decision to follow orders and started to help the man to stand. He asked if he needed to stand all the way up; Monica could have said no, but she did not. Once on his feet the patient collapsed in horrible pain, and despite emergency care from the inexperienced resident doctor he died of peritonitis before noon the following day. Nobody blamed Monica, but of course she blamed herself. The nightmare was compounded by having to assist at the post-mortem and then type up the resultant report.

Some time after this Monica was moved back to the main London hospital. In *An Open Book* she commented merely that being on a different sort of ward she nursed no more of that particular surgeon's patients.

It is easy to imagine how this dreadful event weighed on Monica for the rest of her life.

§

In May 1945, soon after Victory in Europe Day, Monica resigned from the London Homoeopathic without taking her State Finals. In her memoir she gave as reason a rumour she had heard that State Registered nurses would not be released from service for at least five years. What role the tragic death of her patient played can only be guessed at.

She was in any case exhausted and run down, doubtless a result of the excessively hard work and poor wartime nutrition: many of the nurses had stopped menstruating and had boils and septic fingers – at one point Monica had seven all at once, each bandaged separately. In a picture of her taken that summer in a swimsuit, she looked like a skeleton.

Monica never nursed again, but her return to the profession for a full two and a half years argues for a genuine love of nursing rather than a search for copy. 'I thought I was rather a good nurse,' she was to remark many years later. In the decades that followed, she was a natural port of call when reviews or forewords were required for 'nurse' books. She was certainly a very appropriate choice to provide a foreword to a 1956 publication by the New York Public Library of Charles Dickens' prompt copy of *Mrs Gamp*, a character study worked up from *Martin Chuzzlewit* for delivery on stage as part of his reading tours. In this prologue to the prompt (published complete with Dickens' own crossings-out, underlinings and word changes), Monica walks the reader through the original conception of the character and its effect on the Victorian public as a notorious stereotype – drunken and slovenly – of all that was then wrong with the image of nursing. In 1978 she was asked to contribute an introduction to a new edition of Enid Bagnold's haunting nursing journal *A Diary Without Dates*. Like Monica, Enid Bagnold was dismissed from the hospital for writing her book (and, in other strange parallels beyond sharing the name Enid, worked in a factory during the war and was a passionate horse-lover). This 1918 account of life as a VAD in the First World War appeared to Monica not unlike her own experience as a very junior nurse in the next war some twenty years later. She recognised Enid's subservience to the 'rules and caprices of the almighty Sisters', dedicated women only happy when the beds were made with sharp enough corners, and understood Enid's battle not to become like them. She sympathised with Enid's helpless pity for the agony of the wounded soldiers in the days before painkillers and antibiotics, writing that she too had known the grudging allocation of drugs as if part of the cure was to suffer.

In another introduction to a book on nursing, Canadian writer Sheila Mackay Russell's *A Lamp is Heavy* in 1950, Monica wrote of her continued fascination with nurses:

Nursing is a kind of mania; a fever in the blood; an incurable disease which, once contracted, cannot be got out of the system. If it was not like that, there would be no hospital nurses, for compared dispassionately with other professions, the hours are long, the work hard, and the pay inadequate to the amount of concentrated energy required.

(Monica Dickens, Introduction to *A Lamp Is Heavy*, 1954)

She had been thankful to leave hospital at the end of the war, Monica admitted, and thought she had had enough of it, but recognised later that this was not the case. The spell of hospitals still drew her and always would, she wrote, and her time as a nurse had been the most exciting and rewarding years of her life. She was also to observe that nursing had taught her about belonging, hard work, and exhaustion, and being needed. Her eyes had been opened to the lives of others.

A Cottage in the Country

With the end of the war in 1945 and her retreat from nursing, Monica, now thirty, found herself once more ensconced at Chepstow Villas. She remained very close to Henry and Fanny, who the previous year had celebrated their fortieth wedding anniversary, and was to remain lovingly attached to them all their lives. She maintained similarly close ties with other family members, including her brother Bunny's widow Joyce and their little son Christopher. During a week off from the homeopathic hospital while in the throes of writing what was to become her next work, *Thursday Afternoons,* Monica went to stay in Devon with Joyce and worked on the new book all day in the garden; she spent the evenings relaxing in the bath, drinking hot cider as she sang duets with her nephew in his bed across the corridor.

Times were grim. The war was over, but men were returning to find their jobs gone and sometimes their families also. Rationing was still in force, everything was in short supply and everyone was exhausted. Monica's sister Doady and her four children had returned from the country and moved back into number 52 again while they searched for a house in bombed-out London, and as there were no servants to be had Monica and Doady managed the house between them. Chepstow Villas had always meant love and safety for both sisters even after they had left home as adults, as well as for many other family members following the loss of Chilworthy and of Mulberry Walk on the death of Henry's parents. But actually running it turned out to be quite another matter.

Number 52 was supposed to be back to normal, now that Henry had hung up his air raid warden hat and planted a rock garden on the roof of the bomb shelter in the backyard, but the fleet of servants was gone forever. The sisters did their best to keep the inconvenient house clean and the meals coming, climbing up from the basement kitchen with overloaded trays to the dining room and slowly breaking successive pieces of Fanny's china as they fell up and down the back stairs. Monica was in charge of all the cooking and spent a lot of time down below. When she and Doady eventually baulked at carrying up Sunday lunch for nine people,

Henry, described by Monica as 'democratised by the war', finally agreed to eat it in the kitchen.

Looking back on her life thus far in a contribution to a book of memoirs by her *Sunday Chronicle* editor James Drawbell, Monica recognised what her various experiences had given her in place of her initial self-absorption: an intense and lifelong fascination with the vagaries of the human race. Her subterranean domain as a cook had been the perfect lens for viewing the incredible antics of her fellow man. No caricaturist could draw humans as funny as they really were, or tragedian show them as pitiful, she observed. The war, for its part, had thrown her into contact with yet more of the human species than she would otherwise ever have met, whether cooking in a canteen for emergency workers, working on a factory bench or nursing. The other nurses' frequent platitude that in the job they met all sorts was quite true, she discovered. Now back with the family, Monica was looking at even these familiar figures 'with the more discerning eye of a wider experience', finding more there to study and surprise her than she had realised when too used to them. She had been roused to an abiding interest in others:

> *If the observant eye looks outwards instead of inwards how can life ever be dull with the enormous number of quite incredible people one bumps into every day?*

(Monica Dickens, *Drifts My Boat* by James Drawbell, 1947)

Drawbell himself described Monica at this stage as still characterised by her enormous zest for life. But in fact she often felt depressed, no doubt worried about what the future would bring and certainly not enjoying the crowding and endless round of menial tasks at number 52. When not cleaning or cooking, she escaped the chaos with a bolt hole in a borrowed basement flat where she continued to write. It seems there was no further attempt at finding a job, and Monica may have decided once and for all that writing could actually provide a living. When the flat was no longer available she found space in the house of a friend.

Michael Joseph brought out Monica's fifth book, *Thursday Afternoons*, later in 1945. It was her bleakest work so far, possibly still in the process of being written around the time of the traumatic death of her hospital patient. Bleak, but successful, and well received by critics, apart from its surprise ending which was generally disliked. Poet John Betjeman in the *Daily Herald* saw the final scene as melodramatic and a false note, as did an Australian critic who labelled it hasty and incongruous. The *Observer* commented that it was as if the author's great-grandfather had suddenly laid violent hands on Bob Sawyer in *Pickwick Papers*. The *Times of India*, on the other hand, acknowledged the 'wild surprise' but found the novel none the worse for it.

For Betjeman the book was 'devilishly clever' and he pointed out that Monica excelled at laconic description; the acclaimed writer Pamela Hansford Johnson observed that her mind was as sharp as a needle. The *Sphere* referred to the novel's touch of genius, and the *Evening News* declared that Monica was now beyond the stage of reviewers patronisingly recalling that she was a great-granddaughter of the illustrious Charles. She was, in her own right, 'perhaps the best woman novelist in Britain – just Monica Dickens'. General readers were enthusiastic, and *Thursday Afternoons* was amongst the books most in demand at the Central Catholic Library in 1945.

The novel depicts episodes in the life of a handsome hospital doctor, Steven Sheppard, whose innate kindness sows the seeds of his own destruction. Monica had the idea for the story after reading Nathaniel West's *The Day of the Locust*, which had impelled her to examine how those who receive help can actually destroy the helper if that person is not strong enough. Dr Sheppard is the love object of the prissily unattractive Nurse Lake, a character arising from one of a group of nurses Monica had known at the London Homoeopathic who were training to go abroad as missionaries; she described them as 'cowishly aroused' by the unimpressive male staff working in a non-priority hospital during wartime. Set mostly in hospital surroundings in 1939, the rather plotless narrative explores the daily existence of the charismatic doctor as he regrets both his marriage and his profession, dreams of action in the fast-approaching war, and tries his hand at writing – seeking to enter that trance-like state that Monica herself must have experienced, where

the imagined world is the only world, the body is all brain and feels neither heat, cold nor hunger, when...the right, the only words are jumping up and making him bounce on his chair and cry 'This is it!'

(Monica Dickens, *Thursday Afternoons*, 1945)

Monica confessed to a weakness for her doctor hero Steven, despite her very unsympathetic treatment of the pathetic nurse's unrequited love. 'He's the sort of attractive man I always hope to meet but never shall,' she told the BBC TV programme *Kaleidoscope* in 1948. He had entered her head fully formed and requiring no development, she added, and because she knew his tragic fate in advance she felt a sentimental attachment to him all the time she was writing. The tragic fate duly occurs, unaverted by the horrified Nurse Lake, who has entertained fantasies of saving the doctor from drowning or from a gangster's bullet.

Monica's medical bugbears are again present – the rigid nursing hierarchy, the obsession with cuffs – and a number of other touches lifted straight from Monica's own life: the doctor's dog is also called Ugly and, just as she had done, the doctor has rescued him from being chained up in a Cornish farmyard. Also like Monica, the doctor's wife works as a VAD, and Nurse Lake has to go for a meal in the middle of laying out a corpse. The hospital scenes and the various characters are her usual vivid creations, if not always tending to lead anywhere, and seemingly in the book more for the fun of the observation than as a means of advancing the story. A Sister is 'short and square and possessive, with inadequate legs and tiny feet in buckled shoes', a fat junior doctor has 'a face like pink plasticine and grey flannel trousers that were too short and too tight in the thigh' – Monica's usual thumbnail sketches that capture the character in a single line, but also get expanded into credible human beings. The scalpel once again incises into the unattractively aspiring: the comedy, or tragedy, of social striving was by now a definite thread in Monica's work. The *Times Literary Supplement* may have praised the 'life and body' she gave to the minor characters but some of her portraits in the rather depressing *Thursday Afternoons* border on the vicious. She reserves particular invective for those trying to get above themselves, such as the tweedy Mrs Delacroix, who registers as a patient

...with a remote, disinterested air, receiving her folder in her finger-tips with a slight laugh to show how <u>absurd</u> all this was...Breezing into the clinic, she felt how nice it must be for Dr Sheppard to see someone of his own kind in the middle of all the dreary folk, so when she sat down, she crossed her legs very high and made herself quite at ease to show she was his own kind.

(Monica Dickens, *Thursday Afternoons*, 1945)

Again, Monica was far kinder to ordinary working people who know their place: her cooks, charwomen and plumbers were particularly happy portraits, noted the *Times Literary Supplement*.

§

At around this time, along with other women journalists, Monica was invited by the Ministry of Information to visit Bremen and Hamburg in order to write articles about how German women were living. German civilians in these cities were still starving after the end of the war, some living in foul-smelling bunkers, and the experience was harrowing. Monica managed to track down one of Fanny's German relations and, to help with the food situation, stuffed the woman's bag with stale rolls while the other journalists added jewellery and cigarettes. She was feeling pleased to be of some assistance but then pulled herself up short: she was patronising Fanny's *cousin*. On returning home she wrote not a single word about the German women, and as far as she knew neither did any of the other traumatised journalists.

In 1946 came Monica's sixth book, the fourth in four years: *The Happy Prisoner,* dedicated to her brother Bunny's son Christopher Dickens. The central character is a bedridden amputee, originating from a one-legged patient at the London Homoeopathic who used to talk to Monica at night about how it felt to be unable to walk.

She had enjoyed writing it, despite the difficult conditions and hard work at number 52. The book went well from the start. At this stage of her writing career ideas for books would come to Monica all in a flash; not the whole story, just the central idea, and then the story would begin to develop around it until finally she shaped it into a novel, which in fact she found the most tedious part of being an author. She sometimes longed to make a start on an idea that had come to her, but had to hold off until she knew where she was headed. For research she picked the brains of anyone who had the technical knowledge needed, and for routine material she visited the library. Once she got going Monica loved the actual writing – though finding concentration difficult – and was 'pretty sour' with anyone who interrupted her. The best characters usually wrote themselves, she observed, whilst others required plodding at. Characters full of vitality were the best because she knew exactly what they would say and do, although occasionally they got out of hand and began to develop in their own way. In these cases they would not do the things that Monica had planned for them, forcing her to alter the plot. (Monica spotted this problem in other novels: in her introduction to a new edition of Austen's *Emma* in 1947, she asked if Austen planned the gradual softening of the annoying Emma into loveableness, 'or did Emma, as is the way of perfectly conceived characters, take things into her own hands and develop in her own inevitable way?')

The Happy Prisoner, however, had required little in the way of research as Monica had all the medical facts at her fingertips. The central character in this country house novel is floppy-haired Oliver, a Major who has injured his heart and lost a leg in the war and is confined to bed in his family home to recuperate. Although occasionally depressed, he has the comfort and interest of the frequent visitors to his room: his scatty American mother, an efficient but cool young nurse, his awkward, big-boned sister, another sister dreading the return of her husband from war, and a charming ten-year-old cousin who is a horsy Monica-type in boy's clothes and a snake-buckle belt. As he observes the tribulations of his friends and family, Ollie begins to think that he can solve everyone's problems, and meddles disastrously. The story has romance and pathos and, of course, a happy ending for Ollie, with whom no female reader has ever failed to fall in love. It is a far happier and more enjoyable book than *Thursday Afternoons*; Monica appeared to have recovered her equilibrium.

The structure is cohesive, and Monica admitted that she had taken greater care with it than with the books that had been written at the end of a day's work as a nurse or factory hand; she had the opportunity now to sit down for hours on end and to become thoroughly absorbed in writing. Able to recognise her own flaws, Monica had pared the book down to the nth degree:

I had time to go over and over it, pruning, correcting and re-shaping it. Its form is more coherent than my other novels which incline to dart off at a tangent after stray characters who, often, have nothing to do with the story.

(Monica Dickens, *The Best Characters Write Themselves*, How I Write My Novels, 1948)

Because the action of the novel takes place only through Ollie's eyes, nothing can happen without Ollie seeing it, and structurally this made some aspects of the writing very difficult. In other respects it was a useful device: instead of an omniscient narrator explaining everyone's background, characters all recount their lives and problems in person to Ollie as he lies in his bed, and their stories thereby become more immediate and intimate. Monica thought it her best work yet, and in fact began to wonder how *One Pair of Hands* had ever passed muster. Were it not for Compton Mackenzie's reading of the proofs she knew it would have been far worse than it was, and could now recognise that she had taken no trouble with her first book but had simply 'dashed off whatever came into my head'.

The then immensely popular author J. B. Priestley considered *The Happy Prisoner* a light work but full of skill and invention and liveliness, and very good entertainment; *The Illustrated London News* called Monica a born story-teller. For writer Pamela Hansford Johnson, Monica was unfailingly entertaining, with a sharp eye for the amusing trifle and a 'genius for the humours of the commonplace'. Cleverly contrasted characters, praised the *Scotsman*, and a work offering 'endearing appeal'.

Others were not so kind. The respected American writer Sterling North did a hatchet job in his Virginia newspaper, seemingly incensed that Monica was nothing like Charles Dickens but then proceeding to list several points of similarity. Although in common with her famous ancestor she felt and resented the exploitation of the poor, wrote North, it was at a far less perceptive level. She would never create an Oliver Twist because she lacked almost completely the 'Hogarthian bitterness' necessary to rail at social injustice; she had no power as a satirist. However, like Dickens, he continued, her writing could be earthy: her earlier books were crudely written and somewhat vulgar but then so was *The Pickwick Papers*. She had inherited Dickens' broad sense of humour, his slightly provincial point of view, and his real affection for erring mankind. But according to North she was guilty, as was Dickens, of producing caricatures. Her primary objective, like his, was to tell a tale, even if not with the same native genius.

Having criticised Monica for being both like and unlike Charles Dickens, the stern American critic at least concluded that *The Happy Prisoner* was enjoyable for its plot twists, character development and hilarious and affecting incidents. Another US reviewer accused Monica's transatlantic characters of unconvincing Americanisms, while a further pointed drily to the appearance in the book of a vulgar American harpy who was 'as unfavorably drawn an American as any in *Martin Chuzzlewit'*.

The Happy Prisoner proved to be one of Monica's most successful books, and was chosen by the Book Society as one of its Books of the Month. In France, however, it was rejected by three and possibly as many as five publishers in succession, after which literary agent Jenny Bradley in Paris declared herself unhappy with the situation although intending to keep trying. *Prisoner* never did find a French publisher, but succeeded in Italy, and in Germany as *Zwölf um ein Bett* (Twelve Around a Bed).

There was another, far weightier consequence following on from the publication of Monica's sixth work. With its one basic scene of bedridden Ollie receiving successive confidences from family and friends in his room, the work was crying out for a life on the stage and was adapted as a play by John McNair and performed on TV, on radio and in theatres (and Monica was credited with the writing of a televised version for the BBC's *Sunday-Night Theatre* in 1955). In Monica's opinion it was not a very good play, but with its single set and numerous parts for women she could see why it was popular with small repertory companies.

She is likely to have been grateful for the existence of the play in the long run, however, for it was to change the course of her life.

§

By now Monica was writing sometimes sixteen hours a day and believing that work was all-important: she would get up and work and eat, and go to bed and get up again the next morning and go on working. When she saw that she was sleeping and eating merely in order to write, Monica began to question what she was working *for*. What was the aim of it all? she asked herself, recollecting this period a few years later. Surely there should be some fun in it too?

...for the first time I thought what a fool I was being – I was just working for working's sake and having that awful righteous feeling you get when you work hard, as if you were doing better than the person next door who is only lazing in the sun.

(Monica Dickens, *Author By Profession*, 1952)

At number 52 Monica and Doady were starting to quarrel, as they had not done since they were children, over stupid things like burned saucepans. The now ageing Fanny and Henry were increasingly distressed by the overcrowding and the din and ruckus of Doady's three growing boys and daughter Mary. Finally, Doady and her husband Denys discovered a house in Wimbledon and the family departed, leaving number 52 worn out and strangely silent. Her parents found a servant who would live in and Monica realised she might be free to move on. She decided to leave London.

By this time the once presentable Chepstow Villas had considerably deteriorated:

It was a very bad neighbourhood. When my parents bought the house in 1912, it was quite respectable. Then it became like Clapham right on the edge of the slums. In the unlikely event of any guy asking to take me home, I would be too ashamed to say I lived in Chepstow Villas...In my day most of the houses had degenerated into rooming houses, full of alcoholic boxers. There was a brothel across the street. Ours was the only family house on the block, very shabby genteel. The streets began to be a centre for all kinds of strange occult sects, with weird signs on the doors; failures and revolutionaries and penniless students and odd potty people lived there.

(Monica Dickens, *Evening Standard*, 1973; and *Where I Was Young*, 1976)

Walking to the cinema one day, Monica on a sudden whim went into an estate agent's and saw a picture of a cottage for sale in the little village of Hinxworth in North Hertfordshire. The property was three hundred years old and consisted of several farm cottages knocked into one and topped by a heavy thatched roof. One soft summer evening she drove out to have a look at it and found an apricot-coloured house, still lit from the dying sun, amidst a profusion of hollyhocks and roses and phlox. She knew at once she was going to live there.

Bury End, now a listed building, was built in the seventeenth century as a row of three single-storeyed cottages with timber frames and plastered walls. Inside, an eighteenth-century staircase led up to the attics, and the inglenook in what had been the fireplace in the middle cottage went so far back that it was possible to sit on little benches at either side and see up the chimney. In the

106

winter the fire was permanently ablaze. A solid front door led straight into the main room, its old red tiles set directly in the ground. Deep cupboards were built into the equally deep whitewashed walls and overhead ran ancient beams; the windows were low and latticed. The kitchen at the rear overlooked lavender bushes and a cooking-apple tree in the garden, and upstairs the view from the back was of the abundant Hertfordshire farmland.

Monica moved in a few months after seeing the cottage, having spent all her money on buying it with nothing left over for furniture. She took her bed from number 52 and rummaged around a second-hand shop for rugs and an armchair, and three chests because the upstairs ceilings of the cottage inclined too much to have cupboards.

It was 1947, and Monica, still unattached, had reached the grand old age of thirty-two. In those days this was tantamount to spinsterhood, and having taken the then unusual step of buying her own house, others may well have begun to see her in this light – even though Monica was a very attractive young woman who put effort into looking glamorous, perming her hair and still wearing plenty of make-up. A photo taken at the door of the cottage shows her slender and fair-haired, heavily lipsticked, her beautiful eyes gazing wistfully into the distance. Friends asked her if she ever thought about marriage, assuming, to Monica's annoyance, that she lived alone of necessity and not from choice. In her memoir Monica maintained otherwise, declaring that she could not wait to get home to greet her dog Joe whining for her behind the door and her cats converging from the garden, and to rediscover her sense of self in her own place surrounded by her own things.

At weekends the cottage was filled with family and friends, and, when her sister Doady separated from her husband, Doady's offspring during the school holidays as well. Monica did all the work in the cottage herself, to a crazy schedule so that she had free time for her guests; the children were encouraged to help with the jobs they could enjoy. With the ponies and horses kept in her stables she tried to recreate for them the horsy world she had experienced herself at Britwell as a child: caring for the animals, going for a gallop on the downs and attending horse shows. Bunny's young son Christopher was also a frequent visitor and recalled Monica giving them all more or less anything they wanted, yet always keeping up with her writing each day. He would later remember Monica's enormous sense of fun. 'Mont', as the children called her, fell in wholeheartedly with all their games. 'She was the rare kind of grown-up with an open mind into a child's world. She was always ready to take us riding, or play with us – she loved games of any kind,' her niece Mary remembered. Monica enjoyed being an aunt: in a rather sentimental article on aunts in *Woman's Own* in 1951 she wrote of the joy, pride and stimulation to be gained from nephews and nieces, and how she would think she had not lived in vain if they wrote about her with affection in an *in memoriam* column.

Mostly, however, Monica could do as she pleased. It was the first time in her life she had ever lived completely on her own; before, she had been either at number 52, or on holiday somewhere with her family or in a nurses' residence. Now she was mainly alone with her dog and cats. It had taken her over thirty years to discover her need for solitude – or perhaps she had only now acquired a need for it, she mused in *An Open Book*. She employed no domestic help and would rinse out her single plate and mug and make scanty meals out of leftovers from the weekends, fried up with an egg. Reading became more private, more akin to a message to Monica personally instead of being shared and discussed with friends and family. (She was once amazed when she met a man who knew all the same poems that heartened her too, even though the poems were very popular.) As for her own writing, she often did not start until six or eight in the evening, when there was absolute stillness and little risk of being interrupted. She would sit down in front of the open fireplace and write in longhand in exercise books for most of the night, stopping in the early hours to soak in the bath with a cup of tea and a sandwich until either the dawn chorus or the tepid water woke her up. Then she would clamber up the steep stairs on all fours to bed, and sleep until Joe the dog barked at the postman making his way up the path at nine o'clock.

Some nights she made little progress, however. Writing was not like a physical job that you could force yourself to do, she told the author James Leasor, who interviewed her at this time for a book on how a number of contemporary novelists got started. The mind could not be forced to do something in the same way as the body: you had to *want* to do it, to be in the mood, she explained. Monica's method was to keep writing and tearing it up and starting again, over and over, until she did get in the mood. She knew that if she just sat down and waited for the Muse to come, there would be little produced. Her advice to other young writers starting out, as she herself had been advised, was to write exactly what they wanted and to trim it afterwards.

Sometimes she was despondent, feeling 'lonely and unsettled and insecure'. A passage on loneliness in a work she wrote in the cottage may echo some of this unease:

It was bad to be alone. It made you think – futile, distorted, unbearable thoughts. Images of horror that seared into the brain like a branding iron. Memories in the cheating guise of nostalgia. Remorse where none was needed; false regrets...

(Monica Dickens, *Flowers on the Grass*, 1949)

When in this sort of mood, Monica needed to see other people to prove she existed. In London she counted among her friends the ballet dancers Pamela May and Ray Powell, both of whom had danced with the great ballerina Margot Fonteyn, and Ray was later to become an Associate Director of the Australian Ballet. But whether going up to London or visiting local friends Monica would occasionally nod off at dinner parties or have to pull over to the side of the road for a nap because of her topsy-turvy sleeping habits. There was little she could talk about in any case – although keeping up with films and the ballet, which she loved – as she was always doing the same things: riding her horses and gardening, and, of course, writing a book.

Monica's seventh work, *Joy and Josephine*, published in the US as *Portobello Road*, came out in 1948. It was serialised in the now long gone magazine *Home Notes*; to celebrate the latest Monica Dickens, Selfridges on Oxford Street in London devoted a whole window to a display of her books. A well-plotted story of switched babies, the novel features the old Portobello Road almost as one of the characters, and much of Monica's Portobello childhood is resurrected: the ramshackle shops and people, a gang of wayward slum boys, the middle-class family like Monica's who live on the corner of Chepstow Villas and the 'Porto'. And, in an echo of Monica's own crushes, the heroine as a schoolgirl bores her parents to death with constant dinner-table details about the current passion.

After spending her early years as the adopted daughter of a grocer's wife in the Portobello Road, Josephine makes a sensational shift to high society and the guardianship of a fastidious baronet when it appears she may really be his niece switched at birth. Josephine becomes Joy (with careful training from the baronet) and gets suitably engaged to the handsome son of a landed family; then, when war comes, she trains as a fitter and works in a factory, enduring exhausting night shifts and freezing bike rides home just as Monica had done. She is suddenly jerked back to a depth lower than even the corner grocery when a dreadful drunken Irishwoman appears, claiming to be her real mother. (These switches between classes afforded Monica an opportunity to plunge her heroine into different milieus and to have some fun differentiating between slum, lower-middle-class, middle-class and upper-middle-class accents). As the novel draws to an end Joy (or Josephine) is left still in doubt about her real identity and still mourning the love of her life, first encountered as a child in the Portobello Road.

More surprises are in store before the book concludes but by now Joy/Josephine has developed a sturdy individuality which finally makes her independent of her origin and surroundings – a maturation of personality which mirrors that of Monica's earlier heroine Mariana. After trying to be the right person for everyone else, she ultimately succeeds in being herself.

It was a book to enjoy, not to criticise, said the Catholic *Tablet*, nevertheless criticising some contrivances of plot and noticing, as it would, that when the heroine in breaking off her engagement reveals the story of her possibly Catholic origins, her fiancé's parents are relieved to escape a possible papist in the family:

The Drakes, that vigorous old Protestant family, whose ancestors had tortured Edmund Campion – their progeny to be Roman Catholic? It was unthinkable.

(Monica Dickens, *Joy and Josephine*, 1948)

Nevertheless the *Tablet* thought the novel witty, dramatic, and funny, and Monica's work good – but implied that with more effort it might be very good. The *Scotsman* concurred, liking the excellent characterisation but overall dismissing the book as 'novelettish', and the ease with which the heroine slips from one social environment to another remarkable. Monica Dickens 'gets better and better', declared J. B. Priestley, on the other hand. The *Times Literary Supplement* thought Monica made the best of a good idea and that the novel was neatly conceived and 'almost consistently' amusing. Poet John Betjeman, always a fan of Monica, enjoyed its 'rich and humorous' description of street life in the Portobello Road.

Beyond Britain one Australian critic picked out for special enjoyment Monica's treatment of the distress suffered by 'the higher orders' in the face of wartime shortages, as exemplified by the effete baronet on losing the services of his butler:

It was one of the most pitiful sights of the war, people said, to see Rodney on safari in Harrods, trying to track down a kidney...

(Monica Dickens, *Joy and Josephine*, 1948)

But all reviews in Australia praised Monica's skilful management of the complicated plot: '...a vintage product, in style and handling, for those who like their Monica Dickens', summed up the *News* in Adelaide.

By now Monica herself had arrived at a realistic understanding of her own strengths and limitations as a novelist. She admired the accomplished writer Elizabeth Taylor for her dramatisation of everyday life into something significant, and knew that her own work was at its finest when likewise depicting 'small matters'. She believed she ought to stick to this style of writing – even if it meant that she turned out 'the same old stuff' book after book – because it was what she liked and what she did best. She was well aware that critics bewailed the lack of plot in some of her work, but she held firm to the belief that story should arise from character, and not from plot with the characters fitted into it afterwards. The characters in this latest novel were certainly finely drawn, especially Josephine's adoptive parents: the mother hard-working and self-sacrificing, the father a callous brute described with the satirical edge Monica reserved for the cruel and selfish.

Monica's vivid description of the Portobello Road in *Joy and Josephine* captured her old stamping ground so well that some twenty years later the BBC used it in a 1960s programme about the area. After the novel came out Monica thought she had got Portobello out of her system, but just like nursing and hospitals, it was to keep resurfacing in her work.

§

As time went on Monica became very involved in local country activities. At that point Hinxworth was a traditional English village complete with thatched cottages, pub, manor house, post office with shop, war memorial and village hall. There were no buses or trains. Monica became President of the village cricket club, a distinction which she put down to buying maroon blazers for the entire team with the advance for one of her books. Every summer the club played against a team down from London consisting of Monica's friends and family and one or two of her father Henry's middle-aged comrades. A photograph in the local press entitled *Novelist Hits Out* showed Monica, dressed for some reason in an uncricket-worthy but very pretty summer dress and heels, batting energetically with laughing, dark-haired Doady keeping wicket behind her. The locals always won and both teams would end up at the village pub, The Three Horseshoes. As the local celebrity Monica was also called upon to open events, hand out prizes, and address the Women's Institute, of which she was a member. Opening Hinxworth's fête in aid of the Village Hall Fund in July 1949, she was introduced as 'famous the world over', and told the fête-goers that she had only lived in Hinxworth for a year and a half but felt she had lived there all her life. A young girl presented her with a bunch of sweet peas and in true celebrity fashion she then made a gracious tour of the stalls and sideshows accompanied by Henry and Fanny, who were down for the weekend. There were various horsy events in the surrounding area and for a time Monica was treasurer of the nearby Ashwell Horse Show (although quite unable to bookkeep), plus fancy dress judge and organiser of pony rides for children at other local functions.

In some ways Monica seemed to be living the life of a country spinster, if a rather young one. In reality this was far from the case: she was now a famous figure on the literary scene, both in Britain and internationally, her books having been translated into a number of languages (even Finnish). In 1947, in an indication of her standing as an author, she was asked to write the introduction to a new edition of Jane Austen's *Emma*; she reportedly produced the storyline for the 1948 film *Love in Waiting*; and her short story *The Revenge*, about a factory girl who seeks vengeance against a predatory boss, was included in a 1950 volume of literary short stories in the luminous company of H. E. Bates, V. S. Pritchett,

Evelyn Waugh, and Olivia Manning. Monica was even invited to judge a beauty competition during a research trip to a holiday camp in Clacton for her eighth book, and to crown another beauty queen in Canvey Island about a month later.

This was no life of country retirement, as perhaps most clinchingly proved by an appearance on the BBC's *Desert Island Discs* in early 1951. In fact by this stage Monica was pretty much a ubiquitous presence on the airwaves, with frequent appearances on *Woman's Hour, Any Questions, Children's Hour, The Brains Trust, One Minute Please, Don't Quote Me, My Kind of Music,* other game and book shows, and in 1950 her own series of four programmes, *Monica Dickens' Book Club,* in which she recommended new books for family reading. Monica was a popular guest at the BBC, although staff were once asked to watch her for 'carelessness with facts' after she referred to the atomic energy research facility at Harwell as a bomb factory. On another occasion, after turning in a suggestion for a talk on *The Perfect Guest – The Perfect Hostess* ('the people who one likes to have to one's house') it was gently pointed out to their well-bred performer that as most of the BBC's listeners did not stay with each other for the weekend, perhaps she could change the occasion to a tea party or holiday visit.

§

Monica was also becoming well known for her journalism, mainly through her weekly column for *Woman's Own.* This began soon after the war when she was offered the job by Jimmy Drawbell, who became the magazine's first male editor on leaving the *Sunday Chronicle* in 1946. He saw that readers needed colour and excitement in a new era, and good fiction, and his innovations drew in young mothers and working girls and hugely increased the magazine's circulation. Monica's name became almost synonymous with *Woman's Own* and she enjoyed the income and the fans, who flocked around her at publicity events with copies of the magazine for signing. Being a journalist also afforded her access to people and places that interested her, such as the trip to Germany, and she received letters from fans all over the world. Some of these she met in person and maintained contact with into old age.

Monica stayed with *Woman's Own* for some twenty years. In her weekly column, entitled *The Way I See It,* she was allowed to write about anything she wanted: interviews with interesting people, investigations into different kinds of jobs being done by women, articles on everyday problems and sometimes on what the trade then called 'beastlies' – women coping with disabled children or husbands and other difficulties in life. She could do things that other women did not always get the opportunity to do and then write about it, such as getting a treatment at a slimming salon (hardly needed, in Monica's case) – which she enjoyed, even if the woman at the salon did supposedly tell her she was terribly out of proportion. Her column elicited what she described as 'masses of letters' from readers thanking her for helping them, which of course was highly gratifying. Sometimes, when a particular theme had generated a greater than usual number of letters she would ask if she could write on that theme again, only to be refused by what she described as a cynical head office who told her she should consider all those who had *not* written in.

Carrying on with what was probably seen as her trademark gimmick of taking temporary jobs and then writing about the experience, she also did a stint in a cigarette kiosk in the lobby of a big hotel and took a Christmas job in the book department of a large London store (probably Selfridges). A customer told her she could not stand Monica Dickens and did not believe for a minute that she had really done all those cooking and nursing jobs.

There was even a spell at a Lyons Corner House, the very popular restaurant and cafeteria which catered to thousands every day. In her article in *Woman's Own*, and in a talk on the BBC, Monica described her work draining chips out of a bath-sized cauldron of fat and doling them out into equal portions for the harried waitresses to grab as they rushed by, then cutting cabinet puddings into wedges all morning and slapping margarine onto toasted buns all afternoon. She filled jam dishes, made butter pats, prettied up the cream icing on cakes that had got squashed on the way up from the bakery and worked on the bread-and-butter spreading and cutting machine. The chief snag about working in the inferno of a kitchen was the effect of the steam on her hair, Monica commented, so after a stretch grilling Welsh Rarebits she argued her way into being a waitress or 'Nippy', so-called because of the speed with which they nipped around. As a Nippy she was not allowed to wear nail varnish and was subjected to inspections of her hair, stockings and aprons. She was put to work on six tables (as a newcomer, the furthest possible distance away from the kitchen) and an experienced veteran taught her how to hold the loaded trays aloft; after a while Monica taught herself not to put the palm of her hand under the part of the tray where the scalding teapot was. She learned also not to clear the table before the customer had left, in case they took offence and 'stiffed' her out of a tip. Finally she was put on the cafeteria's cold sweet section, where the rule was that nobody could have a second helping but some often tried to sneak back for a second go. The job was hard and tiring, Monica admitted, although claiming to have grown fond of the atmosphere of a big restaurant, the lights and glitter and chink of china and over everything the strains of the live band continuously playing the *Blue Danube*. But she had noticed how many lonely people there were in London, spinning out a cup of tea all afternoon.

Monica may not have worked at the Lyons incognito. In one of her later novels, probably as a joke at her own expense, a manageress at a popular cafeteria recalls that one of her previous workers was a debutante whom she put on teas. 'The newspapers came after her to take her picture, and got everybody upset.'

Articles of this type were interesting enough but most of the rest might now be viewed as thin stuff, although Monica's old friend Charles Pick was to describe her pieces as 'noted for their originality and common-sense approach'. She wrote on topics such as remaining young at heart instead of striving to look younger than your age; talkative women who say nothing; appreciating your children as they grow older; how you make your own luck; women who reveal too much about their husbands; the sacrifices the woman must make on becoming a wife, and other trite themes along these lines. It's easy reading, often funny, but missing the real talent of the novels which had received plaudits from some of the most discerning writers of the era. The apparent dumbing down in these pieces was quite possibly in response to an ethos created by editor Drawbell, who was of his time in his views on women's interests and intellectual capabilities. In his autobiography he described women as 'objects of curiosity and pity' because of their dependency on men, which in his view made them vulnerable and always in need of reassurance, and he was the author of an article entitled *Men Don't Want Clever Wives*. With this kind of attitude it seems likely that Jimmy Drawbell deliberately set the bar rather low for the magazine's content. In his introduction to *Yours Sincerely*, a 1949 collection of *Woman's*

Own pieces by Monica and fellow magazine contributor Beverley Nichols, Drawbell used the word 'unpretentious' to describe the spirit of their writing, presumably the tone he himself had dictated for the magazine.

Doubtless already aware of the then tenor of *Woman's Own*, Monica in subsequent years admitted that when she first started her column she was thinking 'oh, women's magazines' and unconsciously 'writing down'; in her memoir she referred to the advice proffered in her column by her younger, unmarried and childless self as 'facile wisdom'. She did feel that Drawbell helped her journalistic skills, showing her several tricks about how to present an article, such as starting with some sort of statement or story that was the main theme and then elaborating on it, rather than messing around at the beginning with descriptive material and waiting too long to tell the readers what it was all about. He taught her how to relate to the readers, explaining exactly who they were and that it was a dual effort between her and them. The column resulting may well have been tighter and punchier in terms of structure, but there is a yawning chasm between Monica's books – witty, entrancing, occasionally dark, already compared with some seriousness to Dickens' own works – and the limp, conventional offerings in *Woman's Own*. (The columns were nevertheless often referred to as 'much loved', and perhaps they were.)

The earlier pieces in the magazine expressed pretty much the attitudes of the period and now in the twenty-first century make for very dated reading. Monica, at least in the 1940s and '50s and even into the '60s, was certainly no feminist (but at that time, of course, neither was anyone else). On men, and women's desire to cleave to them:

Men are born with a lord and master instinct. They think they are the rulers of the earth, and of course they are. Women are not equipped to rule.

The instinctive desire of woman is to attach herself to a man who will be her provider...The average woman is only too happy to do so – to have the tedious business of coping with the duller mechanics of existence taken off her hands.

Your husband comes first, she wrote in 1951: a wife's aspirations must be subordinated to those of her husband, and even abandoned altogether if they get in the way of domestic happiness. Marriage is the only career worth having, said Monica, and a woman's job can never be more than second-best to marriage so why keep it going when the right man comes along? Don't try to be the boss, came her warning in 1955. Children were prouder of unselfish and devoted Mums than of poised and worldly-wise mothers who worked outside the home, was the assertion in 1959. Any man would rather have his wife at home looking after his children and waiting for him with a decent meal and a sympathetic ear when he gets home from work, she insisted in 1961. 'You can't have deep and safe happiness in marriage and the exciting independence of a career as well.'

Most eyebrow-raising of all was her *Woman's Own* article in 1958 maintaining that truly feminine women were not fitted for politics because they were emotional, sentimental, and illogical. Those women who had battled their way into the House of Commons were doing a wonderful job, Monica conceded, and there were certainly women around with outstanding qualities of leadership, ambition and intelligence – 'But we average, more feminine women, are not built that way.'

Such opinions were the traditionalist views of the period, part of the widespread cultural backlash against the increased independence gained by women during the war. Of a piece was Monica's firm adherence to the sexual double standard: her apparent view that a single woman was not to have a sex life in the way that men could. 'Keeping your standards high never made anyone less desirable,' she wrote in *Let's Be Frank About Petting*:

> Let down the bars once, and there is no reason why you shouldn't do it again. You'll want to do it again. Just petting isn't fun any more. Go on feeling like that, and you are well on the way to becoming a first-class promiscuous tramp. And people will know what you are. It shows.

This model of the chaste, submissive, self-sacrificing woman hardly evokes the way Monica herself had hitherto conducted her own rebellious and independent self, but while there may well have been an element of toeing the *Woman's Own* party line and deliberately spouting the conventional wisdom of the era, nevertheless evidence would emerge that Monica genuinely espoused some of what she said and would try to live up to it. However, perhaps suspecting that she might find her own advice difficult to follow, she did put forward an exception to the rules: the artistic woman. She allowed that dancers, actresses and musicians would find it almost impossible to ignore 'the fire and surge inside' which must be given expression or burst, although not without some sacrifice. In her 1951 item about the necessary subordination of a wife's aspirations she gives the example of a brilliant young novelist friend who puts her husband and children first, eschewing likely fame and fortune, and only writes when she can spare the time from her 'real job' – perhaps Monica's idealistic vision of what she wanted for her own future.

On occasion more interesting and sometimes controversial opinions would surface. One of Monica's particular concerns in the decades after the war was what she saw as a lowering of Britain's moral standards, an element of this being the greater laxity in relations between the sexes, as in her 'petting' article. But her disquiet went beyond this one aspect. In a talk for the BBC Monica claimed a huge reader response to an article on this theme of diminishing standards, a piece she had been 'terribly keen on doing', in which she had discussed the way that those who should be providing a lead in this respect – intellectuals and people 'with names' – were failing to do so. In 1950 she also used her column to present a dire warning of the potential impact of the newly popular television on family life, and indeed on the nation. In *Television – Not for Me!* she begins by contrasting the happy, TV-free homes of Sweden (where television did not arrive until later in the decade) with the sordid slums of Chicago: here, in the midst of poverty, drunkenness and squalor, a refrigerator and a television were always to be found. These modern appliances Monica depicted as symbolic of the unaffordable spending required to attain the new 'essentials of life'. Americans themselves were starting to fear television, she claimed, and were worried about neglect of homework and the amount of time children were spending indoors; sociologists were talking about television changing the pattern of family life because it destroyed conversation, domestic activities and concentration on any work or pastime. In Britain too, Monica warned, children might become a generation unable to read a book or play games outside or amuse themselves with hobbies (a prescient prediction, if television is taken in the wider sense of new technology). She exhorted the British housewife to hold back the onslaught of the evils of television and to cling on to the past in order to protect the nation from descending into depravity. She foretold what might become of women if there were ever to be such a thing as daytime TV:

If they ever start having TV programmes all day long we might become a nation, not of housewives, but of sluts! I don't say we would, but we might.

On the subject of television, however, the letters pouring in this time constituted a storm of protest. Only about one in seven of Monica's readers agreed with her. The editor of the magazine *Practical Television* objected indignantly (as well he might) that her arguments were specious and that television was doing a great deal to enlighten the country's youth. (He ridiculed another of Monica's prescient predictions, which was for a telephone in the future that might enable speakers to see each other – such a device would require equipment the size of a mansion, he spluttered scornfully.)

A later article in *Woman's Own* at the start of the sixties was more accepting of the way that television, for good or ill, had become part of national life, and of the fact that children were learning from it. Television was one of the everyday responsibilities of parenting, Monica now conceded. Parents should restrict viewing hours and teach offspring good taste and the ability to discern the second-rate and the dangerous. But Monica's basic dislike of the medium, at least for children, was abiding:

...the happiness in every house when the TV breaks down and they rediscover all the things like sewing and games and reading...Reading is like breathing. You've just got to read at some time of the day even if it's just in a book propped up while you're making gravy.

Where Monica was producing fiction for a magazine, rather than simplistic advice, the real writer would emerge. A collaborative magazine story published in 1949 was begun by Monica, finished by Beverley Nichols, and an alternative ending provided by the prolific writer Rupert Croft-Cooke. The plot of *You Bet Your Life* concerns beautiful young fortune hunter Anna, who risks everything she has to go to Monte Carlo in hopes of attracting a rich man. In Nichols' ending Anna captures her aged prey and spends all his money; in Croft-Cooke's she also captures the prey but by different means, and the wealthy man is young and attractive. But Monica was given the last word. As a woman, neither ending seemed true to life, she commented. In her version,

119

the rich man pays Anna no attention in the casino but as she is leaving, she is asked to dance by a young, badly dressed English doctor. They marry, live in the suburbs, and have three children. Anna is blissfully happy.

This is quintessential Monica, and certainly one of the reasons her books work so well. They are true to life, and their happy endings are credible. As she wrote before introducing her own ending:

In one story, Anna lost her gamble but won her man (and her money). In the other, she won her gamble and did the same. But Life isn't like that. More often than not, it isn't red or black which turns up, but zero. You don't win or lose outright; you steer a middle course, or something else quite unexpected happens, quite different from what you planned.

This interesting triptych had an unhappy postscript. Rupert Croft-Cooke was gay at a time when the practice of homosexuality was illegal. In 1953, on dubious evidence, he was sentenced to six months' imprisonment for acts of indecency and at around the same time the actor John Gielgud was also convicted and fined for a homosexual offence. Monica, shocked by the news, was sympathetic and concerned that Beverley Nichols (likewise gay but of course not out) might be next. The pressure seemed to be on, she observed. She was right: the Home Office was trying to clamp down.

§

Of interest in the pedestrian *Yours Sincerely* collection of magazine articles is a note hitherto almost completely absent from Monica's novels and comic semi-autobiographies. In one piece in the book, meditating on the nature of happiness and how it can be found in everyday life, Monica provided an unexpected conclusion. A suburban avenue, she wrote,

with its small comings and goings, its work and play and undemanding human relationships can indeed be the road 'to bring us daily nearer God'.

(Monica Dickens with Beverley Nichols, *Yours Sincerely*, 1949)

The line is from John Keble's hymn *New Every Morning is the Love*, which, as in Monica's article, suggests that God can be found in the trivial round and the common task. Although raised as a Catholic, Monica had never preached or made a point of religion in her earlier books. *The Happy Prisoner* was the first work in which religion really figured, if in a fairly prosaic way: bedridden Oliver's sister Heather converts to Catholicism but is not any happier having done so. She struggles with it, mouthing the prayers without properly understanding them, getting up early in the cold and saying ten decades of the rosary, putting more than she can afford into the plate at Mass but without feeling any benefit. Then, suddenly, she experiences a deep sense of peace when she is least expecting it:

I felt it, Ollie. I just felt warm and comfortable and not unhappy about the future any more. It was like someone making a fuss of you when you don't feel well; like someone taking your hand – someone friendly, who you're sure knows more than you do about everything – and saying: 'It's all right; you don't have to worry. I'll look after everything.' That was all. That was my extraordinary experience.

(Monica Dickens, *The Happy Prisoner*, 1946)

Perhaps Monica's own religious feeling in those years was of this nature: a relationship with a personal God who was more of a friend than anything else. Her deeply felt Christianity at this stage of her life was manifesting itself in the compassion for others now increasingly evident in her works; her deep personal belief was also occasionally to start leaking out in her public utterances – and in other journalism. In an article on the Dickensian Christmas for the *Catholic Times* in 1948 she asked whether Christmas was not the one season when everyone's thoughts must 'turn to Christ, though they try to deny Him for the rest of the year'. She argued too that, despite what her great-grandfather's modern detractors and waspish biographers said of him, Charles Dickens was in reality a deeply religious man. Behind his party spirit and his delight in the feasting and hilarity of Christmas, and in himself as the 'inimitable', lay his more sober delight in celebrating with his family 'the birthday feast of the Family to which we all belong'.

The following year, appearing on the BBC's *The Brains Trust*, Monica along with the rest of the celebrities on the panel produced amusing answers to questions such as whether a wife has the right to know what her husband earns, or whether the press encouraged people to think for themselves. But asked what short message she would broadcast to Russia, Monica replied simply: 'Read them the story of Jesus Christ.'

§

In late 1948 Monica sailed to the US aboard the *SS Mauretania* to do some publicity work for American publishers, and taking the opportunity to visit her father's friends the Stockton Whites. On arriving in New York – the first visit to the US since her trip there with Henry in 1935 as an unknown twenty-one-year-old – newspapers asked for her reaction to the charges of anti-Semitism being levelled against the portrayal of Fagin in David Lean's new film version of *Oliver Twist*. The whole thing made her furious, Monica replied, arguing that you might as well ban *The Merchant of Venice* because of Shylock. Jewish Americans disagreed, however, and the film was not shown in the States until 1951, and only then with cuts to Fagin's role. Of David Lean's *Great Expectations*, Monica in 1947 had confidently announced that Dickens would have loved it.

Monica greatly enjoyed herself on the visit, just as she had done in 1935 but even more so because this time she was a real celebrity:

I found it very exciting. It represented excitement to me, because when I came I was somebody special, and everybody was interested in the name of Dickens, and so I was here as somebody with a 'name', living in hotels and having parties given for me...

(Monica Dickens, *American Mosaic*, 1980)

She appeared in various bookstores to sign her works, sometimes mistaken for a representative of Charles Dickens rather than a descendant and herself a famous author – on one occasion being asked to sign a copy of *David Copperfield*. 'Are you *really* William Shakespeare's granddaughter?' asked someone else. In New York she wandered alone around the city talking to strangers. There were intriguing new plays to go to such as Tennessee Williams' *A Streetcar Named Desire*, which she found 'shattering'. She saw her first game of American football on a barroom TV and was captivated by its marching bands and cheerleaders: the game itself seemed to her less rough than a game of English rugby.

On arrival in New York

'The very attractive great-granddaughter of Charles Dickens', as she was described in the *Princeton Alumni Weekly*, also attended a game of Princeton University football in person as the guest of the Stockton Whites. Staying with her father's old friends at their Philadelphia home Monica was interviewed by the *Philadelphia Inquirer,* mostly on the subject of the Dickensian Christmas. Art collector Samuel Stockton White was heir to a dental manufacturing fortune and, rather surprisingly, the model as a muscled youth for Rodin's statue *The Athlete*; Vera was a water-colourist with a growing reputation. Both were to play an important role in Monica's life at a much later date. Nowhere in the world were women so spontaneously welcoming as in America, a sweet-talking Monica told the paper, and she found it delightful. Her great-grandfather would have liked it, she added, apparently forgetting that Dickens had in fact visited America (and had indeed been impressed by the 'singularly beautiful' ladies of New York and the 'unquestionably' very beautiful ladies of Boston.)

Somewhere on this visit thirty-three-year-old Monica fell in love. According to her memoir she 'found out the man was married' and fled on the next boat home, leaving from Montreal in late November. Her broken heart felt literally broken, Monica wrote in her brief account of this unhappy affair, and for the first two days of the return voyage she sat hunched over as if from an operation, arms wrapped around herself to hold everything together.

123

§

In 1949 came *Flowers on the Grass*, Monica's eighth book in ten years, dedicated to her father Henry. The title is taken from the lyrics of an old song: 'Where my caravan has rested, Flowers I leave you on the grass...'

The hero, insouciant artist Daniel, moves from job to job after a tragedy in his life (inspired by a real-life near tragedy suffered by Doady when evacuated at the start of the war).

Monica had long been fascinated by the idea of alternative realities, the path not taken, and what happens to the alternative self after a choice is made in another direction. Was there some sort of parallel existence alongside the known one, perhaps ahead of reality? Was that why some people and places, seen only tangentially to one's own life, seemed so familiar? A happy atmosphere sensed in a house might be because it *was* that alternative life, not because of whoever lived there, she conjectured. She herself often felt a sense of familiarity with glimpsed places, people fleetingly seen – often the same kind of people and places. She had toyed with the idea of writing a story about a man, perhaps one well-known to the public, suddenly glimpsing from a bus someone ordinary putting his key in the lock of a terraced house – then deciding to get off the bus to start a new life of anonymity, but at the same time familiarity, in that very street. In *Flowers on the Grass*, she makes Daniel feature in a series of stories, in each living a different life in a different setting, a stranger to those around him.

The structure of the book is therefore episodic, a series of vignettes in which Daniel briefly appears and affects the lives of others, not always to their advantage. We never hear anything from Daniel's point of view, only from that of those who encounter him, and through these voices his character slowly builds and develops as he comes to terms with the tragedy he has experienced. The format – one possibly suggested to Monica by the episodic nature of the hugely successful *One Pair of Hands*, and to which she would return more than a few times – afforded her the opportunity to introduce an array of very human characters, still sharply defined by class (even now, as the increasingly democratic twentieth century neared its mid point, Monica continued to label characters 'common'). And each scene – a progressive school, a holiday camp (researched by Monica in person), a hospital ward, a Jewish family home in London – has something to say about the realities of postwar Britain.

Other characters are again mined from Monica's own experience. Daniel as a teenager commits an act of rebellion and is expelled from Eton; a woman sleeps soundly after a homeopathic treatment she believes to be a powerful sedative; a pupil at a school where Daniel is teaching has a crush on him and lies around in wait as Monica had done at St Paul's; a nurse can never forget the mistake she made which resulted in the death of a patient. The penultimate chapter, *The Nurses,* affectionately reprises some of Monica's hospital writing, including a harried Monica-like young nurse deeply in love with her profession. This time, however, Monica documents the changing attitudes within nursing, including a Matron shockingly indifferent to the wearing of cuffs.

Directly influenced by Hinxworth, the opening and closing scenes are set in Monica's own cottage:

There it sat, looking as if it had grown out of the earth instead of being built onto it. The thatch was so thick that you could sit on a bench outside in the rain and not get wet. The wood fires were laid on beds of never-cooling ash inside chimneys as wide as a little room. You could trace the traffic of four hundred years by the places where the red tiles were most worn, and the easiest way to go upstairs was on all fours.

Leaning on the white gate, he would study the way the apricot-coloured walls seemed to diffuse from themselves the soaked light of centuries instead of reflecting today's light from the sun, or how the thatch turned up at the corners like dogs' ears..

(Monica Dickens, *Flowers on the Grass,* 1949)

Just like Monica's, the cottage in *Flowers* has a palpably happy atmosphere, and as the novel begins is the contented setting for Daniel and his wife Jane as they await the birth of their first child. Jane fell in love with Daniel, her cousin, as a child of nine when he was completely oblivious; as in *Mariana*, Monica was again writing of an unrequited passion, beginning in childhood, for an unattainable handsome cousin.

Some reviews focused on the vignette form of the novel and the frustration faced by the reader in becoming interested in one set of characters only to be moved on too quickly to the next. The *Times*

Literary Supplement in their review forgave Monica this neglect of one of the 'elementary rules of story-telling' because she was such a natural writer, able to conjure up a scene by implication. For the *Scotsman* the novel was 'an individual and delightful essay in the picaresque', although noting that her pen had a cutting edge on occasion. The *Illustrated London News* found the final scene, in which Daniel offers a poor young couple his cottage to live in, quaintly Dickensian. (In fact this last scene bids a very moving, almost elegiac farewell to the fictional version of Monica's beautiful cottage: its walls 'the indescribable colour of sunlight', the cobbled path to the door between borders of blue primroses and the evening sun striking the kitchen through the apple tree.)

The Canadian Broadcasting Corporation liked the book so much it considered a series. In America, the renowned thriller writer Patricia Highsmith wrote that Monica relished her assortment of characters as much as her great-grandfather had relished his Wellers and Pecksniffs. She found Daniel absorbing, although less in evidence as the book progressed, almost as if all the other characters had run away with the book (which they tended to do, as Monica herself recognised). Highsmith highly recommended *Flowers* to any of her American readers with the 'taste for or curiosity about that admirable and multifarious people – the English'.

The *New York Times* found the novel briskly entertaining, but without emotion or depth. Describing Monica's books as enormously successful in Britain and only moderately so in America, the review summed up *Flowers* as a series of eleven stories so linked together that they 'nearly make a novel'. Each story was an effective characterisation of an interesting person, the reviewer conceded, but within this collection Monica had chosen, as 'so many women writers do', to produce a series of amiable or admirable women and only specimens of weak or foolish men. Jane, Daniel's wife, is sweetly loving; Valerie is a likeable young widow; Doris, the pathetic chambermaid in a third-rate hotel, is kind and loyal while Mumma the Jewish matriarch loves her family (and Daniel) with a selfless devotion. Compared to such women, the review rightly points out, the men make a very poor showing: Ossie the fat and sentimental buffoon, Geoffrey the selfish epileptic who uses his illness to manipulate his family, and Dickie, the pleasant if sadly self-deluded 'Blue Boy' at a holiday camp. In addition, the *New York Times* concluded, each story was

126

somehow drenched in one prevailing tone: sentiment, pathos, or sometimes satire, as in Monica's account of the progressive school in which Daniel is briefly the art teacher, which for the reviewer degenerated into 'angry farce'. Despite these caustic comments *Flowers* was still summed up as sleek and fun, full of bustling life, the product of a natural story-teller with the sense of humour and considerable literary ability of her great-grandfather.

Australian critics were enthusiastic, the Melbourne *Argus* likening the portrayal of Daniel to Charles Dickens' creation of characters so real they lived alongside readers for the rest of their lives. This was a book of great merit, said the critic: unconnected incidents were gathered up into one clear picture, and there was no delving into the past or Daniel's motivations but simply a statement of what is, revealed through his words and actions. Beautifully constructed; written with a skilful, light touch that was endlessly entertaining, said others. Not likely to appeal to men but women readers should enjoy it, weighed in the *Age* in Melbourne (confirming the suspicion that Australian critics thought Monica Dickens was for girls).

Monica was 'lighter in manner and funnier at times than her great-grandfather', according to the *Times of India*, and, through all her lightness of heart, she cared for humanity and wanted to right its wrongs.

Flowers was novelist Pamela Hansford Johnson's choice for a BBC radio literary programme and the Booker Prize winner A. S. Byatt had a particular liking for the book, especially its first chapter, which finishes with a shocking and completely unexpected turn of events (unfortunately given away in at least three reviews – including the *Scotsman* – without the 'spoiler alert' now common). This, Byatt revealed, became forever printed on her mind by its technical mastery. Writing about it many years later Byatt referred to E. M. Forster's comment that it was an extraordinarily difficult thing to convey the real shock and effects of pure accident in fiction – presumably, said Byatt, because the author cannot help shaping the book towards the disaster which of course he or she knows is coming. To her mind Monica Dickens had solved this problem by allowing her catastrophe to come almost at the very start of the book without hint or premonition. Events are conveyed in two 'precise, perfectly imagined, economical sentences'. Byatt wrote that she always had trouble re-

reading this chapter, which remained forever powerful and dramatically shocking.

When Byatt eventually met Monica, she revealed that she had named one of her own characters Daniel in homage to *Flowers on the Grass*, and in her own much later novel *The Virgin in the Garden*, Byatt in her acknowledgments expressed her gratitude to Monica for 'a matter of plotting about which she knows'.

§

As time went by at Hinxworth Monica became fascinated by the local newspaper, the *Hertfordshire Express*, which now that she was a local herself she found gripping for its coverage of fêtes and Water Board meetings. She likely had fond memories of meeting her first journalists at the *Sunday Chronicle* in the late 1930s, with their disordered desks and easy-going transatlantic calls, and perhaps wanted to be one of them. Once again she felt drawn towards taking a job, Monica wrote in *An Open Book*, although in fact she maintained in a much later interview that her interest in a job on a newspaper was actually for research purposes – the first time that she had done so. She approached the *Express* editor at the paper's office in Hitchin (where coincidentally Charles Dickens' oldest granddaughter Mary Angela Dickens, also a writer, once lived and is now buried), and asked to be taken on as a reporter. The paper had never had a female reporter before but the editor, described by Monica in her memoir as cultured and whimsical, decided to take a chance, no doubt intrigued by this offer from a world-famous novelist living on his doorstep. She joined the grubby, untidy office of four unimpressed male reporters who had only one typewriter between them, and was started at the very bottom 'endlessly and tediously' correcting proofs and filling inkwells. She performed other lowly tasks too, like washing up the cracked cups and going out for buns – and making the tea.

After a while permission came for her to revise the badly written announcements and births, deaths and marriages notices, and to rewrite the confused accounts of darts matches and club meetings submitted by local correspondents from the surrounding small towns and villages. Then she was sent out to cover minor events like fêtes and cookery demonstrations, and worked her way through heady stories of new traffic lights and speeches by Council candidates until at last she was allowed to accompany one of the other reporters to learn Court reporting at Sessions and Assizes in Hertford. Once permitted to cover Petty Sessions on her own, Monica attempted to make human interest stories out of the slowly paced proceedings but found her efforts reformatted by the editor to conform to the *Herts Express* standard, which in her opinion made every case come out sounding exactly the same.

As a more seasoned reporter Monica rang around the hospitals once a week to see who had died, interviewed the grieving relatives, and covered football matches, hunt meets, horse shows and amateur theatricals. She rewrote material filched from other newspapers, invented competitions for the Children's Corner and produced reviews of films showing in the local cinema without having seen them. On press days she stayed late to check the proofs one last time and was proud to be the one putting the paper to bed, as the phrase went, although she knew she was only allowed to do it because the others wanted to get home. She felt as if she had produced the whole paper single-handedly, and took her fresh damp copy home to read from cover to cover.

Working on the paper taught her a tremendous amount about writing to a deadline, Monica later observed. She learned how to sit down and write, how to turn it on and cover any subject. In her view everyone who wanted to write needed a stint as a reporter.

She left after several months to write a book about working on a small-town newspaper, disguising it as the *Downingham Post* because she lived in the area. She also deliberately mixed in some fiction with the facts in case people had had their fill of her autobiographical efforts.

My Turn to Make the Tea, originally titled *Slaves of the Lamp*, was published in 1951. There is plenty of authentic detail about life on a provincial newspaper, but the fictional element looms large and it is certainly the least autobiographical of Monica's three 'I' books: in only the first two does she firmly identify herself as Monica Dickens. The 'I' of this book, nicknamed Poppy by her fellow reporters after a blonde cartoon character, is never so identified, although Monica may be faintly hinting when at one point Poppy talks about going back to being a cook. The tone is moreover subtly different, still chatty in style but somehow less personal and believable as a possibly real account.

This 'I' is a young woman living in unpleasant digs in the invented town of Downingham, not a world-famous novelist with her own charming cottage who has taken the job for research. The novel is plotless, a series of amusing scenes reliant for their comedy on the gallery of sub-Dickensian grotesques Poppy encounters at work and round the town, as in this description of the Dame in a pantomime:

We were now in Mother Goose's kitchen, and here is Mother Goose herself in the person of a thin but padded man with a lascivious mouth and bolting eyes, wearing the voluminous, oft-lifted skirts, striped football jersey and red tow top-knot, which showed he was the Dame. I had last seen him singing dirty songs in a London night club, and now here he was to bring joy to the hearts of the kiddies, and the best one could hope for was that they would not understand his jokes.

(Monica Dickens, *My Turn to Make the Tea*, 1951)

The editor in *My Turn to Make the Tea* is not the cultured chance-taker of the real-life *Hertfordshire Express,* but instead a bullish old diehard who scores his pencil through all Poppy's original adjectives and replaces them with standard ones; in Poppy's eyes he seems more like a man who prods pigs with a stick on market day than an editor. Her fellow reporters are a sad bunch of losers who spend their time avoiding the more boring reporting jobs and demanding cups of tea from Poppy. (The joke in the title, of course, is that since she is the only girl in the office it is always her turn to make the tea.) The book later came in for some feminist comment when it was pointed out that Poppy, although apparently a better writer than her male colleagues, simply accepts the fact that she is never given the serious assignments and that her work is never allowed to stand uncorrected. Eventually sacked for trying to prevent a story being printed that would ruin a friend's career, she meekly agrees with the editor that women are a nuisance in an office and goes quietly.

To promote her ninth work Monica appeared on BBC radio's *In Town Tonight* and during the interview talked about her many previous jobs, mentioning her time in the book department of a West End store, where, she joked, she mainly tried to sell her own works. She recalled that people were very vague about what they wanted to read, which she believed came in part from the dearth of book reviewing in provincial newspapers because of the continuing newsprint shortage. But now her own book found an avid readership. *My Turn to Make the Tea* was greeted as a brilliantly accurate representation of life on a small provincial weekly and was relished by budding young reporters such as Bill Hagerty, later to become Acting Editor of the *Daily Mirror* and Chairman of the *British Journalism Review*, who felt strongly drawn to the profession by Monica's fun-filled descriptions of reporting fêtes and magistrates' courts. He subsequently realised that it was obviously part-fictionalised, and indeed on re-reading it as a mature adult saw that it actually made life on a small-town newspaper sound hideous, though accurate in its depiction of the press and machine rooms of the era. How the book had managed to enthuse him and his fellow trainee reporters he was unable to imagine, but in his opinion it had fired the ambition of a generation longing for Fleet Street. The *Times of India* agreed that she had made it sound terrible: 'Miss Dickens does not seem to have liked anyone or anything connected with journalism.' Nevertheless, the book remained popular with would-be journalists well into this century: in 2015, Twitter followers of the *Press Gazette* voted *My Turn to Make the Tea* onto a list of the thirty best books about journalism.

As with Monica's first two semi-autobiographical works readers tended to think *My Turn to Make the Tea* was the gospel truth, although most reviewers saw it for what it was. The *Times Literary Supplement*, for one, suspected fictionalising in that Poppy's landlady and fellow lodgers were so 'entirely novelist's characters', yet still enjoyed the book for its wit and good humour. The *Observer* easily detected the novelisation but wrote that it was 'Vivacious...wherever her eye falls, it finds the exact, significant detail, and her ear for dialogue is unerring...All in all, Miss Dickens is bringing the word 'Dickensian' up to date.' The author had undoubtedly worked for an old-fashioned weekly, commented the lefty *Daily Worker*, continuing pedantically that Miss Dickens should remember that a printer does not screw down but lock up a forme of type; otherwise, full marks – if readers were not looking for anything beneath the surface.

The book does not appear to have made much of an impression in the US (perhaps too British) but in Australia it was variously greeted as both 'witty and sparkling', and a 'type of small talk' that was 'no worse than numerous others of the same ilk'. But in the UK *My Turn To Make The Tea* remained a popular read for decades and as late as 2004 a BBC Radio 4 series was based on the book and was repeated a few years later. Broadcaster Libby Purves included it with *One Pair of Hands* and *One Pair of Feet* as Monica's 'masterworks': small classics, loved and recognised by women like herself half a century younger than Monica, and by their children in turn. All three were vivid and truthful glimpses of a lost world, wrote Purves, but were in no way period curiosities. These were books instantly recognisable by anyone who had ever slaved in a dead-end job because they reproduced the sense of apprenticeship and 'larky comradeship' of the novice and the downtrodden. 'What tyro, in any field, will not cringe in happy recognition of the snubs and errors of her cub reporter?' she asked.

According to a journalist from the *Hertfordshire Express* Monica based her main characters on only thinly disguised actual members of staff. Some of them had not been amused. After the book came out Monica sent copies to the whimsical editor, who thanked her in his cultivated way, and to a reporter she had been friendly with. He did not respond and Monica misguidedly rang him up for his reaction. 'I read some of it,' he replied, 'and thought it was silly.'

Roy

On 10 January 1951 Monica was a guest on BBC radio's *Desert Island Discs*. Host Roy Plomley described Monica for his radio audience as looking like 'a rather intellectual film star' and listed her hobbies as riding and caring for horses, reading and drinking tea in the bath, and doing housework at three in the morning. Monica appeared nervous and worried that the programme would give away rather too much of her character; that was the idea, Plomley responded. She announced apologetically at the start that nearly all of her eight choices of record were sad and nostalgic, but if she had to be sad and lonely on a desert island she might as well enjoy it by having a 'good old sentimental wallow and a lovely cry now and then'.

Not all were sad: she selected a light dance tune, a Christmas carol, some ballet music, a recording of Noel Coward dialogue. Others were, as Monica warned, downright tearjerkers: *The Kerry Dance*, which she admitted made her cry even when she was feeling perfectly happy, so she would 'simply howl' if she heard it when sad and lonely; the French love song *Plaisir d'Amour*, because it was 'beautiful, and sad, and harps on the exquisite note of happy things that are gone forever'; and *Just One of Those Things*, a song that for Monica forever captured the romance that did not quite happen, the wonderful moment that *was* only a moment. Your heart seemed broken, she went on, but with a song like this as background it became almost enjoyable.

Another choice was *Have I Told You Lately That I Love You?*, sung by Gene Autry. In the romantic tropical setting it would be nice to have a man about the place, Monica felt, and by getting the singing cowboy every so often to tell her that he loved her, she could enjoy the illusion of having one.

§

Just as her sad and yearning record choices suggested, Monica was at a low ebb. She was now thirty-six, still single, very handsome with her slender figure and curly fair hair, and a hugely successful author. Nevertheless, despite her achievements and celebrity, Monica's self-esteem was fragile. People could still make her feel inferior and she was easily upset by the occasional rude letter from a reader.

Although continuing to enjoy her cottage in the country Monica had recently made some 'mistakes', as she put it in *An Open Book*, without going into detail. Then suddenly everything seemed to go wrong at once, as if telling her she needed to steer her life in a new direction. One by one her animals died, almost as though deciding they no longer wanted to be with her. A cat was killed falling out of a tree; her dog Joe became ill and died of heart failure, and Monica castigated herself for failing to recognise how sick he was. Her thoroughbred horse broke a leg when she scrambled him up a bank whilst out hunting, and had to be put down. The horse's death revealed to Monica the barbarity of hunting and the cruelty to the fox. It finished hunting for her forever.

She acquired another horse and another dog, and there were other cats, but Monica continued to feel depressed and guilty. Her writing appeared not at its best; she knew too that she had become set in her ways and dictatorial with guests at the cottage. She thought no one loved her.

After previous love affairs Monica was wary, perhaps made circumspect by what sounded like personal experience of the human capacity for self-delusion. In her *Monica Dickens' Book Club* radio series in 1950 she had talked of the ease with which people imagine themselves enamoured, usually with quite the wrong man, merely for the sake of being in love:

You imagine his face so much as your romantic heart wants it to be that it's quite a shock when you do see him and he's all knobbly and wearing the wrong sort of hat. You plan a delightful ardent conversation that never comes off, because he talks all the time about a football match. In your mind, you even write letters to your friends telling them you're engaged. Over and over again you imagine him saying 'I love you' but he never does. If you risk saying it yourself, partly as an experiment to see if it will help along your illusion of romance, it's always a terrible flop and ruins everything.

(Monica Dickens, *Monica Dickens' Book Club*, BBC, 1950)

There had been what she called 'failed attempts' at marrying, perhaps including the man mentioned in her memoir who eventually wearied of calling for Monica at number 52. Everybody who had appeared on the scene expected her to give up writing after marriage; according to Monica's own account she had turned down 'various people' who saw her writing as something she did to fill in time, rather than the most important thing in her life. One man she reported as saying, 'You'll give up all this writing – it will be wonderful, we'll have people in for drinks every night.' Monica knew that if men did not love her as a writer, then they did not really know her at all, and she withdrew. Now her single status was a source of great anxiety: she felt a dread of becoming the type of leathery, horsy old aunt whom parents insisted their adult children go and visit because she had been so good to them when they were young. She could see herself churning out the 'same kind of novel' every two years and telling disbelieving acquaintances that she used to be famous.

That June, boarding a small plane home from Glasgow after seeing the first night of a stage performance of *The Happy Prisoner*, Monica found a seat by the window and was pleased when no one sat down beside her. She was tired, and felt stale and unkempt after her busy day. Armed with the Sunday papers, she only wanted to read and sleep.

The plane was late taking off and at the last minute a passenger boarded and took the only remaining place, the seat next to Monica, and politely introduced himself: Roy Stratton, a Commander in the American navy. In traditional American fashion he then proceeded to pepper Monica with questions about where she was from and what was the population of the towns they were flying over (Monica was to joke that one of his queries was 'Is it true that of 25,000,000 Englishmen, eight and three-quarter thousand are in mental hospitals?'). She answered only in ungracious grunts until she got a good look at him as he stood up after they had landed: he was some years older than she was, solidly built and ruggedly handsome. Monica was moved to offer him a lift to London in the car that was meeting her.

This was the usual account Monica gave of her first meeting with Roy; in others, she related that the flight passed in silence. In any event, shortly thereafter Monica, generally a reluctant clothes shopper, went out to buy some 'dazzling dresses'. A whirlwind courtship had begun.

Roy, for his part, had gone into a bookshop to check out Monica's claim to be a writer and was amazed to find pictures of his attractive new acquaintance on copies of her many novels prominently on display. (In one version of the story he promptly bought a copy of every single one.) Roy was then fifty, with two grown sons from a previous marriage. Born in Indiana, he had enjoyed a happy childhood picnicking, bicycling and fishing with his father before these idyllic years came to an abrupt ending when his father committed suicide. Roy's parents had married when his pregnant mother was only a teenager, and the relationship had ultimately foundered; his alcoholic father became subject to bouts of depression and killed himself by drinking a mixture of carbolic acid and beer. He left only a short note: 'Take care of my son.'

Roy, aged only thirteen, had loved his father deeply. He continued his schooling, learned to play the piano, dabbled at writing short stories, and determined to make his mark in the world – how, he did not quite know, just as Monica had felt as a young woman. In 1916, at the age of sixteen, Roy told his mother he was going out for a walk and together with two friends he jumped a freight train to Ohio, intent on discovering the world outside Indiana. His mother did not see him again for three months. The boys were soon caught by the railway police but Roy escaped, and jumped another train headed for Florida. Finding a clerking job in Jacksonville, he lived at the YMCA and would wander down to the river at weekends to watch the boats and talk

to the US Navy sailors he encountered there. One day he was approached by a recruitment officer who had heard of his interest in the navy, and Roy being underage at only seventeen, the officer found a convenient tramp willing to sign the forms as Roy's supposed father. He was sworn in and three days later the US declared war on Germany. Roy's long and exciting career in the navy had begun.

During World War I Roy served in the European theatre aboard various destroyers; post war he took part in the joint US-British expedition in support of the anti-revolutionary White Russians at Vladivostok in 1919, and was with US naval forces on duty patrol in Mexican waters during an outbreak of bubonic plague in Vera Cruz. Born with a head for detail, Roy was put to administrative work and in 1930 he was appointed to pay clerk after coming top in the relevant examination. As he made his way up the ladder Roy had a number of adventures during his foreign postings, including a friendship with the future Vietnamese leader Ho Chi Minh when Ho was still a struggling young Communist rebel. During the Second World War he was involved in a top secret network of US military personnel and local resistance operating deep in Japanese-occupied China, called the Sino-American Cooperative Organization (SACO). Roy was paymaster to both the 3,000 Americans and the 100,000 Chinese guerrillas and coastal pirates operating together to undermine their Japanese foe by destroying supply depots and blowing up bridges. However, he was more than a mere administrator – the enemy put a price on his head. Roy entered Shanghai as a wanted man only minutes after the end of the war when the Japanese soldiers mounting machine-guns at every corner were quite possibly unaware of the cessation of hostilities. Rendering his situation even more dangerous, his jeep was loaded with cash, a million US dollars and a billion in Chinese currency. Fortunately, he was well protected by Chinese guards and survived unscathed.

Roy also played an important role in preparations for the Normandy invasion of 1944. He retired in 1948 and became a corporate secretary at an independent boys' school in New York, but was called out of retirement in January 1951 for his current mission to Europe analysing the supply systems of the British and German navies.

Roy was musical but, more importantly, was another writer. In 1950, during his short period in retirement, he had published *SACO – The Rice Paddy Navy,* a true account of the secret network's activities in China. He had also written freelance for newspapers and magazines, and when he met Monica he was penning his reports on European navies. Most of his writing output had constituted non-fiction, but Roy being a writer of any ilk was likely a bond for Monica, after former prospective partners had expected her to jettison this critical element of her life.

He was a widower, and twice married. Roy had adopted his first wife Esther's son Donald and the couple then had a son of their own, Roy Junior; in 1937 both boys witnessed the Hindenburg disaster when the family were living in naval quarters close by – young Donald ran to help survivors and was awarded the Navy Civilian Medal for his efforts. Roy's marriage to Esther ended in divorce in 1939 or 1940. Three months after the divorce he married newspaper feature writer Arlene Fleming.

When Roy met Monica on the plane in June 1951 he had just lost his second wife – literally. Arlene had accompanied Roy to England but died suddenly in May of a cerebral haemorrhage; her body was flown home and buried in Arlington National Cemetery in the nation's capital. Monica in *An Open Book* makes no mention of Roy's first and second wives, or of this startlingly recent bereavement only one month before the beginning of their relationship.

§

This was not the first occasion that Monica had felt deeply for someone. She had suffered the painful episode during her 1948 visit to America, falling in love with a married man and jumping on the first boat home to nurse her wounds.

But Monica revealed in her old age that another early love affair had also involved a married man (apparently not always the deal-breaker suggested above) and had been 'one of my first sexual encounters', despite her warnings to *Woman's Own* readers not to go all the way. The affair had been marred by Catholic guilt and Monica's lover accused her of holding back. He was amused to hear her reply that it was a sin.

He laughed. And then he proceeded, during the rest of the affair, to show me why sex is not a sin. I'll be ever grateful to him. He was married but it was all gloriously romantic. We met in dark cafés and that appealed to my sense of drama. Then a cryptic telephone message and we met for a weekend in Cannes. There should be no guilt in life. Life is a short phase, a part of a much bigger journey.

(Monica Dickens, interview, *The Boston Globe*, 1985)

Now, encountering Roy 'like a knight on a white horse', Monica knew she had found her true soul mate. Had she not been to see that dramatisation of her novel *The Happy Prisoner* in Glasgow, they would never have met. They liked each other immediately and decided to marry 'rather quickly' (becoming engaged on their first date, according to one account she gave). He was an unfamiliar type to Monica, with an intriguingly different background to her own, and no New York sophisticate, as she clearly recognised: rather, he was more real and down-to-earth than many other people she knew. Roy was just as enraptured, and wrote an excited letter about Monica to his adult son Roy Junior back in the States. And, unlike previous amours, Roy was delighted that Monica was a writer and would never have thought of asking her to give it up:

> *He was also the first person who ever said, 'I'll do everything I can to further your career and help you, because I'm very proud of what you've done and I want you to do better.'*

(Monica Dickens, *American Mosaic*, 1980)

Monica took Roy to meet Fanny and Henry at number 52, having previously kept his existence quiet: she knew all the gossip that flew around the family grapevine if she mentioned her men friends. Doady advised her to take Roy home when Henry had already had his dinner, so that his mind would not be on it. Monica remembered sadly how, when the terrible news of her brother Bunny's death came in 1936, Henry in a state of shock had wandered around the house in the midst of all the grieving relatives, asking why dinner was so late.

Monica's ever kindly parents were more concerned about what Roy might think of them than the other way round, and to meet his prospective son-in-law Henry dressed up in his old Trinity Hall blazer from Cambridge and his MCC cricket tie, faded from travel and stained with pipe ash and spilled soup. Monica had already broken the news that they were going to be married, and that she was leaving the country – she was in love and would have followed Roy anywhere, she admitted. Luckily the family liked Roy and were pleased to get her off their hands, Monica joked years later. (She noted too that in that period of continued rationing Roy had the added attraction of access to luxuries like Campbell's Soup, Mars Bars and American mayonnaise.)

Monica's friends, on the other hand, many of whom had married a great deal earlier and some of whom were now divorcing, were shocked at the idea of Monica wedding an American and warned against the perils of living in such an outlandish place. A few attacked Roy on the subject of American foreign policy and other matters for which Roy was hardly responsible, even before they offered congratulations on the engagement.

At Hinxworth, Roy's first taste of English village life was sitting in a car in the rain watching the village cricket team play Monica's team of family and friends in between downpours. His second was the Ashwell Horse Show in August, also mired in torrents of rain, where Roy with his Supply Corps skills spent the day in a tent straightening out treasurer Monica's confused handling of the show's finances, and counting the pennies collected from onlookers at the dressage display. A newspaper photo of the event showed a beamingly happy Monica, in fifties-style ankle socks and sensible shoes, fair hair fluffed around her face, holding the bridle of her niece Mary's horse. 'Rains spoiled a most attractive programme,' ran the caption.

One Sunday lunch with Monica's friends at the cottage, Roy was horrified when Monica shouted at a guest who had lit up a cigarette; she had been right about her own increasing crankiness. Roy took her outside, walked her up and down the lane and told her she could not talk to her guests like that. A chastened Monica took his advice and started making an effort to be more polite.

Being on active duty Roy was not permitted to marry outside America, although at one point they did try to get hitched after an excellent lunch while on a trip to France. As only Monica spoke French and Roy could do no more than beam and nod, the Mayor of Beauvais decided it was entrapment and refused to allow the marriage. When Roy eventually had to return to the US they decided that Monica would sail after him for a wedding on the other side of the Atlantic. She needed time to sell the cottage and her car and also had to obtain a permanent immigrant visa, a long and difficult process. Hinxworth was very hard to leave but the fact that she was able to do so convinced Monica, if she needed convincing, that the decision to marry Roy was the right one.

Her niece's and nephews' ponies had been kept at the cottage stables and arrangements were now made to keep them elsewhere. Taking their horsy cottage holidays away from the children seemed like a betrayal and for Monica at their age it would have been a tragedy, as she well knew. To quell the guilt, she played in her mind the far worse vision of the children as adults being reminded to visit old 'Mont' not because she had been so good to them, but because she had given up so much for them.

The cottage was too far from London for weekenders and proved hard to shift. Monica took a heavy loss when she sold. (For sale again in 1990, the cottage's previous ownership was still a selling point, with *Country Life* describing it as the idyllic Grade II-listed former home of Monica Dickens. For her part, Monica never forgot Hinxworth. Decades later, in 1982, she spoke on BBC radio to appeal for funds to restore the village church.)

Notice of the engagement appeared in the *Times* on 16 November 1951 and on the last day of that month Monica set sail on the *SS Mauretania*, alone, to her wedding in America. At Southampton before the ship departed, friends and family crowded into her cabin, 'with flowers and love and tears'. Being a celebrity she was seated at the Captain's table, the centre of attention as an imminent bride. Film stars Laurence Olivier and Vivien Leigh were fellow passengers, on their way to play Caesar and Cleopatra in the US with twenty-seven tons of scenery.

As the *Mauretania* sailed into New York Monica hung over the rail, flanked by two stewardess friends eager to see her intended.

...and there was Roy, standing alone on the end of the Cunard pier.

(Monica Dickens, *Christian Science Monitor*, 1986)

'Off the shelf at last at thirty-six,' as Monica put it. A new life was dawning, one that must have presented at least some doubts. As she wrote in a later article on wives who choose to make a life abroad with their husbands, she had a great admiration for those courageous women who think the world well lost for love:

You have to be absolutely sure that you love the man for whom you are going to give up so much. You have to be certain that he will be able to make up to you for the loss of all the familiar faces and places. You have to know this before you go, because it's too late to find out afterwards. There can be no running home to mother from a distance of three thousand miles or more.

(Monica Dickens, *The World Well Lost*, The Woman's Own Book of Pleasure, 1957)

Navy Wife

In *An Open Book* Monica presented herself as a mature GI bride 'venturing' into the New World for love, and getting a shock from the ugliness of the alien landscape. The journey south from the New York docks with Roy the day she arrived was disturbing, she wrote. In reality it was far from Monica's first visit: she had thoroughly enjoyed the social whirl in New York with Henry in 1935 and again on her trip in 1948 as an established writer. On each of these occasions Monica had travelled beyond the city of New York, so that on arriving in 1951 she would already have been fully acquainted with both the uglinesses and beauties of the New World.

On those previous visits she had been fêted: everyone was interested in the Dickens name and she had been a celebrity living in hotels and the guest of honour at parties. To Monica, America was excitement. She had not thought of it as a place where people really lived, more as somewhere to go for fun. Now no longer merely a curious and excited visitor but on the verge of being a permanent resident, Monica professed to feel a deep dismay. Her horror at the dumps and oil tanks flying past her window was amplified by the terror she felt at the prospect of marriage after her decades of independence.

The wedding took place on the afternoon of 7 December 1951, the day after her arrival, in the rectory of St Paul's Church in Princeton, New Jersey, where Roy had a number of friends. Because Roy was not a Roman Catholic the marriage could not take place in the church proper, but the Catholic chaplain from Princeton University had agreed to perform the ceremony in the vestry. Roy looked very handsome in full naval uniform, and the bride, carrying brown orchids and wearing a toast-coloured suit and veiled brown velvet hat, was given away by her father's old Cambridge friend Sam Stockton White.

The matron-of-honour and best man were Roy's friends and completely unknown to Monica; the bride's entire party consisted of the Stockton Whites up from Philadelphia, two other old friends of her parents and a photographer from *Woman's Own*. The magazine had naturally run a feature on her engagement and now wanted to make the most of the wedding. The reception afterwards was at the home of the best man, and he and his wife subsequently hosted a dinner in honour of the happy couple and also in honour of another guest, the very distinguished Rear Admiral Miles and his wife. Miles had been joint head of the SACO operation in China and was to write his own book on the subject, giving full credit to Roy for his earlier account.

After a New England honeymoon the newly-weds settled into a tiny home in historic Georgetown in Washington DC, a charming area of old wooden houses and red brick pavements. (A charm Monica took entirely for granted: only later did she learn of the 'anxious finagling' Roy had undergone to find a rental in such a desirable place.) Their little home was just one room wide all the way through, bordered on one side by an alley and on the other by a junkyard where Monica in her memoir mentioned making her first black friends.

Washington seemed unreal. Life as a wife began as a succession of parties for Roy's friends to welcome the new bride, and initially Monica enjoyed it all. With her big American refrigerator and dishwasher, housekeeping was a lot more convenient than it had been at home, and coming from Britain where food rationing was still in force she was overwhelmed by the choice in the supermarkets and splurged on food as if starving. After listening to the afternoon soap operas on the radio and being taken in by the adverts she would buy three types of floor cleaner for their tiny kitchen. Outside the home, she worked out how to move around the city on public transport or in Roy's car and eagerly explored Washington's museums, art galleries and department stores.

Gradually the initial excitement abated and Monica was home alone for most of the day, for the first time in her life a wife with a husband leaving each morning and coming home at the same hour each evening. She thought she was ready to be a housewife and to 'do all those conventional things', and was determined to show that Englishwomen were better at it than Americans: she washed and ironed all Roy's shirts herself and polished his shoes and cleaned the silver once a week to demonstrate English superiority. Listening to the soap operas as she ironed made a change from her usual work, and she did no writing. Rather than establishing a life of her own Monica wanted to adapt to being a wife (or the 1950s conception of being a wife), and seemingly to follow the strictures she was laying down in *Woman's Own*.

But of course it did not work out like that. Monica soon became 'pretty miserable' and realised that she was merely playing a part. Just being an ordinary housewife was never going to be enough for her, she finally acknowledged. Her first solution was to try and find work, applying for jobs like dentist's receptionist, but was told that she had the wrong type of visa. Then Roy, in Monica's words the unstuffiest of men, suddenly delivered the startling news that officers' wives did not work. This meant that she could have no income of her own, as it was not immediately possible to get at her money in England and at that time American banks did not provide overdrafts.

She was homesick, and feeling emotional. Compounding her misery Monica also spent hours comparing the differences between America and England, arguing with Roy about pronunciation and use of words, searching for likenesses to England and being critical where they were lacking. (Perhaps she echoed Dickens' sentiments on living in America: an excellent place to make money 'but blow the United States to 'tarnal smash as an Englishman's place of residence'.) Only after several years did Monica recognise how ridiculous it was, within a transatlantic marriage, to criticise the other country's ways: the native person always became defensive even if in agreement.

I took for granted, in my dumb, insular way, that how the British said and did things was right, and it took me much too long to admit that there was no right or wrong, only different.

(Monica Dickens, *Christian Science Monitor*, 1986)

But the worst aspect of Monica's new life were the social duties incumbent upon her as the wife of an American naval officer, which included an outmoded observance of customs long gone in Britain. She was to muse that she seemed fated to find herself in rigidly conventional and proper surroundings – first as a debutante, then as a nurse, and finally as a navy wife in America. Subordinate officers' wives could not sit down before the Admiral's wife did, for instance, or leave an event before she left. As their Admiral's wife was an alcoholic who, in Monica's words, never left until she was carried out feet first at midnight, this proved rather trying. Other wives could be quite snooty, asking what academy Roy had attended, and Monica would have to admit that he had come up through the ranks.

There was in addition the paying of calls. She would be happily painting a ceiling or in bed on a Sunday afternoon when a knock at the door would reveal a Captain and his wife, in full rig, expecting to be given tea.

Infinitely worse was that Monica in her turn was expected to pay unannounced calls on the wives of senior officers, which she described as 'death to a British soul'. She tried refusing but Roy was adamant that it must be done. Monica recalled the advice she had given in her *Woman's Own* columns, years before she was married, instructing her readers how to keep their husband happy by compromising and coming at things from the sides rather than confronting head-on. She now took her own advice by ringing up some wife she was supposed to call on and hanging up if the woman answered; if there was no response, she would rush round to the house and thrust her visiting card through the letter box with a scribbled apology, which counted as having made the call.

Another significant torture was the mandatory lunch at the Officers' Wives Club. A number of the younger wives, under the impression it mattered to their husbands' careers, would buy outfits they could not afford, lacquer their hair to a hard finish and hire a babysitter. This time disregarding her own advice in

145

Woman's Own Monica totally refused to go, but eventually backed down on the pleas of a likeable Admiral's wife. It was worse than she anticipated. She was the only one without a hat, and the zip on the back of her dress was undone. New wives were obliged to stand up and stay standing until they were introduced, which meant that as her surname began with a letter towards the end of the alphabet Monica had to stand for a lengthy period with what seemed like all eyes upon her. If someone was introduced as a new bride, all eyes immediately fixed on the poor woman's stomach to see if she was pregnant. The food was awful and after the meal everyone had to sit through the Vice-President's slides of her trip to Ancient Greece and instructions from a Charm School director on how to lock the hips and raise the bust. When Roy came home, Monica cried.

Cocktail parties were less awful because she went with Roy, but they were all identical. In the US Navy everyone socialised within their own department, so everywhere she went Monica met the same crowd from the Bureau of Supplies and Accounts where Roy worked, and then had to invite them to their own events. When it was her turn to entertain she first had thoughts of offering British food – sausage rolls and cheese straws – but like a coward ended up serving turkey and ham just like everyone else. Despite her experience as a cook Monica could not match the self-assured American women, who seemed to produce beautiful food without effort and without dashing in and out of the kitchen with a red face as she did. Such women tended to intimidate her, except one of these capable hostesses who confided in Monica that all the entertaining and looking perfect was driving her to the edge of a nervous breakdown.

Monica knew she was just not right for that milieu:

I couldn't appear looking svelte and gracious in the living room, and I found that a little hard to cope with. And I didn't have the right kind of small talk. If I had any sophistication, it wasn't in that style. So I felt a little lost and out of place. Well, I've never been very good at just sitting and chatting, doing what Americans call 'visiting', doing things like going to the Officers' Wives Club. I'd never been in great big groups of women like that, all wearing hats. I'd never been into that sort of artificial life. My manners were wrong...

(Monica Dickens, *American Mosaic*, 1980)

She began to worry about what she had lost in coming to America, and who she was turning into. She had enjoyed great popularity in England, where everybody knew her wherever she went because she had been in the press and on television and generally around, and this she had liked. *Woman's Own*, in particular, had increased her visibility to the point where fans would come up and chat in shops. Thousands had written to congratulate her on her marriage. Now she envisioned sinking back into obscurity. On one occasion, on a night out to a restaurant and the theatre with friends of Roy's, Monica was introduced to a journalist and could tell from the woman's blank face that the name meant nothing. 'In my conceited way, I felt very hurt.' It was hitting home that nobody knew who she was, and that she had lost the entrée bestowed by being a celebrity. She had built up a name for herself from that long ago need, which she had experienced even as a child, to be famous, and now it seemed the fame was slipping away. An article was turned down by a Sunday paper. It appeared that in the US she was unknown as a writer, Monica was to say in *An Open Book* (despite the fact that her books had usually sold respectably there, if not to the same extent as in Britain, and had been favourably reviewed. Her marriage to Roy had also been widely reported in the American press). Monica felt lost and unwanted. Trying to adjust to marriage at thirty-six was difficult enough, but trying to do so in a foreign country was 'precarious'.

There were patches of sunlight in the general gloom. In February 1952 Monica spent a weekend with her friends the Stockton Whites in Philadelphia before the couple boarded a liner for a long tour of South America. Later that same year she was evidently being recognised in Washington as at least some kind of celebrity when she spoke at a YWCA event on the subject *From English Woman to American Wife*. The occasion was a luncheon arranged by the YWCA World Fellowship Committee, chaired by the wife of Roy's former superior and old China hand Rear Admiral Miles (who had perhaps brought her influence to bear).

And, give or take the occasional problem, Monica was happy with Roy and found America tremendously stimulating, despite its strangeness to one so quintessentially English. In subsequent years she was to look back and recognise what a great deal she learned when she married an American, including how to be truly hospitable, which she admitted she had not known previously.

Being in America helped her understand how to make friends quickly, and how to be less cagey and more open.

§

As difficult as her early life in America was, Monica began to wonder what it would be like if, instead of the kind and sympathetic Roy, she had married someone selfish and pompous whom she should never have married in the first place. Solving the problem of what to do all day, she began to write again in earnest.

No More Meadows, published in the US as *The Nightingales Are Singing*, came out in 1953. The English title came from the dismal Robert Louis Stevenson quote that 'Times are changed with him who marries; there are no more bypath-meadows, where you may innocently linger, but the road lies long and straight and dusty to the grave.'

The plot, inevitably, concerns an English innocent in her thirties who gets engaged to an American naval officer stationed in England and then goes to the US to marry him. Her bridegroom-to-be Vinson Gaegler is nothing like Roy: small, purse-lipped, and humourless. He does not fit into the English scene: his clothes are all wrong (always an important factor in choice of men for Monica) and the heroine, Christine, is embarrassed by him but agrees to marry when her life appears suddenly empty.

As ever, there are more than a few slices of Monica's own life in the book: as a young woman Christine feels too fat when she goes to Oxford dances and parties; she trains as a nurse; and she sails to her wedding alone on an ocean liner and is married the very next day, knowing none of Vinson's friends at the ceremony. (In a reverse of Monica's situation, the wedding cannot be held in the main part of the church because Vinson is a Catholic and his bride is not.) Christine is overwhelmed by the choice in the supermarkets and bored at home all day but resistant to the social duties required of a US naval officer's wife, which include the appalling ordeal of the stand-up introduction at a wives' luncheon:

What could one do? Where could one look? Christine put her hands behind her back, realising too late that this made her chest stick out too far, and fixed her eyes on a ventilator high up in the wall, while female stares stabbed her like darts from all over the room, and she imagined that she could hear whisperings from three hundred female tongues about this phenomenon who was a bride, and who came from London, England, and who had not got a hat. Were they asking each other if she was pregnant?

(Monica Dickens, *No More Meadows*, 1953)

Again just like Monica, Christine rings up to see if an Admiral and his wife are at home before dashing round to leave a calling card when nobody answers.

The book is distinctive too in that for the first time Monica is franker on the subject of sex. Christine has had a previous lover and admits to feeling the need of a man, and does eventually feel desire for Vinson during their honeymoon. When she and Vinson run into trouble with their marriage, Christine has an affair – a situation which is resolved rather too neatly – but the novel nevertheless ends optimistically, leaving Christine and Vinson with a real hope of papering over the cracks and making a go of their transatlantic union.

Back in Britain *No More Meadows* was serialised on the BBC's *Woman's Hour*. For the *Times Literary Supplement* the work was deceptively akin to women's magazine fiction but was in fact full of shrewd comment, even if the restrictions of naval society were dealt with 'in sledge-hammer fashion'. Other English reviewers, with the delighted anti-Americanism of the 1950s, gleefully embraced Monica's biting commentary on America: 'Here is the American way of life at first hand, from the horrors of television to the purgatory of the visa office and the car-driving test.'

Australian critics were not far behind in savouring the book's criticisms of America. Monica Dickens had neatly reversed the cliché that Americans were a go-ahead, democratic people while the British were tired, down-at-heel, snobbish and conservative, observed the *Brisbane Telegraph,* for in the novel the English wife is lively and unconventional while the American husband is staid and pompous. In fact, the review perceptively pointed out, the sterility of Christine's life in Washington occasionally seems to depress the writer so much that the narrative loses its sparkle. A 'highly entertaining and amusing study of Anglo-American relationships', wrote the *Age* in Melbourne (although critical of Monica's relentless depiction of Vinson as a self-centred prig). Adelaide's *Advertiser* – likewise tending to characterise Monica's novels as especially appealing to women – enjoyed the author's 'satirical and mildly malicious' accounts of American ways.

Certainly Christine finds the American interurban landscape 'ugly, ugly' just as Monica had done. She learns to love America and misses it when she visits England, but initially Monica's heroine focuses on the negatives of American life: the silly soap operas on the radio, the stultifying, clammy heat of a Washington summer, the inflexible racism of Vinson and his mother. The more perceptive American reviewers were understandably hurt. Award-winning writer Helena Caperton deplored Monica's lack of tact in her depiction of Anglo-American relationships, her complete omission of any admirable American characters (not quite true) and the 'sordidly' realistic depiction of only one aspect of social life in the US Navy. She recognised Vinson Gaegler as a type, conceding that such dreary, middle-class naval officers did exist, but wished that such an excellent writer had encountered a few well-bred, representative Americans, 'for she could write of them so charmingly'. One cannot help remembering, Caperton's review continued gently, that so many of our Vinson Gaeglers went onto the beaches of Normandy never to return. Monica Dickens had not intentionally bitten the hand that fed her but she had certainly snapped at it, Caperton concluded, predicting that Monica would irritate American readers with her assumption that the provincial dwellers in Arlington's bungalows were typical of the entire United States Navy.

The *New York Times* was kinder, seeing in Monica's 'honest, sensitive and well-written' work a reinforcement of the belief that the slim hope for freedom and peace in the world lay in a right understanding between the English-speaking democracies. The novel concerned a modern-day transatlantic alliance, the paper observed, not one between a wealthy American bride and an impoverished British aristocrat as in days gone by, but between a solvent GI and his English bride who are both essentially middle-class. Surprisingly, the paper believed that Monica had avoided the obvious clichés about American life, and had written convincingly of Christine and Vinson's efforts to adapt to each other. The novel relied too much on catastrophic coincidence in terms of plot, but it was deftly done and in the critic's opinion Monica's account of an Anglo-American marriage – another of which had produced Sir Winston Churchill, it was pointed out – would find satisfied readers on both sides of the Atlantic.

Being back at her old job of writing helped Monica to bear the life of a naval officer's wife by allowing her deliberately to observe, rather than simply endure. She gave Christine 'all the traumas, all the snubs and insults' that she herself had suffered, and felt better because she had transferred her own problems to her character. In fact the book 'saved' her:

Work was the link between the old life and the new. I was still myself.

(Monica Dickens, *Christian Science Monitor*, 1986)

But of course the book did not help her standing with the other naval wives. As predicted, the Washington women hated it. Monica knew she was hardly popular in any case, perhaps because of her outspokenness. In those early years in America she was frank in her opinions regarding her new home, sounding off in interviews about the spoiling of the beautiful countryside with billboards and the 'frightfully narrow and limited' outlook of Americans she had come across on a trip to Ohio. (To be fair, she also declared her liking for the innumerable electrical appliances and American use of bright colours in the home.)

Roy retired from the navy permanently in October 1952, and afterwards the local heat from the US version of *No More Meadows* made it seem like an excellent time to get out of Washington. If Roy had not intended to retire anyway, after the hostile reception of her book he might have had to, Monica commented. But before this point there had been a momentous event in Monica's life.

§

When the naval wives at the luncheon stared at her stomach, Monica had not been pregnant. She was at least ten years older than any of the other new brides, and wrote in *An Open Book* that in case she was too old to have a child she and Roy decided to adopt. (Monica was only thirty-seven, but possibly aware that her thyroid condition could cause difficulties conceiving.)

American adoption agencies would not even grant them an interview: they were too old, from different religious backgrounds, and at that point Roy was still in the navy, considered an unstable occupation. Once Roy had retired for good they took a lengthy, almost year-long trip back to England, where adoption might be easier. Legislation at the end of the 1940s had recently made adoption more streamlined, although much of it continued to be by informal arrangement through friends and acquaintances or via a doctor or matron. When Monica and Roy were looking, only about a quarter of adoptions were carried out through registered adoption societies. The Strattons used the informal method: a friend of Monica's who was an adoption officer found them a baby 'round the back door somewhere', in Monica's words.

Monica wrote little in her memoir about their search for a child, or the formalities of the adoption. But she did write that when she glimpsed the chubby, grimy child gnawing on a dirty crust of bread on the floor of the foster home, she was flooded with that 'new mother' sense of recognition. She had found her daughter.

§

Monica and Roy took baby Pamela to her new home in America aboard a US naval ship crowded with thousands of troops and their families. Arrival in New York was a day late following bad weather; other women had been prostrated but not Monica, who even managed to type up a few items for *Woman's Own*. During the day she looked after Pamela; in the evenings there was little to do except read and Monica was grateful for several books donated by her old friend Charles Pick. These included Barbara Pym's *Jane and Prudence*, which she loved and thought superior even to the same author's *Excellent Women*, and Balzac's *Cousin Bette*, which she described as fascinating (if interminable).

Back in the US with their new little daughter, Roy and Monica put navy life behind them. They had decided to settle in a small community where they could live quietly and find time to write. Roy already had a property in a pretty village on Cape Cod, the arm of land sticking out into the Atlantic south of Boston. Monica was delighted with the location as along with the house came enough land for a proper garden, and she could have horses again into the bargain. By late October 1953 they were happily ensconced in their new home.

Cape Cod

North Falmouth in 1953 was an unspoiled seaside village with no facilities for tourists. Summer residents in the know were as anxious to keep it a secret as the people who lived there year round.

Describing her new abode for a village newsletter back in England, Monica wrote that everyone had a boat. In winter, the rich went to Florida while the others stayed put, digging themselves out each week when new snow fell. The children went off in the yellow school bus at seven in the morning and were brought back at three to hang round the drug store or the post office, the centre of life for the village since everyone had to come in to collect their letters. At Christmas the man from the hardware store dressed up as Santa and rode an old cow pony to the four corners of the village where all the children were gathered in snow suits, the little ones towed on sleds. They were given presents and everyone cooked hot dogs and sang carols. All the houses were lit with coloured lights, and candles shone in every window down Main Street. Trees were garlanded with little glass lanterns.

For a slow writer, who must live like a hermit for six months to produce a book, it is ideal. New Englanders understand cranks and they are self-sufficient. They will be social with you – or leave you alone, whichever you want!...it isn't corrupt. It isn't sophisticated. People like to live here.

(Monica Dickens, All Saints Coleshill Village Newsletter, Christmas 1967)

When Monica and Roy first arrived the houses in the charming little village were all white or weathered wood, set in green lawns. Their own new home, built in 1812 and once the abode of a sea captain, was white with green shutters and stood at the corner of Old Main Road and Pine Street.

Roy fell in love with the old place in 1946 when on a visit to a former navy friend who lived across the street, and bought it before he met Monica. It was long and narrow, each room leading into the next and most of them facing south, so that during the day they were flooded with light; the western windows were set aflame by the dying sun in the evenings. Monica was delighted with both the sea captain's house and North Falmouth, where there were no neon lights, no barbecue shops and no billboards.

Their first concern was to make the house more habitable, and they embarked on major reconstruction. It had previously been divided into two apartments, and these now needed to be melded back together into a single home. As the work proceeded Monica knuckled down outside, where the plan was to replace what had formerly been a miniature golf course with a garden, greenhouse, terrace, rock garden and vegetable patch. The local tendency was to lawns and small trimmed evergreens but Monica wanted her own garden to be more like a cottage garden in England, with a profusion of roses and other flowers. (Her work apparently paid off: in July 1955 her garden was open to the public as part of the annual Garden Tour sponsored by the Falmouth Garden Club, and Monica would hold annual champagne parties to celebrate the blossoming of her famous night-blooming cereus.)

Digging beds for bulbs and shrubs at the start of the process, Monica kept an eye on 16-month-old Pam as she hurtled around in her American blue jeans. There was little time to think about writing. In any case her mind was a blank, and there were so many other much more enjoyable things to do sorting out her new house and garden.

When eventually the house was finished Monica and Roy had created a beautiful and comfortable place to live. An entire new wing had been added and walls knocked out of the small boxy rooms to open up a sunnier spaciousness. English-style, Monica had installed flowered chintzes, big comfortable chairs and pieces of her antique furniture from the cottage at Hinxworth. A baby grand piano for Roy stood in a corner of the living room and he had his own book-lined writing room towards the rear of the house. The walls of Monica's writing room, at the front of the house, were lined with fitted bookshelves holding her own books and hordes of others, and when Roy later built a corner desk between two windows she was able to gaze out at a different view from each as she wrote. In pride of place near Monica's desk hung a large picture of her father Henry.

A special area in the house was devoted to Dickens memorabilia, which slowly grew over the years: the great man's hat and cane, his two court swords, an etching of him at twenty-one, a photograph with his two daughters, the Luke Fildes painting of Dickens' study *The Empty Chair*, his portrait on a plate, prints from his books, and of course the books themselves – bound volumes of his complete works plus ultimately a collection of over two hundred books written about him. On the wall hung a framed copy of a document entitled *The Great International Walking Match of February 29, 1868*, the 'articles of agreement' drawn up by Dickens for a walking competition in New England between his British tour manager and an American publisher (who won). Elsewhere, framed photographs of Monica jumping hurdles on her horses were also in evidence, and one of a racing horse owned by her publisher Michael Joseph which he had named Monica Dickens in her honour. Upstairs, Monica now had a dressing room fitted with sliding-door cupboards and a multitude of drawers – greatly to her pleasure, used as she was to the hulking dark wardrobes of 1950s England.

With Monica's love of dogs and horses, the new home was naturally not complete without the full complement, now including Bobby the black and white collie and Egbert, a lively little Schipperke dog, both greatly loved by Pamela. The four-stall stables were soon occupied by a pair of horses, with ponies planned for Pamela in the future. As time went on Roy and Monica bought more of the land around them, until finally they had nearly seven acres which they fenced in to make five paddocks and a training ring.

This burgeoning animal husbandry was not appreciated by a number of the locals, and in the mid 1950s there were attempts to change the zoning laws in an effort to force Monica and Roy to get rid of the two horses. Nevertheless, Monica was well liked: neighbours remember her as very friendly and easy to talk to, even if she did have a habit of riding her horses blithely through their backyards, often with a child on another horse in tow. She was outgoing with everyone, they recalled, handymen as much as those in her own social circle. (She made sure not to repeat the mistake of a former resident of her house, an Englishwoman who had flown the Union Jack on the Fourth of July). When Pamela started at North Falmouth's little nursery school and Monica got to know other mothers she began to feel more settled and part of village life, and even, at last, that she belonged in America. In time close friends were made, including a Catholic couple who asked the Strattons to be godparents to their new daughter, for whom they had chosen the middle name of Monica. Going back regularly to England helped. To find that it was still there and people still knew her, and that all her friends still liked her, was reassuring, and she was able to return to the US with equanimity.

Early visitors to Monica's new home included her famous ballet dancer friend from Hinxworth days, Pamela May, who was appearing with the Sadler's Wells in Boston.

§

Monica assumed that now she had a baby she would give up her writing and settle down to being a full-time mother, just as she had (wrongly) assumed she would cease to write when she started nursing, and again on marrying Roy. Although recognising the importance to her of her writing, Monica nevertheless continued to make periodic attempts to put it aside when she believed it the right thing to do.

Then came a proposal from Monica's English agent David Higham: the firm of Rainbird, Maclean was planning a deluxe edition of the works of Charles Dickens in fourteen volumes, and wanted Monica to write a 25,000-word biography for £1000, and for an extra fee to write a short preface to each volume and to advise on content and arrangement. She could ask her father Henry for help with this last, Monica mused, but should she do it? The money aside, would it be of benefit to her standing as a writer? She recognised that it would be a great deal of work and felt disinclined to tackle it – probably through laziness, she acknowledged, owning that she actually knew deplorably little about her forebear's life and that it would require much research. She knew that Charles Pick would rather she spend her time on another novel, but for the moment she did not feel inspired.

She was advised against it, on the grounds that the research necessary would probably only be possible in London and that, taking into account all the work that would be required, £1000 was hardly the kind of remuneration Monica was used to. The same effort spent on bringing out a new novel, with its extra rights and Book Club edition, would bring in a far better sum than might be forthcoming from the Dickens idea. Moreover, critical reviews might well be damaging to Monica's reputation, which was now as good as it had ever been following the publicity attending the recent *No More Meadows*. Monica could see the truth of all this – and was particularly concerned about the possibility of harming her reputation – yet dithered about giving a definite refusal in case she was merely suffering from sloth.

In the event the Rainbird, Maclean edition of Dickens did not transpire. But Monica now wanted to write. Predictably, she found the winters of North Falmouth long and empty, even with Pammie to take care of, and wanted to get back to her desk. Monica was still Britain's best-selling female novelist apart from Daphne du Maurier, and continued to write for *Woman's Own* (including articles about her new daughter; they posed together for a cover). As she admitted around this time, 'Increasingly, as I grow more prolific, my writing is for me the greater part of life.' She became anxious to start another book, but was bereft of ideas.

Eventually, something that Monica wanted to write about started to surface. Just before she left London with baby Pamela there was a visit to the city by a minor foreign ruler, with a procession through the streets. As Monica hurried round the shops she saw people lining up to witness the parade, and it occurred to her to wonder about those with all the time in the world to wait around for a glimpse of someone completely unknown to them. Her first idea was to have a lonely woman of this sort get mixed up in an adventure which would take her out of her solitary existence, but jettisoned this for a more straightforward account of loneliness and dependence. She wanted a departure from the meandering, almost actionless type of book she felt she had been writing that was really only a study of people and how they lived their lives. She had been mulling over the lot of the woman who devotes twenty years of her life to bringing up her children, often at some expense to her marriage, and receives so little return for it after they have left home. (Perhaps Monica was also thinking of Fanny, or even feared this outcome herself now that she was a mother.) She came up with the story of Louise, a widow with nothing to fill her days and no place to call home.

Monica had to move her writing hours around, rising at four a.m. and putting Pam down as late as possible at night so that she would wake later in the mornings. As she worked in those early hours she sometimes heard the wind howling in from the sea, relentlessly blowing around the old elm and pine trees growing outside her writing room. Initially the title was to have been *When the Wind Blows*, duplicating the intended opening words, and a windy night was going to bring the denouement of the story. In the end she called the book *The Winds of Heaven* to reflect the aimless life of the widow, blown this way and that by circumstance and not allowed to settle.

Almost for the first time in her writing career progress was slow, despite the early starts. Being a wife and mother made a difference, Monica was to find. She was also doing her best to put down roots in the local community and was gradually offering her services, volunteering to sign her works at book fairs and contributing her writing skills to the Falmouth Playhouse. In April she warned her publishers that with a visit from her parents expected in August and September, she would not be able to achieve a great deal and the book would not be ready for Christmas publication, though possibly finished by then. She mentioned that the book was being written from the points of view of both Louise, the widow, and of her three daughters, so that the middle-aged outlook would not be overplayed and the daughters' lives and problems could be developed alongside.

As was her habit, Monica did not show her work to anyone before it was finished. If she discussed a book too much while she was writing it, somehow it became spoiled: she would lose interest. Criticism during this period could likewise be fatal:

> *I get discouraged if I get any criticism or if anybody disagrees with a point of view. I can only go on a system of just telling myself all the time that this is going to be a good book and that people are going to like it, and so I go ahead with the writing. Then when I've finished I show it to people and get the criticism and am able to go back and tidy it up.*

(Monica Dickens, *This is Britain*, BBC radio)

The Winds of Heaven, dedicated to Pamela in its first edition, was published in 1955 and was Monica's eleventh work. Left without home or income by the death of her callous husband, the book's lonely heroine Louise is forced to live several months of the year with each of her three daughters in turn, and then spend the winter at a hotel owned by an old school friend. She feels her dependence and uselessness and is indeed a dithery, useless sort of person, often irritating to the reader for not standing up for herself more or trying to find a job to regain some independence, although it is made clear that she is a 'lady' unused to working. Even so, the reader is always on her side, and at the same time just as much on the side of the daughters, who have their own problems. Elements of Monica's own experience are again present: a trip to the junk shops of Portobello Road, the consolations of the Catholic religion, a remembered passion of Louise's for her gym mistress at school. On the trip around Portobello, Louise's grandchild Ellen is deeply affected by a picture of a dying horse on the battlefield, as Monica herself had been as a child, and insists on buying it to take home where it upsets her younger sister.

The pain of feeling unwanted is skilfully conveyed as Louise, staying at her elder daughter's, wonders when to go down to Sunday breakfast, not wanting to be too early and get in the way or too late and cause inconvenience:

She thought about the years when Miriam was a child, and it was Louise who prepared breakfast, and served it out, and gently criticised table manners. How odd it was, the way their roles in life had become reversed, the mother's and the daughter's. For what a short time, it seemed, had Louise been able to look after Miriam. Now it was the other way round. Miriam was responsible for her mother. Louise was the child, and, absurd though she knew it to be, as anxious to be in Miriam's good graces as if her daughter had been an exacting parent.

(Monica Dickens, *The Winds of Heaven*, 1955)

Through a chance encounter during tea at a Lyons cafeteria, Louise meets a sweet and gentle man, a 'little common', who surprisingly turns out to be a writer of lurid thrillers. A bond very slowly develops but the novel is more the story of a mother's relationship with her daughters and what dependence can do to a person's spirit. Satisfyingly, a believable happy ending is still delivered, with the start of a new life for Louise.

The book was serialised in the magazine *Home Notes*, a sister title of *Woman's Own*, and as with so many of Monica's novels was broadcast on *Woman's Hour* (in fourteen parts) and dramatised for radio in 1971. English reviewers loved it. John Betjeman weighed in again, writing in the *Daily Telegraph* that Monica was 'one of the most affectionate and humorous observers of the English scene, particularly of the pretensions of genteel suburban life, that we have. Not only this, but she can always tell a good story, touch the heart with a pleasant sentimental grace...I think *The Winds of Heaven* is her best novel yet.' Elizabeth Bowen wrote in the *Tatler and Bystander* that 'Miss Dickens has chosen a situation perfectly suited to her art – her sense of comedy, her affection for people and her almost uncanny knowledge of their small ways'. She saw in the novel humour at its most kindly, but with the occasional sardonic edge. Monica had, in common with her great-grandfather, a sympathetic preference for the underdog, said Bowen, but at the same time rightly noting that underneath Louise's ditheriness was something indomitable. 'How well she sees the extraordinary in the ordinary, and how familiar she is with *all* kinds of people. Never once does she give us a 'stock' character.' Every page of *The Winds of Heaven* was enjoyable, Bowen concluded, a fine blend of comedy with sheer good sense. Only the *Times Literary Supplement* had reservations: Monica was accused, again, of making too many of her points with a sledge-hammer, and occasionally allowing her gift for caricature to run away with her. Her manipulation of her characters was too slick, it added, although redeemed by the portrait of gentle and sensitive Louise.

In a serious study of Monica Dickens written as an essay for *Nova* magazine in 1970, the respected writer A. S. Byatt found *The Winds of Heaven* restrained in its treatment of the problems of the elderly and yet 'genuinely distressing'. It succeeded because its emotions were understated and because it was *not* sentimental, Byatt argued. Louise's problems are first experienced as merely embarrassing – such as whether or not to make an appearance at a smart party at her daughter Miriam's house or remain in her bedroom – but become frightening when her stay for the winter with her old friend suddenly falls through and she has nowhere to go. Byatt liked the happy ending, which for her was not unrealistic because Louise's sweet and honest character could lead to happiness in exactly this way.

American reviewers tended to focus on the issues raised. One declared that the spirit of the book warranted a social discussion, and that the solution might lie in economic and social reforms. The happy ending of the novel for this reviewer was a Hollywood cop-out, inappropriate to the Lear-like tragedy of the situation, and to be consistent Monica should have left it as expressed on Lear's death, that 'Our present business Is general woe.' The *Boston Sunday Herald* took a different tack, their reviewer refusing to believe that women Louise's age were superannuated. In America, she insisted, thousands of middle-aged women succeed in finding new occupation through their ingenuity and resourcefulness. Critic and novelist Dachine Rainer in the influential *Saturday Review* was the harshest. Mistakenly labelling Monica as Charles Dickens' granddaughter (not unusual in the US), Rainer was of the opinion that heredity had not enabled Monica to produce exceptional work. Making the inevitable comparison, she found *The Winds of Heaven* to be as sordid as Dickens' work but without his brutal social satire, relieving comic sense, or vast compassion. Some scenes were well done, she commented, but in general the characters were not so much good or wicked as just dull.

The book did well in the UK, reportedly selling twice as many copies during its first month as those of any contemporary British woman author, again with the single exception of Daphne du Maurier. On a visit home in early 1955 Monica promoted the book with the standard events. It was translated into Dutch, amongst other languages, and Monica found time for a three-day trip to Holland for lectures to literary societies in The Hague, Rotterdam and Amsterdam. Back in the US, she jetted off again almost immediately, going with Roy to Canada for yet more publicity work.

In France, alas, *Winds* met the usual brick wall. Rejections flooded in from publishers Julliard, Amiot-Dumont, Galliard, Presses de la Cité (twice), Éditions Mondiales and even from the magazine *Elle*. The novel has never been translated into French.

§

When Pam was around two and a half, Monica and Roy found her a little sister in England. They arranged with a social worker to see a child in a children's home who turned out to be as happy and chubby as Pam, but only when she was sitting down: the child's legs were weak and she was unable to stand without pain. Agonised, Monica and Roy felt that others might be better parents to this child than they could be. Describing this anguish decades afterwards, Monica admitted to a lack of courage but also rationalised that had they taken this poor girl they would not have gone away and discovered Prudence, an 'odd little thing' they found clinging to her foster mother. The only person the insecure toddler would look at was Pam, who made her laugh, and it was Pam who decided she should come home with them.

Monica came to believe that love for children sprang from the life that had been shared, and not just from the physical fact of carrying a child in the womb for nine months. The delights and rewards were the same, said Monica, and so were the troubles, with the one addition of forever wondering if others might have been a more suitable match as parents. She gave the girls the usual positive stories about their birth parents giving them up so that they could have a better life, and how they had been specially chosen by Monica and Roy. In the end she saw that it hardly mattered; even though no secret was made of their adoption (Monica mentioned it in *Woman's Own*), it rarely arose. She thought the children became somewhat like her and Roy because they copied the same expressions and mannerisms, and that outsiders saw resemblances in the girls to their parents because they expected to see them. *An Open Book* nevertheless makes clear that becoming the mother of adopted children was not plain sailing, and there had been friction. Monica wrote that as time went on she changed her ideas about the balance between heredity and environment. 'Adoption is not easy...for the child.'

She declared elsewhere that for all the advice she dispensed to mothers in her columns she was unable to carry it out herself: she failed on every count, and did not think she was a particularly good mother. When the girls were tiny she had helpers come in and look after them in the mornings, and looking back she could see how distracted and unavailable she had been. 'I was always working, leaving notes for the children in the kitchen,' Monica told a friend. 'Not that I put work first, but when you're writing, to close the door is the only way to get it done.' When she did come out for a cup of coffee, she would be assailed by a chorus of children's voices complaining that the horses had escaped or the dog had been run over, and with her head still in the book she was writing she did not really want to know. For their part, Pamela and Prudence understood that when their mother was working, her office was like a sanctuary and they were not to open the door. They would come home from school and stand there, wanting to knock and go in to talk to her, and yet knowing that it was simply not allowed. So they in their turn left notes on the table for Monica. As adults, when Monica harked back to the closed door they were quick to tell her she was being too harsh on herself. ('I want to be perfect,' smiled Monica.) And Pamela remembered that her mother was always available in the afternoons to go to the beach with them.

Monica did show signs of being an anxious parent. She sent Pam, who was timid and followed her mother everywhere, to a nearby riding camp at around the age of eight. Pam was nervous about riding the horses at home and Monica thought she might learn to ride on the safe camp ponies and to become more confident. When she dropped her off the camp counsellors advised Monica not to visit until the following weekend, despite living only two miles away. Monica argued the case but agreed. The following day she went riding near the camp in the hope of seeing her daughter; she saw a crowd of shrieking girls milling about at some game and, standing apart, a square figure in a red jacket that might have been Pam. That Sunday Monica used recent rain as an excuse to go back with Pam's rubber boots. Poor Pam screamed when she saw her and hung on to her clothes, begging to be taken home; again the counsellors told Monica to leave and insisted that Pam was adjusting well. Monica had to accept this, knowing that parents have to let go for the sake of the child's future, yet she never forgot and years afterwards would worry about the pain that Pam might have gone through.

Prudence was seemingly a more confident rider, at age twelve winning a prize at a Boston horse show with her palomino, named David Copperfield. A Boston paper helpfully pointed out that Prudence was a descendant of 'Charles Dickens, who wrote the book by that name'.

North Falmouth was an ideal place to bring up a family – the right amount of snow and skating in winter, and long summers of swimming and messing about in boats or playing in the treehouse built for the girls in the garden. Pamela and Prudence (who were both given 'Dickens' as part of their surname) were brought up as Catholics, making their First Holy Communion in the local churches. Eventually both went to boarding school near Boston, coming home for weekends and holidays when the old house, which could sleep twenty, would fill up with family and friends. 'In the evenings Mont conjured up amazing meals with no fuss,' her niece Mary recalled. 'Or she would suddenly grab a hat and dance a polka round the kitchen with the nearest child. She created fun wherever she was.' Monica loved playing card games and board games with the children, which often went on till the early hours as they sang along to the folk tunes and pop songs played on the piano by Roy. Monica would sometimes be caught vacuuming at midnight in order not to miss a minute of the fun.

Monica believed that the most important thing parents could do for their children, and people should do for each other, was to inculcate feelings of self-worth. She was continually shocked that parents did not praise their children, in the belief that praise made them conceited. 'A child needs praise,' she insisted.

§

Fanny and Henry, known to the girls as Gramps, came to Cape Cod every summer for a visit. Even after flying became safer and more comfortable they would still sail over, always on one of the smaller Cunard ships because they knew all the crew in person and were well cared for. Monica would meet them in New York and take them to Cape Cod by train, which gradually discarded its carriages as it flew through Harlem, over the Connecticut River to Providence and across the Cape Cod Canal into North Falmouth. By then the only carriage left was a parlour car of armchairs and little tables, where Henry could enjoy a drink and a sandwich brought by a smiling porter. It was perfect for them. When the train service was discontinued she would drive them to the Cape instead, leaving the road to search for decent places for lunch which also served drinks. Though not an alcoholic Henry loved good wine and liked a gin at certain hours of the day, Monica wrote later, commenting that had her aunts been alive they might well have objected to her mentioning his drinking habits in print, but she could hardly describe her father without reference to the sacred rituals which gave structure to his life. The drive to North Falmouth became as ritualised as Henry's drive from London to Hinxworth had been, with its traditional stops at the same pubs on each occasion.

In Monica's American village Henry would wear his old white tennis trousers and the ancient Panama hat that he had sported on the family's frequent tours in Europe. In the mornings he strolled to the North Falmouth post office to fetch his *Times,* sent by airmail, and following an afternoon sleep under the trees in the garden he would wander round the village talking to locals at work in their gardens. Kind American drivers, not understanding that he enjoyed walking, would stop to offer him a lift. Henry and Fanny had regretted the loss of Hinxworth – without saying so in case it made Monica feel guilty – but now they took pleasure visiting her in the new setting. Henry was taken to the county courthouse to be admired as a colossus of British law, and Fanny would captivate the local women with comic accounts of the servant problem, even if they did not really know what she was talking about. People in Cape Cod loved them. They loved the fact that Henry became more and more like one of his grandfather's characters, and that they were both so English they were barely intelligible. A decade later, in 1964, Henry and Fanny celebrated their sixtieth wedding anniversary with Monica in America, the Dickens clan gathering in North Falmouth for the cutting of the cake with one of Charles Dickens' court swords.

Other regular visitors to Roy and Monica in North Falmouth for summer vacations were Roy's son Roy Junior, wife Toni and three daughters Pamela, Sarah and Susan. Their eldest daughter Pamela had been born just as Roy and Monica were adopting their own baby Pamela in England, and when the young couple sent a cable announcing the birth, Monica wrote in reply that now they could love two Pams instead of one. For the next few decades the two sets of daughters enjoyed each other's company every summer on the Cape as they rode and competed in local horse shows and swam at the private beach that came with the house. Around the kitchen table the talk would be of horses, horses, horses, the girls as obsessed as Monica had been in her own youth.

The long succession of holidays with his father and new English wife brought some of the happiest days of family life for Roy Junior, who had suffered when his parents divorced. His mother, Roy's first wife Esther, believed Roy divorced her because she did not fit the profile Roy wanted to project as he pursued his career in the navy, and certainly Roy's second wife Arlene, a college graduate from a banking family, was far more sophisticated. For a short period Roy Junior, aged ten at the time of the divorce, had gone off the rails, playing truant from school and twice running away from home. He was finally placed in a foster home for two months but managed to get back on track and return to his schooling. These old wounds were now healed as he and his wife and daughters built a contented relationship with Roy and his new family. It was a very happy marriage, Roy Junior commented about Monica and his father.

§

After Monica moved to the US she continued to set much of her work in her native country. Monica's firm belief that she could write nothing without seeing or experiencing it in person meant frequent visits back to Britain to do research and find material. At first she stayed at number 52 with her parents, and then with her publisher Charles Pick and his wife Beryl, before eventually investing in a flat in London. Monica well understood that since the greater part of her readership was in England, she needed to give her *Woman's Own* fans the impression that she was experiencing normal life as they were and that they might run into her any day at the shops. She knew there would likely be some resentment if it were known she had defected to the US; her fan mail was therefore sent on to her in Cape Cod. Her answers were returned to England for posting and had to be written with a 'walking along the Thames yesterday' type of approach. On occasion she found local inspiration for a theme that would also work in Britain, such as a news story in 1957 on the subject of a Scottish restaurant hostess on Cape Cod who had studied hotel management in London for six years and then worked in Buckingham Palace. Monica determined to use this as a basis for a little homily in her *Woman's Own* column about learning a job thoroughly in order to go places. Her talks for the BBC when in England were angled in the same way: 'The editor of the paper she writes for is most anxious that she should not appear to be <u>living</u> in the US,' a senior manager instructed the editor of *Woman's Hour* in 1964.

In the mid 1950s Monica was keen to become better established in continental markets and asked her English agents Pearn, Pollinger and Higham to increase their efforts. They duly wrote to the literary agent Jenny Bradley in Paris, pointing out that not long previously the magazine *Elle* had published an article by Monica entitled *The Contemporary British Girl* (and would subsequently print another of Monica's on the Queen) and that there could be a market in France both for serialisations of Monica's books and for her *Woman's Own* pieces. It was a no to the *Woman's Own* articles from sophisticated *Elle*, but in early 1956 a family magazine accepted seven of them. These were typical fare from Monica's column and included *The Man You Should Marry, Should a Girl Speak First, That Magical First Date, Pity The Woman Whose Love Is Stolen* and *Don't Try To Be The Boss*. The magazine, *Les Veillées Des Chaumières*, then rather shamefacedly inquired if the author would object to her pieces bearing the byline 'Monique' Dickens, owing to their somewhat insular and provincial readership. 'Monique' did not mind at all.

Writing for *Woman's Own* from America ultimately became too difficult as Monica could rarely interview people in England for her column, and in her memoir she wrote that when a young girl in Liverpool wrote in asking for fresh blood on the staff of the magazine Monica lost the job. The recollection of the then editor, however, was that towards the end of 1965 it had obviously become increasingly difficult for a weekly column written at such a distance to sustain its appeal to a British readership in the rapidly changing conditions of the sixties. Although Monica's contract was not renewed, she was asked to contribute some special articles on America at less frequent intervals, which *Woman's Own* was happy to publish, but still not as if she resided there: she had to write as if sent over on assignment. Whatever the true version of events Monica was naturally upset when she lost the column, to the point of tears. With the reduction in income Roy threatened that the horses would have to go (they stayed).

Fortunately, Roy loved going to England just as much as Monica did, and while she was still writing and researching for *Woman's Own* (and beyond) they returned almost every year. Monica was to say that she never really felt she had stopped living there. One winter Pamela and Prudence were sent to the local convent school in Chepstow Villas, wearing English school uniforms that in Monica's opinion did not make them look English. They were given holy pictures by the nuns which they promptly touted for sale in the Portobello Road.

When Monica first returned to her native land for visits it was as though she had landed from another planet; newspapers and television encouraged her to be amusing on the subject of Americans, who in the days before regular transatlantic flights were seen almost as alien beings. Monica appears to have obliged. On that exciting first mission to England to find a child for adoption, starting in November 1952 and extending well into the following year, she was a guest on the BBC's *In Town Tonight* to talk about the US. She told the (possibly apocryphal) story that a young male assistant in a New York store had told her not to worry whether her shoes went with her dress: 'Listen, honey, when you got one of those strapless evening gowns on nobody ain't going to look at your feet.' She also related that an American acquaintance once asked whether she had studied the language before coming over. Yes, Monica had replied, do you think I'm making progress? (A version of this incident featured in *No More Meadows*.)

Despite the funny stories Monica herself had already gone a little native. During the 1952-3 visit she was fined £2 for causing an obstruction in a road in Southampton with a 'large American car', and she published an article haranguing her compatriots for their dress sense. It had given her 'heart pangs' to see British women so dowdy, she wrote in Britain's *Sunday Graphic*, with their attire mostly consisting of trousers, a mud-coloured coat and a head scarf. This was fine in wartime, Monica continued, but Britain was no longer at war. Why did half the women in London dress as if expecting an air raid?

I know it's cold, but it's far colder in most parts of America, and you don't see women going about the streets of New York or Philadelphia or Chicago wearing trousers that make them look like the north end of an elephant headed south. Nor do you see them wearing the drab colours that I see all around me in the London streets. Americans like to wear all the bright colours of the rainbow, but British women seem to favour all the colours of mud.

(Monica Dickens, *Sunday Graphic*, 1952)

The American woman, she asserted, was essentially feminine and did not forget to take care that she looked it. She might not be able to afford to spend a great deal on herself but she looked after her hair and would rather die than be seen without lipstick. Her hands would not show how much washing she had done or how many vegetables she had peeled. She cooked superbly and with imagination, and could spend all day in the kitchen and still manage to come out and greet her guests looking as if she had never seen a hot stove or a sink full of greasy dishes.

Three-quarters of the women in Britain were also weighed down by the hateful word 'housewife', she added, showing signs of feminism at last. In America, in the press and in Congress, women were called 'women' and 'wives'; they were never called just 'housewives'. In Monica's opinion British women had more sense, better skins, finer features, softer voices and usually better legs than Americans.

So why cover all this up with a big brown sack labelled 'housewife'?...Be feminine, be women.

(Monica Dickens, *Sunday Graphic*, 1952)

The article was reproduced without comment in the American press, complete with Monica's forthright opinions on the superiority of British attributes.

The Miseries of the World

Despite the demands of a young family and elderly parents Monica continued to write prolifically, as she was to do throughout her long life. There now emerged from her pen a surprising series of what appeared to be social issue novels, essentially begun by *The Winds of Heaven* and its narrative of an unwanted and ageing mother. Although interleaved with lighter works, she was successively to write about domestic violence, cruelty to animals and children, the isolation of inner-city life and the agony of the suicidal. There was no judgment, only compassion. Monica's books had always been shot through with an instinctive sympathy for the plight of her fellow man; now this concern became the focus of her work.

She was later to maintain that none of her books had a message and that she had never tried to change attitudes with them. She did not think she had inherited Dickens' social conscience, as many believed. Rather, Monica observed, the change from best-selling authoress of light works to a writer with something more serious to say was a natural development, part of her development as a person – adding that she had been criticised as a lightweight and then criticised again for moving away from what had been termed her 'delightful frothy books'. She did not even think that she had a social conscience, and had never written anything with the idea that it might do some good. She wrote about things that interested her, as in her view did Charles Dickens. In writing these far more sombre books she was not trying to effect changes or expose rottenness in society, she insisted, but simply saw a particular theme as the basis for a good story. At the same time, however, Monica wanted to share with others what she had seen for herself, and felt that if it affected people the same way and made them care more, then she had to some degree succeeded.

What impelled this much darker exploration of humanity at this juncture in her life? Monica was happily married, the busy mother of two children, and a very successful writer in her genre: her books invariably found an avid readership and *One Pair of Hands* was still selling between 20,000 and 30,000 copies a year. Life was contented and fulfilling, and there were no skeletons in the closet after a childhood spent in comfort and security. The troubles of her early womanhood were far behind her:

The complexities of youth, the frustrations, the constant search for a man, or the man, the hurts...I gladly leave them behind...I wouldn't want to be twenty again for the world...You look back and wonder how you ever survived.

Her forebear Charles Dickens, of course, had personally experienced misfortune and despair as a boy when his impecunious father withdrew him from school to work in a factory pasting labels onto pots for ten hours a day; when his mother and siblings joined his father in debtors' prison the young Charles was then left to fend for himself, cold and hungry on the streets of London. These early events were a determining force in shaping the man he was to become and the books he was to write. Monica never experienced poverty or abandonment, but as a child at number 52 she had imbibed the poverty and drunkenness of the adjacent Portobello Road, the apparent hopelessness of many lives compared to hers. As a factory hand she had worked side by side with the poor and the uneducated, and in hospitals she had been witness to birth and death and the tragedy of illness. 'My eyes were opened to other people's lives,' Monica had written about nursing. Perhaps, now that she was happy and comfortable, a degree of guilt was surfacing in relation to unasked-for privilege. As the 1950s drew to a close she began to delve into the social ills of the day at a time when concern over such issues was minimal, virtually buried since the thundering novels of her great-grandfather. And, like her forebear, her books were to take the shape of social commentary without any clear solutions. In the words of Keats, perhaps the miseries of the world were now misery to Monica, and would not let her rest.

§

The Angel in the Corner, published in 1956 and dedicated to Prudence, is a bleak story of domestic abuse. Virginia, a fledgling journalist, falls for the wrong man and marries him to avoid being carted off to the US with her selfish mother Helen, who has snared a rich American. Virginia makes a heartfelt argument for wanting to stay in England, where she knows the people and how their minds work, instead of going to another country where she would feel out of place for a long time and where whatever she had learned and begun to believe in would be of scant use – perhaps Monica's own internal argument when considering the same option.

Virginia's layabout husband, Joe, is 'common', a term which has to be explained to the innocent American marrying her mother. Virginia's marriage quickly descends into brutality when Joe orders Virginia to give up her beloved job on a magazine:

Virginia smiled. 'I'll do what I like.' The smile disappeared under his hand as her head jerked backwards and she stumbled to the floor.

It was the first time he had ever hit her. Even as his hand touched her mouth, he had the terrible feeling that now that he had done it once, it would be more easy to do it again.

(Monica Dickens, *The Angel in the Corner*, 1956)

Virginia maintains her struggle to keep her marriage alive in increasingly difficult circumstances, sustained by her vision of an angel in the corner watching over her. But this tale of violence is full of dread, and obviously heading towards the disaster that eventually befalls her.

This was the first appearance in Monica's work, but not the last, of grim scenes and squalid lives in London slums. She had long wanted to write a story set in the city where she had been born and bred. 'I always dreamed of a story in which every scene would unfold in my great city, in its slums, its suburbs, its offices, its shops, its blocks of flats – in Piccadilly Circus, on the Edgware Road, in dirty train stations on the outskirts...'

Angel garnered an array of enthusiastic reviews from broadsheets, upscale magazines and local press alike – some of which compared Monica's descriptions of the contemporary London scene to Dickens' – and in addition unexpectedly warm words (given the subject matter of the novel) from the *Church Times* and the *Catholic Herald*. Frequent references were made to Monica's economy of style: her skilled precision and ability to dash off in a few lines ('almost *sotto voce*', said one review) what another novelist would take a chapter to achieve. The *Spectator* described the book as 'bursting with high spirits, garrulous, warm-hearted, commonplace, easy to sneer at but (at the time of reading at least) extremely vivid'. Miss Dickens was oddly careless at moments, the review continued, and yet stylistic quibbles were swept away by the avalanche of her good nature and ebullience. For the *Times Literary Supplement*, the work radiated professional competence, despite a too predictable ending. Monica's work had once again demonstrated the valuable, intangible quality of sheer likeability, said the *Sphere*. The *Manchester Guardian* stood alone in being sternly unimpressed, labelling the novel 'banal and slipshod'.

A. S. Byatt found the novel to have some of the 'blatant tear-jerking qualities of Charles Dickens', and thought the saintly Virginia a more convincing version of Little Nell. To present-day eyes the overwrought death of Little Nell may actually seem far less affecting than the death of Virginia's dear old nanny Tiny, who first encouraged her to look for the angel in the corner and taught her the little Catholic prayer *Angel of God, My Guardian Dear*. Implicit in Virginia's explanation of why her nanny means so much to her is Monica's deep love of her own long-lost Nanny Gathergood:

> ...people who've had nannies never forget them, not all their lives. When you're little, it's like having something – well, not better than a mother, but something more your own than a mother. Mothers have husbands. They have friends. They go out to parties, or to a job, like Helen. Nannies never go anywhere. The old ones, like Tiny, have no interests except you. You take everything from them, greedily, because you adore them. They're safe and comfortable and always the same...

(Monica Dickens, *The Angel in the Corner*, 1956)

A number of American reviewers were less forgiving than Byatt, finding in Monica a fondness for the melodramatic situation 'without the richness or power to command it to reveal her characters with compassion'. The *New York Times* deemed Monica's talent for atmospheric detail as authentic and satisfying as that of her great-grandfather, and suggested that her theme had cadences of Tennessee Williams' *A Streetcar Named Desire* – only without the power. Miss Dickens had placed upon a brightly-lit stage two figures familiar from Williams' play, said the review: the coarse-grained, dynamic animal with a civilised, finer product at his mercy. In this case, however, the struggle degenerates into ugliness and melodrama, with Virginia reduced to a sort of moronic complacency and Joe thrown back into the jungle before matters can be resolved. Tragedy, when it arrives, has the feel of a clean and decent turn for the better. The theme was too stark for the writer's more innate, naturally lighter touches in the novel, the review concluded, and the reader ends confused between sentimentality and terror.

'Infinitely better than other books by this author,' was the lofty pronouncement from French critic Annie Brierre on reading the novel in English. She liked the clear and solid writing and the way the reader was hooked in, and saw a Dickensian atmosphere in the scenes where Joe and Virginia are running a pub, although conveyed from a more feminine and modern perspective. In her view it would be surprising, nevertheless, if the book received any very good reviews in the serious French papers: for Brierre it was a work destined for a wide and primarily female public looking for amusement, and would require both initial serialisation in a women's magazine and a certain amount of publicity. She understood that a book of Monica's had once been published in French – 'without success, I believe'.

The Angel in the Corner was launched in Britain as a serial in the long gone magazine *Modern Woman*, and, once published, was one of the five top best-sellers during the winter and popular in Europe too. The Strattons arrived in the UK in mid November 1956 for a lengthy promotional visit lasting into the following year, which included a tour of Scandinavia and other European locations. In England Monica engaged in the usual publicising, appearing on radio several times and televised at number 52 for a BBC programme called *Monica Dickens at Home* (which required special equipment for the filming as even then the house had no electricity, only gas). Roy and the girls all appeared in the programme, with Roy revealing that he did the final typing of Monica's books and that this was usually the first time he knew anything about them. Monica hastened to explain that she was generally reluctant to 'exhaust her imagination' by talking out the subject.

Angel was to prove one of Monica's most enduring works and was ultimately translated in Denmark, Norway, Finland, Germany, Holland and Italy, where it became *Virginia e l'angelo* (Virginia and the Angel). In France, where Monica's works had proved a hard sell – *One Pair of Hands* and *Mariana* were the only previous books to have been translated, and there had been no sales of either since 1950 – inquiries came in about *Angel* from leading publishers. Monica's UK agent David Higham at Pearn, Pollinger and Higham considered *Angel* likely to be a far more marketable book in translation than her last two had been, and was anxious for a successful drive in France on his client's behalf. Higham wrote to the agent Jenny Bradley in Paris that Monica and her husband – Monica's 'manager', he added, putting the word in quotes – were both very alive to the possibilities of foreign markets. In early 1957, as Monica's UK visit continued, Higham wrote again to say that their client was proving rather wearing on the issue of foreign rights and asked Jenny for the fullest possible picture in all markets to pass on to her. Fortunately the publisher La Table Ronde had by then made a firm offer and wanted to issue the novel as *Mon bel ange* (My Beautiful Angel), after an initial serialisation in the popular women's magazine *Elle*. (*Elle* advertised its serialisation with the slogan 'England finds its *Bonjour Tristesse*', a reference to the recent best-seller by teenager Françoise Sagan – a novel similar only in that it concerns a young woman who chooses the wrong man, but otherwise an inappropriate comparison given the wholly different tone of both works, and a source of considerable puzzlement to Monica.)

The translator for La Table Ronde boldly asked for extensive cuts to the lengthy *Angel* – tens of lines at a time, or here and there entire pages, and the almost complete deletion of a chapter in which Virginia is convinced she has seen her angel in a vision. This section was 'heavy, dull and pointless', in the brutal opinion of the translator, who sniffed that Monica was given to overuse of dreams and hallucinations in the novel and required constant pruning lest French readers gave up on it (she expressed the hope that Monica did not intend to examine the result in detail). She also carped that the novel was too episodic to justify a title which gave the angel such a starring role.

Understandably, Monica refused the virtual excision of that one chapter and agreed to the other cuts only with reluctance. On eventual receipt of the French translation from La Table Ronde she was gracious enough to praise the presentation, and to aver (a little illogically) that although her French was not very good, she could see that the translation was excellent.

After she had returned to America, La Table Ronde contacted Monica via her agents to work out several publicity ideas for the French launch of *Angel* scheduled for early in 1958. The company wanted her to make a personal visit to Paris in order to get the critics interested, and, if she spoke French, to give media interviews and do book signings. The publishers were confident that *Elle*, having run the serialisation, would agree to do an article when the book was actually out, and the monthly magazine *Marie-Claire* was willing to follow suit if given something entertaining. This proved to be a matter of dredging up the tired old Dickens connection: Monica was asked if she lived in the house where Charles Dickens had lived or was surrounded by his relics, and whether she and Dickens had both been to Paris. If so, *Marie-Claire* could turn out a piece contrasting and comparing their respective reactions to the city.

Monica, perhaps not inclined to do La Table Ronde any favours, replied that she had no plans to visit Paris before the launch date and in any case excused herself from making personal appearances in France on the grounds of limited French, which would not allow her to sustain a TV interview or carry out book signings. She did pass on some biographical details and information about her hobbies: reading ('every worthwhile new novel'), horses, and taking care of her big flower garden in Cape Cod. As for Dickens and Paris, she referred the publisher to collections of his letters and the recent Edgar Johnson biography for 'entertaining comments' about the French capital.

Undaunted, La Table Ronde arranged for the New York correspondent of *France-Soir* to interview Monica at home in North Falmouth, and for some 'amusing' photographs to be taken of Monica and her family to help with the launch. One Edgar Schneider duly turned up and produced a lively account of Monica surrounded by tumbling children, absent-minded husband (in Schneider's opinion a dead ringer for Spencer Tracy), dog Geoffrey and cat Norma, and a variety of horses trotting past the window. England had been re-created in this corner of the New World, wrote Schneider whimsically, noting the display of Charles Dickens portraits across an entire wall and the severe-looking portrait of Monica's father Henry hanging opposite. Monica drew his attention to the portrait of her French grandmother Marie – describing her as the most opposed in the family to Monica taking up the Dickens pen again.

Schneider noted Monica's typewriter on her corner desk, surrounded by piles of white paper and manuscript, and the little mirror to one side in which Monica made faces at herself when lacking inspiration (a frequent occurrence, she claimed). She talked of her intense attachment to her characters and how they led the action in her novels. If they refused to carry out some step ordained by her as author, she preferred to change the circumstances or create new characters rather than allow them to be untrue to themselves. Roy was not allowed to criticise her work before it went for editing, she said; criticism of her books while 'I'm still carrying them in me' caused her as much pain as would insults to her children.

Also flanking the typewriter, Schneider observed, was a giant ashtray: Monica chain-smoked when she wrote, and the desk had been covered in formica to protect it from her cigarette butts.

§

Monica used to complain about book signings when still a newish author and in fact had tried to get out of these events, which she found extremely embarrassing, especially when people walked straight past her. The issue still plagued her, and the necessary publicity work in Britain and Europe during Monica's long visit home in the winter of 1956-7 appears to have been the spark for a heartfelt article entitled *Signing My Way Round Europe* (translated into French and probably intended specifically for that market). A funny but perceptibly bitter look at the perils of the authorial tour, the piece drills down into the humiliation routinely suffered by Monica as she sat at her table in various bookshops waiting for the hordes who never came. Just to see the announcement in a store window that Monica Dickens would be signing copies of her works always plunged her into a deep depression, she wrote. She went to these occasions 'as if to a massacre', and everywhere she had to endure the same torture: indifferent crowds passing the sign in the window, stopping only, if at all, to gaze at the prominent display of the works of a rival author; her table of books hidden away at the back of the shop or in winter placed so as to feel the draft every time the door opened; the signing of a few books tendered by the shop's employees, mobilised for the regulation publicity shot; and then the hours of waiting for someone to buy her books, 'one of the most embarrassing situations in which a writer can find herself'.

There were occasions when her fans did turn out in good number, Monica conceded, but these were generally the readers of

Woman's Own, who did not come to buy her books but to confirm that she actually existed. As she waited, the shop manager would while away the hours by regaling her with the massive sales figures of her fellow authors, and how the crowds who turned up for Paul Gallico had to be forcibly turned out of the shop by police at closing time; or deploring the fact that she had come on their slowest day (after screeds of correspondence with them fixing the exact date for her appearance). In one department store in Stockholm, under the eye of shoppers in the store's café gazing stolidly at Monica in her discomfiture, the manager revealed that too many writers came for signings and that people were fed up with it. In Helsinki, in the best-stocked bookshop in Europe, hordes of fur-booted book lovers thronged the counters but avoided her table as if she had leprosy. 'They're too busy looking at the other books,' explained the manager helpfully.

Book buyers were the same the world over, Monica observed feelingly. The shy ones would try to avoid her eye, wandering around as if in search of something while putting off the moment when they would have to approach her (especially in Britain). But she preferred this type to those who treated her as an inferior species who needed to be put in her place, riffling through her books with an air of disgust and giving her a reproving look before heading off to the other end of the shop to buy a cookbook. Then there were the over-enthusiastic, people who did not really know who she was but who would stand guard over her giving out wrong information about her books; others who insisted they had known her at school – all looking quite aged, Monica noted – and showed her photographs of their children as behind them the queue shuffled; and someone's elderly aunt who wittered on confusingly without buying anything, having only come in order to report back that she had seen Monica. Children requested her autograph on dirty bits of paper and, having got it, asked who she was. ('Oh Miss Dickens,' one woman was to say to Monica in Winnipeg years later, 'I always enjoy your books. I'm a busy mother with small children, and that's why I like your books because they are so easy to put down.')

Fervid Charles Dickens fans would arrive for the afternoon, always claiming some far-fetched connection with the writer and assuming that she would be transported with delight to meet them. Would-be writers brought along their poems and dilapidated manuscripts for help getting them published, or suggested that Monica write the story of their life for a share of the profits. On top of all this Monica had also to suffer offensive remarks made about her within earshot, from the extremely personal – her hair must be dyed, her teeth were false, her lipstick did not go with her hat – to the downright defamatory: her books were all ghostwritten, she was exploiting the name of Dickens, her last book was terrible.

Every time Monica finished a book she vowed no more signings. Every time her publishers talked her into it, with assurances of guaranteed crowds and wildly enthusiastic bookshop managers who had been waiting years for her to visit. Again she would allow herself to be swayed, her article concluded, and on arrival would feel not a flicker of surprise when the said managers received her at the door with regrets that she had chosen their slowest day.

Despite these torments, the promotional tour for *Angel in the Corner* did produce an unexpected bonus. Driving through forest near Oslo, Monica and Roy came upon a herd of ponies running through the trees and when they stopped the car, one trotted over to investigate. Monica decided to buy her for Pamela, but then discovered the animal was in foal. Christening the pony Virginia after her character in *Angel*, Monica made arrangements for shipping but Baby Joe – named after the husband in *Angel* – arrived earlier than expected and mother and foal had to remain in England until Joe was old enough to travel.

§

There was sad news in March 1958: the death of publisher Michael Joseph from heart failure and a perforated ulcer at the age of only sixty.

Monica must have felt bereft at the loss of such an old friend. She had become one of the family, attending the wedding of Michael's daughter in 1948 and being visited in the States by Michael and his third wife Anthea. As she recalled about this occasion,

...he was so charming and sort of – electrical still, it gave me nostalgia for the days when I was this dopey girl of twenty-two, suddenly growing up into reality, and he was so utterly charming and fascinating, and of course I was 'in love' with him in a hero worshipping way, and he made me feel he was quite intrigued with me. Playing a game, he was, but it was fun.

(Monica Dickens, *At the Sign of the Mermaid*, 1986)

Perhaps there is more than a hint here of something a little beyond flirtation with the handsome and elegantly moustached Michael, although Monica's phrasing makes the relationship appear harmless and Michael merely avuncular. She was very pretty and very young when Michael met her, and he had a reputation for passion, with reports of the tempestuous nature of his first marriage to the actress Hermione Gingold.

§

Man Overboard, a lighter, less overtly 'social issue' work, came out that same year. Ben is a young Commander in the British navy, another of the naval officers who frequently feature in Monica's books and who presumably reflect the various naval relatives in her own family (and Roy). Dismissed by the navy after the war, Ben needs to find work to support himself and his likeable young daughter. Aged ten, Amy has a strong imagination and in her daily life acts out a series of parts, successively playing a repressed Victorian child, a World War I bride and a hockey enthusiast with a passion for the captain of the first eleven.

Ben has an affair with a beautiful but frigid TV actress who loses interest when Ben is no longer a naval officer with the potential to provide security and respectability. He takes a series of lowly jobs to survive, including clearing tables at a Lyons-type cafeteria. The jobs provide an opportunity for the episodic narrative that Monica wrote so well, a chance to introduce her usual closely observed characters – Ben's father sits with 'thick thighs apart and his torso laid between them like an egg' – in the series of vignettes that make her novels so akin to the randomness of real life.

Man Overboard was the novel she had always intended to write about the man who gets off the bus on impulse, Monica wrote in her memoir *An Open Book*, only in this instance he gets off a train to enter the lives of a happy family he keeps seeing from the train windows. She invests Ben with her interest in glimpsed lives, the sense that other people are having a more interesting time:

> *Ben...had found out long ago that the fascination of a group of strangers fades as soon as you become part of the group. The discovery, however, did not impair his enjoyment of other people's lives at a distance. Without envy or discontent, he was an appreciative Peeping Tom, yearning after houses glimpsed from a train, basement kitchens, shadows moving behind a blind, lighted front rooms seen from a street at dusk before a silhouetted figure drew the curtains on the intriguing interior.*

(Monica Dickens, *Man Overboard*, 1958)

Predictably, when Ben alights from the train suddenly determined to get to know the family he has idealised from afar, he discovers they are very different from the contented group of his imaginings. He nevertheless finds with them the happiness he was unable to achieve with his cold and calculating TV star. The *Illustrated London News* judged the novel intelligent and lively, but the *Times Literary Supplement* complained that it was wordy and diffuse and in need of some heavy cutting to allow its inner kindliness and compassion to emerge more strongly. For the *Observer*, it would have been a better book had Monica's characters not been such 'characters'. The American *Saturday Review* was similarly unconvinced: 'this book remains a series of clever portraits, crowded and unconvincing as a novel'.

The French, again, failed to take this latest work to its national bosom. *One Pair of Feet, The Fancy, Thursday Afternoons, The Happy Prisoner, Joy and Josephine, Flowers on the Grass, My Turn to Make the Tea, No More Meadows* and *The Winds of Heaven* had all been offered to the French market and had all in their turn been humiliatingly declined by top French publishers, often after they had shown initial interest. *Man Overboard* suffered the same fate.

The normal combined promotion and research visit to the UK followed in early 1959. Monica again appeared on radio and television, and spoke at a booksellers' banquet. She subsequently described *Man Overboard* as not much liked, and in its underwhelming wake she felt low and bereft of ideas, almost as if her writing career were coming to a halt. She described her state of mind as feeling completely lost. Having desperately looked forward to being free of the book during the five months it had taken her to write it, she could not now enjoy the freedom, and suffered from a terrible sort of guilt complex: resentment at having to write, but feeling all wrong when she did not.

But she was soon back at her desk and, after the fairly light-hearted *Man Overboard,* turning her attention in earnest to stronger themes. Both Monica and her publishers had come to the conclusion that it would now be better to go in a different direction. Sales of *Man Overboard* had been disappointing, and Monica realised that during the rapid few months of its writing she had not really been trying. She had experienced the usual difficulty fitting in her writing around the children, the getting up at four o'clock in the morning before they awoke, the furious scribbling during their naps. Only when the girls reached school age was she finally able to return to being more or less a full-time writer without letting the family suffer, working in the evenings as well as the mornings once they were out of the house (having first, in her own words, taken care of the horses, the house, the various animals and her husband).

Monica decided that her next book needed to be 'something big' and 'more important'. Roland Gant, a friend and editor at Michael Joseph, was worried about her next theme and on Monica's behalf spent a wet afternoon trekking around her erstwhile Notting Hill and Portobello territory, taking photographs of the old pubs and houses but also of the Council estates, the increasing demolition in the area and the many new residents. With the influx of immigrants from the Caribbean in the 1950s things were changing rapidly. When Monica went into Gant's office he handed her the photographs and suggested she write a story about changes to an old district, for which she should look no further than her own doorstep.

Monica's imagination was fired and she spent the next month gathering her own information from immigrants, welfare workers and schools before returning home to America to write. She had long ago discovered that it was easier to describe a location when away from it. An over-exact description often failed to capture the essence of a place, Monica observed, whereas concentrating on one salient feature which has remained in the memory – as with people – could bring the whole thing to life.

During her research she had learned that the musty old shops were being replaced by coffee bars and cheap clothes stores, and that the harmless drunks she remembered from her childhood had been replaced by Teddy Boys brandishing bicycle chains, at war with Caribbean immigrants armed with knives. The shivering newcomers had moved into crowded terraced houses and were being exploited by unscrupulous slum landlords. Racial tension had come to a peak with the Notting Hill riot of 1958, when night after night for a period of two weeks mobs of hundreds of white locals carried out attacks on immigrant homes. A number understandably fought back, and were among those arrested for grievous bodily harm and possessing offensive weapons. Notting Hill was the locale, and the riot the inspiration, for Monica's ensuing work *The Heart of London* (dedicated to Roy).

Most of the solidly respectable had moved out of the area, their servants no longer willing to put up with the gloomy basement kitchens. Just a sprinkling of sedate old residents gamely soldiered on, like Monica's parents, who continued to live quietly at number 52. In her book Monica reincarnated the area as Cottingham Park, and included amongst its inhabitants examples of these older remnants living in Georgian houses alongside the slum-dwellers and immigrant 'Spades', as her 1960s characters call the Caribbean newcomers. In place of those who have left, young middle-class families are drifting back in, attracted by the affordable housing and hoping that the area will come up again:

In the old heaving lifts of the Underground, bowler hats began to be seen standing next to beards and duffel coats. Corpse-white girls with seaweed hair, no lipstick and six layers of mascara rubbed shoulders at the ticket window with trim young wives in suits from fashion house boutiques. The children who went through the side streets to the Park once again began to have names like Jeremy and Sarah, and some of them had nannies, although they were not the kind of nanny that Martha's had been, with a moustache and a round grey felt hat; but foreign girls who met their lovers on benches while the children played.

(Monica Dickens, *The Heart of London*, 1961)

The central character Martha is another Monica, a middle-class mother born and bred in the locale with two endearing young daughters. Just as Monica had done, Martha as a horse-mad child coveted a pair of brown riding boots in the window of a second-hand clothes shop. As an adult, she is living the sort of life that Monica might well have lived had she not become a writer and departed London. The story begins with Martha walking home through the streets and past the little shops she knows so well; she sees a girl wearing the hideous hat of her old school, and remembers a mass rebellion when she and her fellow pupils threw the hat into the river at Hammersmith. She allows her children to play cricket with the local slum boys as Fanny had allowed Monica and Doady to play with the rough urchins of Portobello.

The novel continues to follow Martha as the storyline unfolds, and ends with her, but she is only one of a vast panorama of characters living their very different lives in this particular London time and setting. As with the real re-routeing of the A40 in west London during that period, all of the characters are affected by the construction of a transurban expressway cutting a swathe through dingy Cottingham Park, imposing compulsory purchase orders as it goes for the homes of newcomers and older inhabitants alike. Subsidiary plots abound but the focus is on Martha and on Grace Peel, a pretty young teacher in a slum school who is anxious for her deprived young charges: Frankie, an unloved twelve-year-old whose monstrous mother neglects him in favour of his sweet polio-stricken brother Kenny, and Edgar, who struggles to secure an education after his parents abandon him to return to the Caribbean, and then gradually slips into drug addiction and gang warfare. Other characters include a plain and lonely midwife, a stalker and his ashamed but half-excited victim, shopkeepers, a prostitute, a beatnik, and two bewildered old ladies living in splendid decay – all threatened with the loss of their homes and a move to somewhere unknown, all observed with compassion. The novel culminates in a race riot provoked by young upper-class twits. People get hurt.

The story ends with redemption – for some. The reader desperately wants Edgar to be saved from his miserable life, and for the quadriplegic Kenny's horrible mother to let him have an operation to restore movement to his hand and thus be able to go to school. Because this is no fairy story, only one of these hopes is realised. For the rest of the characters Monica lets real life take its likely course. The novel is highly realistic: Monica had clearly done her research well, from the convincing culture and patois of the Caribbean immigrants to the frank details of prostitution, pimping and drug-taking. Cockney characters drop the occasional 'aitch' to establish their Cockneyness, but, as taught by Compton Mackenzie decades before, Monica deliberately does this only once or twice and thereafter relies on turns of phrase to continue the dialect in the mind of the reader.

The incident in the book of a bottle party held in the London tube by upper-class twits was based on an actual occurrence reported at the time in the press. On her various trips home Monica had been appalled by the snobbishness still rife in 1950s Britain, the segregation between grammar school and public school pupils, what she termed the 'young lordlings' at Oxford who thought they owned the world despite the best jobs going to graduates of the red-brick universities. While Monica was never to shake off her own class consciousness, she was always dismayed by real arrogance when she met it. Her own nephews – Doady's boys and Bunny's son Christopher – were at Oxford and Cambridge and she had taken the dialogue for her superior young people word for word from conversations held with these young men. She used to pour them a glass of whisky, let them talk and then go straight upstairs and write it all down. (She knew they would not believe they had ever come out with such 'ghastly snobbish things'.)

The Heart of London was a laborious book to write. Previously Monica had tended not to take prolific notes or do much planning but on this occasion, with the many concurrent stories, she realised the whole project needed to be worked out mathematically. She spent around three months doing this before starting any actual writing: it was vital to know in advance which of the several stories were going to run together and which would be completely separate. In the event the balance changed during the process of writing. She enjoyed the mechanical difficulties and the complications, finding it fun and more of a challenge than the way she usually operated.

Monica's original plan was to have Martha ('she is, of course, pretty well myself') as a Somerset Maugham-ish observer who sees everything happening but has no specific story herself. She then realised that Martha would not see everything that went on and could only have a part in some of the threads, and must therefore have a life of her own. She was duly allotted an alcoholic friend who comes for a disastrous stay with Martha's family. Writing six hours or so every day except Sundays, in fairness to the children, Monica tried to achieve around six pages each day, finishing with about three pages of new material to work on when she sat down cold the following morning. Getting something new down on paper was the hard part but re-writing was fun, she observed – using her Thesaurus to nail the right word, walking around the room making faces in the mirror to find the right expression. Each page was typed out about four times before it was finished, revision being done in this piecemeal way rather than going through the book again as a whole. Monica found that the beginning of her books always needed re-writing to sharpen up the amateurish way she often started before getting into the swing of it. Research should be done afterwards, she believed: better to make progress than worry over whether the train to Scotland goes from Paddington or Kings Cross.

The Heart of London came out in March 1961 and provoked a number of critics on either side of the Atlantic to screeds of appraisal, both good and bad. 'That rousing old cliché 'a slice of life' springs irresistibly to mind,' wrote English historian and classical scholar Peter Green, except that in his opinion one slice would be miserly in comparison with what was dished up in *The Heart of London*. As Monica's proliferating characters stepped in, page after page, Green was forcibly reminded that the author was Charles Dickens' great-granddaughter, with a similar fertility of invention (including the crippled children). He thought it an immensely competent and readable novel of its kind, spelling this out as 'sociological reportage spiced with sentimentality and melodrama', which for Green was not a bad definition of Dickens himself. Perhaps Monica Dickens was most impressive when most casual, he wrote, as in her superb throwaway account of a fashionable coiffeur talking to a client (interestingly, Monica made him the same coiffeur who styled the hair of the beautiful TV star who scorned Ben in *Man Overboard*):

He rested both manicured hands on the sides of her head, looked in the mirror – but at himself, not at Edwina – and said: 'I just have my lady to comb out,' and was gone.

(Monica Dickens, *The Heart of London*, 1961)

Green's parting wish was that Monica would 'ease up on The Great Panorama of Common Life' and provide more of this 'bitchily accurate' satire.

The *Illustrated London News*, meanwhile, easily recognising the setting as Notting Hill, applauded Monica's realistic descriptions of an undisciplined, thoroughly badly run secondary modern school and the teeming tenement life of Caribbean immigrants – but emphasised that this was still a real story, not documentary. *Spectator* critic John Coleman thought Monica's 'bad ambitious novel' belonged to an unfortunate tradition arising from a misconception of the Victorian epic: that if enough sub-plots were kept running and crossing, some 'large energetic truth' was bound to emerge, or at the very least, an image of jostling, super-abundant 'life'. Miss Dickens had chosen to hurl herself into contemporary life via a garbled version of Notting Hill. It was all there – the coloured boy, the brave, pretty teacher, the doomed tart, the ugly district nurse with the heart of gold, and the mackintoshed pervert. In fact there was an amazingly up-to-date allotment of distorted sex, said Coleman. It became not so much a question of not flinching from the sordid as of getting rather a charge out of it. He predicted a large, blind success for the book.

The *Times of India* saw Monica's swirl of characters as stock types and believed that the genre of documentary-fiction necessarily involved superficiality, except in the hands of a genius (not meaning Monica, it can be assumed); it hoped that henceforward she would return to the more 'confined canvasses' which in the past had allowed better scope for her undeniable talent. In the US a Charleston newspaper enjoyed the novel and commented that it should prove of considerable interest to Southerners, who would find that the frank discussion of the problem posed by the 'invasion of Jamaican Negroes' had a certain familiar ring.

This is hardly fair. Although Monica does not avoid the racial stereotyping of her time and culture – she writes of Edgar's 'watermelon smile' and the 'thick lips' of his parents – she does not present immigration as a 'problem', but simply what is happening, and her portrayal of Edgar as a human being deserving of the same compassion and understanding as anyone else was unusual for the era. Her sympathy is entirely with Edgar's vain attempts to learn something at his hopeless school, and with his horrific life at home in the care of callous, drug-addicted foster parents. She makes it abundantly clear that the immigrants, whose high hopes of a better life have been washed away by the English rain, are subject to cruel prejudice and grasping landlords and that the white gangs, equally underprivileged, are just as culpable for the racial violence.

Other US reviews appreciated the calm realism of Monica's approach to social issues, unlike her ancestor's sentimental 'schmaltz', and saw the work as free of the 'tinny respectability' that still pervaded British novels – but in straight contradiction were then apparently shocked by *Heart*'s occasional steamy language and accused Monica of having become Americanised. The *New York Times* noted that, as the novel is set in England, the drama of the new expressway is underplayed, arriving as it does more slowly and more considerately than it might elsewhere. Similarly, the race riots do not 'flare' as they would elsewhere in the world, so much as smoulder and splutter damply and fizzle out. Overall, said the paper, it was a big London novel catching very well the atmosphere of little newsagent shops and misty autumn sunlight, and stood to be a best-seller, although perhaps Monica had overdone some of her characters – her beatnik too far out, her upper-class twits too madly decadent, Frankie's ghastly mother just too ghastly.

§

Monica had probably awaited the British reviews with some glumness. She could admit that she was hurt by criticism, and that authors needed to be 'awfully strong-minded' not to read their reviews. Certain reviews made her furious, particularly when she saw that a book had not even been read, only the blurb and perhaps a couple of pages.

She had come to believe that British reviewers hated books that readers enjoyed, and so because she was a popular writer who sold in the tens of thousands, *The Heart of London* was likely to merit only a terse three lines. For the critics it was an unpardonable crime to make money, she remarked around this time, and popular novelists such as herself and the likes of the 'absolutely brilliant' Paul Gallico received no plaudits. The same held true for Daphne du Maurier, she believed, unless du Maurier wrote a dull book, in which case she would be sure to get a positive review. For *Heart* she predicted condescending reviews to the effect that 'Miss Dickens, with her usual talent for capturing the character of the little man, has given us a book that library readers will enjoy to the full.' The *Sunday Times* and the *Observer* were the worst offenders: if one of their book reviews took up half the page she could be sure that it was a book most people would not want to read, and while the author concerned might be thrilled to have a marvellous review in the Sunday papers, unfortunately the book was unlikely to sell. As far as Monica was concerned, book reviewers should merely be informing the reader what kind of book it was and whether it had succeeded in its aims, so as to clarify for the reader whether or not to spend money on it. Critics were not there to sharpen their wits, she declared, and produce nice polished pieces to show themselves off: let them do so in the *Times Literary Supplement* rather than in the popular Sundays.

American critics, on the other hand, Monica believed to be more honest and less spiteful in their reviews, less remote from reality and what readers wanted than British reviewers (though in the long run she came to think that American critics were just as bad as British). But in such a vast country as America those 'intelligent enough' to want to read books were scattered so diffusely over the country that no group discussion was possible. In Britain almost every intelligent person read one of the two main Sunday papers and everyone was therefore reading and talking about the same books; in the US, she observed, only a small class of 'booky' people were reading the *New York Sunday Times* while the rest were reading the papers of their home cities. This meant no sales from word of mouth and reviews becoming extremely important – to the extent, Monica saw, that quite bad books could be turned into best-sellers. Publicity by publishers could have the same effect, although in her opinion her native country needed to do better on that front. A number of British firms had no marketing specialists at all at this point, something she thought was due for a change.

Monica's own critical favourites as the 1960s got under way were Pamela Hansford Johnson and *Hangover Square* author Patrick Hamilton, and, in the US, John Cheever and John Updike. Reading for Monica was an essential part of life, like breathing, she once remarked. A book was propped up in front of her on the stove as she cooked, and the whole family read at meals.

§

During the writing of *The Heart of London*, her fourteenth work, Monica had as usual been fully engaged on the domestic front. She did her own cooking and housework, but thought cleaning far less important than was generally believed – especially in America, where she considered they made 'a whole saga and a religion' out of it. She cared for her husband and daughters and the current complement of dogs and cats and horses. She worked several hours a day in the garden, swam, took a keen interest in local church and community affairs, which included entertaining the local Brownie troop in her garden, and of course rode, which always cleared her mind as nothing else. The many visitors to the house were greeted with a 'Hello, darling,' and a warm hug. She loved to play, and even after a day of vigorous activity Monica would still be up for a game of rounders with anyone in the house and, after supper, Scrabble at the kitchen table. In fact she suffered almost from a surfeit of energy, which had started after the thyroid pills cured her weight problem in her twenties:

> *Ever since then I've had so much energy I destroy everybody. People come and stay and there's swimming, riding, sailing, ping-pong at one in the morning, and they leave limp and weeping. The only thing I hate is housework. I do it once a year. I won't have servants: I was a servant once myself.*

(Monica Dickens, *The Times*, 1970)

Roy, too, was busy. When he and Monica and the girls celebrated the publication of another book in late 1962, it was not one by Monica.

Turning his hand to mystery stories Roy had produced *The Decorated Corpse*, a detective novel written in collaboration with the Massachusetts State Police. The force had chosen Roy to succeed the well-known writer Ben Benson, who died in 1959 after producing similar collaborative police procedurals throughout the 1950s. To write the book Roy first spent time with the police officers, getting to know their ways and methods: living as a trooper in their barracks, accompanying them to laboratories and crime scenes, attending the State Police Academy and a Harvard seminar on homicide investigation – even attending a criminology conference in London and visiting Scotland Yard. Monica complained that when Roy was working with the police she would come home to find police cars with their blue lights flashing in the driveway and the policemen inside the house having a drink with her husband; she joked that the neighbours all thought he was constantly being arrested.

The Decorated Corpse, from the same publisher as Benson's, was touted in the press as offering 'documentary accuracy' and Roy was reported as planning a series, although in the event only two appeared. In the book two officers investigate the kidnapping of a young girl in New England, encountering murder and intimidation along the way. Roy's writing is factual and unemotional, a step-by-step account of following police procedure to find the answers. Cape Cod is the setting, and North Falmouth and other local places are mentioned, but the principal locations are invented so little local flavour emerges. The story itself is likewise pure invention, though some newspaper reviewers appeared to think it actual reportage. The *New York Times* liked the way the story moved and thought the investigative details interesting in that they were presumably authentic, but deemed the writing and characterisation far below Ben Benson's. As a rider they conceded that Benson's own first book was nothing special and that Roy Stratton 'may, in time, develop as satisfactorily'. The book was nevertheless selected as a Mystery Book of the Month.

Monica was always happy that Roy was an author too, and believed that writers ought to marry writers. 'I couldn't bear to be married to someone who came home at five and started screaming for his meat loaf,' she said. She and Roy wrote in separate parts of the house but, at least on one occasion, Roy asked his wife for help with a romantic passage he was having trouble with, which read something along the lines of,

Oh don't leave me, she whined.

Oh go to hell, he barked cruelly.

Monica could not restrain herself from being 'dreadfully unkind' and writing 'woof woof' in the margin. At various times she claimed both that she and Roy did, and did not, show each other their work, so perhaps she ultimately thought it wiser not to get involved – she admitted to having irritated him by pointing out his split infinitives. In general, her advice to writers was not to talk about a book being worked on, so as to avoid the danger of talking oneself out of it. It was usually fatal to show anyone a work in progress, she warned:

> *Either they will want to please you and say it's marvellous and you know it isn't and you think they're stupid, or they'll pick holes in it which is even worse because people only give destructive criticism...Writers' egos are terribly frail. If someone even suggests you should change a comma you want to put your head in your hands and cry because you're a failure. Writing is the secret agony which you must suffer through alone and it is an agony.*

(Monica Dickens, *A Writer's Double Life*, lecture given at Boston Public Library, 1977)

Roy promoted *The Decorated Corpse* on TV and was subsequently invited to write reviews on books of a similar genre, and at one point to review a work on pirates. The second in his Massachusetts State Police series, *One Among None*, appeared in 1965 and was reviewed as an excellent suspense story and a tight thriller, but turned out to be a flop. After that Roy gave up on thrillers and returned to writing on the subject of his real area of expertise: US Forces activities in China in World War II – although his 1977 non-fiction account of American inter-service rivalry in China, *The Army Navy Game*, was somewhat unkindly criticised by a US Naval War College review as being in desperate need of the editorial skills of his authoress wife Monica Dickens.

§

On the 150th anniversary of Charles Dickens' birth in 1962, Monica, with social justice seemingly still on her mind, had a few sharp words to say about the problems of the present day which she believed Dickens might well have crusaded against had he lived a century and a half later. In his own time Dickens had tried to root out squalor and would find a great deal in need of a clean-up today, she wrote in an article for the British press syndicated in the US. The anachronism of old hospitals and prisons which he had seen built and would be shocked to find still 'darkly standing'; the modern evils of bureaucracy, the plight of the elderly, and the apathy which now greeted news of massacre, flood, famine and the carnage of war. Rather surprisingly, the 11-plus examination was also included on her list of current evils as a 'more modern subtle form of cruelty to children' than the brutality in the ragged schools of the nineteenth century. And, no doubt rather feelingly, Monica cited the crippling taxes which writers at the time saw as destroying artistic creativity: 'Charles Dickens would never hand over without a struggle that nineteen shillings in the pound surtax on his royalties.'

For her next novel, however, she turned to a different evil: cruelty to animals. While in the UK in 1962, driving to a film studio at Elstree to work on a script for a film of *The Heart of London* that was never realised, she used to stop at Borehamwood to visit the Home of Rest for Horses. This was a charity inspired by Anna Sewell's *Black Beauty* where exhausted or ill-treated horses were taken to rest and recover, or to spend their final years grazing in peace. With her love of horses as deeply ingrained as ever, Monica had to write about it. *Cobbler's Dream*, the story of a horse sanctuary, came out in 1963. This was the first of her horsy books and the beginnings of a new fan base of horse-mad young girls which continues to this day.

However, this was no book for dreamy young pony enthusiasts. It opens with a horse having to be shot during a hunt, just as Monica had suffered the loss of her own horse after it broke a femur while out hunting at Hinxworth. The descriptions of cruelty to horses and circus animals – poleaxed in a knacker's yard, worked to death, or packed like sardines in the holds of ships and bound for slaughter in Belgium – are brutal and disturbing. Those of Monica's characters who inflict such torture, such as the vicious young girl Chrissie who blinds one eye of her horse Cobbler's Dream with a whip, are presented with none of her usual forgiveness: Monica obviously had her line in the sand. Other characters have an excess of feeling for animals, rather than not enough. Callie – a young girl similar to Evelyn in *The Happy Prisoner*, Ellen in *The Winds of Heaven* and Amy in *Man Overboard* – is made acutely miserable by the sight of ill-treated horses and lions at the circus, and steals one such horse away to take to the sanctuary. Ex-Borstal stable lad Paul suffers agonies as the horse Cobbler's Dream slowly loses the rest of his sight. Dora, the horse-mad niece of the sanctuary's owner, the Captain, voices what is likely Monica's view of human responsibility towards animals:

God is our only hope. We're the only hope of animals, once we've robbed them of wildness. Horses could kill us if they wanted to, but they make God of us, because they need us. A horse is the most dependent creature there is. We've made him so, and we have got to care, the Captain says.

(Monica Dickens, *Cobbler's Dream*, 1963)

The novel has its sentimentality – broken-down horses badly treated the whole of their working lives at last finding a sunlit sanctuary – but it is well done, and affecting. Most reviews judged it too mawkish, although perhaps critics did not want to admit to enjoying the work. The *New York Times* saw the humans as only auxiliary in *Cobbler's Dream*, and Miss Dickens' heart as being plainly with the horses. In Britain *The Illustrated London News* deemed the book 'uncharacteristically sentimental', with Monica only occasionally pulling herself together to produce a dark shadow or two before returning to golden sunshine on lush green pastures. A. S. Byatt was later to write that *Cobbler's Dream* was too easy, with the ostensibly delinquent Paul very obviously actually a nice young man and his lies clearly a matter of defence, arising from a deprived childhood.

A few of Monica's sporting friends were shocked by her critical attitude to hunting in the book. (One claimed to have stood up for her by attributing it to the menopause.) Otherwise the book did not appear to cause much of a ripple. However, several years later the actor James Bolam, as mad about horses as Monica, suggested to Yorkshire Television that *Cobbler's Dream* be made into a children's series. Yorkshire Television bought the rights and together with the German company TV Munich created the long-running series *Follyfoot*, shown on ITV from 1971.

The setting for *Follyfoot* was found only after much searching: a decrepit farmhouse and outbuildings on the estate of the Earl of Harewood, between Leeds and Harrogate. These were all extensively reconstructed to look more picturesque. When the director realised that the farmyard presented a featureless expanse of cobbles which needed breaking up, he found a lightning-blasted tree nearby and used a heavy crane to move it the half mile to the farm where it was then sunk into seven tons of concrete. Local horses, ponies and donkeys were used to fill the stables and staff brought in to care for them. Stunt horses were occasionally used for storylines requiring special moves.

Monica was initially unenthusiastic about the choice of name for the series, which was probably based on the small village of Follifoot near the filming location. She complained that 'Follyfoot' sounded a bit too much like Merrylegs, the horse in *Black Beauty,* and tried to get the name changed, but Follyfoot it remained. In the end she accepted that viewers would become accustomed to it, as they had done with *Black Beauty* and *Lassie* and *Little Lord Fauntleroy,* and indeed the series became so famous and was so popular that it is hard to imagine it being called anything else.

Several celebrity actors were part of the cast: Desmond Llewellyn, previously James Bond's gadget man, as the farm's owner the Colonel, and character actor Arthur English as the Colonel's ex-batman. Beautiful doe-eyed Gillian Blake played the Colonel's niece Dora and Stephen Hodson played stable hand Steve, both becoming the objects of many a 1970s teenage crush. Producer Tony Essex contributed to the writing. A rotation of notable names directed who ultimately became revered figures in the UK film industry: Stephen Frears, Michael Apted and even the actor David Hemmings, who also appeared in one of the episodes. The series was aimed at young girls in love with horses but also at the newly emerging youth market, and dealt with teen issues such as jealousy and insecurity as well as the overarching theme of giving a second chance to horses and people alike.

Follyfoot was an enormous success and was judged the Best Children's Programme of 1972 by the Society of Film and Television Arts. It was bought by television companies in twenty countries around the world and the theme tune, *The Lightning Tree* by the Settlers, reached number thirty-six in the charts in October 1971. There followed the inevitable spin-off annuals and quiz-books, and now, in the internet age, a vigorous Follyfoot website.

Monica herself was not involved in the programme as other scriptwriters were brought in. A publicity photo with the cast shows Monica as an attractive, smiling woman in the prime of life, blonde hair parted in the middle and swept into an elegant 1970s cascade of curls. Her oldest grandchild, the other Pamela, daughter of her stepson Roy Junior, went on location for a couple of summers to help care for the horses and did stand-ins for the actors in distant riding shots – fuming when the director did not appreciate that if the horses were not properly managed when on camera, then the horse-mad girls watching would be too anxious to concentrate on the storyline.

Cobbler's Dream was not written for children, but after the success of the television series Monica wrote a series of books based on the programme that were specifically aimed at that market: *Follyfoot* in 1971, *Dora at Follyfoot* in 1972, *The Horses of Follyfoot* in 1975, and *Stranger at Follyfoot* in 1976. After a few years *Cobbler's Dream* itself was reissued as *New Arrival at Follyfoot*, and a new edition was published as recently as 2012 to the delight of fans old and new. Abroad, the series was particularly popular in Germany, and was even enjoyed in France as *Le ranch de Follyfoot*.

One happy outcome of a book on horses, Monica discovered, was that for tax purposes she could now write off the keeping of them as a necessary business expense.

§

Monica was rather pleased with *Cobbler's Dream* when it appeared. Then, as she recounted in her memoir, an MP cousin (perhaps Charles Orr-Ewing) casually asked her at a party what she was working on. Monica mentioned her book on cruelty to animals and immediately her cousin grew sombre. It was ridiculous to write about cruelty to animals when she should be writing about cruelty to children, he reportedly told her. Appalling accounts were coming in, leading to frequent discussion in the House of Commons.

The seed had been planted and Monica was left 'germinating', as she put it, although it seemed that she was already thinking along similar lines. In *Cobbler's Dream* she had drawn comparisons between English attitudes towards animals and children, commenting through her characters how lopsided it was that the Royal Society for the Prevention of Cruelty to Animals had been created well before any organisation to protect children. Now she immediately contacted the National Society for the Prevention of Cruelty to Children, the NSPCC, who agreed to let her go round London with their workers. Before joining them she spent a couple of months with the NSPCC equivalent in America.

It was the dreadful English winter of 1962-3, when people died of hypothermia, plumbing seized up and dirty lumps of ice stayed frozen in the streets for weeks. What Monica saw with the NSPCC staff on their rounds was the worst she could possibly see. She sat in freezing flats shivering in thick coat, woolly hat, gloves and jumper, while children with no underwear ran around in the kind of nylon party dresses donated to charity. While she was often ready to die of cold and exhaustion well before the day was over, the dedicated caseworkers would always carry on to one more wretched house, one more desperate family at the top of five flights of stairs. The beat included parts of the Notting Hill area in whose lower stretches Monica had been born and raised, and through which she had bicycled for a year to the Spitfire factory during the war – and which, she now saw, the NSPCC workers knew far better than she ever had.

In *An Open Book*, written nearly fifteen years later, the awful impressions were still fresh. Monica described in harrowing detail the brutal and drunken fathers, the mothers worn out by childbirth, the battered and neglected children shivering with cold in the filthy rooms. She was introduced as a 'student' or caseworker in training to avoid any possible resentment at what might have looked like curiosity, although in the event people welcomed someone new to tell their troubles to. She discovered the value of listening: that while she had nothing to say of any use, nevertheless people were always starved for a sympathetic ear.

When it was time to finish accompanying the caseworkers on their rounds and start writing a book, Monica was reluctant to step back: she wished that she could stay. In any case she had not yet determined on her main characters. She was to uncover one of them in the juvenile court, where she now went to listen to the magistrates and witness the sad parade of children and parents who appeared there. Here she lighted on what she needed for her novel: a dirty, undersized girl with teased, uncombed hair who had been found in a café with several soldiers. When the father told the magistrates his daughter never came home when she was told to, the girl let out a sudden anguished cry: 'What is there to come home for!' Monica used this scene in the court exactly as it happened. Another poor child she wanted to take home with her, a bony, neglected, bed-wetting seven-year-old she had met on her rounds, but instead, 'I only took him back in my head and wrote about him.'

Monica returned to Cape Cod to write her book, surrounded as usual by various animals – the current two cats Paul and Tommy, and Geoffrey the dog – who had to accept less than their usual measure of her attention. She needed absolute quiet when she was working and could not even stand the noise of the dog's stomach rumbling (although she found that if she spoke sharply to Geoffrey the rumbling actually stopped). The book took around six months of writing, in her customary mix of longhand and typing – scrawling an idea quickly by hand to get it down and only typing it up the next day because she was such a slow typist.

Her character Kate was based on the girl she had seen in court; she decided to write about only one case of cruelty in detail, rather than several and risk ending up with a sort of documentary. She wanted to show how people go wrong, and have them pitied, not censured. She made good use of the material picked up on her rounds with the NSPCC, including a caseworker's comment that poverty was a disease and, as with malaria, those affected tended to keep slipping back. The social worker character Johnny Jordan in the book based on the real-life Mr Bowes, called the 'cruelty man' by local children, who had taken Monica with him around London – the description of Johnny is identical to that given of Mr Bowes in *An Open Book*, down to his physical appearance, army background, and reasons for taking up the work (unless Monica was again confusing reality with what she had written in a novel). She included too, through her other main character Emma, the angry reaction of one of the caseworkers when a baby died through neglect. After the book was published the caseworker got in touch to say she had hoped Monica might have forgotten her outburst, or at least left it out, but for Monica it had been one of the most touching aspects: that the indomitable NSPCC were not so case-hardened against the muddle and misery as to lose all humanity.

The original title for the book was to have been *Who Cares*, but because Monica believed that reviewers seized any opportunity to make witty or cutting remarks – which she knew was not so much a review as a chance to take the author down a peg or two – she and her publishers decided that this would be too much of a gift to critics who did not like her. Too tempting with a title like *Who Cares* to simply review it as 'Enough said', Monica observed drily.

The final choice for the title was *Kate and Emma*. The book appeared in 1964, this time published by William Heinemann. The early 1960s had brought a momentous change to Monica's long relationship with the publishing firm of Michael Joseph, begun so long ago with *One Pair of Hands*. Michael himself was sadly gone, and the Canadian newspaper tycoon Roy Thomson had subsequently bought the company. Charles Pick, by then a joint Managing Director, had promptly resigned on principle, highly dubious as to what a newspaper man could possibly know about book publishing. A move to Jonathan Cape was mooted but in 1962 Charles took the post of Deputy Managing Director at William Heinemann, where he was to remain for the next twenty-three years, eventually becoming Managing Director of the Heinemann Group. He took Monica with him, along with other well-known Michael Joseph authors such as Paul Gallico and Richard Gordon of *Doctor in the House* fame, both of whom had become Monica's friends. (In fact Gordon only brought his 'Doctor' books to Michael Joseph after seeing the success with Monica.)

Monica was to remain at Heinemann for many years and enjoyed a fruitful professional and personal relationship with their publicist Nigel Hollis, who in new 1960s style made innovative use of the media to promote Heinemann's authors. Seemingly taking her place at Michael Joseph, Monica's sister Doady was then taken on by the publisher for a series of children's abridgments of Dickens. Later in the decade Doady began to publish children's stories using the names of Monica's daughters, one of these being *Pam and Prudie in the Tree House.*

The subject of *Kate and Emma* is the role of poverty in the ill-treatment of children, seen through the eyes of middle-class magistrate's daughter Emma but directly experienced by slum waif Kate. The two young women form an unlikely yet mostly believable friendship, but their paths diverge as Emma finds a career and what seems to be a suitable marriage while for Kate there is only teenaged pregnancy, too many children and a slide into squalor and despair.

The events of the story are narrated by each in turn. Emma's is the dominant voice, beginning the novel and taking the wider view as she sees other cases of deprivation-driven cruelty when going around with caseworker Mr Jordan (asked to do so by her father in an attempt to make her more aware of the realities of life).

The novel is painful reading as it proceeds towards the inevitable fate of Sammy, Kate's young son, who is probably based on the unhappy little boy Monica had so ached to take home with her during her research. Kate slowly starts to mistreat Sammy as she herself was mistreated as a child; the gripping horror felt by the reader, desperately wanting not to happen what very clearly will happen, but unable to put the book down, is testament to the strength of Monica's writing. Emma discovers Kate's younger children alone and neglected in a cold room, but Sammy is missing and Emma and Johnny Jordan go out into the freezing back garden to look for him. They find him locked in the chicken house:

He was asleep, curled up on the stinking mattress of old chicken dirt and his own filth, one hand under the sharp bone of his cheek, his hair a caked and sticky mass, his delicate eyebrows raised in sleep as if his dreams surprised him.

A rope was tied round his waist...fastened to the wall, long enough to give him a few yards of movement, not to reach the door...On the floor were a dented pan, and an empty jam-jar and a darkened lump of bread so hard that he had been sucking on it before he dropped it in the dirt.

Johnny stood very still...'Bear witness to this,' he said to me. 'Bear witness to what you see.'

(Monica Dickens, *Kate and Emma*, 1964)

Sammy survives, as does Kate and Emma's friendship, but the novel ends bleakly with nothing resolved.

Kate and Emma has been called Monica's most accomplished work. Challenging and without doubt Monica's best, said *Books and Bookmen*. For the *Sunday Telegraph* it was a 'masterly, intricate counterpoint of two Londoners' lives' – although the *Observer* was not convinced by the central premise of their friendship. The *Times of India* wrote of Monica inheriting her ancestor's humour and gifts of observation. The American writer Elizabeth Smart declared that everyone should read it, while for America's *Saturday Review* the lives of the two young women were related with 'exactitude, sympathy, psychological insight, and flashes of humour'. The novel was teeming with convincing character sketches of rich and poor, wise and foolish, stuffily respectable and ineptly criminal, all human and all too human, observed the review. At the same time Monica was 'quite pitiless' in dooming her two vividly real heroines to misery, leaving the reader feeling that rich or poor, it was not possible to win. Other American reviews inevitably compared the squalid detail of the novel to the works of Dickens, seeing in it a similar call for the amelioration of poverty, and judging its social message of equal relevance in the States.

Within ten days of its publication in October 1964 *Kate and Emma* went into its third printing. Monica subsequently commented that cruelty was swept under the bed in those days; social workers knew exactly what was happening and people were aware, but in general most really did not want to know. She believed that writing about cruelty to children had never before been done in novel form. Her rounds of deprived people's homes had helped her understand the behaviour of parents, she continued, and she saw that they were to blame for the misdeeds of the children but were not at fault: such parents were just not mature enough to cope and their utter inadequacy was at times appalling. No matter how often they were helped, they tended to slip back. The social workers had called poverty a disease, and Monica agreed.

Some longtime fans were distressed that Monica had tackled such a subject but in the long run *Kate and Emma* became one of her most successful and memorable books. Two years after its publication the film director Ken Loach produced his gritty, unforgettable 1966 television film *Cathy Come Home*, with its similar depictions of poverty and homelessness and the terror of parents that their children might be taken away from them. Conceivably influenced by *Kate and Emma*, the film led directly to the formation of the homeless charity Crisis.

Much later, in 1978, Monica chose *Kate and Emma* as her best work. It was *Kate and Emma* that she wanted to be remembered for, she was to observe. It was the book that came nearest to her original conception of it.

Following *Kate and Emma* Monica was invited to address the NSPCC in London, and did so in July 1964. She was introduced by its then president Princess Margaret, whom she found delightful and who, to Monica's gratification, laughed loudly at all her jokes. Monica joined her for tea afterwards. Returning to Massachusetts she was met at Boston's Logan Airport by Roy and the girls, both carrying large signs welcoming her back: WE LOVE MONICA DICKENS on one, and HURRAH FOR MONICA DICKENS on the other.

Emma Chisit

In late 1964, to publicise *Kate and Emma*, Monica and Roy embarked on a tour of the major cities of Australia and New Zealand. In the Australian press Monica was reported as shopping for kangaroo skin postcards in Adelaide and showing an interest in Australian hats, which she described as 'fantastic' – diplomatically adding that she thought Australian women could carry it off, and were the smartest dressers in the world. On the subject of finding inspiration, she confided to local journalists that she always had a coffee spoon which had belonged to Charles Dickens in a cup on her desk when she sat down to write.

The Canberra Times was enthusiastic about *Kate and Emma*, finding the alternating first-person voices successfully done and a satisfying way to get Emma's take on events and then the explanation for them from Kate's point of view. Monica Dickens presented the villain of the piece as poverty, rather than individuals, without any sensationalism but also without squeamishness in relaying the detail, the review observed. She had not produced a political tract, there was no railing against the system. She wrote with such insights and sympathy that the novel should be prescribed reading for social workers.

But despite such encouraging reviews Monica found, to her great hurt, that very few people actually turned up for her book signings. As she and Roy drove through Melbourne from the airport she had been excited to see crowds of readers resolutely pouring into bookshops – an uncommon sight in London and even more so in the States, she noted later in a letter from an insalubrious motel in Woolloomooloo in Sydney. Then came the terrible realisation that they did not flock to see Monica Dickens. The old wound reopened, and was made deeper.

The torturous exposure to public ridicule as she sat alone at her table was to remain an abiding feature of the trip and decades later, in *An Open Book*, Monica described her painful humiliation. The same old excuses had surfaced: bookstore managers explained the absence of fans by claiming it was early closing, or pension day, or the Test Match, or any of the other reasons Monica had already heard in bookshops in other parts of the world. The more merciful managers presented her with a small pile of books, making out they were advance orders for signed copies. Monica naturally believed that people were not surging into the shops because they did not like her books.

When and if they did come, Monica recognised in Antipodean book buyers the same types she had met so many times before and, in a reprise of her *Signing My Way Round Europe* article of the late 1950s, she used pretty much the same wording to describe them in her memoir. Here again were those who presented her with another author's paperback thinking she was a sales assistant, or brought her Charles Dickens' books to sign, or claimed to be his distant relatives in the belief that she would be utterly fascinated. There existed plenty of this last pool in Australia, she reported, despite the fact that the two Dickens offspring who had emigrated there had no known descendants. She knew that they came not to meet her and buy her books, but to allow her the pleasure of meeting them. Some of the battier types came in looking like Dickens characters in the flesh, whether by accident or design. Others came to show her their own work in draft, expecting Monica to read hundreds of pages of manuscript on the spot and causing those who might be queuing behind them for her signature to lose heart and wander off. Yet others came just to see what she looked like, and were not impressed. When they did buy a book, it was never for them, always for a wife or a mother, in case Monica might imagine they could possibly want to read it themselves.

The dreaded book signings gave rise to a very celebrated incident which spawned a whole new language. As related in *An Open Book*, a woman approached Monica in a Sydney store with a copy of *Kate and Emma* for a friend. Monica asked if she should include the friend's name when she signed the book.

'Emma Chisit.'

I wrote on the title page, 'To Emma Chisit, with best wishes...'

'No,' she said impatiently. 'Emma Chisit?'

'Twenty-three shillings.'

(Monica Dickens, *An Open Book*, 1978)

The *Sydney Morning Herald* got hold of the story, commenting that the plural of 'emma chisit' must be 'hammer charthay'. Reading this the Australian artist Alistair Morrison was struck with the idea for an Australian-English glossary. The result was his famous *Let Stalk Strine*, written under the pseudonym Afferbeck Lauder (alphabetical order), with Morrison declaring himself professor of Strine studies at Sinny University. Over the years the original incident was attributed to a variety of other writing celebrities, including A. S. Byatt, and was the subject of an exchange of letters in the *Times* as late as 2015.

In spite of the signing fiascos Monica loved Australia, finding the inhabitants friendly, lively and enjoyably informal – being called 'Mon' by strangers and exchanging awful jokes within minutes of meeting. A party was thrown for her by Ray Powell, her old ballet friend from Hinxworth days who was now a ballet master with the Australian Ballet. She loved New Zealand just as much, enjoying what she called its strange contrast of unruly nature and decorous inhabitants, and in Auckland when the city instituted its first ever literary lunch (possibly even the first ever in the whole country), Monica was delighted to be counted amongst the guests.

Henry and Fanny

A short horror story by Monica, *To Reach the Sea*, about a wig with mysteriously growing hair that leads to its owner's death, appeared in the American digest *Ellery Queen's Mystery Magazine* in September 1965. A complete horror novel was to follow, the first of Monica's books set in the US. Monica had long been aware that her books were received in America with, at best, polite attention rather than acclaim. She wanted to write something that would go down well in her adopted country, although recognising this as a challenge. She thought long and hard before going ahead, reluctant to risk her loyal following in Britain. She also did not want to write a book set in America until she could write it 'as an American'. Then she hit upon a good idea for this crucial next work, a horror plot sparked by the predicament of Roy's elderly mother Gracie.

When Monica and Roy moved to North Falmouth, Roy's mother Gracie Stratton moved from Ohio into a little house on the other side of their stable yard to be nearer her son. When Monica was first introduced to Gracie, her future mother-in-law was the ticket lady for a big amusement park and lived in the park grounds right next to the roller coaster. She had loved the job and the excitement of the park and initially felt lost and confused on retiring to the east. Here she took a job in a local gift shop and became involved with the church, but in the long run these were abandoned and the old lady grew lonely. As Monica and Roy were away a great deal they eventually found Gracie a series of live-in companions, not all of them successful. The last of these was a motherly sort but as Gracie began to lose her grip on reality she started to feel that her kindly carer was cruel and controlling. She was not, but Gracie in any case soon afterwards fell ill and had to go into hospital. The situation inspired Monica with an idea for her novel.

Then she discovered the perfect setting. Driving through the countryside to Boston, Monica used to see a beautiful yellow house standing in fields near the road, concealed in summer by thick elms and copper beeches and only emerging into view as the leaves fell in autumn. Opposite to the house on the other side of the highway was more grass and some red barn buildings; the busy road had apparently been cut right through fields belonging to the property.

It was exactly right for the suspense story Monica had been imagining. She could almost see the pale face of a captive, pleading soundlessly for help from a high window. One day she stopped and knocked on the back door of the yellow house to ask permission to use it as the setting for a book.

The house turned out to be of considerable historic interest, having been in the same family since its construction in the early 1800s by a naturalist who was friendly with back-to-nature thinkers such as Ralph Waldo Emerson and Thoreau. These famous men had visited the house, and the rooms still looked much the same as they had done in those far-off days. It was a place of creaking floorboards and hidden cupboards, and Monica could imagine an elderly and nervous inhabitant thinking she could hear the sounds of Emerson sleeping in an upstairs room, just as her character believes in the book. Monica also discovered that after the busy road had indeed been cut through the property, a tunnel was built underneath to allow the cows to go to and from the barn on the other side. Now the cows were gone and the tunnel stood eerily empty as the traffic roared overhead. There was everything here Monica required for her story of an old lady and an evil companion. The current woman of the house, a herbalist, even taught Monica a little about herbal poisoning – a suitable choice for the nefarious doings of the carer in her projected novel, which she was to call *The Room Upstairs*.

Eighty-year-old Sybil, Monica's central character, lives alone in the old yellow house; when she falls and goes into hospital she needs support in the house on her return. Her lawyer grandson Laurie and his new English wife Jess – who flew to America to marry the day after her arrival, has doubts about the marriage, and in private weeps 'stupidly' for England – do what they can to help. They engage carers for Sybil but, just as really occurred with Roy's mother, the first of these turns out to be an alcoholic and has to be let go. The second, the overbearing and dyed-haired Dorothy, begins to take what might be a sinister interest in some of the toxic herbs growing in the garden. Is Dorothy intent on murdering her vulnerable charge?

The style of the book is more impressionistic than usual, the structure perhaps a little awkward. The story is told from the point of view of both the increasingly confused and fearful Sybil and the younger Jess, who is disturbed by what she thinks are apparitions in the house and an atmosphere there which causes trouble between herself and husband Laurie. The book is a page-turner, though it is also about other things: old age and youth, appearance and reality, time gone by and the noise of modern life.

The Room Upstairs was bought by the American publisher Doubleday (whose editors, Monica joked, removed every single comma from her manuscript). She was truly optimistic that it might mean the end of her long run of non-success in the States. One of her books in Britain might sell in excess of 50,000 in hard copies while the same book in America would bring in almost nothing, a fact which had bemused Monica for years. She suspected it was to do with being 'just too British for words', but by now she thought she was properly absorbing the American way of life and had overcome the resistance she had initially felt towards Americans – the way they laughed at different things, and were only superficially friendly and deep down less warm than the English. Some of these aspects of the American character Monica still believed to be the case, only she had come to accept rather than criticise, and judged herself capable of writing from the American point of view. (However, despite confessing to being half-American, and using the odd Americanism in her speech, Monica at this stage insisted that she would never give up her British citizenship.)

Reviews in America were healthy. Doubleday labelled the book a psychological suspense novel, a tag which for one US reviewer served only to cheapen a fine work. It was not simply a thriller, the review observed: it went beyond the gallery of good and evil characters in their setting of the old house and became a struggle between old and new. 'Youth and age, coarseness and gentility, reality and fantasy are sensitively probed in this witty and serious novel by a master writer. Highly recommended,' was the verdict. Other US reviewers saw it more as enjoyable light entertainment with a ghoulish climax, or 'British Gothic' in a Massachusetts setting, although advising readers not to assume they knew what was coming next. Monica Dickens had absorbed New England so well, noted one critic, that people and places were described with the understanding of a native, and Monica's sympathy with the problems and tragedy of ageing was magnificent.

In Britain, Virginia Ironside in the *Daily Mail* described the novel as tremendously funny, in an agonising way, 'and so perceptive you are left half-laughing, half-shuddering with the astuteness of Miss Dickens' observation...not a single sentence that doesn't prick its point right home'. Loneliness, claustrophobia and the fantasies of old age were all summoned up and left lingering in the memory, observed the *Daily Telegraph*.

After the book came out the owners of the yellow house, 'Hillside', near Plymouth, held a celebratory gathering for Monica at the historic property. But despite Monica's high hopes, sales were poor, and the book did not even earn back its advance. At the time of its publication Monica stated that her intention was to set her future works on both sides of the Atlantic, but in the event, no doubt somewhat chastened by the performance of *The Room Upstairs*, she returned to her homeland for most of her settings.

§

Monica's parents made their last trip together to America in 1965. Their summer visits had continued regularly as the years went by, though Fanny spent more and more of the day in bed, and Henry in an armchair by the fire or in a long chair out in the sun in his battered Panama hat. He mislaid his pince-nez glasses and other belongings several times a day and would talk to the lost object, asking it where it was or who the devil had hidden it. At Monica's, where most meals were served in the kitchen and there were clearly no servants, Henry continued to expect lunch and dinner at set times and vaguely thought that staff were cleaning up after him. As he aged, he reverted to calling Monica 'Baby' as he had done when she was a child.

On that last visit they sailed across as usual, Fanny having recently essayed air travel and been unimpressed. However, by this point the transatlantic sea voyages had changed for the worse, the smaller Cunard ships on which Henry and Fanny had been so well looked after now beginning to be retired, together with their solicitous crew. While the older ships were getting down at heel, so too were the passengers: the Dickenses were astounded to discover that some of the diners in First Class did not change for dinner.

On their return to number 52 Fanny increasingly took to her bed there as well, and finally kept to it for good. People still came to see her and to tell her their problems, and Fanny stocked bottles of gin and vermouth in her bedroom to offer them. She continued to produce her witty rhymes for births and marriages, or cases of ill health, despite the depredations of her own emphysema. Even when old and sick, Fanny remained genuinely interested in others and thought about them more than herself, said Monica, and so naturally she received great love in return. Henry would clomp up the stairs every evening to read to his wife from Jane Austen or Jerome K. Jerome, sometimes for hours, even when Fanny hardly knew he was there. Two nurses were brought in to look after her, a day and a night nurse who cared for the old lady tenderly and protected her through her slow fading. Monica wanted to be there for the end and came over to England, but Fanny knew what she was up to and sent her home to America. Fanny Dickens died in June 1966, on the day before her ninetieth birthday and two days after Monica had arrived back in Cape Cod.

Fanny had not had an easy time of it with Henry. They had waited four long years to marry, during which they were not even allowed to ride alone together in a cab. The early years of the marriage were difficult as Fanny tried to forge a relationship with Henry's daunting French mother Marie; she suffered the loss of her baby twins, and then the death of her adult son Bunny. After her mid forties Henry would not dance or play tennis with her or take her out alone on the river at Sonning. Instead, he danced and played tennis with younger women with whom Fanny was expected to be, and was, friends. Monica defended this as not womanising but innocent goings-on, Henry making his own laws. Her mother occasionally voiced some disgruntlement at Henry's behaviour but would immediately retract it, trained as were all the Dickens wives to accept the 'tyrant-child' sons of Marie. The final years of marriage were no doubt a long accommodation with Henry's progressively ritualistic quirks and routines.

Henry only lived a few months longer. He was found once or twice at the foot of the stairs with a book in his hand, on his way up to read to his Fan (it was always 'Fan' or 'M'wife' when she was in favour, and 'Your Mother' when not, said Monica). According to Monica they had adored each other, underneath all the rows and bickering and the dredging up of time-worn grudges against each other's parents. After Fanny went, Henry would talk about their perfect marriage and refuse to admit they had ever exchanged a cross word. He died of a stroke aged eighty-eight on 5 November 1966, at home in Chepstow Villas, the last surviving grandson of Charles Dickens. Monica attended the Requiem Mass held at the Jesuit church in Farm Street on 9 November. For the funeral their housekeeper had a wreath made in the shape of the pince-nez Henry had so often lost and accused her of taking, and after the ceremony Monica saw her take it from the pile of flowers and matter-of-factly throw it into the open grave as though to say, as she had done so often, 'Here you are then.'

§

When Henry died he was an OBE and former President of the Dickens Fellowship, a position he took seriously. In 1946, when newly President, his grandfather Charles was coming under attack in books and the press as a fop, a drunkard, a cruel and unnatural father and a libertine. Henry responded with a robust defence at a Fellowship conference. Dickens' flowered waistcoats were then the fashion, he pointed out, and were sported by Disraeli and several other luminaries of the era. Dickens may have presented his guests with plenty to drink and mixed all kinds of punches, Henry's defence continued, but the great man drank very little himself. Throughout their lives the three Dickens children known to Henry personally never ceased to express their great love and admiration for their father, and as to Dickens being a libertine, Henry's legal opinion (without mentioning Nelly Ternan by name) was that the evidence was not enough to hang a cat on. Henry also stoutly defended his great-aunt Georgina Hogarth, likewise under attack in the press at the time. Far from being a scheming, cold and calculating woman who had ousted her own sister, Dickens' wife Catherine, from Dickens' home, and alienated his children's affections, Henry insisted she had been a sweet, kindly, mid-Victorian woman totally incapable of any such behaviour. Following on from his spirited rebuttal of all the charges against his grandfather at the conference, Henry that same night officially reopened to the public Dickens' old home at Doughty Street in Bloomsbury, which had been closed for the duration of the war and its treasures removed to the country.

Henry enjoyed a long and successful career as a barrister, and had the habits of his time and class, if somewhat dented after the war: the expectation that he would be waited upon by a fleet of servants and that dinner would always be served at eight. But for all that, Henry was the kindest of men. A former pupil in his chambers remembered him as a forthright, courageous and able advocate and in addition as someone who, despite his admirable combative qualities, remained on the best of terms with his opponents. He was immensely kind and helpful to younger men, providing advice and encouragement and, most prized of all, friendship, the pupil recalled. For many years Henry acted for the Medical Defence Union and outside the courts he had been tireless in his efforts on behalf of those less privileged than himself. Too short-sighted to enlist during the First World War like his three brothers – an extremely painful memory for him in later life – Henry had instead done sterling work helping soldiers' families and the men themselves on their return from combat. After serving as an Air Raid Warden during the Second World War, he became very involved in work to improve housing in the poorer part of the borough of Kensington. Homes were desperately needed after the extensive bombing and Henry was instrumental in getting a Council estate of flats built, which was named Henry Dickens Court in his honour and the buildings named after Dickens characters. Henry, by then an Alderman and wearing the traditional fur-lined robe, was amongst those on the platform when the Queen Mother came for the official dedication of the estate and afterwards he had tea with her in Dombey House. On retirement in 1955 Henry was made an Honorary Freeman of the borough, an award recognising significant contribution to public life and then only rarely conferred: one predecessor was Sir Winston Churchill (and Margaret Thatcher was to follow).

Despite his famous lineage and considerable achievements Henry would remark that his claim to fame was being the father of Monica Dickens. His more famous daughter wrote a great deal, and movingly, about Henry in *An Open Book*, far more so than about Fanny, no doubt just as loved but seemingly less of a force in Monica's life. During her childhood Henry had taken her to matches at The Oval; when she was an adult the two of them had gone alone together on cruises and expeditions, Monica often carrying Henry's unwieldy old camera for him up and down the hills, the trips forever punctuated by the frequent loss of Henry's several pairs of pince-nez and the subsequent cables to Bond Street for replacements. At Hinxworth they would drive to the top of the nearby downs and sit in silence gazing at the view, happy and comfortable in each other's company.

On the very last pages of her memoir Monica included a final snapshot of Henry. When she had been kicked out of drama school as a young woman she was reluctant to tell her parents after making such a fuss about going there, and every day she would leave number 52 with her tights and books and wander around or go to the cinema to fill in the hours. One day Henry came upon her reading on a bench in Kensington Gardens. Monica admitted that she had been expelled, and explained that she had thought they might be angry after having paid for the whole term (not quite true, she admitted all those years later: it was because she felt like a fool).

'Angry? I'm delighted. We only let you go because we hoped it wouldn't last long.'

We walked home together.

(Monica Dickens, *An Open Book*, 1978)

The loss of her parents left a hole for Monica like an 'infinite nothing'. For a few months both she and Doady felt that Fanny was still present in some way, at the edge of consciousness, until at last Doady suddenly announced that Fanny was gone. It had taken her mother longer than others to depart, Monica sensed, because she had been so engaged with the living. Much later Monica dreamed that she was sitting in a chilly dark corridor, waiting for her fate to be decided by someone behind a high closed door. When she put out her hand to see if anyone was there, Fanny took it.

'Yes, my darling, I am always there.'

(Monica Dickens, *An Open Book*, 1978)

§

After Fanny and Henry were gone number 52 was sold, and without this mainstay of her childhood Monica for a while felt very lost when in London. Returning to view the house many years afterwards, she was to say that her old home was 'almost haunted by love'.

The Literary Life

In Britain in the mid 1960s Monica, still famous, appeared with Roy in a couple of TV commercials which were part of a series aimed at encouraging women into pubs – with their husbands, of course. In *Monica Dickens and her husband look in at the local* Monica in pencil skirt, cardigan and pearls, short curly hair tightly done, leads Roy into an old English pub that her voiceover announces was once frequented by her great-grandfather. It's fine for lunch when you don't feel like eating in a crowded restaurant, says Monica over a shot of them chatting at a small table. In another ad, appearing both on TV and as stills in a large advertisement in the *Daily Mirror*, Monica and Roy are again drinking in an old pub (possibly the same one). In this she voices a longer, nostalgia-filled narrative about pub-going, talking of the lemonade that she drank in Oxfordshire pubs as a child after riding, and how as a nurse she used to sneak out of the hospital to the Nag's Head to fetch a bottle of beer and a packet of crisps 'for a very charming fractured femur on Men's Surgical'. When in London her preference is always to go to a pub for lunch, Monica avers, launching into a panegyric on the pleasures of pub-going:

> My great-grandfather used to come to this pub and they have these rather splendid pictures of characters from his books dotted around the walls...My husband, being American, likes to poke about and find all the fascinating old places. Galleried courtyards where steaming coach horses once stamped the cobbles. Sociable little taverns by the docks, with crusty bread and a perfect ham, and the river smell seeped into the very timbers of the scarred old bar. Pubs in Bloomsbury where all the great names of English literature have drunk and laughed and argued.

The fact that she had emigrated to the States was again obscured: the voiceover finishes with Monica fondly relating how she still comes home from a ride by way of a pub, with her children now the ones drinking the lemonade and even her horse enjoying a pint of bitter.

The Charles Dickens connection was naturally well to the fore in these commercials, and Dickens as a theme was to prove a centrepiece of Monica's public activities for the next few years in her adopted homeland. She had already relied on her Dickens lineage for various Christmas pieces in the American press, and had presided over the welcoming of attendees at the 56th Annual Dickens Fellowship Conference when it was held in Boston in 1962. Following publication of *The Room Upstairs* she now concentrated for a while on lecturing in the States with Dickens as the main focus. Because the book had not done well, finances were tight, and her American publisher Doubleday suggested that instead of relying on book sales – at that time only one in four Americans bought a book even once a year – she should do what everyone else was doing and go out on the lecture circuit. Over a period of six months or so Monica did just this, following in her great-grandfather's footsteps on his second visit to America nearly a century before and for much the same reason: profit, what Monica later called the 'easy lecture circuit buck'. (She was not the first Dickens descendant to milk the American market: three of Dickens' sons had preceded her.) She gave around sixty lectures in thirty states to a mainly female audience, and continued to give the occasional lecture until well into the next decade. Her fee, as of 1971, was reported to be $600 per event. (The celebrated feminist writer Kate Millett, author of *Sexual Politics*, was getting $1500 and expenses.)

Monica became submerged in what she called 'the fantastic sub-world' of women's clubs, luncheon groups, conventions and assemblies. Some of the women's club buildings were vast, taking up whole city blocks and fitted with their own auditoriums.

Her engagements were more or less divided into two main categories. The first was lectures proper, where she stood on a stage in a hall or theatre facing rows of women challenging her to educate or entertain them, sometimes at ten in the morning. The old ladies sat in the front row in order to hear, but had a tendency to clomp out with their canes to the toilet and then clomp their way in again, watched by the entire audience with far more interest than Monica sensed they were affording her lecture. Several members of the audience, both young and old, invariably nodded off.

The other category was the ever painful after-lunch or after-dinner talk. Monica found the prior small talk at these lengthy dinners excruciating, and if they were taking place at the hotel where she was staying, she would sometimes make an excuse and go upstairs to lie down until the appointed hour. If she mistimed it she had to sit through rambling reports from the secretary and someone's description of their recent trip to Europe. After her own talk ended everyone was as exhausted as Monica, but the winding up of ritual conversation had still to be endured. People came up just to tell her they had an entire set of Dickens at home, and inevitably somebody would enthuse about her being Charles Dickens' great-granddaughter and how they had been brought up on his works and read *A Christmas Carol* aloud every year – and then would bid her goodbye as Miss Dixon.

Her three subjects were initially planned as *Charles Dickens – The Man and the Myth, America is My Cup of Tea,* and *The Facts of Fiction*. Promotional shots showed Monica, now fifty, as an elegant, slender woman in a fringed ear-length bob (not so flattering to her strong features), often formally dressed in a suit. In her myriad interviews with local newspapers – in which she was once described as talking with a decided British accent but lacing her speech with American slang – she went over and over the same old ground of her debutante-turned-char-turned-writer backstory (perhaps by now completely sick of it). She would usually mention that *One Pair of Hands* was still selling 20,000 – 30,000 copies a year, perhaps hoping to reawaken US interest.

She was invariably introduced as Dickens' great-granddaughter but Monica never presented herself as an expert. She took her lecturing material from various biographies, such as Christopher Hibbert's 1967 work *The Making of Charles Dickens*, which she wrote to tell him had been helpful to her. In Britain a few years later she cheerfully admitted to a *Times* journalist that she knew nothing about Dickens: she would read up on things and then present them as family secrets (just as she appears to have done for her BBC broadcasts when a very young woman).

You can get away with it in America...I learnt early on in life that you can bluff your way through anything.

(Monica Dickens, *The Times*, 1970)

Monica was frank about the fact that many in her audience knew far more than she did. Thousands of Dickens fans in England and the United States were able to recite whole pages of his works, Monica told a Dallas newspaper (adding that they were occasionally very hard to stop). Others had never read a single work of Dickens, or perhaps only *A Christmas Carol*. When lecturing, Monica genuinely believed that if she created any interest in reading Dickens for the first time, or in rediscovering him, then she had in some way succeeded.

The Dickens talks, routinely preceded by her no-expert disclaimer, covered aspects of his early and private life and the genesis of a few of his novels: Monica's aim was to make Dickens come alive as a real person rather than remain a myth. She talked of the mobs during his tours in America, of Dickens being the 'Beatle of his day', and how he was seen as a Santa Claus-type figure because of the vitality and humour in his books, while in reality his work had an underlying melancholy. She discussed his relationship with his parents and with his own children, and the estrangement from his wife Kate and erroneous rumours of an affair with his sister-in-law Georgina Hogarth. She referred to the relationship with Nelly Ternan, though in her earlier lectures making it look as if it began after Dickens' separation from his wife (it began well before). By around 1970 Monica was franker and dismissing the affair as 'no secret'.

The lecture on America revolved around the usual topics of differences in customs and pronunciation and table manners, the predictable tack of two nations divided by a common language with plenty of jokes thrown in. The English believe they belong to the most exclusive club in the world, Monica told her audiences, warning that despite the superficial similarity Americans should remember that the English were really very different. They should never argue with the English because the English were always right, she quipped. She mined her experiences as a new bride in a new country – it was only after crossing the Atlantic that she realised American housewives did not spend their mornings drinking Martinis with the Fuller brush man – and would get laughs with her take on American TV commercials and the American use of such terms as 'homemaker' (to her mind patronising) and 'senior citizen' or 'golden age' for the elderly. Round-robin Christmas letters were insulting, she informed her audience, and she disliked the ubiquitous piped music wherever she went.

Naturally Monica also found plenty to applaud for her audience, such as the gracious way Americans accepted compliments and the many courtesies and conveniences of American life. She loved American radio, with its advice, solace and information-giving on every subject, including sex. She claimed to have become extremely Americanised. 'To me the way American people open their minds and hearts to other people is the main reason I have come to love the country so well,' she would finish. She was 'enchanted' with America.

Her *Facts of Fiction* lecture was probably the same as, or similar to, her 1960s article of the same name in which she wrote about the way the facts of an author's life inevitably found their way into his or her works – a point she was often to return to:

Nothing in a novel can be completely invented. Everything must have been seen or heard or felt or read.

(Monica Dickens, *The Facts of Fiction*, Writer, 1968)

In the midst of these peregrinations, in 1967, the Southeastern Massachusetts Technological Institute awarded Monica an honorary doctor of literature degree. Charles Pick sent her a congratulatory cable and letter, one of which ran her to ground in Milwaukee and the other in Kentucky. Monica was more than gratified and actually felt herself blushing as she read the news from the Institute. She returned to Boston for the ceremony.

§

To a degree Monica enjoyed the public speaking and the constant touring, on occasion finding the 'roaming experience' most seductive, and a good excuse not to do any writing. It was fun to lecture on her forebear, or so she told interviewers. 'I've always liked being Charles Dickens' great-granddaughter,' she said of her Dickens talks. But for the most part she would have preferred to be with her family in North Falmouth. Staying in so many hotels kept bringing *Death of a Salesman* to mind, she commented, and she worried that the girls were more in need of her as they entered adolescence. They were still at boarding school from Monday to Friday and at home only at weekends, but during the week there were numerous phone calls. Once the bulk of the lecturing was behind her, Monica was happy to settle back in Cape Cod.

In tandem with beginning her next novel Monica now assumed additional duties as the local lady of letters. She became a regular on a panel of judges for a *Boston Globe* book award, finding most of the other judges hidebound and affectedly highbrow and on one particular panel even anti-fiction, until she talked them out of it. She did not always have the time (or the interest) to read every single book, however, and the husband of a friend used to do this on her behalf and make recommendations. In 1969 she was a guest speaker at the newspaper's annual book festival, part of an unlikely pairing in a dialogue on 'The Novel' with fellow Cape Cod resident Kurt Vonnegut, who had just released *Slaughterhouse Five*. She and Kurt were fellow guests too at a *Meet the Authors* tea at a Cape Cod Writers Conference that same year. The two hit it off and Monica invited Kurt to dinner. 'They are the sweetest, happiest people I know,' Kurt wrote in a letter to a friend. He described how Roy did all the final typing for Monica, and was full of admiration for the Strattons' stables and paddocks and the expansion then under way of their house and guest house. He remarked as well on their 'wonderful breed of dog all their own: poodles crossed with golden retrievers'. (This was the so-called goldendoodle, according to several sources a type first bred by Monica.)

Alongside these various authorial appearances Monica continued her series of literary reviews for the *Boston Globe*, the *New York Times Book Review* and others, initially embarked upon in 1965 and set to carry on for about two decades. Her reviews of non-fiction works dealt mainly with the content rather than the style or approach of the writer. An exception was her review of Wolf Mankowitz's *Dickens of London*, which, while for Monica saying nothing new because to her mind everything that could possibly be said on the subject of Dickens had already been said, was nevertheless an intelligent and readable condensation of Dickens' packed, kaleidoscopic life. A new biographer could only read the best of other books and select and reinterpret, she commented – perhaps the view she had arrived at after considering, and rejecting, the proposal made to her in the early fifties that she herself write a biography of her great-grandfather.

Reviews of fiction were often short and to the point, usually with a fair degree of plot exposition (likely a requirement of the paper), and of course often delivered with a shaft of wit. A number of the English writers of the day earned her approbation, even if in Monica's opinion they mainly wrote about themselves. She admired the 'clean, swinging' style of Edna O'Brien's *August is a*

Wicked Month, reviewed in tandem with Flann O'Brien's *The Dalkey Archive* – no doubt for the fun of the twin surnames and general Irishness – but she was not impressed with Flann O'Brien's 'bog of verbiage' and the apparent whimsy of his unusual writing. The male O'Brien could learn from the female, Monica observed. Margaret Drabble's *The Garrick Year* was 'perceptively deep', with an ecstatic humour that Monica found a joy in those days of the solemn novel. *Watership Down* by Richard Adams was a 'lovely, lovely novel' while the short stories of V. S. Pritchett were 'wonderful and utterly satisfying', his writing superb, and he himself at ease with the difficult art of constructing a short story – economical but complete:

> *All his characters, whether stars or walk-ons, are described in one or two startlingly exact phrases and then left to fend for themselves. His style is not spare or clipped. It flows and wanders...But there is no useless word, no self-indulgent decoration. Surprises, yes, because no one is a stereotype, but once Pritchett's put you in the know, there's instant recognition...*

(Monica Dickens, *The Boston Globe*, 1983)

One review ran into trouble, however. A *Boston Globe* reader accused Monica of a 'serious literary gaffe' when she attributed the famous cakes and ale quote to Falstaff instead of *Twelfth Night*'s Sir Toby Belch.

Those were the better authors. She gave shorter shrift to *Just Barbara*, the life story of Britain's much loved dog trainer and national treasure Barbara Woodhouse. Barbara was lovely, wrote Monica, but no writer, with her naive and simple style and frequent exclamation marks like 'short, sharp yelps'. Yet she liked Barbara's brilliantly successful style with dogs, equally simple and direct, and she ended with 'Good girl, Barbara - what a good girl!'

Commenting on writers on her own side of the Atlantic, Monica took a feminist view of Sue Kaufman's 'hilariously disenchanted' *Diary of a Mad Housewife* in 1967, praising the merciless eye and fearless wit with which Kaufman produced previously unuttered truths about women: 'the secret disillusioned jests we share only with real intimates, often only with ourselves'. Shirley Jackson's *The Lottery* 'should be in every classic collection'. Her exuberant review of Joyce Carol Oates' crammed *A Bloodsmoor Romance* picked up on the deliberately lengthy, nineteenth-century-style diversions which went on and on but were never tedious, the heaped detail on Victorian customs and costumes, and the dig at her own great-grandfather as the foreign visitor who heartily enjoyed America before returning home to publish vicious satires on the New World. The novel might be self-indulgent, but Oates was enjoying herself in a way that Monica coveted, relishing the freedom to move in any direction at her own leisure.

Opportunities also came to review writers who had reviewed Monica themselves, including the intellectual writer Rebecca West who so many years earlier had made Monica the subject of an admiring radio broadcast to the French immediately after the war. West's *The Birds Fall Down* was the best novel of the year so far, Monica wrote in 1966, declaring that this 'long, marvellous' work, written in the most beautiful prose, should make lighter-weight writers cashing in on the spy fiction boom hang their heads in shame. For Monica, West's genius was to make a highly complex novel, in terms of its intricately laid out Russian background, as simple as the story of its beleaguered young heroine. She was similarly riveted by a collection of stories from Patricia Highsmith, who in the 1950s had recommended Monica's work to her fellow Americans. Highsmith's expertise at subtle horror rendered her stories 'unbearably believable' and 'marvellously unbearable'.

In the late 1970s Monica thought that a great deal of modern writing was extremely bad, the result, she believed, of grammar not being taught in schools and authors not understanding the importance of sentence structure for clarity. She could not understand why so many really bad books were published, and was alarmed by the proliferation of second-rate romances and by the success of poor work. Her own early reading had included Dickens (naturally), Galsworthy, Robert Louis Stevenson, and Siegfried Sassoon and the romantic poets; as an adult, she did not care for Gothic novels, historical romances, mystery, science fiction or humour, 'as they are designed for people who may never read anything better'. She also disliked introspective novels by authors 'who have very little to say beyond a self-conscious examination of themselves and their neuroses'. At the same time, though, Monica was optimistic about the future of fiction, convinced there would always be an avid audience for a good novel.

§

One of her funniest reviews was of what Monica considered a seamy novel by Charles Jackson, author of *The Lost Weekend*, the groundbreaking autobiographical work on the topic of alcoholism. Jackson had been brave to give readers an account of a stupendous bender in his first book, Monica noted in her 1967 piece *A 'Lust Weekend'*, but now Jackson's latest work was simply following safely along in the wake of a new trend – pornography, despite publishers announcing that porn was on the way out:

...nay, has already picked up its scattered underwear and departed, shoes in hand.

(Monica Dickens, *The Boston Globe*, 1967)

Jackson had now written a novel about a nymphomaniac,

which takes this quarter's prize for the greatest number of sexually descriptive words adding up to the least titillation....There is also a lot of questionable stuff about the aesthetic qualities of the male physique, and one episode with a state trooper in a patrol car, which, as a long admirer of Mr Jackson, I believe he must have written tongue in cheek.

(Monica Dickens, *The Boston Globe*, 1967)

His publishers should also do him the service of editing out his confusion between the verbs lie and lay – in or out of the summerhouse, she concluded acidly.

In fact Monica by now had become seriously concerned about the rise of pornography. The seeds of her unease had been in evidence as early as 1950, when she remarked in her BBC radio series *Monica Dickens' Book Club* that it had been necessary to read quite a few books before she came upon any fit for family reading or quoting on air. She was no prude, she said,

and I know quite a lot about the seamy side of life, but I know too that is only one side of life. The world is full of squalor, but it is full of splendour too, and I can't see any literary merit in writing a novel about all the most unsavoury characters you can think of, bringing in as many rude words as you think you can get away with. It isn't even like life.

(Monica Dickens, *Monica Dickens' Book Club*, BBC, 1950)

The appearance in Monica's own *Heart of London* of a character who makes obscene phone calls had arisen from concern about what she saw as an increase in London life of 'furtive vice', in her view perhaps a result of the nanny State trying to push vice underground, or possibly because of increased repression around sex. Monica was therefore in favour of more openness and of sex education in schools. However, out and out pornography was another matter. She spoke of her own *One Pair of Hands* as a 'clean' book recommended for teenagers, and while on her lecture tour she would mention that whatever his themes, Dickens' books too were 'clean' (although in the same lecture she herself brought up the homoerotic overtones in *David Copperfield*, and on BBC radio had once referred to Nancy in *Oliver Twist* as syphilitic). She was appalled by some television, 'the straight filth that gets by, excused by being called satire', and by pornography in books. In Britain Monica's views on television and pornography were well known and she was seen as something of a moral force in the nation: in 1964 one of the adherents of Mary Whitehouse's budding campaign to clean up British TV wrote to Monica for support. (Her response, if any, is not known.) While in Australia Monica had likewise spoken out on the subject. 'If you put enough dirt into a book it will be a best-seller in America,' she told the press – although she did not approve of censorship: it would 'not stop people from reading dirty books; education of the public is the only way to stop filth'.

In the end she set out her concerns in a 1968 article for the *Boston Globe* entitled *How, Alas, to Write a Hit.* Pornography was 'energetically alive' and crowding the best-seller lists, she wrote: all the new novels at the library spontaneously fell open at the steamy bits. The dirtier the books became, the dirtier the public wanted them. Time was when it was enough to get the hero and heroine through the bedroom door and then let the reader's imagination take over, whereas now they must be bedded, undressed and examined in prolonged detail. Why did people waste so much valuable time reading about sex when they could be doing it? she asked. However, Monica knew the real reason for this 'crescendo of crud': sex sells. Repeating the statistic that had sent her on her lecture tour, she observed that only one in four Americans bought even a single book a year. The enterprising Harold Robbins had therefore conceived the brilliant idea that tapping into the vast non-reading public could make a million, said Monica, and so was born the non-book for non-readers.

Monica's particular contumely was reserved for the real writers who had joined the gold rush. For her this included 'talented, articulate authors' such as Gore Vidal and John Updike, who used to get better reviews than royalties but were now going after the big sex sales. Of Updike she wrote:

Woe, woe that a man who can write with such pure beauty should try to solicit his readers' sympathy or even interest in an improbable stud like the slab-faced hero of 'Couples'....Bunkum. Go for the great non-readers, but don't let's pretend it's art.

(Monica Dickens, *The Boston Globe*, 1968)

These views were not in tune with prevailing liberal mores. In 1970, on a panel of writers at a book show in Kansas, Monica announced that she preferred to see 'the good Anglo-Saxon four-letter words rather than a lot of beating around the bush and mealy-mouthing', but subsequently continued at such length on the topic of pornography and Danish sex books that the other two writers staged a brief walkout in mock protest. Surprisingly, though, Monica later had positive words to say on Erica Jong's controversial *Fear of Flying*, the provocative 1974 novel about a married woman who decides to indulge her sexual fantasies with another man. A 'brilliantly articulate picture' of a neurotic woman, Monica wrote, '...the wit is dazzling'.

Her own works, of course, could never be accused of explicitness, and were usually considered appropriate for a young readership: a number, including at least *One Pair of Feet* and *The Happy Prisoner*, were abridged for schools. Over time, despite the increasing frankness of her output in the 1960s, Monica in fact earned such a reputation for innocuousness that schoolgirls were rumoured to encase rather more sultry works in a Monica Dickens book-jacket – a report greeted with delight by Monica.

§

With each book Monica said it was the last, but whenever she vowed to write no more Roy bought her a new pen or a more comfortable chair or devised some new method of encouragement. He built her the special corner desk in their home at North Falmouth, where out of one window she could distract herself from her work by watching the villagers walking by or from the other, enjoy the garden with the horses grazing peacefully beyond.

Perhaps looking for her next subject, Monica in late 1966 requested an interview with the famous Helen Keller, deaf-blind since an illness as a toddler. There was a Dickens connection which Monica may well have been aware of: during her great-grandfather's tour of America in 1842 he had been greatly impressed with the work done at the Perkins Institution for the Blind in Boston, particularly the education slowly being imparted there to a young deaf-blind girl. The story goes that a few decades later Helen Keller's mother read Dickens' lengthy account of this in his *American Notes* and immediately understood that the school might be able to help her own daughter. At her request a teacher was sent from Perkins, the famed Annie Sullivan, who taught Helen Keller how to communicate. Helen went on to become a celebrated author and political activist. In the event Monica's request was not possible to grant as Helen, by then fairly elderly, was no longer up to receiving visitors. In the reply to Monica's letter came a grateful mention of Dickens' role in Helen's life: 'How she would have enjoyed seeing you...!' wrote Helen's close friend and carer in her response.

Instead, Monica started a novel set in the 1930s, thinking that this was the one era she knew well that she had not yet put in a book, and also that she had become too removed from current English lives and needed to return to what she had lived through herself. Or perhaps, Monica mused in her memoir, it was the loss of her parents and a desire to return to the time when they were so invincibly alive.

Sitting in Boston Public Library, reading old magazines and going through microfilms to summon up the events of those far-off years, Monica came across the tragedy of the R101 airship. At that point the largest flying craft in the world, the reputedly safe R101 crashed in France in 1930 on its maiden flight overseas, killing forty-eight of the fifty-four people on board. This was the story she wanted to write.

As was her habit, Monica returned to England for research, visiting Cardington in Bedfordshire whence the airship had departed on its doomed flight and where the bodies of the dead were laid to rest in a mass grave after a memorial service in St Paul's in London. She found the cemetery still a troubled place, she wrote in her memoir, even after so many far worse air disasters since.

Leaving Cardington in the heavy rain, Monica drove to nearby Hinxworth to take one more look at the village and her beloved old cottage. There were changes, inevitably: trees cut down in the lanes where she used to walk, the Post Office grocery moved to a house next to the village hall where she had led the Women's Institute in Twenty Questions. Her old home, once the only apricot-coloured cottage in the county, had been painted white with black beams just like every other period cottage in Hertfordshire. The greengage tree in the garden was gone but what remained – the rosemary bushes by the door, the flowers and the cooking apple tree – still seemed like hers. She felt the house reproaching her, and did not attempt to go in.

Walking past her old stables, Monica turned down the green lane which had been the starting point of countless rides and for a moment wished that she had stayed in this dear familiar haunt. But only for a moment. Had she not gone, she would not have the love and companionship and 'stimulating conflict' of her life in America. Instead, she would be the fifty-year-old maiden aunt she had so dreaded turning into.

That moment of regret at leaving England is perhaps reflected in the doubt experienced by the two characters in Monica's novels who crossed the Atlantic to marry and start a new life: Christine in *No More Meadows* and Jess in *The Room Upstairs*. In each case the marriage endured, perhaps more equivocally for Christine – a character created early on in Monica's own marriage – but more obviously happily for the later Jess.

§

The heroine Monica created for her novel set around the crash of the R101 is a clumsy, self-conscious girl resurrected from Monica's own youth. Thinking back to that time, she discovered the hurt buried beneath *One Pair of Hands*, and remembered how badly she had felt being overweight and the insecurity she had suffered. Her two-year period as a cook and maid had been more than a mere whim, Monica reflected: it had been an attempt to eliminate insecurity by masking it with new experience. Now, some thirty years later, she gave her character Charlotte her own awkwardness at those unhappy country house weekends as a debutante. At a snooty weekend party Charlotte wishes she was just one of the maids instead of a guest:

...she could turn down beds and fill hot water bottles and then go away and take her shoes off in the kitchen and laugh and say terrible coarse things about the guests.

(Monica Dickens, *The Landlord's Daughter*, 1968)

She gave even more of her own experience, perhaps the greatest amount of autobiographical detail in any of the novels yet. Just as in Monica's childhood, the young Charlotte and her sister are placed beneath a mattress to protect them from the Zeppelin bombs; she endures vast, aunt-ridden Christmas parties where the children act in little plays, and enjoys summer holidays digging in the sand on Belgian beaches. At school she has a pash for an older girl who is captain of cricket; as a debutante she sits out one dance in the ladies' cloakroom and then gives the whole thing up. Her dashing older brother lends her his sporty car. Charlotte is called Charlie by her family, who like Monica's are forever bestowing nicknames, and as a young working woman Charlotte lives in a village not unlike Hinxworth, in a country cottage which she describes as 'her cave, her shell'. The intermittent narrator of the book, Charlotte's future husband, even pushes a reporter over a headstone and breaks the man's camera as Henry's brother had done following the funeral of Monica's grandfather. And, as with the Dickens' own terrifying butler at number 52, the face of a butler in *The Landlord's Daughter* masks 'seething plans for his own night of the long knives'. It was more than merely a novel set in the thirties, with its rigid class distinction and formal BBC announcers: it was a return journey to Monica's most formative years.

Monica's publisher had told her that *The Room Upstairs* did not have enough plot so in *The Landlord's Daughter* she went to town, though fearing that it might end up as melodrama. The plot is certainly melodramatic, and yet still believable – just. Charlie becomes a games mistress at a girl's school and falls in love with Peter, a crewman on the R101 (which in fact never becomes the focus of the story). He turns out to be a brutal murderer, but Charlie hides him in her cottage, unsure whether he truly loves her or only stays because she has come across the evidence to turn him in. The work is structured in an unusual way, told not through Charlie's eyes as it occurs, but in retrospect in the 1960s through the witty and civilised voice of her eventual husband James. The question of the murderer's love for her is only resolved after all their deaths.

The Landlord's Daughter – a title originating from Alfred Noyes' romantic poem *The Highwayman* (which Monica had memorised as a girl because it had a horse in it) – came out in September 1968, published in the UK by Heinemann. Monica in any case liked the word 'daughter' in a title, believing that good words such as 'daughter', 'meadow' or 'angel' attracted potential readers.

She was relieved that Heinemann's Editorial Director Roland Gant enjoyed the book. There was nothing more marvellous, said Monica, than to 'slog and agonise' for months and then finally surface to hear a word of praise. The publisher in the US was again Doubleday, who gave her a $12,500 advance – not bad going, Monica thought, considering Doubleday had not recovered their advance for *The Room Upstairs*. American critics liked the intriguing plot and enjoyed the evocation of the thirties and, to their ears, the exotic English spoken by the different classes. One in-depth review considered the novel one of Monica's most successful, difficult to classify, and imbued with an extraordinary flavour from the way it is told rather than from what happens. Monica had achieved a Jekyll and Hyde effect, the reviewer observed, a juxtaposition of drawing-room gentility and stableyard passions, gentle humour and macabre events, daydream and nightmare. The slow mounting of suspense was an impressive achievement, the shuffling between past and present adeptly managed. The novel was a succession of triumphs: stumbling blocks set up and skirted with finesse to form an unusual and engrossing piece of fiction.

In places the writing is intense. Peter threatens to disfigure Charlie with a pan of boiling water:

He held the pan steady, so close that the hot edge burned her chin. She watched the scalding water in horror...With an effort as great as a corpse thrusting aside its gravestone, she brought up her hands and pushed pan and water across the room, scattering them both with stinging drops, then ducked and ran through the house and up the dark stairs. She lay on the bed and heard the stairs creak, step by step slowly, as he came up to kill her.

She lay on her back and watched him come towards the bed. He put his hand on her, and she shivered.

'You're ready for it, aren't you?' he said. 'It's always best after a fight.'

(Monica Dickens, *The Landlord's Daughter*, 1968)

In Britain, the *Daily Telegraph* liked the 'complicated and grisly' plot and *Books and Bookmen* admired Monica's sure touch with characters and their neat and accurate placing in the social structure. The novel did well. On a visit to London to launch the book that autumn, Monica was summed up by a *Guardian* interviewer as the quintessential lady novelist: fair, fluffy, faintly scatty, frivolous. On the other hand – as the interviewer noted – this 'scatty' writer had sold over 10,000,000 copies of her eighteen novels in thirty years.

Holidaying together in their beloved Bahamas after she had finished writing *The Landlord's Daughter*, Monica and Roy impulsively bought a house boat, which they planned to keep tied up at a friend's dock with a wonderful beach. The boat should more properly have been named *Landlord's Daughter*, Monica considered, but she christened it *52* instead and confidently looked forward to getting a book out of the whole experience in the future.

The glamorous and far-flung holidays, as well as the frequent trips back to England, no doubt derived from Monica's healthy sales figures. She and Roy took various European cruises, including one to Venice where she professed herself thrilled to see two corpulent German tourists fall into the Grand Canal and flounder like whales. The Bahamas remained their most popular destination, and Monica was there in February 1971 when two old Scotsmen in a decrepit boat were towed in after surviving a disastrous transatlantic crossing which had lasted six months. Monica was amongst the first to talk to the men about their experience and, ever the writer, even on holiday on a sun-kissed tropical island, she wrote the adventure up in a long article for the *Boston Globe*.

§

In the late 1960s Monica and her niece Mary, a budding writer, decided to collaborate, and together wrote three television dramas which they submitted to the BBC. The Television Script Unit was not impressed. The two longer plays were predictable, reported a reader for the unit, peopled with stock characters that could be summed up in two words and suffering from a 'fatal lack of freshness'. The third and shorter play was deemed to have a 'certain grotesque power' and was offered to Thirty-Minute Theatre, but ultimately all three were rejected. An internal memo was withering. Monica and Mary's dramas were from a 'well-known stable...with no classical pretensions', wrote the BBC writer Gerard Tyrrell, although spotting that the work included some shrewd sketching and good writing, if a bit on the 'magaziney' side, and that the shorter drama did have interesting and amusing characters. He agreed that the plots in the two longer plays were predictable, but in a way that was similar to how real life sometimes played out: 'That is why this kind of writing is popular with simple people: it confirms their experience of life. Monica Dickens' great-grandfather did quite well out of that sort of thing.'

More BBC rejections were to come. During mainly the late 1960s and early '70s Monica's most popular novels consistently received the thumbs down for BBC television dramatisation, despite recognition of the quality of the writing. Monica Dickens was out of fashion. In a few instances staging difficulties or other obstacles made the works unsuitable for the drama slots in mind, but BBC readers' comments were in any case dismissive. *Man Overboard* was 'unparalleled dreariness', *The Room Upstairs* was witless, *Flowers in the Grass* lacked plot, and *The Heart of London*, already rejected in 1961 as unsuitable for an afternoon serial, was castigated as shallow. *The Winds of Heaven* was full of predictable caricatures, *Thursday Afternoons* was (again) completely plotless. *The Happy Prisoner*, although previously produced as a successful ninety-minute television play by the BBC producer and director Douglas Allen, was now dismissed by Allen as unsuitable for a serial because of its static setting around Oliver's bed, plus lack of plot and overdrawn characterisation 'almost to the point of farce'.

No More Meadows, at least, was assessed as having much to recommend it, and both *Mariana* and *The Landlord's Daughter* were possibles, but it was *Kate and Emma* that received the most plaudits and did ultimately get dramatised by the BBC for Radio 4's Saturday Night Theatre (as in the end was *The Winds of Heaven*). Allen felt that *Kate and Emma* was a sociological documentary drama more suited to the *Cathy Come Home* team but nevertheless was written

...with such human warmth and understanding, relieved, quite often, with flashes of humour, that it is a masterpiece.

The Listeners

Ever since her first meeting with Charles Pick in the 1930s Monica had relied on his love and support and bolstering of her fragile writer's ego. She maintained in her memoir that without the luck of meeting a publisher like Charles she might not have continued to turn out books, however many nice new pens Roy provided for her (though Charles himself believed her urge to write was so strong that it would always have prevailed). He was one of her best friends. Talking to Monica about her next book one day over lunch in the late 1960s, Charles suggested finding some new, strong social issue as a theme. Monica, according to *An Open Book*, was feeling her usual fogginess and lack of imagination between novels and could think of nothing to offer in response. Perhaps a life and death issue, Charles prompted, and mentioned the Samaritans, the British organisation of volunteers who take telephone calls from people contemplating suicide.

Monica 'stopped listening' as Charles' proposal sank in – again, as fairly frequently in her memoir, she described an idea coming to her as someone else's random or serendipitous suggestion that then takes root. In fact Monica had already had her own thoughts on the lonely and the desperate who might be tempted to take their own lives. In her 1951 novel *My Turn to Make the Tea* two of the characters were a quiet couple who without each other might have gone under:

...they had not much, but without each other they might be the quietly agonised kind who are found in the river, or in a gas-filled room, the surprisingly brave yet logical act of someone who sees no reason for living.

(Monica Dickens, *My Turn to Make the Tea*, 1951)

Yet again Monica returned for research to England, staying in the tiny flat in Kensington that she and Roy had bought as a pied-à-terre after the sale of number 52. She arranged to meet Chad Varah, the founder of the Samaritans. This unconventional Anglican priest had first encountered suicide as an assistant curate in 1935, when conducting a church service at the funeral of a fourteen-year-old girl who committed suicide because she had started her periods and thought she had a sexually transmitted disease. This had a profound effect on Chad, and he vowed to do what he could both to further sex education and to help those contemplating suicide and with nowhere to turn. He founded the Samaritans in 1953 with the stated aim of 'befriending' the suicidal and despairing, and, with the help of some publicity in the *Daily Mail*, soon began to get calls. By 1966 eighty branches were in operation across Britain and the suicide rate had gone down.

The Samaritan headquarters was in London in the crypt of Chad's church, St Stephen Walbrook in the City. Here, in one of the tiny rooms set up for whoever needed help to come and talk privately to the volunteers, Monica interviewed Chad for the book she now intended to write about loneliness and depression and 'alienated people':

I wanted to write a novel about estranged individuals with few human contacts, who are more or less neurotic and marginal. Society is so geared to achievement, to everyone coping. Lots of people don't fit into the pattern. They fear the institution riddled by experts and formidable social workers.

(Monica Dickens, *The Boston Globe*, 1972)

She discussed with Chad the numerous reasons for suicide, how everyone has the potential to carry it out and how many do find themselves on the brink at some point in their lives. Chad had adopted the simple expedient of organising for someone always to be available to those who desperately needed a sympathetic ear – not trained counsellors, but ordinary men and women.

He suggested that if Monica was going to write a book she might as well become a Samaritan herself and get her information from direct experience, as he was too busy to sit and answer all her questions. Monica, realising or having already decided that she wanted to try this, asked him if she was the right type. He told her she could try.

'We took to one another very much,' Chad was to recall. 'I admired her writing as I did her grandfather's [sic].' He knew the right kind of person had to volunteer, one who would make things better, not worse; volunteers also needed to have a sense of humour. It seemed to him that Monica was right for the role and perhaps meant to be a Samaritan. The idea was simply to listen and not to judge or advise, although volunteers could suggest referral to professionals. They were discouraged from trying to influence callers in matters of politics, philosophy or religion. This was 'befriending', which might involve meetings in person as well as listening on the telephone. Each Samaritan used only their first name with the callers, plus a number to distinguish them from other volunteers with the same name. No surnames were used, to avoid being contacted outside the centre: calls at home would be unfair to the volunteer but likewise to the caller, who might get an annoyed spouse or a confused child and be left worse off than before.

Monica duly attended the preparation course, a series of lectures, seminars and discussions on the subject of suicide. She later recalled that she had slept through most of it, having usually just stepped off a transatlantic flight. Chad delivered one lecture in which he told several very filthy jokes, designed to weed out any who might be shocked or offended. She then underwent a test call using another volunteer and was convinced she had failed, by giving the wrong sort of answer and not listening enough – her natural inclination was to talk, Monica admitted. She also played the role of a suicidal caller herself and in Chad's eyes demonstrated such knowledge of human nature and 'tremendous histrionic ability' (despite being thrown out of drama school) that the volunteer taking the pretend call was quite overcome.

She passed the selection procedure, doubtless because she did well but in Monica's own mind primarily because the organisation wanted her to write a book in order to spread the word. In her own view she was over-talkative, noisy and opinionated, too intent on wanting to fix people's lives (although she did possess the required sense of humour, even in the worst situations).

She began to work her shifts, and did so intensively for a straight two months, day and night. Over time it slowly dawned that she could not live other people's lives for them, and that the best help was simply to offer support. Calls were about anything and everything: loneliness, marital troubles, alcohol and drug addiction – and of course sexuality. At this stage the only part of the work Monica was dubious about was the Samaritan willingness to listen to sexually explicit or sexually aggressive callers, and other volunteers felt the same way. Chad solved this general problem by selecting a small number of volunteers who had no objection and giving them the generic name of Brenda. Whenever reluctant volunteers such as Monica received a call of this nature, he or she politely responded that they were not trained for that kind of call and requested the person to ring again and ask for Brenda.

Only one emergency telephone existed when Monica started working there in 1968, the black, old-fashioned type of instrument that now to Monica appeared full of menace. It was on this line that those on the very brink of suicide would call, and the person's life might depend on her response. Despite all the training and preparation, Monica instinctively knew that she would be unable to cope if someone threatened to kill themselves. After a month or so listening to other volunteers answering on that line, the day inevitably came when she was alone in the centre and a young girl rang up threatening suicide because she was pregnant. Monica not only did not know what to say but physically could not talk, in fact actually saw black. She blurted out something inappropriate and the girl hung up.

Horrified, Monica ran up the stairs of the crypt and out to the nearest Tube station, her inner voice asking her how she had dared to become a Samaritan and telling her that she was only pretending to care for people in order to write it up into a book. She was convinced that the girl was going to commit suicide, and then so would she because she would never be able to forget it.

Halfway down the escalator, another volunteer who had run out in pursuit grabbed Monica by the arm and led her back to the centre. It could happen to anybody with their first suicide call, they comforted her. The volunteers helped each other as well as the callers, and the words of reassurance that Monica received from the other Samaritans, without judgment, was a novel experience of feeling accepted as herself without the need for pretence. She stayed, but she did have to pay for what she called her arrogance in assuming that she was a suitable person to be a Samaritan just because she wanted to. The 'short, intensely awful' conversation with the young girl, and her own ineptitude, played itself over and over in Monica's head every night as she lay in bed. Even after she found out that the girl had called back the same afternoon and talked to someone else, Monica still felt sick and guilty. She remained obsessed, the girl's voice and her own imbecilic one following her wherever she went until finally she suffered a panic attack. The physical symptoms of the attack were similar to that of a broken heart, she learned, recalling the pain she had experienced on discovering that the man she had fallen in love with in America was married: on that occasion, and this, she had literally to hold herself tightly to keep from shattering.

To extinguish the voices from this painful episode Monica returned to North Falmouth and wrote her book, not only to assuage her own guilt but also in the hope of encouraging those in desperation to use the service, and to alert readers – in a palatable way, through fiction – to the horror that was out there. She wanted to share what she had seen herself, and if it affected others the way it had her and made them care more, then Monica felt she would have succeeded.

The Listeners came out in 1970, published by Doubleday in the US as *The End of the Line* because in America the original title was already taken. The book was dedicated to 'Chad Varah, Samaritan Number 1'. Following came the line from the Roman playwright Terence: 'I am a man: I count nothing human alien to me.' This was Chad's favourite quotation, one Monica had suggested using as appropriate to Chad, the book and the Samaritan movement as a whole.

In *The Listeners* Monica spells out the compulsion of being a Samaritan:

To work as a Samaritan was an intensification of the focus of living, direct and clear. You knew what you had to do. You knew why you were there. Could even sometimes begin to grope towards an idea of who you were, as the pretence and defences fell away before the urgent truth of human contact.

(Monica Dickens, *The Listeners*, 1970)

The novel – the characters all invented, though rumoured to be based on actual callers – is another of Monica's plotless series of vignettes, but with at least an element of progression in the lives of both the ministered to and the ministering: young wife Sarah, a 1960s figure in mini-skirt, coloured tights and lower eyelashes painted onto her cheeks, learns how to be a Samaritan and to have a more honest relationship with her husband; lesbian Billie, drinking to ease the pain of her relationship with a callous girlfriend, finds real friendship; longtime Samaritan volunteer Paul falls in love but is too compassionate to leave his alcoholic wife;

and potential suicide Tim, damaged and alienated after a childhood in care, recovers some equilibrium through Paul's befriending. The reader rightly suspects that one or more of the desperate callers might end by committing suicide, and it is a testament to Monica's skill as a writer that which one or how many remains entirely unforeseeable.

Victoria, a Samaritan volunteer recovering from an unhappy love affair, is often Monica's voice in the book:

Victoria stayed on the emergency telephone all afternoon. It was exhausting, compulsive, satisfying, because it drained you of yourself. It drained you into simplicity. Nothing existed except this contract between two people. A cry of despair. An answer of love.

(Monica Dickens, *The Listeners*, 1970)

The novel is an uncomfortable read, the desperate characters disturbingly real and sad, even if at times the work is somewhat like a recruitment tool or pamphlet on the Samaritans. There are descriptions of how to get accepted into the service, how the training is done, how home life is affected, how the Samaritans' private lives can become intertwined with those of their clients. In fact Monica reveals very deftly how the Samaritan volunteers have problems and conflicts just as the callers do, the only difference being that they have learned how to cope with life and have the gift of sharing themselves. Paul's wife resents his commitment and complains that she hates it when he tries to play Jesus, jumping out of bed in the middle of the night,

with that glad crusading face, dashing out to put your finger on the artery of some poor bugger who isn't even allowed to die in peace...

(Monica Dickens, *The Listeners*, 1970)

The ending, as with *Kate and Emma*, is bleak: not much is resolved for either callers or volunteers. The work closes on a somewhat mystical note, a suggestion that the wise and enigmatic director of the Samaritan branch in this nameless town is an 'agent of God' and that the volunteers are his messengers. Meanwhile, the work of the group continues as, in the final paragraph, someone answers the telephone to another caller:

'Samaritans – can I help you? Oh, I'm sorry...I'm sorry. Don't cry. It's all right...Yes, I know, it's terrible when you can't sleep. I know...I know...It's all right...Yes, I'm here. I'll wait. I'm listening...'

(Monica Dickens, *The Listeners*, 1970)

Critical reaction in Britain was mixed, a number of fans still yearning for a return to the comic works of Monica's youth. The *Observer*, for one, commented that the weighty serious-mindedness currently inspiring the works of Monica Dickens might be morally admirable, but it left the weary reader gasping for a return to the frivolous, less crusading spirit of thirty years ago. The *Illustrated London News*, on the other hand, saw the novel as being of a higher order than anything Monica had done previously, engrossing and touching, and judged that she had clearly been moved by her own experiences and had succeeded in conveying this in the work. *Books and Bookmen* knew there was none better than Monica, 'that astute social observer', to write about the Samaritans, and *The Contemporary Review* praised the work as vividly observed and excelling in its frank, naturalistic and often 'downright vulgar' dialogue.

In the States Monica publicised the work (and the Samaritans) by visiting several major cities. At least one American reviewer was put off by the novel's 'hopeless view of forlorn humans at the limit of endurance'. The author's ability was such that the readers were caught up in the despair and futility of the characters' lives, the critic wrote, and grasped at the most pitiful shred of hope only to find it dashed. The difficulty about the characters was the lack of a possible solution to their dilemmas, which made *The End of the Line* realistic, but depressing. The review advised readers to have on hand as antidote any novel by the other Dickens, who had also described the down-and-out but at least in an optimistic vein.

However, Lael Wertenbaker, American author of the famed *Death of a Man*, the 1950s account of her husband's illness which broke through taboos on writing about death, was more impressed. It took a particular literary gift to create unlovely and unimportant people in a way which made them vivid and worth reading about, she observed. It required a special compassion, combined with an unblinking ability to treat the facts of human life with truth and humour, and in her opinion Monica had the gift as much as her great-grandfather Charles. In Monica's fascinating and gripping novel Wertenbaker felt that each cameo was as realised as a Hogarth drawing, each vignette and relationship sharp and convincing. Not one had the chill unreality of a case history. The cast of characters was large and the stories fragmentary, which might have resulted in confusion except for the clarity of the writing and the sure and delicate weaving of the various tales. As with Charles Dickens – although stating she was not equating the two – Wertenbaker wanted a sequel to the book in order to keep reading about the characters and to meet more of them.

Australian critic John Whitwell, of the *Canberra Times*, was also impressed (and suspected a 'sympathetic genetic endowment'). Starting with her early autobiographical works, he wrote, Monica Dickens had tempered a wicked sense of the absurd with a concern for people of every sort and condition. With *The Listeners*, she had produced a book hard to put down because of the way she conveyed the humanity of both the desperate and those who came to their succour. Miss Dickens 'glosses over nothing, and yet the wit and colour of her writing makes it anything but a gloomy and over-earnest novel'.

The book sold respectably at home and abroad, with reports of new volunteers being inspired to join the Samaritans. In England there was some discussion of a press serialisation of the book and of a TV dramatisation, but Monica feared that a TV version might be badly done or be aimed at a 'popular' audience and therefore put off other types of people from reading the actual book. In the event a TV play did appear in the early 1970s and in addition a later series, *The Befrienders*, starring Megs Jenkins.

In America in 1985 a lengthy excerpt from the novel was included in a report issued by the US National Conference on Youth Suicide.

§

Monica in June 1970 was once again a guest on *Desert Island Discs*. On this occasion, in stark contrast to the self-confessedly sad choices of her 1951 appearance, a far more ebullient Monica selected positive and even rousing music. One choice was the *Trumpet Voluntary*, played on the organ by her sister Doady's son Nicholas Danby, because it reminded her of walking down the aisle with Roy. The wedding song *This is My Lovely Day* Monica described as a nostalgic choice (perhaps one equally inspired by the husband to whom she had now been so happily married for nearly twenty years). She stressed her natural optimism, which had always ruled her life, and that she would therefore be confident of rescue from the island.

The word 'sad', in such evidence in 1951, was not uttered once in the programme – although Monica did include as her last choice the plaintive song about the First World War *Far, Far from Wipers*, because its single male voice was so affecting. The only piece selected for the second time was *Plaisir d'Amour*, the reason on this occasion being that Monica loved it and could never hear it enough, and not, as in 1951, because it was about happy times gone forever. Other choices were Bach, Mozart, *Scarborough Fair* by Simon and Garfunkel, and Dylan Thomas discussing the lecture circuit in America, which Monica found highly amusing and a wonderful use of language. Prompted by the programme's host Roy Plomley, Monica recounted memories of her grandfather and his of Charles Dickens and talked of her own debutante-to-writer trajectory, her life in the US, her later more serious novels versus the earlier works and how on the island she would eat anything, including trees. Her chosen luxuries were an unlimited supply of paper and a permanently sharp pencil so as not to waste all the free time, and Roget's Thesaurus because she was unable to write without it.

In 1971 Monica also appeared on *This is Your Life*, the long-running and hugely popular programme which 'surprised' a celebrity with an account of his or her life, arranging for friends and family to appear in the studio. While the recording of Monica's programme is no longer available, it is known at least that her fellow writer from the Michael Joseph stable, Richard Gordon, was a guest – as was her dear old friend Charles Pick.

The programme was heavily criticised by *Punch* TV critic Bernard Hollowood, whether as regards that particular episode or because he disliked the format anyway and suddenly decided to say so. He wrote in his review that Miss Monica Dickens was 'conned' into an appearance, and had 'suffered the routine confrontations with predictable astonishment and emotion'; as viewers were not allowed to see what happened after the show, he continued, they could only guess at the problems created for Miss Dickens by Thames Television's interference in her family affairs.

The programme was built on a lie and constituted a threat to individual freedom, thundered Hollowood, although Monica Dickens, 'charming and talented, gave it – or lent it – a cachet it does not deserve'.

A complaint to the Press Council about his comments was subsequently lodged by Thames Television. The show's famous host Eamonn Andrews, together with its producer, alleged that in publishing the review *Punch* had failed to maintain the character of the British Press in accordance with the highest professional standards. Hollowood's statements were wholly false, Thames's legal representation insisted to the Press Council. Asked if she had anything to say, Monica replied that she thought the *Punch* article 'fair comment'. The complaint was not upheld, the Council noting that the editor of *Punch* had offered one of the complainants an opportunity to rebut the views expressed by Hollowood (apparently not taken). Despite the strong language of Hollowood's review, the Council decided, like Monica, that it did not go beyond the bounds of fair comment.

§

Monica told Roy Plomley that she had written *The Listeners* because she was fascinated by the Samaritans and believed wholeheartedly in their aims. She would rather spend time with the Samaritans 'than anything else in life'. Indeed, two years after she had written *The Listeners* she continued to work with them whenever she and Roy visited London, and in fact tried to find excuses to travel to the UK so that she could do so. Usually, after finishing a book on a particular subject Monica had written it out of her system, but this time her interest had grown, not lessened. She had become engrossed in the work of the Samaritans for its own sake and missed both the company and acceptingness of her fellow volunteers, and the peculiar satisfaction of having nothing to do except give her whole attention to another human being who needed her. Not because of *who* she was, Monica explained in an account of this period, but *what* she was: the person who was there for them.

Her trips to London always began with a visit to the Samaritans. Once she had reassured herself that she still had a place in that quietly-spoken group in the crypt at St Stephen's she could pursue her other business, just doing a shift there whenever needed. It was like being hooked on heroin, she was later to remark, admitting that she had become fanatical about the Samaritans and the idea of augmenting the impersonal welfare state with human contact. Her work with the organisation became more important than the book it gave rise to, Monica told the English journalist Catherine Stott.

Chad once observed that Monica was the ideal listener and befriender. 'She felt with people, and they saw themselves reflected in her, in her benevolent way. People would reveal to her all of themselves.' It was the first occasion Monica believed herself really useful to those in need, and she loved the feeling. She had never before been 'riskily involved' in this way with her fellow man, talking intimately with all defences down: even as a nurse, Monica realised, there had been the shield of the uniform and the practical requirements of the job. In everyday life she had always been diffident about trying to help, fearing to be thought intrusive, and always feeling inadequate. With the Samaritans she was actually part of a system of support.

A client visiting the church once told Monica that her life had been saved by one of the other volunteers, someone whom Monica immediately regarded with 'awe and envy', wondering if anybody would ever be able to say that about *her*.

§

Interviewed by the *Chicago Tribune* in late 1970, Monica explained for American readers what the Samaritans were, and how joining them had impelled her to write *The End of the Line*. The *Chicago Tribune* interviewer, Roy Petty, noted that Monica became 'wound up' as she held forth on the subject of the group's work with the troubled and the homeless. She had ceased to promote her book, wrote Petty, and instead was expounding 'an idea so important to her she allowed it to steal time from her multiple careers of wife, mother and author'. Monica caught herself in mid flow and laughingly admitted that she was a fanatic.

She let drop in the interview that, when at home in the States, she volunteered with a similar scheme offering help in the local main town of Falmouth (distinct from North Falmouth). Drug use amongst teenagers had skyrocketed in the 1960s and an emergency drug hotline had been set up for a summer, but then calls began coming in from worried parents, potential suicides, pregnant girls and others with problems unrelated to drug use. More lines were installed and the operation made permanent.

The group had adopted a very rigid training programme similar to that of the Samaritans, Monica told the interviewer, and also the Samaritan principle that it should not be psychologists, ministers, or social workers answering the phones but ordinary people willing to listen without lecturing or judging. For the training Monica had suggested the Chad Varah expedient of telling filthy jokes to see which of the applicants were shocked or offended, and of course they selected Monica for the task – it was thought that a nice lady with an English accent recounting dirty stories would have more shock value, which according to Monica it did, especially for the younger volunteers.

It seems likely from her account of this scheme – the way in which the group closely followed the Samaritan model at a time when the concept was completely unknown in the US – that it had been strongly influenced by Monica. This apparent early attempt at a Samaritan-like body in Falmouth (and whatever ultimately became of it, perhaps failure) is not mentioned in *An Open Book*. Instead, Monica was to describe her later, official launch of the US Samaritans as an idea that only occurred to her when an American volunteer in London casually remarked that something similar ought to be started in the US:

> *Although she was not serious, the remark stuck on me like a burr, and its seed germinated, in the way of chance ideas that are going to change your life.*

(Monica Dickens, *Befriending*, 1996)

While genuinely seeing the need for the Samaritans in America, Monica also admitted that she had personal reasons for wanting to start the organisation there: because she wanted a branch to belong to, and to feel that sense of acceptance and connectedness not just on the sporadic trips to London, but where she spent the majority of her time.

She consulted Chad, who was in favour. Having seen his original idea grow and branches spring up all over the UK and in many other countries, he was naturally keen to see the Samaritans established in America. Others she talked to were less certain, objecting that psychoanalysts would fight her for what they saw as their customers, that she would have difficulties finding volunteers and funding, that any volunteers she did find would be useless and in need of professional supervision, that talking to callers in person would be risky in such a violent society, and so on and so on.

But Monica persisted, becoming 'tyrannised', as she put it, by the conviction that her life's work was to bring the Samaritans to America. With messianic fervour she started to believe that she had been put on this earth not to write, but to fulfil that one mission. The naysayers she found hurtful and daunting; fortunately others were more open-minded. As she attempted to raise interest in the idea in the US she had to explain from scratch what the Samaritans and befriending were, exactly, to American ears unused to the concept, and looking back she was to reflect that her idea may well have been viewed as 'the impractical obsession of a crazy Englishwoman with a glittering eye' (though adding that in those days Americans tended to think the British knew best). She was careful to stress that she was trying to develop something in America that was needed and right for the country, and not imposing something alien from outside.

A public meeting to discuss the idea was finally held in Boston, with Monica, now in her late fifties, not at her best because she was trying to recover from plastic surgery. For some while she had been bothered by what she called her baggy Dickensian eyelids, and with perfect timing the plastic surgeon had announced that he could only fit her in immediately before this crucial event. She wore large dark glasses to hide her black eyes and felt at a disadvantage being unable to see the audience and gauge reactions. The meeting went well, but was only one step further along the path to her goal, not the instant galvaniser that Monica admitted she had naively hoped for. As various options were mooted – attaching the projected service to a church, or affiliating with a university counselling clinic, or becoming part of the emergency mental health system – Monica's eyes began to itch painfully, and she felt a terrible urge to rub at the scars. Attachment to an existing body was not what she saw as needed: she wanted a simple independent agency on the English model. Luckily, this was finally suggested by someone in the audience, and Monica, weeping, took her burning eyes home for alleviation with iced cloths.

But it was to be a long process, despite Monica's eagerness to get started. A steering committee was created which decided to hold another public meeting to get volunteers, funding, publicity, and sanction from relevant Boston professionals. This took place in October 1973, with Monica suffering surprising jitteriness beforehand about addressing what might be several hundred people. It was incomprehensible to her, after giving so many public talks around the world and across the US. In the event attendance was very disappointing, but a *Boston Globe* journalist in the audience followed up with a useful article which produced potential volunteers and even their first caller in distress.

During the meeting someone asked if the Samaritans intended to ensure racial balance amongst the volunteers. Monica could have kicked herself. It was insane that this had not occurred to her, she admitted. In her own mind it only served to demonstrate how unsuited she was to introduce a new idea to a country 'still alien' to her after more than twenty years. Much later she saw that if she had obeyed this stringent directive and waited for equal numbers of black and white, the Samaritans would never have got started in America. In the end they had a number of excellent black volunteers and plenty more calling for help, if not as many of either as they wanted.

Monica wrote frequent letters to Chad, who encouraged her to keep going and who came over to visit during the long months of frustrated waiting for things to start moving. He accompanied Monica as she drove the seventy miles to Boston in her much loved Saab (Roy had another), and trudged around with her seeing people who might be of help. There were times when she felt the task was too huge and her ignorance too great, and she was tempted to consider the 'contemptible relief' of giving up:

My life was already in shreds, my friends abandoned, my horse unridden, my garden unweeded, my house uncleaned, my writing put aside, my husband neglected. I drove the seventy miles to and from Boston almost every day.

(Monica Dickens, *Befriending*, 1996)

She also knew she was boring people. At parties she would be asked about the Samaritans and what she was doing.

At first, I started to tell them, until I realised that they didn't want to know. All they wanted was to have asked. 'There, I've shown interest, but what's she carrying on about? Gone a bit fanatic. I didn't ask for a sermon.'

(Monica Dickens, *Befriending*, 1996)

Nevertheless, she kept on, giving press interviews and appearing on TV to promote the Samaritans instead of her own works. Then, at last, a location was secured: Boston's old Arlington Street Unitarian Church, built in 1861. In the long, low room in the basement of the church, offered free for a year but rented thereafter, the heating pipes groaned and hissed and dripped boiling water onto the heads of the volunteers as rats scurried brazenly underfoot. Wooden boards were placed across the pools of water that seeped up after rain. Monica and the others divided up the space with curtains and, all in that one room, took telephone calls, held meetings, selected and trained more volunteers and 'half killed with befriending' any innocent who ventured down the stairs. Because they always had a pot of coffee brewing, street dwellers were regular visitors and often slept outside the entrance, so that staff had to climb over them to get in. They were a source of wonderful dirty jokes, a colleague recalled, and one old man used to bring in a dog which never failed to vomit over the sofa. Monica became 'the ultimate befriender to them all', said the colleague, her energy and enthusiasm described as so infectious that volunteers turned up in droves.

Chad Varah and Monica outside the church

For funding they appealed to banks, businesses, and insurance companies. One brave graduate student volunteer had a crack at writing a funding proposal and scored an astonishing ten thousand dollars from a charity foundation. There were plenty of refusals and rejections but Monica was not deterred and simply went on to the next possibility. Often, potential donors wanted facts and figures, and at the outset these were lacking. On one occasion a large corporation was obviously interested but finally asked Monica how she knew it would work. Monica just smiled. 'I know.' They got the grant.

Eventually Monica collected twenty-two volunteers whom she trained with the help of professionals and what she could remember of her own instruction in London. On 4 April 1974 the first Samaritans in America went into operation, a full five years after Monica had been inspired in London by hearing a client say that she owed her life to a Samaritan volunteer.

As the founder of the Samaritans in America she was Monica 12, the US being the twelfth country in the world to start a branch. Interviewed by the media, Monica tried to sound knowledgeable. The various points she attempted to get across fused into the simple message that help was on hand for the suicidal, and soon the calls began to flow in.

§

It was hard work. There were too few volunteers, so at night the group initially used an answering service. If a caller in need of help agreed to give his number, the service contacted the volunteer on duty and asked them to call the distressed person from their home phone. If it was Monica (and it often was), she leapt out of bed to answer the telephone in the next room before it woke anybody else, and then sat shivering on the floor by the lukewarm radiator because she had not stopped to grab something warm to wrap around her.

Early May saw a brief respite from Monica's cares when Roy threw a surprise party for her fifty-ninth birthday. Returning from another tiring day in Boston, Monica saw the cars in the road and lights ablaze in the house and realised what was happening. Her first exhausted thought was to wonder who was going to do all the washing-up, but of course she had a wonderful time and acknowledged how lucky she was, and how nice to be fifty-nine.

After three months the answering service was dispensed with when it became possible to have a volunteer in the church every night. Until a rule was instituted that everyone had to take a turn, only a few were able or willing to do the night shift. If someone had to cancel, it seemed so difficult to find a last-minute replacement that often Monica would just do it herself. She would ring Roy, again, to say that she would not be home that night. She admitted later to being too exhausted, and monomaniac, to see that someone else might have been found. Sometimes she stayed in Boston a day and a night and most of the following day as well, telling Roy she would be home by seven because it sounded better than eight, and then driving the seventy miles home too fast and taking risks.

The publicity machine had to be kept rolling and Monica was at the forefront, unashamedly using the Dickens name, both her great-grandfather's and her own. (By this point Chad was discreetly prevented from making media appearances as he tended to harp on about sex.) Appearing repeatedly in press, on radio, on TV, and at various institutions, Monica kept explaining the basics: what suicide was about, what was needed in the way of help, and specifically what 'befriending' meant and how it was distinct from counselling, with its overtones of advice:

We believe that low-key befriending is more helpful...than professional counselling...Many suicidal people don't really need a psychiatrist. There's nothing wrong with them. If a person has a lot of trouble in life or has made a lot of mistakes or can't cope with a situation, it doesn't mean he's mentally ill...They don't diagnose, they don't preach, they don't make judgments. They're just there to be a friend.

(Monica Dickens, *Boston Herald American*, 1974)

Fearing to alienate American professionals Monica was always careful to clarify that the Samaritans were not opposed to psychiatry, and would happily refer clients to psychiatrists if advisable.

Finding new volunteers was as much a part of the publicity as advertising the service. She used Chad's slogan for recruiting volunteers who were quiet and unassuming – 'Are you ordinary enough to be a Samaritan?' – and stressed that they needed to have the capacity to forge relationships with others. She accepted only around one in four.

Eventually the organisation expanded into more of the church basement and Monica was joined by two fellow directors: the energetic Shirley Karnovsky, who had studied psychology, and Sally Casper. Before this Monica had been director by default, discovering the difficulties of leadership in the process. She had never been in control or authority over anything in her life, she realised, even as a marginally senior nurse, as she was still carefully supervised by someone yet more senior.

Always in my different jobs, I had been a cog, being told what to do and how to do it, knocking off without a backward glance at knocking off time, taking risks that might get me sacked, but not risking responsibility.

I must be a natural cog. That was why I had liked being a servant, a factory hand, a nurse, a very junior reporter, a lowly volunteer with the London Samaritans...

(Monica Dickens, *Befriending*, 1996)

Changing up from a cog was uncomfortable. Monica confessed that she did not know how to be the boss without being bossy, or when to stick to difficult decisions and when to give way and be more flexible. Her fellow volunteers had been reassuring when she made that first terrible mistake in London but now, in her anxiety over the responsibility the new American organisation had to their callers, she knew she was jumping on her volunteers' errors and making them just as anxious. And, having always previously been on the side of the workers, she had not realised that to a boss criticism and disagreement from below were hurtful, and that casual comments could come across as personal. She became defensive over suggestions for change and panicked if someone grumbled, fearing defection; at meetings she asked for complaints but then brushed them aside, after which nobody would contribute. Naturally they were all too nice to tell her, Monica reflected later.

This was Monica's own highly critical summation of her managerial abilities but it was not a picture her fellow directors would necessarily have recognised. She was remembered as a highly conscientious supervisor, and according to Chad Varah the attitude of her volunteer staff was one of 'affection and awe'. With

Shirley Karnovsky she discussed in great detail, almost obsessively so, the progress of volunteers such as 'Pat 105' or 'Carol 64', demonstrating her concern for their well-being and development. She gave her volunteers opportunities and room to grow: with a 'Just do it', she encouraged Sally Casper, only in her twenties when they first started, to tackle daunting tasks such as going to London to represent the Boston Samaritans at a conference. Volunteer Paulette Chapman Loomis, whose own daughter had committed suicide at the age of fourteen, remembered Monica as 'wise and gracious'; she never forgot Monica's lesson that she could neither control nor take responsibility for all the world's sadness, but that kindness and sympathetic listening could often make a vital difference.

However, despite her intrinsic kindness Monica was not afraid to dismiss volunteers unable to measure up to Samaritan requirements. For the good of the organisation they had to go.

Once Sally and Shirley were on board as fellow directors everything seemed to become a great deal easier. Sharing the load rendered Monica less anxious, and through observing their management styles she became less 'critical and paranoid', in her own words. Sally was gentle and Shirley's method was to laugh; Monica recognised that it was probably laughing that got them all through that exhausting first year of crises and money worries and inordinate volumes of work. She grew extremely fond of witty Shirley Karnovsky, whom she nicknamed 'Shoil', and her husband Morris, a respected Harvard Medical School biologist. The couple became close friends and were regularly invited to North Falmouth for meals, walks and riding.

Sally remembered that she, Monica and Shirley were virtually one person with three bodies, a triumvirate totally focused and committed to the cause. When they had worked late into the evening Monica would frequently take the much younger Sally back to Cape Cod for the night, racing the seventy miles like a demon. When they arrived, Roy, hungry for a meal, would make a round of very strong gins with mint from the garden while Monica set up a game of Scrabble to keep everyone entertained as she cooked. She whisked around the kitchen emptying the dishwasher and producing something elegant but unfussy such as sole meunière. Sally recalled her own long and careful thinking to arrive at a good choice of word for the game, while in contrast

Monica periodically drifted over to the board to add something stunning without any contemplation whatsoever. After dinner the others generally called it a day but Monica would stay up writing until two in the morning, then rise at five to muck out the horses before waking Sally, grabbing a few slices of toast for the two of them and setting off back to Boston for another day at the Samaritans. Not surprisingly, Monica was always very trim and fit, Sally remembered, with thighs like steel from all the riding.

At the centre Monica was ruthlessly efficient and never wasted a minute, although not a perfectionist: some things might be worth doing but not necessarily worth doing well, she declared. There was no time to worry about accuracy or spelling errors in articles written for the press, for instance: she saw that as the editor's job, and told Sally that if she expected everything in a newspaper to be correct then she would have a miserable life. (Characteristically, she had refused to delay the opening of the Samaritans until everything was perfectly lined up, as some had wanted, but plunged straight in as soon as it seemed feasible.)

Callers and visitors to the church basement in Boston were the same dispirited, confused, deeply depressed individuals that Monica had encountered in London, as well as those just temporarily demoralised by life – made desperate by grief, or lonely and unable to find friends, or addicted to drugs or alcohol. This being America there were a few Mafia-related calls, one from a woman claiming to be held captive after witnessing her husband's murder by the Mob.

Monica reflected on how fortunate her own life had been:

Sometimes I feel guilty about the luck I had – the more I work with the Samaritans and see the end products of really bad childhoods, I realise what security we had as children, and how you carry it around to a lesser or greater degree for the rest of your life.

(Monica Dickens, *The Times*, 1978)

The callers made plain to her what harm could be inflicted by living without friendship, that sense of belonging that even just one friend, not necessarily close, could bestow. This was what was missing for suicidal people, Monica believed: the sense of belonging somewhere that she herself had experienced when working below stairs and as a nurse. They may be working with others but 'feel they are not connecting – they feel invisible'. Not belonging anywhere meant being worth nothing, not even to yourself.

Day and night came the voices over the telephone, sad or agitated or defeated, many of them threatening suicide. To Monica such calls were not depressing. They were naturally saddening, because nothing could be done other than offer sympathy, but listening and befriending did make a small difference and was therefore heartening. She had learned that most suicide attempts were not so much a cry for help as a plea for attention, and that there was nothing wrong with this, since everyone needs attention. Monica and her colleagues did not 'talk people out of it' but rather helped them to talk themselves out of it, she said: most of the callers did not really want to die, but merely saw death as the only way to escape the pain of their situation.

Although Monica maintained that she was not depressed by her interactions with clients, there was nevertheless an inevitable effect on volunteers' emotions and mental well-being, and she and the other Samaritans worked with a succession of psychiatrists to understand the dynamics of suicide and how to conduct the relationships they built up with callers. Monica was not one for jargon, however, even objecting to the phrase 'burn-out' in relation to their exhaustion. She certainly regretted attending one 'group sensitivity session' on the advice of a psychotherapist who said it would make them all better at the work. This turned out to involve humiliating exercises and role-playing which led to everyone losing control. Afterwards they felt worse, not better, Monica commented, and she took to avoiding a colleague she had gone through it with.

By the end of the second year the centre had talked to around six thousand people of all ages and was receiving approximately a hundred calls and visits a day. Monica and her fellow directors continued filling in gaps on the daytime shifts and spending many extra nights at the church, and, in addition, somehow found time to help set up support groups for bereaved families and suicide prevention schemes in prisons. They also went out to give talks at schools and hospitals and top universities. Monica reflected later that she was not that nervous talking at some of these 'surprisingly high-class places', such as Harvard, mainly because she was then unaware how little she actually knew on the subject of suicide. Nevertheless, she was inevitably seen as something of an expert, and in 1975 was asked to review an academic work, *A Handbook for the Study of Suicide*, developed for a post-graduate programme on Suicidology at the prestigious Johns Hopkins School of Medicine in Baltimore. In her review she complained about 'one or two turgidly technical contributions' to the book (perhaps to be expected in an academic work).

Monica and her colleagues did not mind the effort involved in spreading the word – talking to people was preferable to doing paperwork – but for Monica at home things were falling apart. Roy understood Monica's continuing commitment to the Samaritan cause but it became no easier for her to call and tell him she would be late back, or staying the night again, and no easier for him to get the message.

If he was angry, I felt misunderstood. If he was not angry, I felt he should be. If he was sad, I felt guilty.

(Monica Dickens, *Befriending*, 1996)

She was not following her own advice to the other volunteers to put their families first. One of her daughters tried to tell her to be at home more, but she could never get to the end of the sentence because Monica did not want to hear it. She did not believe she could do it.

During the summer of 1976 the house in North Falmouth was bursting with family and friends: children and teenagers playing music, slamming in and out of the refrigerator, trailing sand and wet towels and generally getting in Roy's way. Monica was forever absent, not there to keep him company or mediate between the generations. Roy was a strong supporter of her work (his own father having committed suicide) and he himself was Chairman of the Samaritans board, but one night when she came home extremely late after two suicide emergencies and an hour's visit to a depressed man, he told her that he was desperate too.

Roy was clearly suffering neglect, and Monica felt guilty. She tried to stay at home more but still had to make the long journey to Boston three or four times a week, and still felt driven to do her share of work for the enterprise she had started and believed herself responsible for (although at the same time honest enough to see there might be an element of vanity in it). When a historic blizzard struck in January 1978 she did not come home for six days. The storm hit Cape Cod before it reached Boston and this time Roy phoned to tell Monica not to return: had she done so, she might well have been one of the thousands of drivers stranded in their cars for hours and even days, waiting for rescue. A number died, from the bitter cold or from carbon monoxide poisoning if they had turned the engine on for warmth, or from exposure if they had left their cars.

In the end something had to give. Monica was exhausted, guilty, and sleep-deprived, often dropping off during meetings and training sessions. The moment had arrived to step back; she was aware in any case that founders of movements should eventually take a background role before they become inflexible. She resigned her full directorship.

Under her drive and tutelage the first Samaritan branch in the US had developed into an enormously successful operation, and after only a year in existence was the second busiest branch in the world. Numerous Samaritan leaders and interested people from all over the globe had visited both Boston and Monica herself at home in North Falmouth.

After she left, callers frequently mistook Shirley Karnovsky's voice for Monica's, Shirley remembered, and would groan when they discovered she was no longer available.

§

This was not the end of the Samaritans for Monica. She had grown concerned about the desperation on Cape Cod where she lived. The suicide rate there and on the islands of Martha's Vineyard and Nantucket was exceptionally high, surprisingly so considering their status as holiday meccas. For the permanent residents, however, the isolated winters were very different from the touristy summers: older couples retiring to the Cape found themselves with nothing to do and no one to talk to, so that loneliness and depression set in, and out of season the younger generation often suffered from unemployment. Suicide could result. At each end of the canal which separates the Cape from the rest of Massachusetts stands a soaring bridge, high enough to kill anyone who jumps. The railings were built at a tempting waist height, so that many did jump. Addressing the graduating class at the local high school in 1978, Monica advised these young adults to get away, if only for a short time, just to try somewhere else. However beautiful Cape Cod was it could become a trap, she warned:

There are people who feel so depressed and frustrated that they may go to the middle of one of the bridges and think about jumping. I'm not saying that living on the Cape will kill you, although it is true that the suicide rate for the Cape and Islands is estimated to be three times the national average. But I am saying that the Cape is not all there is of the world. Cape Cod can be one of the finest places in the world to live – if you've lived in other places.

(Monica Dickens, high school graduation address, 1978)

The Cape obviously needed its own Samaritan centre and before she knew it, and despite her decision to step back and be more at home with Roy and the family, Monica was again enmeshed in steering committees, fund raising, public meetings, publicity, and the welcoming of hesitant volunteers. It kept her busy, but it was only after she stopped the long commute to Boston that she realised how punishing it had been. If she had started the Samaritans in Boston to have somewhere to belong to when she was not in London, Monica subsequently mused, then perhaps she started the Samaritans in Cape Cod in order not to meet death falling asleep on the way to Boston. (In fact Monica did once fall asleep at the wheel after picking up a friend at Boston's Logan Airport a few years later. Luckily the friend managed to grab the steering wheel and swerve them back onto the road. Monica begged that Roy not be told.)

Establishing a group on the Cape was slightly easier as by then the Samaritan concept was more generally known, but the Cape Cod volunteers were reluctant to shift from their home ground and if Monica wanted them to get direct experience she had to take them to the Boston centre herself. She was still there a fair amount anyway, and now she had to add two nights a month observing the new recruits as they gained confidence in the art of listening to the problems of others – including sex. (Monica had overcome her reluctance to take these kinds of calls, often masturbatory in nature, the same old fantasies trotted out by the same old voices. When trainee volunteers began their apprenticeship, she noted, some sort of grapevine seemed to tell sex callers that fresh meat was on hand.)

The location Monica secured for the Cape Cod centre was St Barnabas Church in the old part of the nearby main town of Falmouth. Once again they were in a single room in the basement, this time even smaller. The telephone company refused to install a line into the church, so Monica and her family spent a cold wet day digging a deep, fifty-yard trench across the church lawn. They laid the wire in themselves and stamped back the earth. By November 1977 the telephone was connected, and the Samaritans on Cape Cod had its modest beginning.

To begin with there were hardly any calls. Locals on the Cape were suspicious and afraid of gossip. Monica ran around the neighbourhood in a panic, trying to find ways to raise their profile as the volunteers dozed or knitted by the silent telephones. She worried that perhaps those critics had been right when they complained that a suicide prevention service could not possibly be needed in a seaside paradise. It took several months for the Cape Codders to learn to trust, and for the calls and visits to begin and the need for a sympathetic ear to show itself on the Cape the same as anywhere else. Monica kept the publicity going, again explaining, as she had done to the high schoolers, why a specific need existed in their locality:

There is a great feeling of isolation on the Cape. There is a self-induced feeling of being trapped. People believe they are on an island.

(Monica Dickens, *The Sunday Republican*, 1978)

Sometimes the volunteers were called to go to someone threatening to jump from one of the high road bridges over the canal. (None ever tried from the single rail bridge.) To leap from the bridges was almost certain death: the fall from over a hundred and thirty-five feet into turbulent, swiftly flowing water was like 'hitting a concrete pavement from a skyscraper,' as Monica put it. Bodies had been recovered with every bone broken. The beautiful bridges seemed to exercise a dark fascination, drawing miserable and disturbed individuals like a magnet, and the more deaths occurred, the more the legend grew. By 1979, after more than sixty deaths since police started keeping records in 1963, 'going to the bridge' had become Cape Cod's euphemism for committing suicide.

Monica and her group of Samaritans got permission from the Army Corps of Engineers to put up signs at each end of both bridges. Nobody wanted to use the word 'suicide' in a tourism area, so the signs, which everyone would see entering or leaving the Cape, eventually read DESPERATE? CALL THE SAMARITANS, followed by the telephone number. The new signs resulted in numerous calls, some from people who saw them every day crossing the bridges to work, some from those who saw them for the first time on going to the bridge intending to die. But still they jumped.

The obvious thing to Monica was to erect a higher railing, and when a repair and strengthening plan for the bridges was announced she saw her chance. At a public environmental impact meeting, when the discussions of traffic flow, paint and salt corrosion had finally drawn to a close, Monica shakily rose to her feet and introduced the question of suicide. Again, despite her extensive experience of public talking, she was dry-mouthed and trembling, knowing it might be perhaps the most important speech she would ever have to make. The engineers invited her to the front and she talked for a short while both to them and to the sparse audience, telling them why it was literally vital to build a higher fence: how so many despairing people were tempted by the low railing to jump, how many lives could have been saved, and what 'going to the bridge' meant. How people might go there but not really want to die. One unhappy woman had driven to a bridge, she recounted, climbed onto the railing and was part way over, on her stomach on the rail, when she changed her mind. She was able to grab some cables. As it was winter the woman was wearing gloves and managed to stay hanging there, her feet over the water, until luckily spotted by a man driving by who was strong enough to reach over and grab her under the arms and lug her to safety.

The engineers listened politely. Asked whether would-be suicides would not simply go elsewhere, she explained that if baulked at the first try people tended not to switch plans so easily, and would have time to retreat and find help. Others raised the potential problem of added wind resistance with higher barriers. It seemed hopeless, and Monica did not expect to hear anything further. But when the final report on the renovation programme was issued, it described in loving detail the new twelve-foot-high curved steel barrier that was to be installed on each bridge.

From the moment the barriers were erected, suicide from both bridges was virtually eliminated. One of these, the Bourne Bridge, became the first major road bridge in the US even to have a suicide barrier. As if to prove Monica's point, one further suicide was only made possible in 1984 when a man squeezed through a damaged part of the new fence awaiting repair.

Monica received letters from all over the country, and from Britain too, asking how she got the government to spend the time and money. There were a few calls about spoiling the view, and one from an annoyed woman who asked why Monica had put up the barriers – it had stopped her from jumping.

A historical marker was eventually erected in honour of Monica at the side of Scenic Highway (US 6) which runs along the Cape Cod Canal. The inscription reads:

Monica Dickens Stratton
Founder of the Samaritans, USA
1915-1992

Through her efforts suicide barriers were placed
on the canal bridges.

§

In her memoir Monica included surprisingly little about starting the Samaritans in America. In the late 1970s she wrote a full account of her experiences but could not find a publisher. After her death the manuscript was edited by the American historian Professor Carlton Jackson and issued as a small work entitled *Befriending: The American Samaritans*. In this Monica described in detail the many sad cases she had dealt with, including talking through a megaphone from below to a man on one of the bridges who then did jump, but fortunately survived. (She told Chad about it, and he innocently asked if she had managed to talk him down. 'The opposite, actually,' was Monica's dry reply.)

The tragic parade of the depressed and the defeated in *Befriending* is an echo of that in the fictional *Listeners*, but the true account in *Befriending*, with its frank admissions of self-doubt, nervousness and ignorance, leaves an indelible impression of heroic commitment.

Over time Monica moved more and more into the background of the groups she started in America, having eventually been involved in the creation of fourteen other branches around the nation and at least one in Canada. (In Washington DC, trying to launch a branch there at a meeting in the British Embassy, Monica had tea with Barbara Bush.) In the end, though, she was happy to let others take the movement forward and achieve things 'beyond my range', yet still contributing on various fronts. In 1979, for instance, she was asked to be an expert voice on an American Psychiatric Association audio education course entitled

Management of the Suicidal Patient. But she always kept on doing the one thing she had essentially wanted to do since discovering the work of the Samaritans in London:

> *...sit by the telephone and have the privilege of sharing someone's life at what may be one of its worst times.*

(Monica Dickens, *Befriending*, 1996)

The Samaritans changed her life, said Monica. Writing was not enough, 'too egocentric a way of life to be honourable', too selfish an occupation. For Monica, becoming a Samaritan was simply the most important thing she had ever done. In 1981 she was awarded the MBE, Member of the Most Excellent Order of the British Empire, for welfare services to the community in Boston, USA. On the tenth anniversary of the Cape Cod group a Massachusetts Congressman, mentioning Monica by name as the founder and as the instigator of greater safety on the bridges, called on his colleagues in Congress to join him in saluting the Samaritans of Cape Cod. His words, and the name of Monica Dickens, are in the Congressional Record. The Samaritans in America continue their work to this day.

§

Monica's involvement with the Samaritans was reflected in her subsequent horror story *Activity Time*, a sombre tale of a confused old man, Dick, who lives alone in a US trailer park beneath a bridge used by suicidal jumpers. Taken to a nursing home, he watches in terror as two callous nurses lay out a corpse who Dick thinks is still alive, and therefore believes he is witnessing a murder as they stuff cotton up the man's nose. After the gruesome procedure – all too credibly described – Dick's deliberate fall from his bed as he tries to escape from the home is described as a suicidal leap:

> *He had a leg over the rail in the teeth of the wind, straining in an agony that almost burst his heart...he pitched over the rail and was a long time falling without breath before he hit the black waters of the shining linoleum...*

(Monica Dickens, *Activity Time*, 1984)

Taking Stock

The next generation of Dickenses had grown up, and Monica's niece Mary, daughter of sister Doady, was now a writer who had published her first book – after encouragement from Charles Pick. On hearing about some of the peculiar jobs Mary had taken in her youth Charles had asked her to lunch and suggested she write a book about it, just as he had suggested to Monica all those years ago. In 1972 Mary duly produced *A Single Girl*, a sexual coming-of-age story revolving around an inexperienced Londoner. Mary had enjoyed many a horsy holiday at Hinxworth as a child and in watching Monica write had developed the interest in becoming an author herself. As adults they had grown even closer. 'That clever, happy girl,' said Monica of her niece's venture into authorship. Mary was her dearest friend, she was to state in *An Open Book*, and of all her mother Fanny's grandchildren the one most like Fanny: able to produce the same little verses and turning into the writer that Fanny might have become, had she been granted the opportunity. For her part, Mary once said that being around Monica was like wearing X-ray specs because of the way Monica helped her to see further into life. When Mary travelled to America to promote her book in 1973 she and Monica talked of collaborating on a novel (despite the BBC's earlier rejection of their jointly-written three plays). This seems not to have transpired but the two of them appeared that same year as a double act on the BBC's *Jack de Manio Requests the Pleasure*, a radio programme before a live audience, to present their choices of prose and poetry.

To new writers like Mary, embarking on 'this career of heartbreak and great joy', Monica's advice was to write about what they knew, which would be far easier than trying to imagine something totally unknown or characters never encountered in real life. She also stipulated both grammar and spontaneity, while admitting the contradiction. Although it might sound 'dreadfully old-fashioned and conventional', to Monica a book was unreadable if the author did not know enough grammar to construct a decent sentence. If he or she did understand grammar, on the other hand, it was perfectly fine to break the rules as long as it was for effect.

Then, don't be too careful. Don't try to write marvellous polished paragraphs in the first draft. Get it all out on paper. You can always go back and back and polish and polish afterwards. The life and spirit of a book comes in at the first draft. Once it is in there it will stay.

(Monica Dickens, *A Writer's Double Life*, lecture given at Boston Public Library, 1977)

Another family event of moment followed. In January 1974 Monica's daughter Pamela married her English fiancé Robert Swift, the wedding taking place in London. Pamela looked beautiful, Monica wrote: her daughter was suddenly so mature and content and sure of herself, starting on a completely new and independent chapter of her life. Now they were closer, because their relationship was on an equal footing. She had been very touched to see Pamela walking up the aisle with Roy and very proud to have raised her, with all the various mistakes and successes, and love on both sides, to reach this happy finale.

Two years later Pamela and her new husband moved to the US, greatly to Monica's joy. In America Monica believed they could be freer and more confident and have better chances in life. In the long run they were to return to the UK but Prudence elected to keep America her home, and worked for many years as a legal secretary for a large insurance firm in Springfield, Massachusetts. According to her mother Prudence was the 'all-American' daughter, whereas Pamela she accused of speaking with a Cockney accent.

While in her homeland Monica was interviewed at her South Kensington flat by David Taylor from *Punch,* to which she had occasionally contributed over the years, and was sketched as she talked by the magazine's famous cartoonist ffolkes. Taylor described Monica as 'animated, sympathetic and apt to nod encouragingly', and possessed of a facility with words that made him think twice about his syntax. During the interview she dwelt on the use of proper English versus American slang, which continued to fascinate her, and told Taylor that with her natural optimism she still enjoyed London despite the gloom cast by the country's then economic crisis. Both Taylor and ffolkes enjoyed the interview (particularly as Monica set out some excellent whisky after the initial tea) and Taylor acknowledged in his piece that they had been 'greatly obliged and entertained by Monica Dickens who is, in short, nice'. The cartoon appeared along with the article in mid January 1974, ffolkes' drawing showing Monica in sharp profile and her humorous, lined face looking caustic.

§

Despite her happy years and numerous friends in North Falmouth, Monica in the mid 1970s started to consider returning to England. Roy was open to the idea, believing that if they sold up on Cape Cod he would rather live in England than elsewhere in the US. Perhaps, with the girls now gone, Monica was feeling the isolation of her position and the pull of home. But in the end they stayed put, and in 1976 Monica finally took US citizenship. She admitted that she had held out against this for a long time, but eventually declared, publicly at least, that she had taken on American ways of thinking and doing things, and did not really want to live anywhere else. (On another occasion she stated that she had taken the step for tax reasons.)

One difference in attitude between the two cultures was illustrated for Monica by the response to her changing accent. The English commented that she had an American accent as if it were a disease, she observed, whilst in America people always told her they loved her darling British accent as if it were a rare merit. She described her feelings about becoming a citizen for an American book on the immigrant experience, stating how glad she was to be a citizen of the 'sanest country in the world' and how much she liked its ideals:

I think that Americans are still very idealistic, much more so than other countries. I think they make wonderful friendships. I like the warmth, I like the depth of feeling, that people are open to each other on a far deeper level than they are in England. And I like the fact that people here can get anywhere. You can be born with very little and come from a fairly poor family, and you really can make it if you're intelligent and hard-working. In England that is still difficult.

(Monica Dickens, *American Mosaic,* 1980)

Some of the above is in contradiction to opinions expressed elsewhere and, given her yearnings for home only a few years earlier, Monica was likely more ambivalent than she admitted. Not long afterwards, on a canal holiday with Roy in the South of France, her fellow American passengers came in for some sardonic remarks: the woman who claimed to be a psychiatric social worker but read comic books with her mouth hanging open, and the rest of the passengers boasting to each other about their cars and boats. Americans were so insecure, observed Monica, that they were afraid of not being liked if they had no possessions.

§

Monica described her dedication to the Samaritans as 'a whole new obsession discovered in middle age', the chance to go on working hard, find new friends and still feel of use in the world. It made her feel vigorous and happy with her life – though claiming that the Samaritans played hell with her writing career.

The truth was that even as she doggedly pursued that one shining goal throughout the 1970s Monica never ceased to produce. There was, however, a general shift during the period towards non-fiction and books for children, no doubt less demanding to write than full-length novels. In response to the popularity of the TV series Monica published her four *Follyfoot* works for the juvenile market, taking the opportunity in the process to voice a few of her own opinions about animals and topics such as vivisection (in books for children she could say what she liked on such topics, Monica commented). Not all of the Follyfoot books were appreciated by the critics: one reviewer found the first of the series schmaltzy, cheap, corny and emotional, and (surprisingly) marred by the constant use of the expletive 'goddam' by one of the characters.

At around the same time Monica also brought out two works of historical fiction for children: *The Great Fire*, published in 1970, and *The Great Escape*, published in 1971. The first tells the story of two children caught up in the Great Fire of London in 1666: Peter, orphaned in the plague and now carrying on his father's old job of ferrying people across the dangerous Thames in a small boat, and his friend Lucy, daughter of a nobleman. Peter finds a new home with Lucy's old nurse, who lives on London Bridge, and when the fire breaks out and sweeps ever closer he manages to get Lucy and the nurse away from the burning bridge in his boat. A *Boston Globe* review described the book as a 'corking good choice' for children just learning to read fluently (even though it scarily features a young girl with her hair on fire). The second tale, an equally exciting story set in the French Revolution, is about aristocratic 11-

year-old Chantal whose life and that of her parents is in danger from the mob. Marcel, her father's nasty manservant, promises to help the family but betrays them. Chantal manages to escape and lives with the family's washerwoman and her son, and eventually helps her imprisoned parents escape from a tumbril on their way to the guillotine. The story is believable, and again possibly rather frightening to children as Chantal rescues her parents only just in time to save them from having their heads cut off.

These were not Monica's first foray into the world of young people's literature. She had written a number of short stories for children's anthologies produced by Lady Cynthia Asquith in the late 1940s and 1950s, and in 1968 had adapted the movie musical *My Fair Lady* for teenaged readers. This went beyond the movie, or indeed the original Pygmalion, to expand more on the characters – the reader meets Alfred Doolittle's love interest, the alarming Prunella Hardcastle, and Professor Higgins has a butler nicknamed Nutters. At the Professor's house, Eliza, naturally, echoes Monica's sentiments about having more fun below stairs than above. The tale is told comically and simply but without talking down to the young audience and Monica has fun with the cockney dialogue, including this from Eliza's friend Bill in the flower market: 'E gimme a narf cra-own fer a narf duzzy nornchis.'

Continuing to concentrate on the youth market Monica also rolled out her *World's End* series, four books revolving around a family of children who have been left on their own in the country because their father is sailing the world and their mother is in hospital. Together with a menagerie of rescued animals – one of them a horse called Oliver Twist – they live in an old pub, the World's End, and have a variety of adventures as they try to stay together. The children have distinct personalities, plenty of spirit and a jaundiced eye for grown-ups, especially their sneering aunt and uncle. The oldest girl, Carrie, has an overwhelming love of horses which can cause friction with her siblings, but in general it is all for one and one for all. Monica catches the magic of children living together and caring for animals, an enchanted existence conjured up from her own long-ago days at the cottage in Britwell Salome as a young girl. She observed that when she started to write books for children she instinctively tried to resurrect that world of no grown-ups and no restrictions, and without consciously deciding to do so, came up with storylines that kept the adults absent and the children alone with their animals.

The *World's End* series had everything needed for popularity, wrote the *Times Literary Supplement*: easy professional story-telling with many neat and some humorous touches, bold, simple characterisation, a general sense of being 'the right sort of people', if a bit hard up, and above all, the 'irresistible odour of horsiness'. It was light reading, and nothing wrong with that, the review concluded, though critical of the fact that Monica in *World's End in Winter* dealt too easily with the distressing human predicament of a young girl in a wheelchair. An *English Journal* review of *The House at World's End* declared it a 'delightful romp with strong ecological overtones'.

Monica prepared the books for the American market by translating them into American, which as she described it meant altering nearly every word and 'hauling in about ten people to check them'. A film of the series was planned in Britain, and Monica produced a script. Some big names from classic British comedy were bandied around for casting: Alastair Sim, Joan Greenwood, Joyce Grenfell. The appointed producer, Stuart Lyons, proudly showed Monica a children's film he had previously been involved with, *The Amazing Mr Blunden*. Unfortunately, she thought it appalling, and worried what he would do with the current project. She wanted a good cast of attractive children, not like those from the *Mr Blunden* film who in her opinion were too fat and, of course, common.

However, she knew she would have no say in it, and was glad to have had the chance to work on the script even if it was thrown out. For unknown reasons the film never saw the light of day at all, and neither did a contemplated fifth *World's End* book. But *Follyfoot*, both books and TV, continued to do well, with Monica still receiving sackfuls of fan letters from children all over Europe. She was naturally gratified, and not above gently pointing out this happy outcome to her publishers, who had originally tried to persuade her against horsy themes.

She was far from finished with her first passion. In 1973 came the children's book *Talking of Horses,* a work possibly sparked by the animal themes of the *World's End* series. Written in an often dreamlike, stream-of-consciousness flow, the book is Monica's paean to the horse: her own, other people's, history, grooming, riding, horse lovers, horse haters, anything and everything equine:

You and your horse. His strength and beauty. Your knowledge and patience and determination. And understanding. And love. That's what fuses the two of you into this marvellous partnership that makes you wonder, What can heaven offer any better than what you have here on earth?

(Monica Dickens, *Talking of Horses*, 1973)

§

Not content with her clutch of children's books as she struggled to get the Samaritans off the ground in the States, Monica also wrote the text for a 1972 book on Cape Cod with photographs by William Berchen. She enjoyed the research, which at one point included walking along the span of the vertical-lift railway bridge over the Cape Cod Canal when it had been raised to allow big ships to pass under.

The resultant volume is a strange hybrid of classically beautiful images of the Cape from Berchen, both colour and monochrome – and a rude dose of social realism from Monica. She was obviously more concerned to depict the reality of life in this seeming paradise, though still pointing up its magical beauty, the joy of riding on deserted beaches, and the enchantment of Martha's Vineyard and Nantucket. The reality, according to Monica, is dire. She describes the ruination of the landscape by tourism, the traffic jams, the suicides from the bridges, the lonely widows who turn to drink after their husbands die on retiring to the Cape, the poverty-stricken inhabitants who vacate their houses for the summer visitors and have to move in with Grandma, the lack of winter jobs, the summer jobs 'snapped up by eager young college boys and girls who were bright and attractive. And white.' Even these summer workers do not escape trouble: occasionally the jobs fall through and the high school girls and college girls turn prostitute in the car parks for the price of a meal or a bed for the night. She details the social unrest of the times, the sit-ins and car blockades mounted by the underprivileged of Cape Cod. This saga of misery is interspersed with little vignettes of hapless tourists: 'Eric and Eleanor Boomhower' sampling an over-priced restaurant, an unmarried couple forced to register at a motel, a restless widow sitting in her hotel lobby in all her jewellery because she does not trust the maids enough to leave it in her bedroom. Colourful Provincetown comes in for criticism:

266

Provincetown, at once the most sophisticated and most wild place on the Cape, is where the drifters drift to and pile up. In other towns they stay for a while and drift on. In Provincetown they stay for months and even years, sharing a dilapidated house, spreading venereal disease and hepatitis, caught up in the laissez-faire mystique of this ravaged little fishing village...

(Monica Dickens, *Cape Cod*, 1972)

According to Monica the only good thing about Provincetown is that it keeps the tourists away from the rest of the Cape. For those who remember the old Provincetown, she goes on, the 'garish melée of tawdry shops' and the old barns crammed with junk art are nothing less than tragedy.

Few would want to buy this as a coffee table book, and Monica states at the start that it is neither guidebook nor eulogy. (Books about the Cape were apt to be maudlin, she wrote elsewhere: 'soppy ravings' about cranberry juice, which to Monica was only good in vodka, and clamming at sunset, which ruined the nails.) Reviewers were puzzled; one believed Monica was aiming at a casualness that did not come off, and was merely irritating.

The clue to Monica's diatribe may lie in the Cape's history, and her own. She had arrived in the early 1950s, just as the construction of the Mid-Cape Highway was opening up the area to tourism. President Kennedy's summers on the Cape then added to the allure, but Monica, at least in retrospect, was more clear-sighted about what this meant: spoliation. In 1968 she had reviewed *The Cape Cod Years of John Fitzgerald Kennedy*, by Falmouth author Leo Damore, and was impressed by Damore's prediction that eventually the locals would tire of the trippers trying to catch a glimpse of their vacationing president. She approved of the way the author chronicled the worrying growth of the Cape into a 'surf-n-sand-n-hippie heaven', and admired the book's superb pictures:

For me, the most poignant are of Cape Cod as it once was when its wealth came in from the sea, not the highways: a handful of houses where now there are a hundred, clean empty beaches where now the bodies sprawl like maggots in a garbage can.

(Monica Dickens, *The Boston Globe*, 1968)

As the years went by, Monica must have witnessed the mutation of the Cape, its apparent morphing from a place of forest, dunes and lobster boats into a threatened hell of motels and shopping strips. Her concern in writing so brutally in the Berchen book was clearly to sound the alarm.

Its beauty is endogenous. It is not enhanced by man. But neither has its essence been destroyed. Yet.

(Monica Dickens, *Cape Cod*, 1972)

This threat has yet to materialise: though tourism is a mainstay of the economy, farming and fishing continue and the natural landscape is little changed. The Cape is still magical. Perhaps Monica's had been a warning voice.

§

Monica's only adult novel of the decade, *Last Year When I Was Young*, was published in 1974. Several characters had been hanging around at the edge of her mind, one a quiet young man in a white jacket who seemed to be a male nurse. She made him a private nurse so that the book could be in the episodic style always close to her heart. The novel was also an attempt to rid her brain of some lines of long-lingering poetry, just as she had tried to blot out Noyes' line 'the landlord's black-eyed daughter' by using most of it in the title of her 1968 novel. This time it was lines from Hilaire Belloc's *Dedicatory Ode* that Monica sought to expunge: 'There's nothing worth the wear of winning, But laughter and the love of friends.' It failed to stop the lines from reverberating in her head, the last line still dominating, but it was one she profoundly believed in anyway.

The idea of writing about a male nurse and those he cared for had been sparked, or furthered, by a comment from a male nurse friend: that it was always assumed male nurses were 'queer', in the parlance of the time. Rather than use the word nurse, the friend would tell people his job was to 'look after' his private patients in their homes. He knew it was ridiculous, he told Monica, but he was tired of all the raised eyebrows.

In Monica's novel, written in the first person, the young male nurse Richard is straight but has to put up with this reaction whenever he takes on a new job:

A male nurse could be six foot two with the physique of a boxer and a jaw like a glacial boulder, and the eyebrow would still go up.

(Monica Dickens, *Last Year When I Was Young*, 1974)

He moves aimlessly from post to post, 'looking after' his ill or dying male patients, who are Monica's standard array of believable and funny characters. One of them has cosmetic surgery on his eyes, the detail likely to have been based on Monica's own recent experience of plastic surgery. Richard is full of energy and finds his quiet days at the bedside irksome; he is in love with Fanny, who has been having an affair with a married man and now seems to want only friendship with Richard. He quotes the Belloc line to her and is unhappy that to Fanny they are more friends than lovers; he wants to possess her totally. In a possibly too pat ending he gets his wish, but not in a way he would have wanted.

Other concerns of Monica's at this period of her life, when she was so intensely involved with the Samaritans, are present in the novel – Richard when taking the Tube around London sees notices regarding delays on various lines due to frequent suicides:

They kept the writing on the board, and filled in the name of the station as appropriate.

(Monica Dickens, *Last Year When I Was Young*, 1974)

There is a curious episode in which Richard seems to make contact with his dead girlfriend Millie through a medium and runs away in turmoil, then reluctantly returns to see if it will happen again, wanting yet also dreading it. It does not happen, and Richard realises, as Monica's sister Doady had done on the death of their mother, that Millie is simply not there. She has passed 'beyond that limbo where the dead hover politely before they go right away'.

Reviews were split. The *Daily Telegraph* talked of 'the whiff of real life' emanating from the pages of the book, much as novelist Rebecca West had remarked in the 1940s, and the Catholic *Tablet* declared the novel often moving and always entertaining. The *Oxford Mail*, perhaps overstating it, went so far as to say it was possibly the best thing Monica had done. The *Irish Times*, on the other hand, thought its 'grisly sentimentality' made it a novel that Monica Dickens' large and faithful public might prefer to forget.

§

Monica, now sixty-three, was described by the *Boston Globe* around this time as a 'tall, reed-thin woman with a cap of blonde hair that frames a face etched with lines like trails in a ski slope', never still even when sitting. 'Hands flutter, legs cross and uncross. She is tireless and tiring to all but the hale and hearty.' Indeed, though singularly focused on her launch of the Samaritans in America throughout the early 1970s, indefatigable Monica had not only produced her several books and a number of articles but also found time when in Britain to appear on BBC programmes such as *Wogan's World* and *The Book Programme* with Robert Robinson. In the mid 1970s, however, she still yearned to write 'one really good book that says something about life, that really comes to mean something to people'.

As the decade progressed through its second half Charles Pick began to nag at her to start something new, and although Monica herself experienced the urge, nothing came to mind. She decided instead that now was the moment to write her autobiography. (Perhaps catching fire from Monica, Roy, too, decided to write one but never finished it.)

She had little time to spare, with much of the day still taken up with driving the seventy miles to Boston and back. Charles suggested using a tape recorder to make notes while she drove, a method Monica may already have employed with previous work. Whenever she got tired she simply pulled over and went to sleep. When it came to transferring her notes to paper there was far too much, and Monica decided to concentrate only on those parts of her life which had influenced her writing. As she wrote, Monica had the terrible feeling of 'Who cares?', and was haunted by the thought that nobody would read it except the type of fan who read all her books and sent her kind letters.

She decided not to go back and read the books she had written about the earlier parts of her life:

Not only were they written by that person at that time, they were also exaggerated a bit, in order to tell a good story. Now one is remembering it from a mature viewpoint.

(Monica Dickens, *The Times*, 1978)

However, parts of *An Open Book*, published in 1978, are very similar to the early autobiographical works and Monica admitted that she became confused between what she had written in those books and what actually happened. It is likely that Monica did turn to her early works, if not to re-read them in their entirety then to jog her memory: some of the wording in the memoir regarding her period as a local reporter, in particular, is almost identical to passages in *My Turn to Make the Tea*. And, although nominally a memoir, Monica as a born novelist was unable to resist the temptation to include long sections of dialogue which could not possibly have been remembered after so many years, and were either invented or culled from her own books.

Looking back as she wrote, Monica saw that in her youth she had frequently been unhappy, something that had not come out in the autobiographical works and that she now made clear in this more realistic account. She had to relive other emotions, too, and it helped her to come to terms with losing her parents: she was surprised by how much Henry and Fanny kept 'popping up' in the book. She learned properly to appreciate the security of her childhood.

Henry and Fanny do appear frequently, Fanny painted as the writer of clever plays and rhyme and coming across as the likely source of Monica's own warm concern for others, Henry depicted (perhaps somewhat repetitively) as the absent-minded and irascible old gentleman whose endearing faults were merely the eccentricities of a member of the upper classes. 'He can't help himself, Miss,' Monica reports hearing from indulgent servants.

But it was still a selective memoir, as she states at the outset, with some gentle finessing of the facts (no doubt in the interests of a better story), as with the 'expulsion' from St Paul's. A few critics argued that *An Open Book* was a long way from doing any such thing as laying open her life, and did not go deep enough beneath the surface. In Canada one review regretted Monica's reticence about her personal life, her children and her friends, while in the US the *Boston Globe* complained that ultimately readers do not feel they know her any better than an acquaintance at a cocktail party. This is perhaps unfair, as Monica's deep love for her parents is touchingly expressed, but it is true that the more personal aspects of her life are glossed over or omitted: her early love affairs, her marriage to Roy, her children, her strong religious feeling. The chapter on the Samaritans, one of the most meaningful experiences of her life, is a short one, with the founding of the Cape Cod branch not even mentioned. But the book is warm and funny, evocative and beautifully written, and as much a social commentary on changing times as the story of one life. 'Entertaining, interesting, alternately grave and gay,' declared one Australian critic. 'A rare slice of social history and a warm self-portrait,' applauded the *Daily Express* in England. To celebrate its publication a Foyles Literary Luncheon was given in Monica's honour at the Dorchester Hotel in London, attended by writers Margaret Drabble, Richard Gordon, Beverley Nichols and Edna O'Brien, and by Monica's old friend Roy Plomley. The book was still selling well in 1980, and in 1981 was narrated in an abridged form on the BBC's *Woman's Hour.*

To publicise the memoir Monica and Roy decided on a second tour of around two months' duration to Australia and New Zealand, with a return via Canada for yet more promotion. Just before departure, they celebrated the 25th anniversary of their arrival in North Falmouth with a massive party for the whole village. A local reporter wrote up the occasion:

In the crisp air of the early September evening the setting was as picturesque as a planned movie set...the white rails of the fences, behind the first fence to the north two beautiful but somewhat nervous horses and, posed magnificently on a little slope, Charlie the dog...Commander Stratton in red coat and white trousers, Mrs. Stratton in a long, flowing red robe.

(*Falmouth Enterprise*)

§

Heinemann's representative in Australia had arranged plenty of publicity on TV and radio but Monica's enjoyment of Melbourne and other cities in Australia was marred, yet again, by what she perceived as the same lack of interest at her book signings that she had suffered in 1964 when on tour promoting *Kate and Emma*. Embarrassed and fuming, she would sit at her table waiting for a crowd that never showed. She was told that even the popular writer Wilbur Smith suffered the same ignominy and would become irate; her own reaction, she said, was to sulk and find a hidden corner somewhere to sit and read. Some occasions appear to have been more successful than others, at least: a newspaper account of one event in a Melbourne bookshop sounded reasonably lively, with dozens of fans showing up. Monica, described as fair, extremely slim, and friendly, was reported as chatting easily and remarking on how open and ready everyone was to talk about books, unlike the British. A woman returned with a just-signed book to ask if Monica would mind writing in the name of her daughter's pony and Monica cheerfully obliged, throwing in a little sketch of her own pony; she suggested to an old lady worried by the price of *An Open Book* that it could be borrowed from the library; and smiled 'wanly' when an old man observed that the only fault with Charles Dickens was that he was not a Scot.

But by the time they reached Sydney Monica had become depressed by the low turnout in the bookstores, despite several successful talks and healthy sales at various literary lunches. She complained to her British publishers by phone but later apologised, admitting that she had been gratified by the many fans at other events who had taken the trouble to bring along their copies of her older books for signing. At one literary luncheon a nondescript woman had risen and spoken very simply about what Monica's books had meant to her; Monica was doubtless touched (though later joking that it was such excellent propaganda she thought the woman had been paid as a plant).

Reviews of *An Open Book* in Australia were warm, and in truth Monica had a loyal following in Australia and New Zealand. The *Canberra Times* highlighted what it saw as the work's most engaging aspect, the mature Monica's capacity for self-appraisal – her willingness to understand and be critical of her mistakes and inadequacies in life, as when she bungled her first suicidal phone call as a Samaritan. This reviewer observantly noted that *An Open Book* also made clear that many of Monica's later novels were as 'heavily' autobiographical as the very first had been. 'One begins to wonder, indeed, whether she had begun to live life in order that she might then write about it.' And if the book occasionally came across as smug, the review concluded, it still managed to leave a good impression.

Once in New Zealand, Monica could see that Australia had in fact gone well, and her depression lifted. The country bestowed some memorable moments: a Dunedin TV station on South Island which flew Monica and Roy in a four-seater plane over incredible snowy mountains and high pastures to tape sessions for a women's programme; an excellent literary lunch in Wellington that sold piles of books; and a TV interview held in a field due to a strike, Monica holding forth in a gale with nose and eyes streaming. Her spirits were raised by the number of readers who talked to her of identifying with the characters in her books, and of getting through some difficult period because they were immersed in one of her novels. *Kate and Emma* was the most cited.

Overall, the Antipodean tour proved a happy time for Monica and Roy, now in his late seventies but in excellent health. In Sydney they met up with Monica's old Hinxworth friend Ray Powell, now Associate Director of the Australian Ballet, who took them to watch a rehearsal at the new Opera House. In New Zealand they greatly enjoyed a week on their own, driving over mountains and taking the tourist boat on an underground river to see the roof at the famous Waitomo Caves lit up by millions of glow-worms. Monica and Roy felt very in tune and content with each other, and Monica was glad they had decided to travel before the frailty of old age set in.

§

As the trip drew to a close Monica began to mull over her next work, pondering domestic abuse as a subject but feeling uncertain. Another possibility was the First World War, which fascinated Monica when she considered the carnage and brainwashing and yet absence of large-scale mutiny. Again she hesitated. The success of her memoir had left Monica less willing to keep churning out novel after novel. When longtime fans had written to say they felt they had shared her life and that she was part of theirs, it encouraged her to carry on in the same vein and indeed to get better, but equally to feel that she had achieved a great deal in her professional life. Now, perhaps, she could write only when she wanted to and not when she thought she ought to.

In fact after *An Open Book* Monica realised she wanted to stay away from fiction for a while. That same year she had co-edited *Is Anyone There?*, a collection of stories on the subject of loneliness which had been produced in aid of the Samaritans, but she did not contribute any of the tales herself. She yearned to do something like a biography that would require months of research in a library, and result in a work that could be taken seriously. She considered writing about Jane Austen, but believed it had all been done much better already – although the writer V. S. Naipaul might have disagreed. After reading Monica's introduction to the 1947 edition of *Emma* he wrote to his sister that it had proved better reading than the book itself.

Eventually Monica embarked upon a family saga set in the mill towns of New England, which, although fiction, did require the type of research she was feeling drawn to. But after working on it for ten months the story had only advanced from 1895 to 1896, and the saga was proving too great a project to fit in with the way Monica was now living her life. She did not, after all, have the time for the research necessary to do a proper job, let alone the actual writing. She had struggled with it for a long period on returning from a visit to England, trying to force herself to continue with the self-imposed task and being disappointed with the result. Monica only managed to escape the gloom this threw her into with the realisation that she did not have to keep up the effort, and by May 1980 she had abandoned it. It would be a greater disappointment for her publishers, she believed, to produce something non-credible merely to show that she could knock out a hefty novel and stay in the public eye. She hardly needed to keep proving herself, Monica finally decided.

§

By 1983 it was nearly a decade since Monica's last work of fiction for adults, and she was again searching for inspiration. She sensed that producing more non-fiction on subjects that interested her personally – perhaps thinking of her then unpublishable account of launching the Samaritans in America – would not work. As for fiction, in her own view and that of her publishers she was encountering the same difficulty that had bedevilled her in the 1960s, that of having become too removed from English life and experience to write a convincing novel set in her birthplace. Back then, with *The Landlord's Daughter*, Monica had solved the problem by writing about an English era she knew well, the 1930s. Now, although wary at the thought of a return to fiction, she contemplated writing a novel set in another era just as well known to her from her frequent visits to Britain, the 1950s. She did not anticipate massive sales but knew that her many loyal readers still thought of her primarily as a novelist, and in light of the ages of this readership the fifties would be an appropriate period to set a book in.

No such novel ever materialised. Monica was hijacked by a family trauma which led her in a new direction.

Monica's daughter Pamela had given birth to twin boys, and Monica took pleasure in her new role of proud grandmother when she and Pamela pushed the twins round the mall in their double pushchair. One night when the babies were almost a year old, little Steve woke up with a rash everywhere on his body, from the top of his head to the soles of his feet. He was burning up with fever. The doctor on call told Pam on the phone to bring the baby in the following day, at which Pam's husband Bob grabbed the receiver and lost his temper. The doctor agreed to meet them in the hospital emergency room, where he angrily refused to speak to Bob, and they were sent home with a diagnosis of some kind of virus and instructions to give the baby a mild dose of aspirin and a cool bath.

It was indeed a virus, but of a 'vicious and malevolent nature', Monica wrote later. In the next few days Steve's temperature shot up even higher, his rash was a brilliant sunburned red and he was admitted to hospital. In a tiny isolation room the naked baby clung to his mother, the rash on his back inflamed into raised sores. His closed eyes were crusted and suppurating, and his constant moaning cry was hoarse and ragged from a throat raw with thrush. His hand was connected to an intravenous drip and wrapped in a boxing glove of bandages. His head lolled backwards on his crumpled scarlet neck.

When the baby's fingertips and toes began to peel, the virus was positively identified as the rare and terrible Kawasaki disease – potentially fatal or, if the child lives, potentially leading to brain damage. Pamela held the baby continuously, day and night, unable to go for a meal or a shower without Steve screaming non-stop. Fortunately, with high-dose aspirin treatment he slowly started to improve and after around three weeks Pam brought him home. He was still sick and underweight and dull-eyed, his head half shaved for the intravenous needles, but he was alive and cured with no apparent after-effects.

On Monica's first visit to Pamela and Steve at Boston's Children's Hospital, she was exhausted from looking after Steve's twin James at her own home and too shocked by what was happening in the baby's room to take much notice of her surroundings. The next time she went there Monica took advantage of mother and baby falling asleep to go exploring and start talking to other parents. After Steve was taken home Pam was no longer a hospital mother but Monica, inevitably, had become passionately interested in the women who still were. She had watched Pamela grow 'brave and strong' in the face of her child's potentially fatal illness, and wanted to know more about the courage of parents in this terrible predicament.

She heard about a doctor caring for child cancer patients at Massachusetts General Hospital, Dr John Truman, and went to see him. She was afraid she might be seen as a nuisance, but instead was met with warmth and reassurance. Dr Truman agreed to let Monica follow the work of his clinic and talk to sick children and teenagers and their parents, past and present. This she did for the next two or three years, without really asking herself what the purpose was or what the market for a potential book might be. She wanted to know how ordinary people 'become giants'; she was attracted to them and kept going back to hear story after story. Not because she was curious, or morbid, Monica explained in the book that she eventually wrote, but because she needed to be with the parents and hear them talk. She was 'drawn to the magnet of their strength' and wanted to write a testimony to them. And, just as much, to the commitment and day in, day out work of doctors, nurses and researchers which so often went unrecorded.

In the hospital Monica again experienced that nostalgic sense of belonging, the feeling of being once more a part of that urgent, purposeful world which had been hers as a young nurse in London. This time she was only a listener, and it was painful to hear the stories and painful for those doing the telling. The book, too, is painful and harrowing to read. It includes the well-known story of Chad Green, the boy with leukaemia whose parents withdrew him from treatment at Massachusetts General and took him to Mexico, where he died while taking the natural but ineffective medicine laetrile. It is not clear if Monica ever had contact with the Greens personally, but she talked to numerous families at the hospital and wrote feelingly about their disbelief, agony, and endurance.

The resultant work, *Miracles of Courage*, was published in the US in 1985 and condensed in the American edition of *Reader's Digest* the following year. British publishers were initially hesitant, fearing that childhood cancer would not attract many readers, but eventually *Miracles* appeared there also. Much media interest followed and Monica, who had hired a publicity manager in Boston, received plenty of coverage, talking to the US press and appearing on *Woman's Hour* in the UK.

Miracles of Courage is structured more or less thematically, covering the effect of a child's illness on a marriage and on siblings, on the ill child, and on fathers versus mothers, plus other related themes. The result is that individual stories are presented piecemeal rather than in dedicated narratives. One review talked of getting only 'scrappy, idiosyncratic glimpses' into the world of families coping with a child's illness, finding the stories of courage and fortitude too bitty and therefore difficult to follow in terms of chronology. But in Britain Sally Vincent of *New Society* liked the book a great deal because it was an account of ordinary human beings who had risen above the worst circumstances by relying on their own bravery, and not on divinity or any other type of crutch. She declared it should be compulsory reading for the two-thirds of men who statistically were unable to cope with serious illness in their children, and equally compulsory for those who were 'squeamish and sentimental'.

The book did well, and Monica donated part of the royalties from a second printing of the book in 1987 to a charity raising money for the first of the UK's Ronald McDonald Houses, which provide accommodation for parents to stay near their ill child.

§

Her grandson had luckily recovered, but Monica was to suffer another traumatic experience involving a child during the period that she was shadowing at the clinic. When she and Roy were returning from a short winter trip to Harbour Island in the Bahamas and were awaiting their plane at the very basic airport at Eleuthera, she heard a cry for a doctor or a nurse. Looking inside the airport shed she saw what appeared to be a group of panicking women in a corner. Although her nursing career had been over for many decades and she knew that her skills were long gone, Monica as in a dream went inside and announced that she was a nurse. People parted for her as if she were a saviour; if they only knew, she thought. A middle-aged woman held a swaddled baby in her lap, the baby's young mother sobbing next to her. The older woman announced that it was dead, and Monica could see that the child had turned blue. Monica had just taken a cardiopulmonary resuscitation course a few weeks previously and the special technique for mouth-to-mouth on a baby was still fresh in her mind: she took the little body and began to perform it. The baby felt cold, and the grandmother kept saying it was no use, he was dead, but Monica persisted. She heard the words of the instructor in her head, telling them to keep going as long as they had the strength. She was sure she could perform a miracle. 'When I did not, it was more surprising than if I had.'

As a nurse Monica had touched dead bodies at the hospital, but she had never kissed a dead person. On the plane finally leaving the island, her mouth continued to feel the tight cold skin of the tiny nose and stubborn lips that refused to breathe for her. Completely despondent, she felt she had failed the course instructor, even though she had learned after ceasing her efforts that the baby was born with a heart defect and had twice before been close to death.

Her thoughts went to Dr Truman and the nurses at the clinic, and how they must sometimes lose the fight.

The Dickens Connection

Charles Dickens was an unremitting presence in Monica's life, from her earliest memory of being taken as a child to put flowers on his grave in Westminster Abbey, to the lifelong label of 'Charles Dickens' great-granddaughter' and the constant and at times invidious comparisons with him as an author. She sat in his chair for inspiration when writing *One Pair of Hands,* collected Dickens memorabilia, maintained steady links with the Dickens Fellowship and lectured on him around America.

Monica's relationship with her ancestor was an ambivalent one. She was thankful that the great name had been instrumental in her getting published, frustrated that the relationship was to dog her all her days. She grew increasingly irritated with what she saw as Dickens' flaws as a writer: his wordiness, the complexity of his plots and what she called the 'skippable parts – the flowery, Victorian sentiment'. Yet she genuinely admired his gifts, which understandably became more impressive to her as she matured.

Monica appears never to have responded to the frequent comparisons made by critics between her writing and that of her great-grandfather, and with the passing of time book reviewers themselves finally wearied of the game. On the publication of her memoir in 1978 the perceptive Australian journalist Pamela Ruskin wrote in Melbourne's *The Age* that after Monica's twenty-nine works the relationship had lost its freshness as a publicity exercise, and that Miss Dickens was surely entitled to be judged on her merits without the continuous revelation of this 'over-stretched umbilical tie'. Ruskin also scented in the memoir something of Monica's ambivalence about Dickens, noting that it was obvious that Monica had no particular interest in the great man and did not appear to be an avid reader of his works.

But one aspect of the relationship remained constant, especially when in America: Monica's willingness to make the most of the Dickens connection.

It was on becoming famous for *One Pair of Hands* that Monica was first invited to hold forth on the subject of her great-grandfather. Many more requests were to follow, mostly from the BBC, and often at Christmas time. As an established author she also became a star turn at Dickens Fellowship celebrations and various other Dickens-related events, such as the luncheon in 1945 marking the 133rd anniversary of his birth. She was wont to think of herself as a true Dickensian, Monica declared to the assembly in her response to the toast, and liked to return to Dickens to 'recuperate' from modern novels, but confessed to feeling nervous lest she reveal her ignorance of the name of Mrs Jellyby's second cousin before such a knowledgeable audience. Not long afterwards she was asked to voice the commentary to a newsreel about the centenary dinner of the *News Chronicle*, edited by Charles Dickens in its early incarnation as the *Daily News*; the film showed Monica herself attending the dinner in glamorous evening dress. A few years later she was guest of honour at the Fellowship's annual dinner in Portsmouth, resplendent in royal blue velvet as she read aloud excerpts from *David Copperfield*.

Monica appears to have willingly accepted these early invitations, though careful to disclaim any expertise (and indeed the BBC broadcasts were often weak pieces, similar to her *Woman's Own* journalism). However, as in her American lectures in the decades to come, Monica would occasionally imply inside knowledge from tales handed down within the family – despite the later statement in her memoir that she had never talked to her rather forbidding grandfather Sir Henry Fielding Dickens about his famous parent. In a broadcast for the BBC's North American Service in 1946, for instance, Monica related how as a twenty-year-old she had gaily kissed the top of Sir Henry's bald head while chatting to him about her first ever trip to the States, and how Sir Henry had brought out some of Dickens' own letters from America to show her – evidence of a little artistic licence, as when Monica was twenty Sir Henry had already been dead for two years.

But it was in America that Dickens as Monica's own private cottage industry truly kicked in. During her 1948 visit there as a young woman the Christmas issue of *Life* featured a lengthy biography by Monica of her great-grandfather, a well-crafted account produced for a discerning American readership – *Life*, though generally light in tone, set a high standard and attracted many of the best American writers. The item was finely calibrated to her market and made skilful use of the tenuous link with her ancestor, weaving in what again appear to be family reminiscences:

> *I remember Grandfather telling us once how, when he and his family*
> *were playing a memory game of repeating a long string of words to*
> *which each person added one more, his father suddenly came out with*
> *'Warren's Blacking, 30, Strand'. His strange look and tone haunted*
> *my grandfather though he did not know why, for Charles Dickens had*
> *never spoken, even to his wife, of the nightmare years he spent as a*
> *small boy in the blacking factory.*

(Monica Dickens, *My Great-grandfather Charles Dickens*, Life, 1948)

This incident can be found in her grandfather Sir Henry Dickens' *Recollections*, although of course Monica may have heard it from Sir Henry's own lips as well. Still with an air of relaying family anecdote, she gave the story (likewise in *Recollections*) of how as a young parliamentary reporter Dickens had invented a speedy version of shorthand and later taught it to his son Henry, getting him to practise by delivering parodies of the bombastic speeches he had reported in his youth and making Henry laugh so much that he was incapable of writing anything down. Her grandfather adored him, she said, describing Dickens' emotion on learning of Henry's winning the best mathematical scholarship of his year at Trinity Hall, Cambridge – yet another *Recollections* anecdote. Her grandfather was with Dickens a great deal towards the end, wrote Monica, and used to maintain that his father taught him more than he ever learned in all the rest of his life. He could imitate his father's recitation of *A Christmas Carol* – this time, a fact certainly coming from her own memory – and now her father carried on the tradition for the current generation of children every Christmas, and Dickens' desk and chair resided in Monica's family home as their most cherished possessions.

On the subject of Dickens' feelings for the young actress Nelly Ternan, Monica played safe with her doubtless more puritanical readers, even though the story had broken in the 1930s with the publication of franker biographies. No one had ever proved anything more than friendship between them, Monica stoutly maintained. She admitted that Dickens treated his wife badly, then offered the common excuse for this that Catherine was dull and stupid, given to moping in corners at parties with her hair coming loose, and a 'painfully inadequate' partner for the ebullient young writer. (*Life* rather unkindly printed a pair of photographs side by side showing a corpulent older Catherine next to a picture of Nelly's pretty sister dressed in a short skirt for the stage.) Dickens could be moody and selfish, Monica conceded, but despite his faults she argued that he was essentially a Christian man who was kind and loath to offend, as when he inserted a sympathetic Jewish character into *Our Mutual Friend* after a Jewish lady complained about the criminal Fagin in *Oliver Twist*. She cited too Dickens' reluctance to write a poor review of a new book when the author was ill and needed the money.

Continuing to play to her audience, Monica attempted to massage Dickens' well-known criticisms of America into something more palatable. Monica merely stated that it was all there in Dickens' subsequent novel *Martin Chuzzlewit*, and it was little wonder that Americans censured him for this poor return of their hospitality. 'He loved and admired the people, but he hardly remembered to say that.' (Having tried to excuse her ancestor with this comment Monica should perhaps have omitted mentioning Dickens' description in his *American Notes* of the gobbets of spittle flying past his train window from the passengers in the next carriage, and how a member of the State Senate in Pennsylvania blew his nose with his fingers onto the carpet.) She did refer to Dickens' expression of horror at slavery, and his tirades against the inadequate copyright laws which had allowed his works to be pirated in the States, but this last she diplomatically attributed to the same over-enthusiasm with which he campaigned against social ills in his novels. She finished her *Life* article with a touching description of Dickens' second tour of the States in 1867, when in the face of his failing health – the effects of a slight stroke, which had greatly affected the whole of his left side, and ultimately heart and eyesight as well – he nevertheless toured the north-eastern states, reciting long passages of his works from memory and needing fortification with eggnog before and during each performance. Americans forgave him his criticism in *Martin Chuzzlewit* and *American Notes* and his reception this time was tremendous, Monica declared. (The impetus for the tour was Dickens' shortness of funds, in fact, rather than a selfless love of the American public.)

This was writing on Dickens of a reasonable calibre, but Monica in her new life in America was to find herself regularly producing rather more popular items on one particular aspect of the Dickens myth: the jolly Christmas.

Her visit to the US in 1948 had also spawned the first of many saccharine Christmas articles for the American market, all well padded with her forebear's effusions. In this, Monica described how she created something of the old-fashioned Christmas beloved by her great-grandfather: making a plum pudding from an old family recipe, full of raisins, fruits and spices and studded with sixpenny bits for the children, then doused in beer and brandy and placed in an old crock to age. This Christmas she intended to throw a party for her niece and nephews and forty children from the village where she lived, she wrote, each of them to receive his or her own present. There would be champagne for the grown-ups, and (presumably non-alcoholic) cider for the young ones as they gathered to listen to *A Christmas Carol* being read aloud for the one hundred and fifth year 'at the hearthside in the home of a Dickens somewhere in England'. She and her sister and brother had been afraid of the ghost of Marley when young, said Monica, just as her grandfather must have been when he listened to Dickens himself,

who re-created his own characters with the eloquence that brought him additional fame, fortune and popularity on both sides of the Atlantic. For no matter where work or whim found him wandering, Charles Dickens always turned homeward to be in the bosom of his family at Christmas time. He considered this the pleasure and duty of every man with a family...when he said that Christmas comes but once a year, he was voicing a fact that unhappily is too true. When the warmth of the Yule season stays with us the year around, we shall make this earth a very different place.

(Monica Dickens, *Philadelphia Enquirer*, 1948)

All of this was obviously slanted to her audience and heralded a long line of similar Christmas froth resting on the Dickens name. In the first two decades after her marriage and move to the US, few (if any) Christmases were to pass without something from Monica appearing in the media about either *A Christmas Carol* or the traditional Dickens Christmas, whether because she was approached to do so and wanted to oblige, or because in some way she felt it incumbent upon her as his descendant to keep churning it out – or simply because it was a useful money-spinner. Whatever the reason, writing or talking about the Dickens celebrations, and

A Christmas Carol in particular, was for many years to be a relentless feature of Monica's Christmases in America. In 1961 came a radio show, *Christmas with Charles Dickens*, and successive pieces over the years offered her recipes for Christmas pudding, roast goose, and Dickens' Milk Punch, and more childhood memories of tasting the pudding mixture and how her grandmother would hide sixpences in her hand as she served it up to ensure each child received one in his slice.

Inevitably, as a result of this stream of seasonal Dickensiana, Monica began to be seen as a *Carol* expert in the States and was quizzed about films and dramatisations. Interviewed after attending a Boston performance of the American playwright Israel Horovitz's *A Christmas Carol: Scrooge and Marley*, she told the press that with Scrooge being such a larger-than-life role, Dickens in a stage adaptation would probably have played the part himself. Of the 1970 movie musical *Scrooge* Monica commented that actor Albert Finney in the main role had brought out things in the character she had never seen before, and (perhaps deadpan) much that Charles Dickens probably had not realised either. Not for the first time, Monica was also asked how her ancestor might have reacted to seeing his work on film. She responded firmly, again, that she always thought that he would be tremendously pleased, and nowadays would likely have been a foremost television writer himself. Alec Guinness' unusual rendition of Marley's Ghost she declared absolutely marvellous, though adding (perhaps even more deadpan) that she had never before seen anyone play the role as a homosexual. In the mid 1970s, at the request of an old war compadre of Roy's, she appeared at a Dickens Evening in Galveston, Texas to introduce readings of *Carol* and to hand out prizes for the best essay on her great-grandfather.

However, as time rolled on there began to emerge definite signs of testiness. A spread in the local press in December 1955, for example, showed Monica expressively reading *Carol* to neighbouring children, daughter Pam sitting open-mouthed in her lap. (Her daughters on growing older became 'politely uninterested' in having Dickens read to them.) On this occasion, in fact the third Christmas Monica had read aloud from *Carol* to the locals, she was reported as commenting that the plots of Dickens' major works were usually too complicated. In late 1960 came a Christmas Day article for the *Boston Globe* on the genesis of *Carol*, angled to engage her American readers by starting with Dickens' letter to a professor at Harvard regarding the birth of the famous story, and bringing in the success of his *Carol* readings on his triumphant second tour of America. Dickens had the idea for the story while lecturing to factory workers in Manchester, Monica wrote, helpfully explaining that this was possibly the rainiest, most depressing town in England. She filled out the article with excerpts from *Carol* but this time, towards the end, came what appears to be Monica's own view of the world's most celebrated Christmas tale:

To some modern readers, conditioned to terse prose and to the school of stating what is to the exclusion of what should be, it could seem too long, too wordy, too fantastic, too sentimental, too preachy.

(Monica Dickens, *The Boston Globe*, 1960)

Millions of others find it perfect, she finished tactfully, an enchanting picture of the ideal Christmas.

As the years went by it became more and more evident that neither Dickens nor *Carol* counted as Monica's favourite reading. Some of her pieces and interviews, as with her 1960 comment above that Dickens was sentimental and preachy, began to evince downright irritation with *A Christmas Carol* and its fans – including suspicion of the enthusiasts who told her they too read *Carol* aloud to their children every year. A full reading took five hours, Monica pointed out caustically. (A recital of the entire work in its original form has actually been timed at three hours, and Dickens himself shortened it to one and a half in his public readings.) Tiny Tim was a cliché, she complained outright on one occasion, and Scrooge's fear of death even gets a waspish mention by a character in her novel *The Landlord's Daughter*:

I have always thought that Scrooge overdid the hysteria. 'Am I that man who lay upon the bed? No Spirit, oh no, no!' The old boy had only a few more years to go, at best.

(Monica Dickens, *The Landlord's Daughter*, 1968)

In tandem with the Christmas banalities Monica also produced more serious Dickens items for both sides of the Atlantic, mostly without allowing her own opinions to sneak in (with the exception of her 1956 foreword to the publication of Dickens' prompt copy of his Mrs Gamp reading, in which she did let slip that her family pride was not too blind to admit that these days Dickens might not be to everybody's taste). Her workmanlike introduction to a US-published facsimile of Dickens' manuscript of *Carol* in 1967 mainly concentrated on the genesis of the work, and allowed that it was 'loved and treasured by every literate home'. For the British market she produced the straightforwardly eulogistic foreword to London Transport's 1970 publication *The London of Charles Dickens*, a guide to the remaining landmarks of Dickens' literary London. In the run-up to that Christmas Monica also dutifully signed all 250 very expensive leather-bound copies of a facsimile reproduction of the original manuscript for Dickens' other famous Christmas story *The Cricket On the Hearth*. Later in the decade she wrote a brief and professional introduction to John Greaves' *Dickens at Doughty Street*, focusing on the books her ancestor wrote at the house and the death there of his beloved young sister-in-law Mary Hogarth, the probable inspiration for the fictional death of Little Nell in *The Old Curiosity Shop*.

But, perhaps fed by the long years of her own Christmas inanity, Monica in interviews and elsewhere became ever more frankly critical, declaring that *Carol* was the worst of her great-grandfather's works and that his books were 'too terribly long' and in need of editing. Her lengthy, carefully argued introduction to an American edition of *Hard Times* in 1972 castigated Dickens for his failure to understand trade unionism (his attitude described as 'confused and short-sighted') and made the not wholly original point that his villains, those whom readers are meant to abhor, are the characters enjoyed the most because the funniest, while the heroes and heroines are palely tedious but at least generally do the reader the favour of dying young.

Within the same introduction, however, appeared what looked like genuine appreciation of the richness of Dickens' *Hard Times* creations Gradgrind, Bounderby and Mrs Sparsit, and Monica finished the piece by quoting Thackeray's words in praise of Dickens: 'There's no writing against such power as this – One has no chance!...it is unsurpassed – it is stupendous!'

The following year Monica was appointed a Vice-President of the Dickens Fellowship. She sent a message from the US expressing her gratitude to the organisation for keeping Dickens 'alive and real and significant to millions of people'. By 1984, when she provided a reading from *Carol* in aid of the Samaritans for a Cape Cod radio station, Monica in the last decade of her life had seemingly become more reconciled to Dickens and his most popular work, if still not a total enthusiast. In the interview beforehand she talked again of her grandfather reading *Carol* aloud when she was a child, and to her mind probably giving a fair imitation of his father Charles. As to why the story was so beloved, she observed that perhaps it was something slightly different to everyone. The story was very simple, 'perhaps quite corny', but she enjoyed reading it because of the opportunity it provided to indulge in plain old-fashioned sentiment, a chance to laugh and cry. And Dickens' words were so marvellous, she continued, his choice of words 'just unbelievable....so visual':

When you're reading it or listening to it, it's creating pictures that run through your head, which is what he did with words...If you analyse his choice of adjectives, he never picks the easy, ordinary, flat, commonplace adjective. It's always something with colour or smell or feel to it.

(Monica Dickens, WQRC, 1984)

She had come to feel more at one with Dickens, she commented elsewhere, fully recognising his genius at last and feeling a greater identification:

I feel very close to my great-grandfather. I feel he is alive. I understand his thinking, his tremendous vitality, his energy...My great-grandfather was a genius. He made make-believe people real...The great mind always stands out. I'm not talking about talent. I'm talking about genius.

(Monica Dickens, *The Boston Globe*, 1985)

Monica's own rendition of *Carol*, still available, was based on her grandfather's tones as he read the old tale and may therefore contain echoes of the great Dickens himself.

§

In 1981 Monica published her short story *A Modern Christmas Carol*, the second time she had used the title. The first of her present-day takes on the old story had been written many years previously for Britain's *Evening News* and had featured the sour and selfish widow Mrs Marley, to whom the spirits of Christmas Past and Present appear and effect their usual transformation. Now, writing for the December 1981 issue of the American *Ladies' Home Journal,* Monica's second tale by that name brought in a potential suicide. A young woman, Laura, is lonely and unhappy after leaving her husband because he would not conform to her expectations. As she drives to her family's home on Cape Cod for Christmas she is filled with bitterness, and dreading the holiday. Crossing the bridge over the canal Laura muses on the ease of suicide from its great height although not yet contemplating it herself, despite a familiar grey depression creeping over her as she greets her loving family. For a moment she feels at one with them all when together they sing the mournful lyrics of *The Kerry Dance* (one of the sad songs Monica had chosen for *Desert Island Discs* in 1951), but soon she is again engulfed by anger and hopelessness. After a needless quarrel, Laura flees her family and attempts to jump off the bridge.

She is saved by a stranger, a rough workman, who hauls her to safety and takes her to a diner to talk, then returns her to her family. He quietly disappears from their kitchen as slowly Laura realises she is surrounded by love, and is finally able to talk to her estranged husband on the telephone.

A note at the end of the tale explains that it was based on real events, and that Monica Dickens is the founder of the American Samaritans. The number of the Cape Cod branch was appended.

Roy

In February 1985, with Monica and the family at his side, Roy Stratton died from a stroke at the age of eighty-four.

He had been suffering from Wegener's disease, a serious inflammation which can affect the sinuses, lungs, and kidneys. Towards the end Roy was almost blind and suffering from untreatable severe pneumonia, the final stage of Wegener's. Despite his illness, and before the disease became so severe that he was bedridden, Roy had continued to play the piano. Monica arranged for the grand piano in the front library to be moved into Roy's writing room at the rear of the house, and several times a day he would sit down to play, sprinkling plenty of bad notes throughout his favourite ragtime tunes because he could no longer see the music, but greatly enjoying himself. His son Roy Junior frequently came to visit and together they sang old pub songs that Roy had learned in England, and reminisced about the happy times their families had spent together in North Falmouth.

After Roy's death a non-religious memorial service was held in the large living room in the house. Old navy friends voiced their recollections of wartime adventures with Roy, and what his comradeship had meant to them.

There was no funeral. Roy willed his body to Harvard Medical School.

§

Roy was fifteen years older than Monica, and she had always known that he must die before her. After he became ill and as his condition worsened, Monica cancelled a number of planned trips to England and nursed him herself with the family's help. Morphine eased his way. It was the best kind of death, she was to write later. No pain, no panic or crisis. His spirit left lightly, 'like a mote drifting through the open window and over his beloved garden'.

Monica wrote in her memoir that she was unable to describe her feelings about her husband and children: 'How define one's life blood?' She did write of the anguish of widowhood and her feelings for Roy in an article in 1986, the year after his death. She had known the end was near, she wrote, and thought she was prepared, but instead had been 'shattered, confused, terrified, lost', not able to see the point of getting up in the morning or eating. There was nothing to live for. She wandered, restless and muddled, catching glimpses of the back of his head in a crowd or a hint of his voice. When she was not sobbing she walked around crying without sound, her face a mask of tears. She wore his clothes, sat for hours in his chair, and walked on their beach calling out to the wind and the gulls for an answer to Roy's disappearance.

His vanishing also led to anger, which turned into poisonous guilt, and she began to torture herself with all the things she imagined she had done wrong. She knew they had enjoyed thirty-four 'gloriously happy' years together, but refused to think about the happy memories – or the times Roy had been so intractable she could have wrung his neck. In her grieving mind he was always patient and kind while she was selfish, bossy, and irritable.

...one day you wake up and you feel good and you think I shouldn't be feeling good, I'm supposed to be a grieving widow, and you torture yourself in the most extraordinary way. If you remember the good and happy memories, that's so painful, you tend to block them out, you're not ready for them. Guilt comes creeping into your brain because the good things aren't there.

(Monica Dickens, interview with Mavis Nicholson, 1991)

Two months after Roy died she was driving the seventy miles home from Boston, remembering the many times during his illness when she had driven fast along that road, taking chances because she was late and Roy would be hungry and worried, and angry because he was worried. Now she was free not to hurry.

Free. The idea was so startling that she pulled over to think it through. Despite devastating loss, she had also been given the gift of great freedom. She had better use it, Monica thought. It was the first of several small turning points that enabled her, step by step, to pull her life together. Another was a vivid dream in which Roy told her to heal her guilt, that regrets were driving a space between them. The guilt did not stop immediately, but Monica began to feel again the possibility of joy in life, sensing this too as a way to reach Roy once more. During therapeutic hours in the garden she found herself meticulously coiling the hose in the irksome way that Roy had done; she felt him very close.

It took Monica a long time to talk easily about Roy, to remember him as he really was without self-indulgent regrets arriving to cloud the bright memories. She found comfort in Henry Scott Holland's lines that 'Death is nothing at all...I have only slipped away into the next room...I am I and you are you...Whatever we were to each other, that we are still.'

§

When Monica was a young nurse she had seen people die, patients she had learned to love. At the moment of death she felt that the person disappeared and the body no longer mattered because the spirit she loved had departed. To witness this happening was to Monica a sign that the essence, the spirit of the person, journeyed on to exist elsewhere. Other nurses told her of seeing a fuzzy light, the size of a dandelion, leaving the body and moving outwards before suddenly disappearing. This, her instinct told her, was the spirit embarking on its next journey.

Believing that the spirit continues was enough to keep her going. For Monica, spirit was linked to infinity, and had she not believed this, death would have been terrifying. But she was convinced that death should not be feared, even loving life as she did. She wanted to come back and live again, and maybe she had already done so, she reflected: perhaps people fell in love and spent the rest of their lives together because they had loved in a previous existence. The tremendous rapport sometimes experienced with a stranger might come from already having known each other in some other time and space.

This interest in the idea of reincarnation, which Chad Varah likewise espoused, had been with Monica for a while. She occasionally led a few of her Samaritan colleagues in guided meditations aimed at discovering past lives, even if not altogether seriously. Once, visiting a medium, she was introduced to the spirit of Charles Dickens, coming through with the voice of a man of ninety or so. As Dickens had died at fifty-seven, scepticism on that occasion prevailed and Monica would happily relate the story as a joke, but her underlying belief remained. Elements of these ideas had surfaced in her writing, as when Richard tried to contact the spirit of his dead girlfriend in *Last Year When I Was Young*.

With Monica's faith in reincarnation, death seemed natural to her. Nevertheless it was hard to accept that Roy had gone, leaving nothing but a devastating black hole. She was shocked out of her senses by the intolerable fact that he was simply not there.

You somehow fantasise the person you love will die and still be there. That's the shocker. The person who dies is not there. What hurts is the disappearance. It's permanent.

(Monica Dickens, *The Boston Globe*, 1985)

Dying was progression to a higher level, Monica believed. Destructive emotions are discarded with the old garment of the body. Roy's spirit had new work to do, she wrote, and so did she,

...to make the most of the rest of my life until I join him, in the next room.

(Monica Dickens, *Reader's Digest*, 1986)

Return

'In the great scheme of things, my husband's death was not a tragedy,' Monica reflected a few months after his going. She had been distraught in the months that followed, but at the point of death she had not thrown herself across his body and covered him with kisses, she said, or begged him to return to her. She did not feel peace, just an immediate sense of loss. There was relief, but with it came tension: what was she to do with the rest of her days? She knew immediately that the structure of her life was gone, and had the exhausting thought, even at the moment of Roy's passing, that now she must make the effort to rebuild it.

It was not long before she decided to sell up in North Falmouth. The Cape's lonely marshes and beautiful beaches had been her home for the last thirty-odd years, and she dearly loved it. When she first arrived with Roy and settled down she thought it would be her home forever:

I would live and die on this narrow sandy land of long, long summers...

(Monica Dickens, *Christian Science Monitor*, 1986)

She had initially intended to stay. She and Roy had often talked about what would happen when one of them died. If it was Monica, Roy joked, he was going to start doing the cooking his way. Monica's plan, more seriously, was to remain on her beloved Cape Cod, living in just part of the house and letting a school for disabled children use the rest. But before long she understood that she did not want to be there without Roy: it no longer seemed like her house, and it did not seem to want her. The house had belonged to the two of them together, and so much of it had been Roy's creative input. Now it was too big, and needed painting, and the estimate from the painters was for the enormous sum of $10,000. Cape Cod was filling up with traffic and tourists and the village was being spoiled by developers. She was aware of the maxim not to take any serious steps for at least a year after a bereavement, but she wanted to escape, and quickly, once her mind was made up. With time, she recognised that it was the pain she wanted to escape from, not the house.

Monica, now seventy, also saw that if she stayed on for another few years she might become too old to move, and that it was better to cut the ties while she still had the energy to begin again. There was no point going elsewhere in America where she knew nobody; it had to be somewhere she already belonged. What she needed was to start a third life, she mused, a return to living by herself in a place she could make her own – somewhere fairly small in the country, probably in England. She would miss her step-family and her friends, but they would be sure to visit. After the initial trauma of Roy's loss she also needed to get back to her writing: 'I had two books to finish, and work saved me again.' An additional consideration was the likelihood of finding more work in England, as without Roy's navy pension Monica worried that she might not be so well off. She knew in any case that authors should be where their readers were.

The decision to return to England was made easier by the same resolution on the part of her daughter Pamela, who was moving back from the US with her husband and twin boys to live near Devizes. Prudence remained in America, where she was to make her mark working at Cape Cod's Oceanographic Institute.

The house in North Falmouth, with the garden by now a wilderness, was sold through Sotheby's for $650,000 and ultimately became a bed-and-breakfast. Monica's beloved horse Robin was given to one of Roy's granddaughters, and most of her belongings to whoever wanted them: better for people to have these things now, said Monica, than after she died. She rid herself of an enormous number of books she knew she was unlikely to read again, a good excuse to buy new ones. With great relief Monica also disposed of her mother's silver tea service, which she had never cleaned and, because of her fetish for not employing servants, neither had anyone else. Finally, freedom, thought Monica as she said goodbye to it – and was promptly presented with a silver tea service by the *Boston Globe* as a leaving gift.

§

She returned to Britain in style on the QE2. After having travelled to America by ship to start her great adventure in 1951, she wanted to start this new adventure decades later in the same way. In contrast to her convivial departure thirty-five years previously, however, for security reasons family and friends of half a lifetime were not allowed aboard to bid her farewell.

Love and tears, but no streamers thrown. As the tugs nudged us out into the Hudson, we passed the end of the pier where Roy had stood. Well, that was that. Life goes in chapters, I repeat bravely, and I must start a new one or be lost.

(Monica Dickens, *Christian Science Monitor*, 1986)

The voyage seemed to Monica 'extraordinary, to say the least', with its modern menu of non-stop lectures, films, demonstrations, dancing, discos, comedians, singers, show-girls and full-blown casinos. She 'cruised about alone, being enigmatic', meeting people here and there whom she often never saw again because of the vast number of passengers on the large vessel. It was fun but five days was enough, Monica remarked, commenting that in general she found the Americans on board a better type than the British, who tended to be on tours from the North Country and 'pretty thick'. Some ancient stewards complained to her about present-day passengers. 'Different class of people travelling,' they told Monica, who included this comment in an article she wrote about returning to Britain.

The five days on the QE2 were a 'limbo transition' between the old life and the new, a period Monica had planned to use to prepare her thoughts and feelings, 'a good way to mutate'. In the event not much thinking was done: Monica found her shipboard existence a constant striving merely to keep up with the relentless pace of meals and activities. She was eventually roused by the sight of the full moon over the western cliffs of the Isle of Wight, and the welcome appearance of members of her family waiting for her on freezing Southampton docks.

§

Monica's niece Mary had discovered the ideal place for her in the Berkshire village of Brightwalton: a thatched cottage very reminiscent of her old place at Hinxworth but even older. It had the perfect address, Lavender Cottage in Pudding Lane, and was surrounded by breathtakingly beautiful downland hills and green, brown and yellow fields rolling away into the misty distance. 'I'm going to be the old lady of Pudding Lane,' she told her journalist friend Valerie Grove the week she arrived, although to Valerie it would have been more in character had Monica dashed around the countryside in a sports car. Brightwalton was also the perfect location: close to friends and family, and, coincidentally, to the horsy paradise of her childhood. Her home-to-be was just right, an idyllic setting for whatever life was to bring:

...And there was Lavender Cottage, facing the soft, rain-swept view, clean, empty, and cold, as I had left the Cape Cod house, and waiting, as I am, to see what will happen now.

(Monica Dickens, *Christian Science Monitor*, 1986)

The cottage required a new kitchen and new windows, including one over the writing desk for Monica to enjoy the view, and she wanted a wood-burning stove in the dining room. She set about grappling with plumbers, carpenters and the local planning committee. While waiting for the cottage to be ready Monica stayed at her niece Mary's in a room over the garage, where she could be alone to write or be with Mary and her family as she chose. On finally moving in she filled the cottage with a miscellany of English and American furniture, some of it the same pieces bought so many years ago for Hinxworth. In the living area Roy's photograph stood on the dining table, along with a nephew's carving of a pair of old riding boots, and on the walls hung the portraits of her American horses John and Robin that Roy had arranged to have painted for her. On a shelf above the fireplace stood two bronze horses and several pink lustre jugs collected over the years in the Portobello Road.

Her new home was pretty and comfortable, but it was hard being on her own:

It was very, very difficult setting up the cottage without Roy and I kept thinking, oh this is pointless – why am I doing this just for me? You have to try and find all the positive things about starting a new independent life.

(Monica Dickens, interview with Mavis Nicholson, 1991)

At least she had the company of her two dogs Rosie and Mollie, once released from their long spell in quarantine, and Monica confidently expected some cats to turn up from somewhere. There were no horses, despite the vow in her 1973 work *Talking of Horses* that she would keep them as long as she was able to hobble about with a bucket and a wheelbarrow, and that when she could no longer hobble, she intended to roll her wheelchair out to the fence of the field where they grazed and simply watch them. Sometimes, when unable to sleep, Monica recited the names of the fifty-odd horses she had loved over her life: Chips, Jenny, Gemma, Little David, Meg...

There were naturally changes in Britain, though after the frequent trips home over the past thirty-five years Monica was not unduly surprised by what she encountered. People had changed mostly for the better, she observed in an upbeat article for *Reader's Digest* in 1987, and in other writing. Her countrymen had kept their common sense and humour and gained a more 'enlightened kindness': they were emerging from reticence and stuffiness to quicker friendships and a more sensitive awareness of each other. They were no longer afraid to discuss ideas and ideals. More of them were quietly helping the old, the sick and the disabled. It seemed like the old class structure had almost gone, even if in Berkshire Monica still came across upper-class types 'with those extraordinary hooting voices' who lived completely in a world of their own. (She admitted that with the general smoothing out of the classes her own cut-glass tones, never quite lost, made her feel 'rather out of place'.) It appeared that England had become more democratic than America:

I think we finally woke up. There has gradually been a wonderful democratic revolution. I feel very hopeful about England.

(Monica Dickens, interview with John Ezard, 1989)

She noted in her *Reader's Digest* piece that the British still laughed at themselves and poked fun at the establishment: in Monica's opinion TV programmes like *Spitting Image* and *Yes, Minister* could only have originated in her homeland. However, good old British pessimism remained very much in evidence, she observed: people continued to expect the worst of the weather, even on glorious sunny days, and complained about racial tensions and the country being ruined by politicians. English friends told her she must be mad to move back.

Privately, however, Monica was horrified to discover how much negativism and pessimism there actually was in her home country.

She recognised it as the English way but was no longer accustomed to it, her natural optimism having only grown during her years in America. Now that she was again in England, Monica made it her mission to go around

...spreading sweetness and light and infuriating everybody by saying it's going to be a gorgeous day tomorrow. If you say it's going to be a gorgeous day tomorrow, it will be.

(Monica Dickens, interview with David Cook, 1988)

Another cause for dismay was the increased traffic and dirt of London, which meant that for Monica the Tottenham Court Road 'had rather lost its charm'. She was astonished to see the 1980s punks, with their 'tortured psychedelic hair and threateningly unsexual clothes'. (Not wanting to feel scared by them, and guessing that they wanted attention, Monica made a point of approaching punks to say she loved their hair and asking them how they did it. Some of them responded, others melted away.) Travelling around the country she was depressed to learn about the loss of unskilled jobs in the north because of new technology, but also encouraged by the way people were retraining themselves.

Despite everything, she was genuinely glad to be back, and refused to be over-critical because to her mind it was a sure way of getting old. She had expected to feel lonely and strange, and did have some difficulty finding what she needed and knowing the right terminology for things or whether prices were too high. She felt 'clumsy and inept' for not knowing anything about British car insurance or what the word 'Girobank' meant. But she had been welcomed in the village, and in nearby Wantage market it was wonderful to hear the vegetable man calling out his wares in exactly the same accents she had heard in the Portobello Road in the London of her youth. It was also difficult to understand how she had survived so long without BBC radio.

Inevitably, Monica missed America and wondered if she had done the right thing. She was 'traumatised' by the return to England, badly missing dear old friends (although making one or two trips over to see them, as they did to her) and pondering if she had been insane to cut herself off from those she loved. But she knew that it had needed to be done.

§

She remained intensely interested in the doings of the Samaritans back in Massachusetts, writing frequently to 'Shoil' Karnovsky about old colleagues and what was happening: she was particularly worried and saddened by the administrative breakdown at the Cape group which had ensued after her departure. In England, although initially reluctant to be sucked back in, Monica ultimately elected to continue her involvement and began to volunteer with the local group. The lack of provision for mental health in the NHS and the dearth of drug clinics came as a shock. It constrained British Samaritans in their efforts to help, Monica believed, and in other ways too they seemed some way behind US groups. She happily broke the British rules, complaining that it should hardly be necessary to ask a supervisor before handing out the Family Planning telephone number to a pregnant sixteen-year-old. There were other differences. Some of her fellow volunteers seemed too emotional, having been over-encouraged in the new spirit of the times to talk about their feelings. Monica knew she was just as capable of demonstrativeness, but nowadays if it was a slow shift she just wanted to read her *Daily Mail* in peace and not have to suffer a 'fat woman demanding hugs all the time'.

As time went on she gave talks on the Samaritans' behalf, helped with fund-raising for Samaritan organisations abroad, attended conferences – at which she encouraged the more radical voices – and presided over the opening of new branches such as at nearby Newbury in 1986. However, she refused to accompany Chad Varah to Russia, which in the late 1980s had recently admitted to a high suicide rate among the young and wanted a Samaritan-type service. Although greatly interested in such a project Monica was now somewhat disillusioned and disappointed by Chad, whom she described as over-focused on sex issues and tending to be dictatorial. She expressed the hope that he would not sell the Samaritans to the Russians as a sex hotline.

Apart from the Samaritans Monica found time for frequent radio appearances, turning up on *Woman's Hour, The Gardening Quiz, Midweek, You and Yours,* and, on a programme entitled *The Night Before Christmas,* narrating the dreaded *Carol.* In 1988 she was the celebrity on *Down Your Way,* making a pilgrimage to the scenes of her horse-mad childhood at the beloved old cottage in nearby Oxfordshire. For TV she took part in a *Bookmark* special on the phenomenal success of *Reader's Digest,* for which Monica had written more than a few times. On the literary front, she appeared at Brighton Festival and the Cheltenham Festival of Literature, and was a judge for the Sunday Express Book of the Year Award, the Southern Arts Literature Prize, the Betty Trask Prize and the Whitbread Book Awards (her private verdict on Salman Rushdie's winning *Satanic Verses* was that it was 'impenetrable', although along with other contemporary writers she protested the fatwa issued against Rushdie in 1989).

Charitable work was not neglected. Monica presented a new variety of rose, Great Expectations, to youngsters at a charity for children with speech difficulties, and in 1988 spent a week at Great Ormond Street Hospital in search of material for a *Reader's Digest* article in support of the hospital's appeal for desperately needed funding. (Monica was yet again following in Charles Dickens' footsteps. In 1852 he too had written an article on the newly founded hospital in an effort to attract donations.) Her week in that part of London may have roused old memories: Monica had worked to raise funds at the hospital as a very young woman in the 1930s, and the building was close to the London Homeopathic on Queen Square where she was a nurse in the 1940s.

Unflagging, Monica also contacted her old school St Paul's to suggest an annual short story competition with substantial prizes in the form of books. For the initial years of its existence Monica herself read and judged the near hundreds of entries, awarded the prizes on Governors Day in person and on one occasion ran an informal workshop to discuss story-writing in general and the girls' work in particular. The competition continues to this day. Returning to St Paul's to give a talk in 1988 on an anniversary of its opening, Monica recounted to the girls the story of her rebellious streak as a pupil but, for this audience at least, describing the years as happy ones. She had thrived in the demanding atmosphere, she said, learning to work hard and love poetry and to value her friendships. Looking back, she saw her own generation as tougher, needing to strive for their independence and value, and that she herself had had to compete in the world 'in a masculine way'. Positive words rounded off her speech:

The word is Yes. Yes to life, to that living instinct. Life is full of potential.

(Monica Dickens, address to St Paul's Girls' School, 1988)

Life *was* full of potential. In addition to her public activities Monica greatly enjoyed visits from friends and family, and the constant beauty of the Berkshire Downs around her. 'There are many more good times than bad,' she wrote of widowhood. She was convinced that one had to grow and move forward, not cling to the old life and stay grieving. In her own words, Monica had settled into being 'me' instead of 'us' but with Roy as a part of her inner being. To others she remained the personification of fun, certainly to her dear niece Mary, for whom Monica could not possibly be described as an old lady when she had the mind and spirit of somebody years younger. 'Young, slim and quick-moving', wrote the *Observer*, interviewing seventy-one-year-old Monica for their series *A Room of My Own*.

However, even though her new life was interesting and exciting, Monica was starting to think about her own demise. This too was an exciting thought, she discovered. She continued to believe that the spirit lived on and that reincarnation made the most sense; she hoped to live again and perhaps find Roy for a second time. Still troubled by regrets, Monica's thoughts would turn to a holiday the two of them had taken in Barbados and how she had written all day on the hotel balcony, refusing to go to the noisy bar with Roy. She agonised over her selfishness; if only she had known how it would come back and haunt her. But she understood that she was allowing the good things about their life to recede, and her more selfish actions, though much fewer in number, to inundate her. Being able to perceive this was a sign that she was getting better, Monica recognised, and felt that Roy was helping.

§

Monica naturally continued to write, which she always termed her salvation. Through a new and energetic agent she was asked to write a newspaper column called *Real Life*, short pieces about ordinary people in unordinary situations or stories behind the news. No hard stuff or hot news and lots of interviewing, she told a friend, adding that it was just up her street. She was to find her own subjects and intended to describe her impressions on returning to England (to include mention of seeing a pub in London called *The Surprise*, outside which stood a blackboard announcing 'Surprise of the Day: meat stew with veg').

The novels continued to come. If free of other activities Monica now wrote for as long as she wanted, though still finding excuses to procrastinate: running outside to pull up weeds in the garden, or deciding that the dogs were in need of an outing. Her best time to write was from around five in the evening until ten or eleven, and she greatly relished the valid excuse this provided to refuse invitations to dinner.

Within the first two years of her return Monica published a series of four fantasy adventure books for children centring around Favour, the centuries-old spirit of a heroic horse (an idea which initially came to Monica, along with other ideas for plots, on those long drives to and from Boston). Favour's mission is to protect the innocent from evil, and in the first of the series, *The Messenger*, he summons young Rose to help with a dangerous task. She is sent on further quests in the next three books of the series, *Ballad of Favour*, *The Haunting of Bellamy 4*, and *Cry of A Seagull*. In each Rose must complete her supernatural task while trying to cope with the complications of everyday life in her mother's hotel, so that a riveting fantasy tale is interleaved with the problems of an ordinary teenager.

An intriguing aspect of the series is that Monica gives Rose the ability to enter into the minds of others and understand how they think and what it is to be poor, or sick, or of a different race:

Rose was inside Linda. She could feel her emotions and what it was like to be her, but at the same time she was still Rose and could observe her.

(Monica Dickens, *Ballad of Favour*, 1985)

A non-fiction work followed in 1986 with the American publication of *A View From the Seesaw*, a collaboration begun in America between Monica and the totally paralysed Lou Sternburg, who lived not far from Boston. Monica does not appear in the book; it is Lou's voice that mainly tells the story of the polio that utterly changed his life in the 1950s when stricken as a young husband with two small children. The extent of Monica's collaboration is not clear, although the rhythm and cadence of her style are detectable. The account is a frank one, with Lou detailing the onset of the illness, the horrific experience of being in an iron lung and his dependency on and occasional manipulation of his long-suffering wife Dottie, who cared for him for thirty years. In order to breathe Lou was confined to a bed which see-sawed up and down, making his diaphragm expand and contract with the motion and thereby forcing the lungs to expand and contract in their turn and keep the breath coming.

Monica had become close to Lou and Dottie and remained concerned about them after she had left, asking her friend Shirley to visit. Lou was depressed, unable to see any reason to live, although he recovered his spirits a little in the run-up to the publication of *Seesaw* with its attendant publicity. He died the following year. Monica was to write again about profound disability in a *Reader's Digest* article two years later on the Irish author and poet Christy Nolan.

Then, in May 1988, came Monica's first novel for adults in fourteen years: *Dear Doctor Lily*, a tale ostensibly about a friendship between two very different young Englishwomen who both marry Americans and discover a new culture. It was the first book to make a stab at capturing some of her American neighbours, Monica commented from the safety of England.

Lily and Ida meet during a flight delay en route to the US, where Ida is to marry Buddy, an undersized, not very attractive airman whom she is not sure she loves – not dissimilar to the American husband in Monica's *No More Meadows* written in the 1950s. Ida's marriage runs into trouble, but Lily's to her own American is for a long period ecstatically happy – almost unreally so. Familiar themes slowly emerge as the somewhat meandering, occasionally random-seeming early chapters of the novel unfold: the surprises of living in America for the two English girls, their differing experiences, Lily's fears about tourism spoiling Cape Cod and the delight of galloping a horse along a Cape Cod beach. Then slowly the story becomes something else. The similarities between Lily and Monica become pointed: Lily has married a handsome American a few years older, a divorced man with offspring from a previous marriage. Together they have two daughters and move to live permanently on Cape Cod.

Lily has always felt a deep concern for the unhappy people she encounters – a suicidal girl, a man whose son has died in a fire – and because of this tendency to want to help, is given the ironic nickname of 'Doctor Lily' by Ida. The happiness of Lily and Paul's marriage is gradually eroded by Lily's commitment to a Samaritan-like organisation called Crisis, seventy miles away in Boston. Some of her character Lily's motives are genuinely good, a desire to help, Monica commented about the work, 'but she also has this need to be indispensable, which is very insidious'. The suicide prevention and friendship work at Crisis takes over Lily's life and she begins to neglect her husband and daughters. As with Monica, she fails to talk down a man threatening to jump off one of the Cape Cod Canal bridges; the man survives, mainly injuring only the soles of his feet because he had been drinking and his body fell in a relaxed way. This detail is identical to that of the real event, as is the stormy trip out in a Coast Guard boat to shout to the man from below through a megaphone.

Like Roy, Paul tells Lily he is desperate to have her more at home. The story builds to a climax, and tragedy strikes: her husband Paul dies from an injury incurred directly as a result of Lily's work with the agency.

Thereafter Monica is unashamedly telling her own recent history through her characters, the original framework of the friendship between Lily and Ida having virtually disappeared. Monica's descriptions of Lily's anguish on losing her husband are Monica's own, down to the very words used in her article on widowhood. Tears pour soundlessly; Lily too wanders the seashore, crying 'Where are you?' at the seagulls; she too abandons her home on Cape Cod because it was 'ours', not hers, and returns to England. Just as Monica had bought Lavender Cottage on Pudding Lane, so Lily buys Daisy Cottage in Pie Lane.

Lily feels the torture of regret:

...she would be awake all night in a cocoon of guilt and regrets, remembering, sorrowing, reminding herself deliberately of all the things with which she could chastise herself.

Selfish. Arrogantly sure of his love and admiration. Impatient when he was ill. Consumed by the work at Crisis. Always home late, talking about her day, not Paul's. 'I'm desperate too,' she had to hear him say, again and again...

(Monica Dickens, *Dear Doctor Lily*, 1988)

Those first few months and years alone are recounted exactly as Monica had personally experienced them: the slow awakening to the idea of freedom and the beauty of nature, Lily's sense that Paul is near, in that she finds herself carrying out tasks in his meticulous way rather than her own slapdash one – including the careful winding of a garden hose. Seen through Lily's eyes, Monica's sentiments about returning to England find expression, including her surprise at the punks on the streets and also some fairly critical comments on life in Britain: everything is slower than in America, appliances and gadgets fall apart more quickly, workmen disappear for weeks at a time and the BBC is riddled with dialects.

Eventually, on her own and learning to live again, Lily is sucked back into helping others. There is a glimpse that her life will always be like this from now on, although she must learn to let people do things their way and not be 'Dear Doctor Lily'. The novel ends with lines from the Gerard Manley Hopkins poem *As Kingfishers Catch Fire, Dragonflies Draw Flame*, implying that whatever the consequences, Lily – and presumably Monica – can only do as her nature bids her: 'Crying What I do is me: for that I came...'

Monica commented that the book was an exploration of becoming dangerously over-involved, drunk with philanthropy and suffused with one's own power to do good. She confessed that in America she had often bent the Samaritans' strictly enforced rules of no personal visits to the desperate, and no inviting them to volunteers' homes. By so doing she knew she had been self-indulgent, imagining she was essential and could fix someone else's life for them. When working on the novel Monica was also still in the throes of her self-reproach for 'all the things, real or imagined, I had done wrong'. She admitted that in writing *Dear*

Doctor Lily she had been seeking to exorcise her guilt over neglecting Roy for the Samaritans (adding that he rarely complained, and had offered wonderful encouragement and support). The link between her own life and Lily's guilt was freely acknowledged:

> *The idea of someone's good works destroying their home must have arisen out of my own somewhat irrational guilt when Roy died. One of the great grief problems is guilt. It is dangerous, it is useless, it is unfair on the dead to think of them up there judging us – but it has to be lived through. I have a lot to be guilty about. I got involved with starting the Samaritans out there, and got hooked into it. It was a huge job. Roy was good about it, but it was hard on the family. There were dark murmurs of 'Mum, you should give Dad more time.' And it came back on me when he died.*

(Monica Dickens, *The Times*, 1988)

Through the character of Lily, Monica minutely relived what she now recognised as an occasionally wrong-headed obsession, as well as the pain of her neglect and loss of Roy and the shock of her departure from America. A year or so after the book was published, she was able to talk of having now reached the 'safe ground': allowing herself to be happy alone, yet equally happy to recall the wonderful life she and Roy had enjoyed together.

An excellent novel by an accomplished writer, wrote the *Canberra Times*. 'Warm, generous and effortlessly readable,' said Britain's *Evening Standard*, while Victoria Glendinning in the *Times* wrote that the one pair of hands had not lost its skill, although finding Monica's treatment of her troubled characters curiously undisturbing and contained, and wishing Monica would let life's 'grief and terrors out of their labelled cages'. The *Times Literary Supplement* was generally critical, rightly detecting the novel's confessional flavour and that it might have worked better as straight autobiography.

Another reviewer referred to her alter ego Lily as a 'loathsome social worker', Monica wrily noted.

§

Emergent in *Dear Doctor Lily* was Monica's new thinking about life after death. Both Lily and her husband Paul believe in reincarnation, and at his mother's funeral service Paul thinks of his mother,

...as she moved faster than light away from the contented personality and neat body she had discarded in favour of whatever came next.

(Monica Dickens, *Dear Doctor Lily*, 1988)

He and Lily believe they are so in love with each other because they have met in a previous life. When Paul dies, Lily sees his dearly loved body become, from one moment to the next, 'no more than an abandoned, empty casing':

Instinctively, they all looked towards the open window, where bright specks of dust drifted out into the sunlight.

(Monica Dickens, *Dear Doctor Lily*, 1988)

Monica had by now left the Catholic Church; when this point came is uncertain. As early as the 1950s she had told the Belfast-born writer Brian Moore that, as a Catholic herself, she appreciated his skilful treatment in a recent novel of the 'worst type' of Irish priest. Praising Moore's subsequent work *Fergus*, a tale of Catholic repression and guilt, Monica in 1970 confided to Moore that she too had been indoctrinated by the Catholic Church ('tho' not, thank God, in Belfast'). Towards the end of that decade Monica preached at a Christian Unitarian church, King's Chapel in Boston, so presumably at this stage still retained some elements of the Christian faith, but not long after losing Roy she spoke publicly about her changed belief that death meant not Heaven and choirs of angels but the spirit embarking upon its next journey. She also talked of having been brainwashed by her religion, of having suffered from Catholic guilt as a young woman which had made it hard to adjust to having a sex life – 'The Catholic Church nagged at me' – although ultimately coming to feel that sex was a beautiful thing. Now, in her maturity, the nature of Monica's altered religious views were perhaps expressed by Lily's prayers being directed to

...the God within herself, which was the only one she knew.

(Monica Dickens, *Dear Doctor Lily*, 1988)

§

As 1989 got under way Monica joined a group of writers urging the Government not to dismantle the Net Book Agreement, a price fixing mechanism which she and the other writers believed was a fair system. Fearing that the disbanding of the Agreement would cause chaos and force small bookstores and publishers out of business, the group – which included Antonia Fraser, William Golding, Hammond Innes, Penelope Lively, and David Lodge – wrote a joint letter to the Office of Fair Trading arguing against its dissolution. Their efforts were in vain. The Agreement was abandoned by several large book chains in the 1990s and was eventually ruled illegal.

In May 1989 came *Enchantment,* Monica's twenty-second novel for adults. The central character Tim was partially modelled on Michael Ryan, perpetrator of the Hungerford massacre in 1987. The gun-obsessed Ryan shot and killed sixteen people and injured many others in and around this small Berkshire town less than twenty miles from where Monica now lived. Monica told the broadcaster Libby Purves that she wanted to research Ryan's type of character because it was very much something of the day. But it was never her intention to exploit what happened at Hungerford, and the massacre was not mentioned on the book jacket of the novel's first edition. Her interest lay in exploring how to spot the signs of someone 'boiling up to potential danger', in the same way that the signs of suicidal inclinations could be spotted. She sensed that with Ryan it was not a question of evil, which she did not believe in; she saw the terrible events perpetrated by Ryan as more about error. He had led such a lonely, friendless existence that his inner life must have been commensurately intense, she conjectured. For Monica it was important not to be dismissive of such individuals, to try and understand each other as best as one could.

Tim, similar in character to the loner of the same name in Monica's 1970 novel *The Listeners,* is self-conscious, friendless, unattractive to women and a habitual liar and fantasist. Like Ryan, he is interested in survival skills, and enrols on a survival course and a paintball-type war game day. His parents appear closely based on Ryan's: indulgent mother, perfectionist father who in common with Ryan's is a building supervisor with the local council. Monica makes Tim a player of fantasy adventure games, which in the pre-internet 1980s were played by post. When the Hungerford massacre occurred Monica had in fact already started a novel focusing on a character who plays fantasy games, which she had learned about from her nephews and tried out for herself. There was some evidence that Ryan too played these games and Monica kept it as a feature of Tim's world. In her hands this esoteric world achieves new heights of silliness:

Tim had chosen the character of Blch, a gallant warlord, disguised as a travelling minstrel and teller of tales, whose mission was to penetrate ever deeper and deeper into the terrible treacherous land where corpses walked among the living, and the dread Captain Necrotic and his skeletal army were to be vanquished, not by brute strength and foolish courage, but only by the gambits of the swift zoetic rapier, which Blch must in the end (it might take months at this rate) discover.

(Monica Dickens, *Enchantment*, 1989)

However, unlike Ryan, Tim is not obsessed by guns, even if his heady experience at the war game inflames his libido enough to be masterful with his dowdy new girlfriend Helen. The plot, if there is one, is the tale of Tim's slowly growing relationship with Helen as he tries to deal with the emptiness of his life and with his difficulty distinguishing reality from fantasy. He is in debt to a local thug, and searching for work after being sacked from his job in the fabric department of a large store. As the novel progresses and Tim's isolation and alienation increase there comes a sense that he is heading for some cataclysmic event, particularly when early on there is mention of a sniper shooting at people on a housing estate. But Monica does not go down this road. Instead, Tim is saved by love, not only love from the tolerant Helen, but also from her beautiful autistic son with whom Tim manages to communicate. The message appears to be that disaster can be averted with human love and understanding.

As research Monica went on a survival course, sporting camouflage as she wriggled through bushes, fired a paint gun and learned to abseil (in her seventies). She found it fun, certainly more fun than the endless hours she had spent throwing dice for her moves as she tried to master the fantasy gaming.

Tim is not exactly a sympathetic character but the pain of living his ineffectual, lonely life is so well conveyed that the reader raises a cheer for his occasional triumphs, as when he captures the enemy flag during the war games or copes well with Helen's son. The relationship with Helen seems so leaden that its gradual awakening is a dawning pleasure, as is the moment of Tim's breakthrough with her severely withdrawn child. What might have been a depressing novel becomes uplifting, and a credible alternative to the Hungerford atrocity is expertly played out.

For the *Sunday Express* the book was touching, with all of 'Miss Dickens' celebrated homely charm'. John Ezard in the *Guardian* praised it as the most astonishing of all her forty-five books and, the comparisons still coming, recognised something Dickensian in the pitch of Monica's 'splendid curiosity about the infinite reach of the small expectations of ordinary people'. In 1990 the novel was discussed on BBC radio's *Speaking Volumes*, hosted that day by longtime fan P. D. James (who was perhaps instrumental in selecting the book). Monica told a friend the panel had said wonderful things about it – but had also referred to her seventy-four-year-old self as being eighty and 'very good for her age'.

§

That same year, 1989, Monica's publishers threw a party to celebrate fifty years since the appearance of her first work, presenting her with a painting of a pair of writing hands. Monica was already in proud possession of a full shelf of trophies: Charles Pick used to give his major authors a leather-bound edition of each of their hard-cover titles, and after a lifetime of writing Monica had amassed more than most.

Still the books kept coming. *Closed at Dusk* in 1990 was a crime or mystery thriller, if not conventionally so, revolving around a threat to the likeable Taylor family. The gardens of their eighteenth-century mansion are open to the public and the family employ several staff, one of whom, helpful and personable Jo working in the tea room, is not all she seems. As Jo insinuates herself into the good graces of the family the peace of the house and gardens is rocked by a series of incidents, possibly instigated by Jo, which include a tragic death in a fire and the loss of a beloved pet. It is revealed that Jo has determined to wreak revenge on the daughter of the house, Tessa, for stealing her husband, and Tessa's young son Rob may be the target. But as the magic of the charming Taylors begins to work its effect on her, Jo gradually becomes less hell-bent on retribution and the reader remains unsure until the very end whether Rob will really become Jo's victim.

The writing is oblique, glancing, similar to Monica's early thriller *The Room Upstairs* in 1966. Things are suggested rather than stated and then casually confirmed at a later point, leaving the reader in a state of uncertainty which impels further reading. Interior monologue is often Jo's, a Monica-like voice which has the effect, perhaps intentional, of rendering a possible homicidal maniac understandable and even cosy.

Closed at Dusk holds the usual traces of Monica's own life: a beloved son in the family dies in the First World War and leaves his mother permanently grieving, as Monica's grandmother Lady Dickens had mourned for her son Cedric, and there is a dearly loved old nanny. But the focus is on telling the story, competently done if with the odd credibility gap, as when the young boy Rob suspects Jo of doing away with the dog yet retains his trust in her. The ending is melodramatic and, as often happened with Monica's endings, seemingly rushed. 'Creepy...a story of love, hate and murder, tinged with the supernatural', approved the *Sunday Express*.

§

In late 1989 Monica was diagnosed with cancer of the colon. After surgery in December she was slow to recover, still unable at the end of January to sit upright at her typewriter, although making progress and psyching herself up to get back to work on her current novel. She had been left with a colostomy, and was disappointed to learn after a barium X-ray in April 1990 that healing was slow and she was not yet ready to be returned to normal. Uncertainty about the next operation meant that talks and other events scheduled for the following month had to be cancelled.

By mid May Monica was recuperating from another stay in hospital – most likely the operation she had been waiting for – and feeling foggy. For a while she suffered frustration, and even a sense of humiliation, because unable to achieve much when trying to write. Another hospital stay of ten days swiftly followed for what Monica was convinced would be the last part of her treatment. Home again in June, she confidently announced (at least to some) that she felt fine and knew she would never be ill again – no time, for one thing. All her usual activities had been resumed, she declared, including the Samaritans and working on the novel that had been left half finished when she became ill, and she was enjoying the return of her health and energy. It was hard going, but Monica was pleased to have a task on hand that needed doing. She felt sure enough of her health to plan a Christmas visit to the States to see Prudence and Roy's grandchildren, and old friends like the Karnovskys.

Her dogs Mollie and Rosie, retrieved from where they had been separately farmed out, were blissfully happy to be home again with 'Mum'. Towards the end of a gloriously hot summer Monica took her usual relaxing month in Devon, where she regularly rented the same cottage by the sea and had friends to stay as well as time alone to work.

At the beginning of her illness Monica generally made light of the situation. After one of her colon operations she joked that it was 'just a semi-colon, not a full stop', and because she downplayed her illness some of her circle did not realise the gravity of the condition or even become aware of any decline. When she underwent radiotherapy treatment at a hospital in nearby Reading she continued to work when she could, researching articles for *Reader's Digest* on being a cancer patient, and taking her place amongst a clutch of celebrity authors each writing a chapter of a thriller for the *Observer Magazine*'s 1990 marking of the centenary of Agatha Christie's birth. There was the occasional public appearance, as when she travelled to London to present the prizes at Great Ormond Street Hospital's School of Nursing annual awards ceremony.

A few social occasions were necessarily refused, such as a publisher's party for the writer Wilbur Smith, but as often as she could it was business as usual. Monica even lamented that she was no longer being asked to judge book awards, which she believed was due to being old and square and speaking for the genuine reader. In her opinion the big prizes these days were going to books she thought 'trendy...difficult, pretentious, porno, dead boring'. She had struggled with reading the 1989 Man Booker prize winner Kazuo Ishiguro's *Remains of the Day*, which she thought very dull, and was surprised at the universal acclaim just because, in her words, a Japanese writer was capable of emulating the fussy voice of an old-school English butler.

Family and friends continued to visit Monica in Lavender Cottage and at her Devon retreat. Close family were naturally more aware of the support she required. Daughter Pamela and niece Mary would take the animals when Monica was in hospital and afterwards have her to stay, while Prudence came from the States when she could. During one hospital stay Prudence was 'really marvellous', looking after the dogs in Monica's cottage for two weeks and spending hours at her mother's bedside.

In the event the planned trip to the US at the end of 1990 proved over-optimistic. Monica wrote to Shirley Karnovsky that the visit was off because another hospital stay was required. She had been feeling so well, everything at last settling down, when it was discovered that a previously healed area had come asunder. This meant a repair and a second colostomy for a short while to allow things to get better, to be reversed somewhere around Christmas. A biopsy for the presence of more cancer – and Monica was certain there was none – would take place in November.

Monica admitted to feeling briefly depressed but then started accommodating herself to the new situation, buying books and planning her next work so that she could be reading and researching as she recuperated.

§

Scarred, Monica's twenty-fourth novel, was published in 1991 after a rewrite of her original ending 'to make everyone pleased with me'. The story of a young man who blames his troubles in life on a facial scar, the novel features much that had so deeply affected Monica over the years: hospitals and nurses, in this instance a plastic surgery unit; selfless mothers of sick children; loneliness and suicide. There is a growing sense of menace as Mark, the scarred young man who has suffered a loveless father, becomes obsessed with plastic surgeon Peter and begins to stalk him. As his obsession grows the reader feels less and less sympathy with Mark, perhaps because there seems to be an increasing dislike of her character on the part of Monica herself. A final confrontation between Mark and Peter on a lonely beach decides their fate.

As ever, and despite her illness, Monica did her research thoroughly, consulting the Disfigurement Guidance Centre in Fife and the eminent Scots plastic surgeon John Kirk to produce accurate details of current treatments for burns and scars. The opening scene originally featured quarrelling children from New Zealand and Monica checked with her New Zealand author friend Noel Virtue for likely epithets they might hurl at each other – although ultimately rejecting his suggested 'chook's bum', amongst others, and changing the children to Canadians so that the scene would be more easily understood. *Scarred*, initially titled *The Scar,* was well received, if arguably not one of Monica's more credible works. Highly readable, full of warmth and feeling held in check by careful observation of facts and some effective suspense, came the verdict from the *Times Literary Supplement*, whilst the *Observer* talked of Monica's sensitive and convincing portrayal of the strains of lengthy hospitalisation – though critical of the work's 'lack of psychological and structural complexity'. The *Sunday Times* praised the plot, research and human understanding of the novel, and wondered that Monica Dickens had not yet achieved a presence in the *Oxford Companion to English Literature*.

She is there now.

§

In 1991, slowly recovering from the operations of the previous autumn and winter, Monica settled down to work and getting back into circulation. She appeared on Radio 4's literary programme *Parodies Lost* in January, and in April gave an interview to the Dickens biographer Claire Tomalin. After the 1990 publication of *The Invisible Woman*, Tomalin's account of Charles Dickens' relationship with the young actress Ellen Ternan, Monica had written to say that she found it entirely convincing and suggested that they meet. The event was postponed because of hospital treatment, but Monica did not forget and the meeting now took place in Lavender Cottage. A beautiful place, Tomalin observed, though remote for a frail person on her own.

Despite her illness Monica did not give the impression of frailty, however, as she discussed ideas for future books and talked of catching the train for a day's research in London before dashing home again to entertain friends, and of meetings with her publishers and visits from Pamela and Prudence and her old colleague Chad Varah. Tomalin was impressed by Monica's courage, energy, and warmth. 'She was as lively as a girl, her strong face framed in glossy hair; her rooms full of books, her garden bright with flowers, everything neat and shining.' As they did the washing-up together after lunch Monica suddenly gave Claire a squeeze and said, 'I knew I should like you, lovey,' a maternal gesture which her visitor found deeply touching.

Another interview followed in the summer with TV presenter Mavis Nicholson. Sitting in the sunny back garden of Lavender Cottage, Monica was thin but relaxed and smiling; daughter Pamela and the twins, now sturdy boys on the verge of adolescence, were with her. She chatted to Mavis about widowhood and her return to England, and how glad she was that Roy had not been around to witness her illness. She talked freely about her cancer – 'large chunks' had been removed, Monica stated calmly – and of the love and help she had received from her daughters and from sister Doady, niece Mary and all her nephews. She admitted making a conscious decision to let Pamela and Prudence do the helping they wanted to do, and not to be a difficult old lady. Living in England, Pamela had been a constant presence and Monica felt that they had become extremely close, cutting out a 'lot of nonsense' and getting down to basics. She remembered with fondness their intimacy during Pam's pregnancy – more exciting to Monica than most grandmothers, she believed, because she had never experienced pregnancy herself. That and going to jail were a couple of the things she had failed to achieve, Monica joked.

There was no fear of death, she told Mavis. During her illness she had at one point been close to death from severe dehydration, and as she started to go she had realised something about the process of dying:

It was like I'd been packing and I was starting out on this journey. Roy was there at the other end, welcoming me quite calmly as if I'd just been away for a day...It's made me very unafraid of dying. I do begin to see that it's the next adventure.

(Monica Dickens, interview with Mavis Nicholson, 1991)

Meanwhile, she was enjoying life, savouring the pleasures of old age without any regret for the past. Those who went on about the way things used to be turned into terrible bores, Monica commented, and in any case the old days had not been much better: people lived in misery and squalor, and even the rich were freezing cold each winter. With her advancing years she had also discovered that it was possible to keep on making new friends, of all ages, and in fact making them more quickly than ever because of the subconscious realisation that little time might remain. She no longer bothered doing things she did not want to do, such as going to boring dinner parties, when as a younger woman she had feared refusing invitations lest she ceased to be loved or no one bought her books. Monica no longer cared, and preferred not to waste time on anything unproductive. Now she spent most of her hours working because she had the hours available, but equally she was more than willing to drop everything and run up to London to see a play she was interested in. Gone were the days when she worried that not working meant she might be a failure.

There isn't time in this life to do everything I want to do. I desperately want to be a paramedic on an ambulance, and I can't do that now, so I'll have to come back.

(Monica Dickens, interview with Mavis Nicholson, 1991)

It seemed that the worst was over. Monica still worked hard at her writing, if beginning to ease up a little. In November she made plans to see friends in Brighton the following January, when she would be in the area to interview an anorexic woman for a *Reader's Digest* article; at Christmas she and Claire Tomalin went to Gad's Hill School, at Dickens' former residence, to present prizes to children who had written the best ending to Dickens' unfinished *Mystery of Edwin Drood*.

But by early January 1992 the visit to Brighton had to be cancelled: Monica was not feeling well enough to cope with the long drive and the amount of work the trip would involve. She managed to appear on BBC Radio 3's *What's The Big Idea*, but in March she reported to friends that despite an all-clear from a CT scan, there was a small tumour 'hanging about' on the bone of her sacrum and that she was returning to hospital to have it dealt with. Monica was aware that she would be in a great deal of pain afterwards; as ever, she played it down, announcing that she would simply request stronger pain medication.

When this and other setbacks occurred Monica's natural good cheer remained in evidence, outwardly at least, and her nephew

Christopher would remember her determination and conviction that everything would turn out well. In hospital Monica was still full of ideas for the future, her journalist friend Valerie Grove recalled. After finishing *Scarred* she asked a friend 'What shall I write about next?' and in one of her last letters to Valerie she discussed having another go at writing about nurses:

Not the nitty-gritty of the NHS, economics, etc. but the human elements. Satisfactions, needs, joys, effect on home life.

(Monica Dickens, as quoted by Valerie Grove, *Reader's Digest*, 1993)

The nurses adored her. 'She was very special to them,' said Monica's niece Mary. 'Not just because she had been a nurse, or because she was famous. They confided in her as a friend, about boyfriend troubles.' Even when she was gravely ill, said another old friend, Monica's curiosity and compassion extended to those who cared for her, making them feel important in the way that she always had with everyone who surrounded her.

On Christmas Day 1992, at the private Dunedin Hospital in Reading, Monica died at the age of seventy-seven.

§

Obituaries appeared worldwide, more than a few reflecting that Monica had died on the very holiday so celebrated, even invented, by Charles Dickens. For the *Times* Monica's work, 'if never in the first rank of literature', had something of her great-grandfather's flair for allowing a glimpse into unseen worlds such as that below stairs, and even worlds of squalor that became enjoyable to read about because the writing was so good. Charles Pick in the *Independent* wrote of Monica's humour and deep understanding of human behaviour, while in other obituaries she was 'a dickens of a character' and a 'maid-of-all-docufiction'. Writer John Mortimer remembered her as a wonderful person and a very funny writer, and the *Daily Telegraph* recalled her voice as benevolent, humorous and of 'unmistakable middle class decency'.

In her will Monica bequeathed $1000 to the Samaritans in Boston and a sum to her nephew and godson Nicholas Danby; the residue of her estate was divided equally between her daughters and her stepson Roy Stratton. Her literary estate went to her niece Mary, to be held in trust for Pamela and Prudence, and her collection of Dickens memorabilia to her niece and nephews, including her brother Bunny's son Christopher. Monica left her body, as Roy had done, to medical science, though at least one obituary reported that Monica had been cremated and her ashes scattered.

A memorial service was held on 29 January 1993 at St Mary Abbots in Kensington; it was requested that donations be sent to the Imperial Cancer Research Fund. Monica's talented organist nephew Nicholas Danby played Stanford's Prelude in G, William Russell's Voluntary in G, and Mendelssohn's Andante in D. There were readings from *An Open Book* and *Thursday Afternoons*, a lesson from Monica's cousin Lord Orr-Ewing, and an address from Monica's dear friend Sarah Hollis, wife of publicist Nigel. The writer P. D. James spoke of Monica's compassion and true literary artistry, and how Monica had written about the miseries as well as the joys of life, for she had experienced them herself. 'She was a popular writer in the best sense of the word, responsive to her readers, wanting to share her vision, her understanding...and her life.' If she had to choose one word to describe Monica, it would be 'warmth', and when she considered Monica's subject matter over the years she could only conclude that Charles Dickens would have been very proud of his great-granddaughter.

Samaritan founder Chad Varah also spoke, reflecting that it was Monica's very qualities as a writer that had assured her success as a Samaritan: her powers of observation, the ability to see through appearances and pretence to the reality underneath, without any disapproval or superiority. Her shrewdness and insight were always humane, her gentle mockery without malice.

In America another memorial service was held in February in the chapel of St Barnabas Memorial Church on Main Street in Falmouth, where Monica had started up her local branch of the Samaritans in the 1970s. The service, 'A Celebration and Remembrance Honoring the Life of Monica Dickens Stratton', was attended by around two hundred. Monica's son-in-law, Pamela's husband Robert Swift, read the same lines of Henry Scott Holland that had comforted Monica in her widowhood. Roy's granddaughter Susan read excerpts from *Talking of Horses*, and Monica's colleague from the Boston Samaritans, Shirley Karnovsky, talked of their shared experiences and of the infectious enthusiasm which had inspired the success of the Samaritans in America.

Now, even in the twenty-first century, Monica remains well remembered in North Falmouth both as a friend and as the founder of the Cape Cod Samaritans. The organisation instituted a Monica Dickens Community Service Award in her honour, and a Monica Dickens Golf Tournament is still held every year. Whenever another former colleague from the Boston Samaritans, Sally Casper, sees the night-blooming cereus in her garden, it is her dearly loved old friend she remembers and the champagne parties Monica used to throw to celebrate the arrival of the blooms.

Chepstow Villas

One last book was to come: *One of the Family*, published posthumously by Viking in 1993, a somewhat unconvincing tale of a charming interloper who insinuates himself into a happy London home. Running parallel is a subplot based on the 1907 real-life murder of department store owner William Whiteley, fact and fiction skilfully intertwined.

Writing at a time when she must have been well aware of her own imminent demise, Monica in this final work returned directly to the wellspring of her life: her family, and the love and happiness she had known as a child. The fictional Morleys, living at number 72 (rather than 52) Chepstow Villas in the early years of the twentieth century, are a partial re-creation of the Dickenses: benevolent father, gentle mother to whom everyone takes their troubles, a daughter with a social conscience who is on equal terms with the servants. Stump cricket, the mixture of cricket and squash invented by Monica's father Henry, is played in the backyard on Sundays. The beloved and indulged little son of the family, Dicky, runs wild with urchin friends around nearby Portobello, careering in a pack over backyard walls and outhouse roofs to see how far they can get without being yelled at. When Dicky is in bed at night he is occasionally woken, as was Monica as a child, by the Saturday carousers as they come 'caterwauling down the Lane...with howls of song and hawking coughs'.

The family are the descendants of a famous Victorian writer, E. A. Morley, whose devotees have formed an Admirers' Association and dress up as characters from his novels at the Annual Dinner. As within the Dickens clan the famous forebear is taken for granted, although the family are nevertheless proud of him and willingly turn out for the Dinner. Morley is no Dickens, however: he is depicted as something of a lightweight, and Monica may be having some fun at her own expense with this somewhat familiar description:

He wrote mostly about ordinary men and women...he involved his readers in real-life dramas that just might have happened to them. Once released, his stored-up feeling for England and its people poured out in scenes that somehow seemed more real than reality. 'Life as it ought to be' was how Harper's Monthly announced their E. A. Morley serialisations. No preaching or moralising. Good and bad brought to life so humanly...He was 'The People's Story-teller'.

(Monica Dickens, *One of the Family*, 1993)

The storyline focuses on the Morleys' increasing fondness for herbalist practitioner Toby as he worms his way into their circle, with some interesting sidetracks into the rise of feminism and the plight of the unmarried mother in the Edwardian era. The twists and turns as the novel progresses make it difficult to get a handle on the beguiling Toby, who is never clearly a villain, but might be. Through his negligence a tragic death eventually occurs in the family, and the grief caused by this loss seems to echo the terrible time the Dickenses endured after the loss of Monica's older brother Bunny in the thirties. In a poignant end to the novel the Morleys' oldest son asks his brave, stricken father what can ever make it right again:

'This family,' his father said. 'This house.'

Then he settled his top hat and went down the hearth-stoned steps, clanged the front gate and turned briskly left down Chepstow Villas.

(Monica Dickens, *One of the Family*, 1993)

Last Word

With her books selling in the millions and constantly reissued throughout her life, and beyond, where does Monica Dickens belong in the canon of English literature? Often dismissed as a lightweight, too much of a best-seller and no competition for her great-grandfather, she is hardly mentioned in studies of twentieth-century writing – and yet she impressed many of the most respected authors of the era: John Betjeman, Elizabeth Bowen, Pamela Hansford Johnson, J. B. Priestley, Rebecca West, and more recently A. S. Byatt and P. D. James, some of whom *did* liken her to Charles Dickens. She was certainly as prolific, and like her great-grandfather, Monica's humour derived from what people are and how they behave. Her straightforward morality was likewise comparable, in that the good and the decent were generally rewarded with love and happiness. These aspects of Monica's writing rendered her an old-fashioned figure ultimately out of tune with the introspection of late-twentieth-century literature – if not with readers. She had more to say on life and love than was necessarily perceived by superficial critics: profound observations that were conveyed in engaging stories and beautifully simple language.

Monica's skill as a writer lay in her ability to limn characters that were instantly recognisable, said her publisher Charles Pick, a comment echoed by John Betjeman's observation that she could etch a character in a single sentence. Her love and compassion for the characters she created, her humour, and her humanity were consistently singled out for mention by the best critics. She was funny, observant, tender, interested in the people she described, wrote Betjeman, 'a writer of such talent, humanity and skill that she really does inherit some of her ancestor's genius'; for Betjeman, she had always been brushed aside as a best-seller and never taken with the seriousness she deserved. One of the tenderest souls in English fiction, warm and understanding to her creations, said the *Sunday Times*. For J. B. Priestley Monica had 'the family eye for a comic character' and for Elizabeth Bowen her novels were rare pieces of literature. In Claire Tomalin's view, Monica's work showed a breadth of understanding and the capacity, echoing that

323

of her great-grandfather, to create and sympathise with odd, marginal characters.

In *The Lady's Not for Moaning,* the penetrating essay written on Monica Dickens for *Nova* magazine in 1970, A. S. Byatt gave her work its first real literary evaluation since that of Rebecca West immediately after the war. For Byatt the novels varied: some were more believable than others, and technically the work could be inconsistent. Nevertheless, Monica Dickens offered 'information, insight, and a certain kind of artistic pleasure' that were absent elsewhere.

As a writer Monica Dickens had never been seriously discussed because she was too popular, Byatt observed. However, in Byatt's view her realistic romantic novels offered not sex and shopping escapism, but consolation as an ordinary hero or heroine journeyed through credible difficulties to mostly credible conventional happy endings. The tragedies of everyday life were thus made bearable. Her heroes and heroines were saved, or at least enabled to go on living, by love. As her career continued, the scope of Monica's social concerns had 'steadily widened and deepened' until for Byatt some of her later subject matter put the novelists of the fifties and early sixties – in her opinion mainly preoccupied with describing middle-class attitudes to sex, and the meaninglessness of modern work – to shame. Monica's rather Victorian choice of what constituted a social problem led her to highlight issues not seen in literature since Dickens himself: abject poverty, homelessness, the problems of the elderly. This kind of anachronistic writing was in the Victorian tradition of George Eliot and Monica's own great-grandfather, Byatt continued, writers unafraid to include dissection of a social evil in a novel with a traditional happy ending, and as such was very unlike the modern-day novel. Monica's treatment of social issues was not always successfully done, in Byatt's view: her social documentary could be wooden, but was excused by her concern to present the facts rather than her personal vision of them. Monica's Victorian assumptions about the existence of love and charity might also lead her into occasional 'excesses of sentiment or contrived happiness', said Byatt, but such assumptions meant that Monica Dickens could describe experiences – such as love – not easily conveyed by the doubting modern novelist.

Monica was 'thrilled to be taken seriously' by A. S. Byatt, though feeling that the article had missed the humour in her work. Personally, she was realistic about her gifts as a writer, and felt uncomfortable in literary circles. 'I just have a little knack with words,' she said. She never bracketed herself with her forebear and would have been the first to agree with the sometimes sneering comparisons. Monica believed her brain worked far more like her German mother Fanny's, the family scribbler. To Monica, Dickens was for the most part the object of an almost fearful veneration, an unearthly being whose genius was unfathomable. She did not believe genius of his sort was inheritable. 'Maybe I've inherited a writing talent, but not the gift.'

The classic writer who gave Monica the greatest joy was not Dickens, but Austen. In her 1947 introduction to *Emma*, Monica wrote of the utter thrill and pleasure awaiting those who had yet to discover the novel. The word-perfect, obsessive devotees were apt to forget that Austen had written the book to be read for *the first time*. She envied those making their first enchanted entry into the world of Jane Austen, a world in which they would find delight for the rest of their lives. Her own favourite character in *Emma* was Emma's hypochondriac father Mr Woodhouse, who for Monica was more than a bore and a nuisance: he was the possessor of a wistful quality which made his daughter's devotion credible (and, to Monica's nursing eye, was probably suffering from a gastric ulcer). In an introduction to an edition of *Mansfield Park* in 1972 she talked of Austen as a genius whose characters lived and breathed and were recognisable in our own lives today. Austen's plots might be conventional, said Monica, and *Mansfield Park* a species of drawing-room comedy, but the books were really about people, transmitted fresh, alive, and still startlingly original. This for Monica was the essence of Austen's genius and why her work had lasted: 'the very stuff of life is here', she wrote, unconsciously echoing the comment by Rebecca West about Monica's own books. Her only reservation was that, in the same way that Dickens could not create a credible good woman, so Austen failed with good men.

Monica when young listed among her favourite modern writers Elizabeth Bowen, Somerset Maugham, E. M. Forster and Robert Louis Stevenson. Forty years afterwards, in the 1980s, she talked of her love for Anita Brookner, Isabel Colegate, Molly Keane, Anne Tyler and the 'extremely good' Margaret Drabble. She recognised the importance of reading her fellow women novelists to find out what they were up to, and to learn from others. What she found unreadable were 'serious-minded' feminist books. 'I have a hard time with them.'

§

For her own part she understood the art of writing extremely well, and what writing gave her. For Monica, it was an 'enchanted land' enabling life to be lived twice, once when it happened and once when she wrote about it. As such, it could be cathartic, a way of sublimating the trauma of bad or difficult times by putting them in a book. For a writer nothing was wasted: boredom, tragedy, anger, pain, everything was usable, just as Dickens constantly reproduced a wretched childhood through his myriad fictional waifs. As for her readers, she hoped they would be entertained, and recognise life in her books. If her basic aim in writing could be crystallised, Monica observed, it was to make ordinary lives seem special.

She discovered that people would always talk to her if they thought they were going to see themselves in print, though they never spotted it if so because of the distorted vision they had of themselves. Bores would tell her that she should write a book about them, to which Monica might suggest they wrote it themselves; the reply was usually that they were too busy – implying that she was not.

In fact she knew that putting people into books exactly as they were in real life did not work, and neither could dialogue be transferred verbatim, as it never came out credibly:

You have to embellish or change a little bit or romanticise or exaggerate or play down...Very real-sounding dialogue in a book or play is not actually the way real people talk. It has to be manipulated or manoeuvred so it comes out sounding like real dialogue.

(Monica Dickens, *A Writer's Double Life,* lecture given in Boston Public Library, 1977)

In the same way, facts turned unconvincing when presented as fiction. After an unidentified 'shattering experience' involving one of her daughters, Monica had written the episode into a novel in order to come to terms with it; an editor removed it from the draft as not believable. The rest of the novel – all fantasy – rang true, the editor told her.

On technique, Monica once modestly stated that she did not really know what it was but believed that character, plot and style were equally important and should not compete with each other (though at other times declaring that character was the most vital). However, it is clear that Monica could certainly spot technique when she saw it: she commented that Austen, for example, did not fully introduce the garrulous Miss Bates until nineteen chapters into *Emma* in order to avoid swamping her main characters with too many colourful subsidiary characters at the outset.

A book did not fully exist until it was read, said Monica, and was merely marks on paper. It was a two-way business of author and reader, and the reader had to contribute something before it came fully to life. The idea that symbols on the page transmitted meaning was fascinating to her. The resultant ideas and pictures received in the reader's brain might end up very similar to the ones the writer originally had in *his* mind if the black marks were in the right order – and might express some significant concept never before fully apprehended by the reader:

I think it's the most miraculous and mysterious process. The reader receives an idea or a joke with, ideally, 'Yes, that's what I've always thought but I never really thought about thinking it.' To my mind one of the functions of the writer towards society is not only giving people new insights but making them aware of things they never really quite knew that they knew.

(Monica Dickens, *A Writer's Double Life*, lecture given in Boston Public Library, 1977)

Beginning to write a new book was extremely difficult and took at least a month to get into. She loved the research part – the investigating, interviewing and taking notes – but it was 'death' to sit down and write it. She had to plough through at least two hours of writing and discarding before it began to 'come'. Once into it, however, Monica sat down every day for several hours feeling as if she could write for ever. 'You always think the next book is going to be really good, the next book is going to be it.'

The physical act of writing was uncomfortable:

When you are writing, you are physically ill. Ill from sitting cramped in the same position for four to five hours, from over-smoking if you're foolish enough to smoke, from drinking too much coffee, from agonising over your inadequacies, from seeing the beautiful day outside and not being able to go out and enjoy it. But if you're not writing and you do go out and enjoy the day, you can't, because then you're riddled with guilt, because you ought to be writing. If you have the writing malady, you can't shake it off, you must go on writing.

(Monica Dickens, *A Writer's Double Life*, lecture given in Boston Public Library, 1977)

Over the years Monica became aware that she repeated herself, that the same things cropped up book after book, and therefore represented her own insecurities and bêtes noires. Books were often disappointments when completed: during the writing it was the most important thing in the world, she said, otherwise a writer would not do it, but then when published it was never as good as anticipated. Monica would recall how 'agonised and frenzied' she had been and wonder what it had all been about:

Something happens between your head and your hand. Glory dims. Tragedy dwindles to a cliché. Humour falls with a thud. Love melts to sentiment.

(Monica Dickens, *The Boston Globe*, 1971)

Despite the agony and disappointments, writing was nevertheless sublime pleasure, a world to retreat to whatever was happening in her life. She recognised that it was a cop-out, an excuse 'to live perpetually in fantasy land, where you can create, direct and watch the products of your own head'. She knew it was selfish, but had to do it.

Monica's life was in her books. Being accepted as a writer was her greatest satisfaction in life, she wrote to a fan: feeling that she had put her experiences, observations and emotions to some tangible use – however inadequate. In writing fiction there was only one's own experience: all fictional characters were an extension of the writer, because characters could not have a thought unless the author had thought it first. Nothing in a novel was completely invented:

There is no fiction. All fiction is fact, moulded, manipulated and enriched by the author's imagination.

(Monica Dickens, *The Facts of Fiction*, Writer, 1968)

A writer must give her heroine her own thoughts and emotions, because, as Monica wrote in her introduction to *Emma* in 1947, 'Of whom else's can you be sure?'

§

I walk among people, staring without meeting eyes, as one must, in a crowd, or go crazy. But I am going crazy anyway, wondering about the story there must be inside each body, if only I knew...Sometimes they let you have a peep. But they shut the hatch quickly...

(Monica Dickens, *The Boston Globe*, 1971)

So wrote Monica, intensely curious her whole life about her fellow human beings. A strong character, she was born with a stubbornness that enabled her to withstand family objections to an insignificant descendant taking up the Dickens pen again, and to achieve all that she did in her crowded span of years. Throughout her life she was determined to succeed, remembered Charles Pick, though Monica always modestly put much of her success down to unbelievable luck (while also seeing luck as opportunity that must be grasped). When things went wrong, her attitude was a brisk 'What's next?', said Charles. Her longtime colleague at the Samaritans in Boston, Shirley Karnovsky, recalled the same. 'Monica never felt rejected by a refusal of financial support, but simply put it aside and went on to the next.' If she did not know something she bluffed her way through it:

When I was a nurse I found out one of the basic rules of life, that if somebody says to you...do you know how to do so-and-so, you always say yes and then rush off and try and find out how to do it.

(Monica Dickens, *Desert Island Discs*, BBC, 1970)

But this innate toughness – and personal ambition – was tempered by an immense compassion for others, evident throughout her work and in her life. After the good fortune of a secure and loving childhood, and jobs like nursing which gave her that all-important sense of belonging, Monica became intensely aware of what the absence of these things could mean to the soul. Her response was to offer understanding, and above all, love. She had her failings: in private discourse Monica was sometimes a little less than kind about her fellow man, and all her life she retained a streak of class consciousness and a particular dislike of social climbers; her compassion also failed her, understandably, when it came to man's cruelty to animals. But it was the love that is remembered. 'That warm, welcoming hug of hers embodied her vitality and energy, and epitomised her capacity to love,' said her friend Valerie Grove.

Monica was a listener, ever open to others and reluctant to talk about herself. Broadcaster Libby Purves remembered a degree of difficulty in interviewing Monica because of her way of turning the focus away from her own doings – asking Purves about her love of sailing, and whether the studio staff had to work night shifts. She also made people laugh and treated them with huge warmth. Her rarest gift, wrote Valerie Grove, was to make people into their best selves. 'She was someone other people wished – with love, not envy – they could be like.' The former *Sunday Express* literary editor Graham Lord described Monica as a lovely woman with an infectious sense of humour, recalling how she once mended the broken zip on his trousers when he had visited for an interview, then thanked him for his subsequent article in a letter addressed to 'Lord of the Flies'. Monica had ten times her fair share of kindness and generosity, said Lord, and his spirit soared whenever he met her.

She spent her money generously, on home and family and horses, often quietly helping others through difficult times or paying the fares for family members to visit America. In one instance that came to light, Monica assisted a poverty-stricken family in Nottinghamshire after visiting the local colliery and meeting the father, who had been disabled in a pit accident; thereafter Christmas never arrived without a parcel from Monica. Other acts of loving kindness are known only to their recipients.

Claire Tomalin believed that Dickens would have wholeheartedly approved of Monica: her open-mindedness, her fighting spirit, her practicality and generous nature, and the tremendous success of her writing. Shirley Karnovsky cherished her old friend's physical and intellectual energy, her determination to get things done, as much as her sense of humour and caring attitude. She was so fortunate in having worked with Monica, said Shirley at the memorial service, to have had her friendship and the good things they had enjoyed together: the parties and dinners, the swimming, the riding, the daffodils in Monica's garden and her menagerie of animals. She would never forget Monica,

...and the way she always greeted you with arms outstretched, saying 'Hello darling.'

———

Bibliography and sources

Selected fiction by Monica Dickens (with page numbers)

A Modern Christmas Carol, reprinted in The Evening News Collection, Chapmans, 1991, pg 288

A Modern Christmas Carol, Ladies' Home Journal, December 1981, pg 289

Activity Time, The Penguin Book of Horror Stories, 1984, pg 259

Cobbler's Dream, Michael Joseph, 1963, pg 193

Closed at Dusk, Michael Joseph, Viking, 1990, pg 311

Cry of a Seagull (for children), Armada, Collins, 1986, pg 303

Dear Doctor Lily, Viking, 1988, pg 304

Enchantment, Viking, 1989, pg 309

Flowers on the Grass, Michael Joseph, 1949, pg 124

Follyfoot series, Macmillan, Heinemann, Mammoth, 1971 – 1976, pg 196

Joy and Josephine, Michael Joseph, 1948, pg 109

Kate and Emma, Heinemann,1964, pg 198

Last Year When I Was Young, Heinemann, 1974, pg 268

Love Below Stairs, Lilliput, August 1939, pg 57

Man Overboard, Michael Joseph, 1958, pg 180

Mariana, (US: *The Moon Was Low*), Michael Joseph, 1940, pg 60

My Fair Lady (for children), Scholastic Book Services, 1967, pg 264

My Turn to Make the Tea, Michael Joseph, 1951, pg 129

No More Meadows (US: The Nightingales Are Singing), 1953, pg 148

One of the Family (posthumous), Viking, 1993, pg 321

Scarred, Viking, 1991, pg 314

The Angel in the Corner, Michael Joseph, 1956, pg 171

The Ballad of Favour (for children), Armada, Collins, Fontana, 1985, pg 303

The Fancy (US: *Edward's Fancy*), Michael Joseph, 1943, pg 81

The Great Escape (for children), Kaye and Ward, 1971, pg 263

The Great Fire (for children), Kaye and Ward, 1970, pg 263

The Happy Prisoner, Michael Joseph, 1946, pg 102

The Haunting of Bellamy 4 (for children), Armada, Collins, 1986, pg 303

The Heart of London, Michael Joseph, 1961, pg 183

The Landlord's Daughter, Heinemann, Heron, 1968, pg 225

The Listeners (US: *The End of the Line*), Heinemann, 1970, pg 235

The Messenger (for children), Armada, 1985, pg 303

The Revenge, The Pick of Today's Short Stories, Odhams Press, 1950, pg 112

The Room Upstairs, Heinemann, 1966, pg 206

The Winds of Heaven, Michael Joseph, 1955, pg 159

Thursday Afternoons, Michael Joseph, 1945, pg 99

To Reach the Sea, Ellery Queen's Mystery Magazine, September 1965, pg 205

World's End series, Heinemann, Macmillan, Mammoth, Pan, 1970 – 1973, pg 264

Non-fiction and memoir by Monica Dickens

A modern Dickens writes about returning to the land of her great-grandfather, Christian Science Monitor, March 1986

A Woman's Best Friend, New York Times Book Review, 1986

A View From the Seesaw (in collaboration with Lou Sternburg), Dodd, Mead & Company, 1986, pg 304

An Open Book, Heinemann, 1978, pg 271

Befriending: The American Samaritans, Bowling Green State University Popular Press, 1996, pg 258

Cape Cod, with photographer William Berchen, Viking Press – New York, 1972

Coming Home, Reader's Digest, October 1987

Christmas in Cape Cod, All Saints Coleshill Village Newsletter 22, Christmas 1967

Dickens' Christmas, The Catholic Times, 17 December 1948

First Loves, When We Were Young: Memories of Childhood, David and Charles, 1987, pg 85

Foreword to *Mrs Gamp: A Facsimile of the Author's Prompt Copy,* The New York Public Library, 1956

Foreword to *The London of Charles Dickens*, London Transport, 1970

Introduction to *A Diary Without Dates,* by Enid Bagnold, Virago, 1978

Introduction to *A Lamp Is Heavy*, by Sheila MacKay Russell, Angus and Robertson, 1954

Introduction to *Dickens at Doughty Street*, by John Greaves, Elm Tree Books, Hamish Hamilton, 1975

Introduction to *Emma*, by Jane Austen, Williams & Norgate, 1947

Introduction to *Hard Times,* by Charles Dickens, Imprint Society, 1972

Introduction to *Mansfield Park*, by Jane Austen, Pan Books, 1972

Life in a Civilian Hospital, The Listener, 23 March 1944

Making the Most of Life, Woman's Journal, 1944

Miracles of Courage, Dodd, Mead & Company, 1985, pg 278

My First Book, The Author, Fall 1992

My Great-grandfather Charles Dickens, Life magazine, December 1948

My Widowhood, Reader's Digest, January 1987

My Work in a Factory, BBC, 1942

One Pair of Feet, Michael Joseph, 1942, pg 68

One Pair of Hands, Michael Joseph, 1939, pg 48

One Pair of Hands, Services Guild Edition, 1945 (includes missing Chapter 16), pg 53

Talking of Horses, Heinemann, 1973, pg 265

The Best Characters Write Themselves, How I Write My Novels, Spearman Publishers, 1948

The Facts of Fiction, Writer, 1 June 1968

The World Well Lost, The Woman's Own Book of Pleasure, Hurst and Blackett, 1957

Your Husband Comes First, Woman's Own, July 1951

Yours Sincerely, with Beverley Nichols, George Newnes, 1949

Correspondence

With Christopher Hibbert, Howard Gotlieb Archival Centre, Boston University, c. 1967

With Shirley Karnovsky, 1970 – 1992

With Laurie Lee, British Library Archives and Manuscripts, 1964

With Brian Moore, University of Calgary Special Collections, c. 1955, 1971

With Charles Pick, Charles Pick Archive, University of East Anglia, c. 1939 – 1985

With Alexander Raju, 1977 – 1978

With Noel Virtue, Alexander Turnbull Library, New Zealand, 1988 – 1992

Interviews and lectures

A Christmas Carol, by Charles Dickens, reading, 1984 (https://www.youtube.com/watch?v=24_JPgAL7lg&t=2569s)

A Writer's Double Life, lecture for the National Endowment for the Humanities, Boston Public Library, 1977

Address to St Paul's Girls' School, 1988

BBC, talks and guest appearances, 1942 – 1974

Interview with David Cook, 1988

Interview with Leigh Crutchley, BBC, 1964

Interview, Chicago Tribune, 1970

Interview, Evening Standard, 1973

Interview with Mavis Nicholson, *In With Mavis*, 1991 (https://www.youtube.com/watch?v=latLvJEOL-4 https://www.youtube.com/watch?v=EgN1bZeVjck)

Interview with James Leasor, *Author By Profession*, Cleaver-Hume Press, 1952

Interview with Binny Lum, 1964

Interview, *Reviewers Hate Success Says Monica Dickens*, Books and Bookmen, March 1961

Interview with David Taylor, Punch, January 1974

News Chronicle Centenary news film commentary, 1946
(https://www.youtube.com/watch?v=gghp4B6KeO0)

Bibliography and other sources

Adelaide Mail, 1940

American Journal of Nursing, November 1942

American Mosaic, Joan Morrison and Charlotte Fox Zabusky, E. P. Dutton, 1980

At the Sign of the Mermaid: Fifty Years of Michael Joseph, Michael Joseph, 1986

Barnes, Colin, *A Bit of a Rebel – But Living up to the Family's Good Name*, 1971

BBC Written Archives Centre

Beattie, Graham, former CEO Penguin Books NZ, memories of Monica Dickens, 2011

Betjeman, John, *Nowadays it's MISS Dickens*, The Daily Herald, 14 January 1944

Boston Globe, 1954 – 1993

Bowen, Elizabeth, Tatler and Bystander reviews, 1 December 1943, 2 March 1955

Brooke, Michael, review, *The Lamp Still Burns* (1943), BFI screenonline (http://www.screenonline.org.uk/film/id/852521/index.html)

Burns, James, *New Zealand Writing, 1964*, Books Abroad, Vol. 39, 1965

Byatt, A. S., *An Interview with A. S. Byatt*, Jenny Newman and James Friel, 2003 (https://www.cercles.com/interviews/byatt.html)

Byatt, A. S., *The Lady's Not for Moaning*, Nova, 1970

Camm, F. J., *Frills Rush In...!*, Practical Television, September – October 1950

Canberra Times, 1964

Casper, Sally, memories of Monica Dickens, March 2017

Christy, Marion, *Illness Makes Giants of Ordinary People*, Boston Globe Company, May 1985

Daily Express, 1938 – 1966

Daily Gleaner, Jamaica, August – September 1936

Daily Mirror, 1966

Daily Worker, 1951

Delap, Lucy, *'Campaigns of Curiosity': Class Crossing and Role Reversal in British Domestic Service, 1890-1950*, Left History, Vol. 12, No. 2 , 2007

Delap, Lucy, *Knowing Their Place: Domestic Service in Twentieth Century Britain,* Oxford University Press, 2011

Dickens, Fanny, interview with Housewife magazine, March 1954

Dickens, Charles, *American Notes for General Circulation*, Chapman & Hall, 1842

Dickens, Henry Fielding, *Memories of My Father*, Victor Gollancz, 1928

Dickens, Henry Fielding, *The Recollections of Sir Henry Dickens*, Heinemann, 1934

Dickensian, 1945 – 1993

Drawbell, James Wedgwood, *Drifts My Boat*, Hutchinson & Co, 1947

Drawbell, James Wedgwood, *The Long Year*, Alan Wingate, 1958

Drawbell, James Wedgwood, *The Sun Within Us*, Collins, 1963

Falmouth Enterprise, 1950 – 1992

Free-lance Writer and Photographer, *Monica Dickens, From Court-to-Kitchen-to-Pen*, October 1949

Great Ormond Street Hospital's Archives

Green, Peter, review, *The Heart of London*, Saturday Review, 15 April 1961

Grove, Valerie, *Unforgettable Monica Dickens*, Reader's Digest, December 1993

Grove, Valerie (as Valerie Jenkins), *Where I Was Young*, Hart-Davis, MacGibbon, 1976

Guardian, 1958 – 2001

Hagerty, Bill, *Blood, sweat and tea,* British Journalism Review, Vol. 27, No. 2, June 2016

Hallam, Julia, *Nursing the Image: Media, Image and Professional Identity*, Routledge, 2000

Hartley, Jenny, *Millions Like Us: British Women's Fiction of the Second World War*, Virago Press, 1997

Highsmith, Patricia, review, *Flowers on the Grass*, Saturday Review, 7 October 1950

Hollowood, Bernard, *This Is Your Life*, Punch, 28 April 1971

Institut Mémoires de l'Edition Contemporaine (IMEC), Table Ronde (La), Dossiers Monica Dickens

Jackson, Carlton, Professor of History, Western Kentucky University, Introduction and Epilogue to *Befriending*

Jenkins, Hilary, *History of the London Homoeopathic Hospital*, British Homoeopathic Journal, October 1989

Johnson, Patricia, memories of Monica Dickens, 2017

Joseph, Richard, *Michael Joseph, Master of Words*, Ashford Press Publishing, 1986

Karnovsky, Morris and Shirley, memories of Monica Dickens, 2017

Knight, Terence, *Behind the Headlines: The Story of a Hertfordshire Newspaper*, Authorgraphics, 1987

Liverpool Daily Post, 1939

Lord, Graham, *Lord's Ladies and Gentlemen*, Fern Hill Books, 2012

Illustrated London News, 1946 – 1970

Mackenzie, Compton, Foreword to *One Pair of Hands*, Michael Joseph, 1939

Mackenzie, Compton, *My Life and Times, 1939 – 1946*, Octave 8, Chatto & Windus, 1969

McGahan, Katy, review, *Life in Her Hands (1951)*, BFI screenonline (http://www.screenonline.org.uk/film/id/1337968/)

Naipaul, V. S., Letter 21 September 1949, *Between Father and Son: Family Letters*, Picador, 2012

Nella Braddy Henney Collection, Box 8, Perkins School For The Blind Archives

North, Sterling, *Dickens' Granddaughter*, Richmond Times-Dispatch, 27 July 1947

New York Times, 1939 – 1992

New Zealand Herald, 1939 – 1940

Observer, 1958 – 2001

Oswell, David, *And what might our children become? Future visions, governance and the child television audience in postwar Britain*, Screen 40:1, Spring 1999

Paulina, St Paul's Girls' School magazine, 1932 – 1988

Philadelphia Enquirer, 1935 – 1948

Philips, Deborah, *Women's Fiction 1945 – 2005, Writing Romance*, Bloomsbury Academic, January 2008

Pick, Charles, *Chance Meeting*, Charles Pick Archive, University of East Anglia

Picture Post, July 1953

Plain, Gill, *Literature of the 1940s: War, Postwar and 'Peace'*, Edinburgh University Press, September 2013

Princeton Alumni Weekly, November 1948

Purves, Libby, *Tales of Experience*, The Times, 1988; Foreword to *Chronicle of a Working Life*, The History Press, 2004; Monica Dickens obituary, 1992

Rainer, Dachine, *Mother and Daughters*, Saturday Review, 20 August 1955

San Diego Union, 1977

San Francisco Chronicle, 1940

Saturday Review, 1939 – 1966

Scotsman, 1940 – 1949

St John, John, *William Heinemann: A Century of Publishing, 1890 – 1990*, Heinemann, 1990

St Paul's Girls' School records

Stott, Catherine, *The Novelist Who Knows Nothing*, Guardian, 21 April 1970

Stratton, Roy III, *Where We Came From*, 1999

Swift, Pamela, *Keeping Up...With Youth*, Parade, 1971

Sydney Morning Herald, 1964 – 1978

Tablet, review, *Joy and Josephine*, 1948

Times, 1915 – 1992

Times Literary Supplement, 1939 – 1993

Times of India, 1949 – 1951

Tomalin, Claire, Monica Dickens obituary, *Independent*, 1992

Tomalin, Claire, *The Invisible Woman: The Story of Nellie Ternan and Charles Dickens*, Penguin, 1990

US Bureau of Supplies and Accounts Monthly Newsletter, January 1953

Varah, Chad, *The Samaritans: Befriending the Suicidal*, Constable and Company, 1980

Vincent, Sally, review, *Miracles of Courage*, New Society, March 1987

Vonnegut, Kurt, *Letters*, Vintage Classics, 2013

West, Rebecca, *Chronique des Lettres et des Arts en Angleterre*, Rebecca West papers, Department of Special Collections and University Archives, University of Tulsa

William A. Bradley Literary Agency Records, Harry Ransom Center, University of Texas, Austin

Williams, Shirley, *Climbing the Bookshelves: The Autobiography of Shirley Williams*, Virago, 2009

Woman's Own, 1949 – 1973

Also by Anne Wellman:

BETTY: The Story of Betty MacDonald, Author of *The Egg and I*

In 1945 Betty MacDonald published *The Egg and I*, a lightly fictionalised account of her life as the wife of a chicken farmer in the remote American Northwest in the 1920s. The book was an immediate success, selling a million copies in less than a year, and was eventually translated into over thirty languages. A Hollywood movie of the book appeared two years later and at least eight further movies based on the popular *Egg and I* characters Ma and Pa Kettle were to follow.

In the decade following, Betty wrote a number of highly popular children's books (*Mrs Piggle-Wiggle* being the best known) and three more semi-autobiographical works. Her four comic memoirs of a life in the West and Northwest range from a rough mining community in Montana to the lush Olympic Peninsula and the bright lights of big city Seattle, and her life may even be viewed as a paradigm of early twentieth-century American experience: pioneering, homesteading, the Great Depression, war, and finally prosperity.

This is Betty's true story.

Available from:

In the UK: http://www.amazon.co.uk/dp/1493662422

In the US: http://www.amazon.com/dp/1493662422

Also available in other Amazon markets

Printed in Great Britain
by Amazon

46984097R00208